The Sudan—Contested National Identities

INDIANA SERIES IN MIDDLE EAST STUDIES

Mark Tessler, general editor

The Sudan—Contested National Identities

Ann Mosely Lesch

Indiana University Press
Bloomington and Indianapolis

James Currey
Oxford

First published in North America by

Indiana University Press
601 North Morton Street
Bloomington, Indiana 47404-3797 USA

and in the United Kingdom by
James Currey Ltd.
73 Botley Road
Oxford OX2 0BS, UK

The paper used in this publication meets the minimum requirements of American National Standard for Information Sciences—Permanence of Paper for Printed Library Materials, ANSI Z39.48-1984.

Manufactured in the United States of America

Library of Congress Cataloging-in-Publication Data

Lesch, Ann Mosely.
The Sudan : contested national identities / Ann Mosely Lesch.
p.   cm. — (Indiana series in Middle East studies).
Includes bibliographical references (p.   ) and index.
ISBN 0-253-33432-2 (cl. : alk. paper). — ISBN 0-253-21227-8 (pbk. : alk. paper)
1. Sudan—Politics and government—1956- 2. Sudan—Ethnic relations—Political aspects. 3. Islam and politics—Sudan.
I. Title. II. Series.
DT157.5.L47   1998
320.9624—dc21   98-34099

1   2   3   4   5   03   02   01   00   99   98

British Library Cataloguing in Publication Data

Lesch, Ann Mosely
The Sudan : contested national identities
1. Sudan — Politics and government — 1956-1985 2. Sudan — Politics and government — 1985-
I. Title
320.9'624'09045
ISBN 0-85255-824-4 (James Currey cloth)
ISBN 0-85255-823-6 (James Currey paper)

To the memory of my sister Patricia

the courage of my mother Ruth

the perseverance of my brother-in-law Phil

and the future of my niece Laura

and nephew Todd

Contents

Appendix: The Changing Composition of Governments

Maps

Tables

Preface

In this study I focus on the identity crisis that has bedeviled the Sudanese political system for decades and peaked with the seizure of power by the National Islamic Front (NIF) in 1989. I use the term "Islamist" to describe an organization such as NIF, which has an exclusivist vision, based on a particular reading of religious doctrine, that it seeks to impose upon the political system and population. "Islamist" would not apply to Islamic-based political forces such as the Democratic Unionist Party and the Umma Party: while based on an Islamic ethos and cultural traditions, these parties have displayed flexibility in implementing their religious beliefs in the political arena and a willingness to share power with peoples of differing faiths and doctrines. Indeed, the suppression of these non-Islamist Muslim movements is a crucial—and often overlooked—aspect of the policy of the current regime.

I concentrate on the internal politics of the Sudan and the intricacies of north-north and north-south relations in this study. I have neither attempted to provide a comprehensive overview of the economic and cultural life of the Sudan nor dwelled on foreign policy issues. I have written several articles on Sudanese foreign policy in the 1980s and 1990s, which are referenced in the bibliography. Those articles complement this analysis, which seeks to elucidate the internal forces at work inside that strife-torn country.

I wish to express my appreciation for the financial support that enabled me to focus on researching and writing. I spent two months in the summer of 1990 as a guest scholar at the Woodrow Wilson Center for International Scholars and the next twelve months conducting research on the dynamics of the Sudanese civil war and external intervention in that war, on a grant from the United States Institute of Peace. The month that I spent at the Rockefeller Foundation's Bellagio Center in March 1996 enabled me to complete the conceptualization of the manuscript and finalize the organization of the book chapters, while residing in a peaceful and exquisitely beautiful setting. I received a second grant from the U.S. Institute of Peace for seven months in 1996-1997, during which I delved deeper into the negotiations concerning the civil war and also completed the manuscript. Throughout those years Villanova University granted me released time from teaching as well as sabbaticals in the spring of 1996 and spring of 1997. Without that time to concentrate, I could not have completed this study.

I wish to thank Janet Rabinowitch and Dee Mortensen at Indiana University Press for their careful attention to the manuscript at its several stages, as well as IUP's meticulous copyeditor Ruth Albright and cartographer Jim Hull for the elegantly redrawn maps. I appreciated the comments on an earlier draft by Carolyn Fluehr-Lobban and Robert O. Collins, and the often-pointed reactions to particular chapters by colleagues at Villanova and Sudan specialists elsewhere—none of whom bear responsibility for the errors of fact or interpretation that may remain in the text. I would particularly like to thank the Sudanese intellectuals and political activists who have patiently tutored me in the intricacies of Sudanese politics ever since I first visited Khartoum in early 1978 as a neophyte program officer at the Ford Foundation. I feel badly that I have not been able to reciprocate by helping them after so many were forced into exile, often living in difficult and alienating situations overseas.

The final year of writing this book coincided with the illness of my sister Patricia, whose cancer was diagnosed in late April 1996, just as I returned from Bellagio and from a side trip to Jordan and Israel. Even as I revised and improved the manuscript—working on it early in the morning or late at night while I visited her, and frantically focusing on completing the editing when I was not with her—her life faded away. Her gentle smile and dignity will remain with me and with her family to support and sustain us.

Abbreviations

CANS	Civil Authority for the New Sudan
DOP	declaration of principles
DUP	Democratic Unionist Party
GGC	Graduates' General Congress
HEC	High Executive Council
ICF	Islamic Charter Front
IGAD	Intergovernmental Authority on Development
IGADD	Intergovernmental Authority on Drought and Desertification
ILO	International Labor Organization
IMF	International Monetary Fund
JMC	Joint Military Command
KUSU	Khartoum University Student Union
LC	Legitimate Command
LRA	Lord's Resistance Army
MP	member of parliament
NDA	National Democratic Alliance
NGO	nongovernmental organization
NIF	National Islamic Front
OAU	Organization of African Unity
PDF	Popular Defense Force
PDP	Peoples' Democratic Party
POW	prisoner of war
RCC	Revolutionary Command Council
SAC	Sudan African Congress
SAF	Sudanese Allied Forces
SANU	Sudan African National Union
SAPCO	Sudan African Peoples Congress Organization
SCP	Sudanese Communist Party
SF	Southern Front
SNP	Sudan National Party
SPFP	Sudanese Peoples' Federal Party
SPLA	Sudan Peoples' Liberation Army

SPLM	Sudan Peoples' Liberation Movement
SRS	Sudan Rural Solidarity
SSIM	South Sudan Independence Movement
SSPA	Southern Sudanese Political Association
SSU	Sudanese Socialist Union
TMC	Transitional Military Council
TNA	Transitional National Assembly
UN	United Nations
USAP	Union of Sudan African Parties

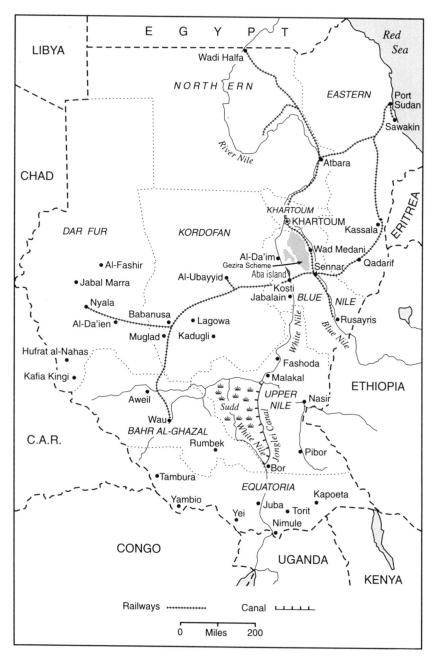

Map 1. SUDAN AND ITS REGIONS
Map information provided by Dr A. Trilsbach, Department of Geography, University of Durham.

PART ONE

Background and Context

1

The Problem of National Identity

THIS STUDY addresses the difficulty of achieving a consensus within the Sudan concerning its national identity. From that difficulty flows the problem of structuring a constitutional system that its diverse citizenry would view as legitimate. Alternative definitions of national identity and of majority and minority are proposed by political groups and leaders within the Sudan, based on varying racial, linguistic, and religious criteria. As the lines of conflict have intensified, those categories have hardened and become highly politicized.

Racial, linguistic, and religious categories have become the basis for crucially important power relationships that have resulted in the peoples who live in the northern and central Nile Valley wielding disproportionate political and economic power. Those citizens' Arab-Islamic image of the Sudanese nation excludes citizens who reside on the geographic and/or ethnic margins: persons who define themselves as African rather than Arab, ethnically or linguistically. Those who reside in the south generally adhere to Christianity or traditional African beliefs, whereas the ethnic minorities in the north are largely Muslim. Their marginalization has intensified as political, economic, and cultural power has remained concentrated in the hands of the Muslim Arab core and as the central government has intensified its drive to spread Islam and Arabic. In reaction, disaffection and revolts by the marginalized peoples have deepened and widened. Originally expressed by those in the south who are both African and non-Muslim, the revolt now includes many Muslim Africans who think that their ethnicity and particular forms of Islamic practices are denigrated and suppressed by the current ruling elite.

Recently a process of rethinking the political alignments has begun that may, in time, cut across the divide and lead to the restructuring of power based on inclusive concepts of national identity. At present, that realignment is partial, tentative, and largely theoretical.

ETHNICITY AND NATION

These issues of identity need to be placed in a wider analytical context. What is actually meant by ethnicity and nationality? What are the components of national identity and to what extent are those fixed or malleable? Must a nation-state be constructed on the basis of one ethnic group? If so, what options—such as self-determination and/or secession—might be available to subordinated peoples?

Some analysts consider that ethnic groups are based on long-standing bonds that stress the significance of residence on the same territory and common language, religion, or skin color.[1] Those markers of sameness and difference are seen as fundamental to social groups. Members of the group perceive their common ethnicity as biologically determined: the familial kinship unit forms a bloodline from which the group's solidarity is derived. Similar and related groups form a people, who assume particular cultural characteristics that are incorporated into their sense of nationhood. In a nation-state, a people controls its own political system, which is separate and distinct from other nation-states that comprise other peoples.

A contrasting view posits that "ethnic identity is an attitude"[2] that people deliberately shape and reshape. Elites and leaders (re)structure ethnic identity for instrumental reasons, such as to enhance their own power and to mobilize the populace behind their political goals. Identity can be manipulated and certain aspects can be more salient at certain times and in certain contexts. A complex ethnopolitics can emerge in which political leaders seek to control the actions of members of their own ethnic group and to affect the relative power and position of their group vis-à-vis others.[3] Symbolic, organizational, and coercive steps can be taken to inculcate a sense of solidarity among people of similar ethnicity so that they will accord priority to their common identity and function as a political unit. Interethnic competition can be intense for a role in and/or control over core public institutions such as the government, armed forces, legislature, and civil service, and over the distribution of economic values.

Even without deliberate manipulation, of course, shifts take place in religion, language, and economic structures over time. But this approach emphasizes that social identities are inherently situational and in flux. In that perspective, since the concept of ethnicity or peoplehood is contingent, the idea of a nation is also a construct. Geoff Eley and Ronald Suny assert that[4]

> a creative political action is required to transform a segmented and disunited population into a coherent nationality, and though potential communities of this kind may clearly precede such interventions . . . , the interventions remain responsible for combining the materials into a larger collectivity.

Conscious action can be taken by a government to create a national language out of diverse dialects and then to inculcate that unified language through the educational system and other cultural vehicles. The construction of civic buildings and monuments, the composition of self-consciously nationalist music based on folk songs and dances, and the establishment of literary societies and publishing houses are all part of that nationalist production. Civic rituals can be developed that are based on events from recent history or from the distant past. Those events are reinterpreted in light of contemporary political circumstances. Religious tenets and practices can be transformed into the conceptual underpinnings for a nation-state. In that sense, language, culture, history, and religion are not fixed factors that serve as preconditions for nationhood, but rather are tools used to "imagine" the nation.[5]

The voluntarist concept should not be taken to its extreme, making it appear that any ruling elite can create a nation *de novo* without a social or cultural base. Anthony D. Smith argues that "nations [must] be founded upon ethnic cores, if they are to endure."[6] Political leaders will find it difficult to construct a national identity in a territory in which citizens lack any sense of common social characteristics and values. Smith concludes that "without some ethnic lineage the nation-to-be could fall apart."[7] He adds:[8]

> To turn a motley horde of people into an institutionalized nation, to give them a sense of belonging and identity, to unify and integrate them, to give them a sense of authenticity and autonomy and fit them for self-rule, all require a symbolic framework in and through which they can be mobilized and stabilized.

Symbolic solidarity can be provided by a mythology of the past, which can take the form of a sense of nostalgia for an idealized way of life or a myth of descent from a common ancestor or ruling dynasty.[9] In this manner, people create a shared history, the memory of which enhances their sense of ethnic consciousness and their perception of difference from others. In Smith's view, the particular configuration of "myths, memories, values and symbols" is the "core of ethnicity."[10] When a religious tradition is a key component of that ethnicity, the solidarity can be particularly strong. Sacred texts, shrines, and languages create shared meanings and provide powerful vehicles to convey a sense of community and of the individual's role within that community. Endogenous marriage and special clothing, foods, and customs set members apart and invoke a sense of unique worth.

The creation of boundaries between the self and the other is an important aspect of building and reinforcing an ethnic identity. Fredrick Barth argued that ethnic groups seek to emphasize their selfhood in relation to the stranger, the foreigner. Language and religion, for example, unify a people but also separate them from others with whom they cannot communicate or share beliefs and rituals.[11] Distinguishing markers also include dress, skin color, and names. Systems of symbolic solidarity separate communities from each other. As a result, groups that reside in one territory can be divided by religion, language, and race:

they may then develop rival histories and incompatible genealogical myths. Karl Deutsch noted that residents may work side by side and share everyday experiences but lack a common culture: their interpretation of historical and current events may be radically different and lead them to be "bitterly opposed."[12]

The existence of ethnic markers is insufficient in itself to denote political difference. A deliberate effort must be made to create or enhance cultural and social bonds by deepening networks of social communication and consciously fostering shared values.[13] Self-awareness as a group may initially emerge in response to an outside threat or arise from competition with neighboring ethnic groups.[14] Such conflicts may help to instill a sense of ethnic solidarity in peoples who were previously highly competitive among themselves: Smith cites the Hausa and Kurds, who were sharply divided internally despite cultural commonalities but began to overcome those divisions and to define themselves as a nation when they faced external threats. Interstate or internal war deepens the demarcation between the self and the other. Mutual dependence in battle establishes an esprit de corps among the participants, and the battles themselves can assume mythic dimensions. The symbolic value of a particular territory can be deepened when its control is contested; such warfare, in turn, "sharpen[s] and politicize[s]" ethnic differences.[15]

ETHNIC AND TERRITORIAL NATIONALISM

A politicized ethnic awareness can lead to the emergence of a movement to create a nation-state. But there is considerable conceptual confusion over the idea of a nation-state since the term has two distinct meanings. Smith calls these the "ethnic model" and the "territorial model."[16] They differ conceptually and in their operationalization.

According to the ethnic model, a state should be coterminous with one self-defined ethnic group. The German romantics, for example, asserted that their organic nation had the natural right to form a state that would incorporate all ethnic Germans.[17] Similarly, Somali nationalists argue that their nation-state should encompass all areas where Somalis live, even though they are now part of neighboring states' territories. According to this approach, Indonesia, Israel, and Turkey should be defined, respectively, by their Javanese, Jewish, and Turkic ethnic cores. At its extreme, this can lead to militant irredentism and to the attempt to create an ethnically pure nation-state, uncontaminated by alien peoples. Operationalizing organic nationalism causes serious difficulties for ethnic minorities. The leaders of the dominant ethnic groups can seek a homogeneity that represses differences and promotes intolerance. Exclusivist policies can deny minorities the use of their language, discriminate against their religious beliefs, or even block them from citizenship. In the above-mentioned cases, asserting an ethnic nation-state automatically excludes Slavs and Jews in a Germanic union, Kurds and Greeks in Turkey, and Muslim and Christian Arabs in Israel. That denial and delegitization can lead to "fierce opposition from ethnic minorities."[18]

In contrast, according to the territorial model, residents in a particular territory have a common allegiance to the state, irrespective of their ethnicity. This integrative approach emphasizes the legal equality of citizen-residents. Loyalty to a place provides the basis for national sentiments in, for example, Switzerland and the United States and in a significant number of anticolonial struggles in Latin America, Asia, and Africa.[19] In the United States, citizens are expected to adhere to common political ideals, rather than to have a common descent. In newly independent countries this approach seeks to create an overarching political culture out of various traditions and ethnic groups. For example, the Indian National Congress sought to turn geographically defined India into a civic nation that would unite Hindus, Muslims, and the numerous ethnic and caste-based groups. The limitations of territorial nationalism can be shown in the inability of Indian nationalists to prevent the eruption of Muslim-Hindu tensions that led to the creation of Pakistan by Muslim ethnic nationalists. Moreover, ethnopolitics in independent India have flared into violence as politicized religious, linguistic, and regional groups compete for power, resources, and political symbols.

The problem of creating a territorial nation-state has been particularly acute in former colonies, partly as a result of the policies adopted by the imperial power.[20] The ruler created and defined the geographic space without taking into account preexisting social solidarities. Moreover, colonial rule itself exacerbated divisions: groups interacted politically that had not had hierarchical and/or competitive relations in the past; the colonizer fostered ethnic particularities in its search for historical kinship groups on which to devolve authority; and its divide-and-rule policies set peoples against each other. Thus, ethnopolitical tensions were often entrenched by the time independence was achieved. A sense of loyalty based on residence in the territory of the newly independent state tended to be restricted to a small number of intelligentsia and politicians.

This means that if a new state is an artificial conglomeration of previously competing or isolated groups, political leaders can encounter serious difficulties in creating an overarching loyalty. Residing on the same land provides an insufficient basis for solidarity. The civic model of citizenship based on residence in the territory has difficulty mobilizing people once the colonial ruler has been expelled. In fact, in order to integrate the citizenry, governments often resort to the politics of ethnic identity. They revitalize particular ethnic sentiments and rewrite history from a nativist standpoint. After examining attempts to form new civic political cultures in Zaire, Uganda, and Nigeria, Smith concludes:[21]

The record to date does not lend support to the view that such territorial "crea-
tions" possess the resources and stability, let alone the ability, to furnish acceptable political cultures that transcend ethnicity or to gain legitimacy from
the political domination and culture of the predominant ethnic community.

Moreover, that effort to integrate the citizenry may cause a government to
believe that it enhances territorial solidarity when its policies actually promote
one ethnic group's definition of the nation. For example, the U.S. constitution
posits a territorial nationalism in which birth automatically confers citizenship.
However, its political culture was originally defined by white male Protestant
elites who assumed that the wider society would absorb their cultural values and
religious symbols.[22] Recent attempts to reimagine that identity in ways that are
inclusive of racial, cultural, and gender differences have caused significant tension and defensive reactions. The Soviet Union called itself multinational, but
the Russian ethnic core was paramount: for example, the effort to spread the
Russian language throughout the USSR was termed "internationalist" whereas
other European and Asian languages were deprecated as local and particular.[23]
Thus, politically dominant groups tend to ignore their own specificity and ethnicity: they see their assimilationist behavior as a positive means to draw the
other groups into a higher global civilization, rather than as the imposition of
their national culture and values on those peoples.

THE CONTROL MODEL

The duality of ethnic and territorial criteria for the determination of membership in the nation-state can be related to two contrasting models for rule
termed the control model and the pluralist model. According to Rasma Karklins,
"the control model's intent is to make ethnic diversity and its political conse-
quences disappear by defining it away and by exercising structural control."[24] A
control model is likely to emerge in the ethnically defined nation-state, where
one ethnic group assumes the right to rule and to craft the country in its image.
However, it can also emerge out of territorial nationalism if leaders of one ethnic
group try to impose their cultural values as the overarching civic political culture. In either situation, minorities are placed in a separate niche or are actively
suppressed. Thus, the Iraqi government has at times accorded limited self-rule
and language rights to the Kurds, whereas at other times it has tried to eradicate
them. Similarly, the Turkish government has tried to make Kurds invisible by
calling them mountain Turks and banning their language and cultural symbols.
It is not surprising that a government seeks to centralize the political system and
integrate the society within its borders. But, under the control model, additional
steps are taken to efface differences. Leaders of the dominant group assume that
they have a "civilizing mission in relation to the smaller and [in their view] 'his-

tory-less' peoples" in their midst.[25] The latter should welcome assimilation into the "national" culture and identity.

In the control model the state tries to undermine and even destroy other ethnic national groups that exist within its boundaries, whether by assimilation or repression. That results in the structural inequality of marginalized peoples, which can also be seen as a form of internal colonialism.[26] Protests by Scots denote the reaffirmation of a people faced with self-perceived economic and cultural threats. Peripheralized Bretons resist the Parisian core of French nationalism and Basques refuse Castillian dominance of Spanish identity. The control model thereby promotes homogeneity and stability in the short run but intensifies ethnic awareness and discontent in the long run, providing evidence that it is counterproductive to try to eradicate ethnic differences.

Karklins discovered in the Latvian-Russian relationship that the very assertion by the marginalized Latvians of their cultural values and political rights relativized the dominant Russian culture. That shift, in turn, unsettled and threatened the Russians who had controlled Latvia.[27] In those contexts, conflict arose from the power relations between ethnic groups and from attempts to assimilate or marginalize peoples, not from the mere existence of ethnic differences:[28]

> If a minority's essential cultural, religious, or linguistic values are seen as immaterial or contrary to those of the majority polity (as is the case for Irish Catholics in Northern Ireland, Tamils in Sri Lanka, and Kurds in Turkey), it should not be surprising that there is, in return, little acceptance by that minority of the values or legitimacy of the majority's state.

The control model can be implemented in democracies as well as autocracies. For example, the principle of majority vote is fundamental to democracy. But, if one politically cohesive group has a numerical majority in the legislative and executive bodies, then the minority is always outvoted and underrepresented. This is a critical problem in Northern Ireland, where the Catholic minority fears the automatic Protestant majority. It was a major issue between the Greek majority and Turkish minority on Cyprus until the Turkish invasion in 1974 led to de facto territorial partition. It also poses problems in the United States, where restructuring congressional districts to increase minority representation conflicts with the norm of individual rather than group-based rights.

THE ETHNIC PLURALIST MODEL

Before examining the repercussions of the control model, which can lead disadvantaged groups to call for self-determination and/or secession, the ethnic pluralist model should be addressed. Adherents of that approach seek to recognize and accommodate group differences within the political system, rather than to suppress or deny such distinctions. Instead of positing a zero-sum political game in which the majority group wins and the minority loses, the ethnic pluralist model envisions the state as combining equal rights under the law for all citizens with special provisions to ensure representation for the country's diverse groups. Karlins argues that this model requires that[29]

> majorities develop an enlightened view of self-interest as tied to the common interest. For power sharing to work, there must be a political culture that sees ... the granting of rights to minorities as strengthening of the rights of everybody in the state. ... The majority needs to be sensitive to minority concerns and accept real or symbolic claims as legitimate. Ignoring or trying to undermine minority interests will create the opposite effect.

Two-fold safeguards need to be built into an ethnic pluralist system.[30] First, equality before the law and regulations to prohibit discrimination are essential. Those establish a national consensus that supports principles of human rights. In that contest, there must be equity in access to governmental authority, services, and employment. Individual rights and group rights are intertwined: exercise of the individual's right to religious freedom is implemented through an institution such as a church or a mosque; language rights require schools and publishing houses; and an individual's security may require having adequate numbers of police forces that are drawn from that person's group.

Second, there must be recognition of the particular cultures and aspirations of the groups that live within the overarching society and polity. That recognition can be based on corporate rights and/or geographically based rights. Corporate rights can include the autonomy for religious communities in the Ottoman Empire or the special school systems for minority groups that were mandated in central Europe after World War I. They can also involve affirmative action programs to overcome discrimination against racial minorities and women, as in the United States. Jordan's guaranteed parliamentary seats for ethnic and religious minorities and Lebanon's communal representation enable each distinct group to acquire a stake in political life and governance. Geographically based rights may be important for certain minorities that live in relatively compact territories inside the state. Political autonomy can protect a minority group by decentralizing authority and reducing the ability of the central government to control and assimilate the minority. Autonomy remains consistent with the ultimate sovereignty and territorial integrity of the country. In fact, "decentralization can make possible the coexistence of multiple nationalities within the territory of one state."[31]

Varying degrees and forms of autonomy have been instituted for indigenous peoples such as Native Americans in the United States, First Nations in

Canada, Lapps in Finland, and Maoris in New Zealand. The UN Declaration on the Rights of Indigenous Peoples (1993) asserts their right to semiautonomous areas and freedom of choice in the pursuit of their own economic, social, religious, and cultural development.[32] To protect their identities in the long term, however, they need to acquire political and economic power not only at the local and regional levels but at the center as well. Self-rule provides the possibility that[33]

> autonomous ethnic control over the homeland's resources and budget would restructure the economy to support the interests of, and so preserve intact, the community which otherwise would suffer further decline and assimilation or deprivation.

Such a federal system can enable "communities to exercise meaningful . . . control over their own affairs" and increase their "real and perceived participation in the political process."[34] They can set policies for education, language use, and economic development at the local and regional level. Localities and regions must, however, operate within the overall authority of the central government and must enforce laws emanating from that government. Powers shared between the center and the region may include the exploitation of natural resources and the operation of ports, airports, and communications facilities. Control over natural resources is highly contested, as demonstrated by the battles between the central government and ethnically defined regions over oil rights and revenues in Nigeria, Iraq, and the Sudan.

Language and education are particularly important symbolic elements in ethnic autonomy, since culture is transmitted through those vehicles. They are also essential components of freedom of expression and association. The UNESCO Convention against Discrimination in Education (1960) upholds the right of members of national minorities to establish their own educational systems that use or teach in their own languages. However, the convention emphasizes that this right must not "prejudice national sovereignty" or prevent minorities from "understanding the culture and language of the community as a whole."[35] This indicates the delicate relationship among the center, region(s), and linguistic groups. For example, a central government is likely to require proficiency in the official language of the state for employment in the civil service or armed forces, and universities are likely to teach in that language. Such measures are seen as essential for political and social unity and administrative efficiency, but they leave linguistic minorities disadvantaged and facing de facto discrimination. For example, Arab citizens of Israel, whose primary language is Arabic, must be fluent in Hebrew for university-level studies and employment in the civil service. Moreover, when a nonindigenous language is used as the lingua franca, as in sub-Saharan African countries that employ English or French in administration and education, popular resentment can be whipped up against using the language of the former colonial ruler.

The international legal scholar Hurst Hannum emphasizes that the combination of individual and group-based rights is essential for a stable ethnic pluralist system: there must be equality before the law at the national level alongside recognition of specific minority rights. Recognition of minority rights within particular geographic enclaves should not provide an excuse to abandon the principle of nondiscrimination at the countrywide level. Thus, the minority treaties promulgated after World War I asserted the link between those rights: the principles of equality of treatment, nondiscrimination, and citizenship must be upheld by the governments and minorities must also have the right to use their own languages, operate their own charitable, religious, and social institutions, obtain state support for their schools, and gain some territorial autonomy. Hannum comments:[36]

> Ultimately, one must resolve the inherent tension between the obligation of every society to recognize pluralism and diversity and the desire of every culture—whether majority, minority, or indigenous—to perpetuate its values and enforce conformity. The appropriate role of the state is to mediate between these competing forces, setting the parameters within which the resulting conflict will be creative rather than destructive.

Balancing the creative and destructive elements of the nation-state is extremely difficult in those multiethnic contexts, since a government is likely to be dominated by a particular ethnic group and to express that group's values. The commitment to pluralist values requires time and effort. In postcolonial states where legitimacy is fragile, the political arena is highly contentious, and governments feel insecure, it is difficult for power-sharing systems to emerge and be sustained. Governments and politicians are less likely to mediate group differences than to reinforce their ethnic and regional bases in ways that undermine pluralism. It is all too easy to shift into the control model and to harden the lines of difference. The pursuit of assimilationist policies and nonrecognition of the cogency of group demands make those demands even more insistent. The process accelerates the delegitimization of the political system in the eyes of marginalized groups and can lead to civil strife and demands for self-determination and/ or secession.

SELF-DETERMINATION AND SECESSION

Self-determination is generally defined under international law as the attaining of independence by a self-defined national group. That formulation passed through two phases in the twentieth century: the first phase stressed ethnic nationalism and the second emphasized territorial nationalism.[37] During the first phase, as the multiethnic Ottoman, Austro-Hungarian, and Russian empires disintegrated during World War I, the victorious powers argued that ethnic groups within those empires could express their right to self-determination through achieving political independence. Each newly independent state should represent a particular ethnic group. Minority ethnic groups did not have the right to secede from the new states, but minority treaties were expected to guarantee their group rights.

The second phase came during the decolonization process after World War II. The right of self-determination was enshrined in the human rights covenants, the Declaration on Decolonization by the UN General Assembly (1960), and the African Charter on Human and Peoples' Rights (1981). Those documents limited self-determination to ending colonial rule and assumed that civic, territorial nationalism would underpin allegiance to the new states. They opposed undermining the territorial integrity of independent countries by allowing ethnic minority groups to secede. Self-determination was a one-time action that would not apply to the postcolonial political situation. Minority groups must remain within the borders of the existing state after the end of colonial rule. Thus, neither the first nor the second phase in the articulation of the right of self-determination embraced the concept of secession from an independent state.

Enforced inclusion is contested by leaders of ethnic groups who assert that the right to self-determination cannot be subordinated to the principle of territorial integrity. They argue that they have the right to choose to remain within the country, to create an autonomous region, or to secede and form a separate state. Nonetheless, since governments play the decisive role in the UN system, they reject the right of secession, arguing that it would lead to the disintegration of many existing states and the destabilization of the international community. This perspective is echoed by analysts such as Amitai Etzioni who fear that secession does not resolve the underlying problem but rather leads "to further schisms and more ethnic strife."[38]

Nonetheless, the UN General Assembly Declaration on Principles of International Law concerning Friendly Relations and Cooperation among States (1970) introduced phrasing that suggested a conditional right to secede. That declaration opposed disrupting the unity of "states conducting themselves in compliance with the principle of equal rights . . . and thus possessed of a government representing the whole people belonging to the territory without distinction as to race, creed, or colour."[39] Although the declaration asserts that territorial integrity is the principal value, it indicates that a government which fails to uphold equal rights and nondiscrimination could be faced with legitimate claims to secession. This corresponds to the League of Nations' justification of

the secession of Finland on the grounds that the Russian government had op-
pressed the Finnish people. In other words, if a government shifts from a pluralist approach to the control model, which denies the legitimacy of differences,
then a minority could have the right to secede. In practice, the separation of
Rwanda from Burundi was endorsed by the international community in 1962,
as was the secession of East Pakistan in 1971 to form Bangladesh. The recent
breakups of the Soviet Union, Czechoslovakia, and Yugoslavia as well as the pro-
independence referendum in Eritrea have also been recognized by the UN. But
those are still viewed as exceptions: the international community generally continues to assert the principle of territorial unity over the right of secession.

Analysts such as Michael Lind argue that holding together a territorial state
by force is worse than allowing groups to secede. He argues that one should neither automatically favor secessionist movements nor offer "reflexive support for
multinational political entities, especially despotic ones"[40] that crush minorities.
Lind maintains that the problem is becoming more serious as[41]

> dominant elites, seeking new formulas for legitimacy to replace fading secular
> and socialist philosophies, make more concessions to the national and religious
> sentiments of ethnic majorities ... [which then heighten discrimination
> against minorities and make] minority nationalisms ... more bitter and in-
> tense in response.

In his view, denying minorities the right of secession intensifies strife: "Op-
pressed nations seeking to escape from a multinational empire should not be
told that they will be free to vote on everything except their independence."[42]

The key problem becomes the form of rule: where an ethnic pluralist system
is in place, minorities are unlikely to seek to secede. They would find constitutional means to achieve representation and meet group goals. Self-determination might be achieved through regional autonomy rather than secession. Such
political systems can contain centrifugal forces in a multiethnic state partly
by establishing institutions that represent the diverse groups and by fostering
"tolerance for those with different backgrounds and cultures."[43] This important
interpretation of the meaning of self-determination is rarely recognized by analysts and politicians. Rather, self-determination is generally identified with secession. In fact, secession should be seen as one possible outcome of the act of
self-determination and not necessarily the most likely outcome.

The difficulty of disengaging ethnic and territorial nationalism is indicated
in this analysis. Politicians often invoke ethnicity as a basis for their political
movements that seek self-assertion and independence. That generates tension
with the territorial nationalist assumption that the residents of the given territory are equal citizens. In reaction to the exclusiveness inherent in the ethnic
nation-state and in the effort to restructure a territorial nation into an ethnic-

based state, minorities assert their right of self-determination. They may seek the codification of their rights as citizens, including the establishment of a geographically decentralized political system. They may also insist that the right of self-determination include the right to secede. Crafting an ethnic pluralist system that respects minority aspirations and creates an overarching identity for the country is a difficult process.

ETHNIC COMPOSITION OF THE SUDAN

The Sudan is the largest country in Africa, covering a million square miles. It is a land of extraordinary diversity, and analysts classify its twenty-six million residents among more than fifty ethnic groups, which they subdivide into at least 570 distinct peoples. The largest groups are self-defined (in descending order) as Arab, Dinka, Beja, Nuer, Nuba, Nubian, Fur, Bari, Azande, Moru, and Shilluk.[44] Table I indicates the wide variety of peoples, many of which lack sharp boundaries and change nomenclature over time. "Naming" them in this table emphasizes their diversity, but also risks unduly emphasizing the idea that they are permanent or central to sociopolitical life.

Moreover, although 40 percent of the population identifies itself as Arab, the actual meaning of the term remains ambiguous. A generally accepted definition would include peoples who speak the Arabic language and claim to have originated in Arabia, even though that genealogy is largely fictional. Many indigenous peoples call themselves Arab since, over the centuries, they adopted the Arabic language, customs, and Islam. In that sense, most Arabs in the Sudan are really Arabized Nubians, Dinka, Nuba, Shilluk, Fur, or Beja. Moreover, Arabs are not homogeneous socially: some have nomadic origins and others are based on riverine villages. Even among those categories there is considerable diversity, which urbanization, labor migration, and long-distance trade patterns have magnified over hundreds of years.

Nonetheless, Muslim Arabs from the Nile Valley have dominated the political, economic, and cultural life of the Sudan. They hold the main government posts in the capital city, the majority of seats in all the parliaments, and the senior positions in the armed forces. They lead the educational institutions, trade unions, industries, and businesses. As the largest and most centrally located ethnic group, Arabs wield a disproportionate influence over policy-making and over the cultural identity of the country. It is not surprising that they have, therefore, tried to shape the identity of the country in their own image: Arab culturally and Muslim in its religion.

The non-Arab ethnic groups in the north comprise a quarter of the population, but are scattered in outlying territories. Beja are concentrated in the east along the Red Sea, where they merge with similar peoples in Eritrea. They retain

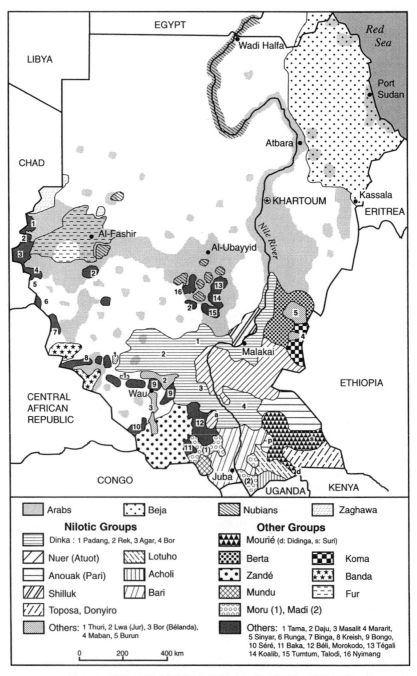

Map 2. SUDAN'S ETHNIC AND LINGUISTIC GROUPS
Source: Marc Lavergne, ed. *Le Soudan Contemporain*. (Paris: Lermoc/Karthala, 1989).

Table 1. The Diverse Sudanese Peoples

I. *Southern Peoples* (34%)
    A. Nilotic linguistic groups: Dinka (10%), Nuer (5%), Shilluk (1%), Anouak, Acholi, Bor Bélanda, Jur, Shilluk Lwo, Pari
    B. Nilo-Hamitic linguistic groups: Bari-speaking (Bari, Kuku, Pojulu, Kakwa, Nyangwara, Mundari; 2%), Nyepo, Lokoyo, Luluba, Latuko, Logit, Lango, Toposa, Domjiro, Jiye, Mourle Group
    C. Sudanic linguistic groups: Azande (2%), Muru (1%), Ndogo, Sere, Mundo, Biri (Balanda/Fertit), Madi, Bongo (Fertit), Baka, Feroge

II. *Arabized Peoples of Northern Sudan* (40%)
    A. Ja'aliyin Arab: Danagla Arabs, Hassaniya, Kawahla, Gima, Husainat
    B. Juhayna Arab: Jamala (Kababish, Shukriya), Baqqara (Silaim, Hawazma, Misiriya, Humr, Rizaiqat, Ta'aisha, Bani Rashid, Rashaida, Habaniya)
    C. Gezira Arab: Mesellimiya, Halawin, Rufa'a
    D. Zibaidiya Arab
    E. Hawawir Arab (Berber stock): Hawawit, Jellaba, Hawara, Korobat
    F. Mixed Arab-Nubian: Shaiqiya, Manasir, Rubatab, Mirifab
    G. Christian Arab: Copt, Syrian Orthodox.

III. *Non-Arabized Peoples of Northern Sudan* (26%)
    A. Beja (6%): Beni Amer, Amarar, Bisharin, Hadendowa
    B. Dar Fur: Fur (2%), Daju, Beigo, Zaghawa, Berti, Masalit, Gimr, Tama
    C. Nuba (5%): over 50 groups, including Nyimang, Temein, Katla, Tima, Tegali, Koalib-Moro (Heiban, Shwai, Otoro, Tira, Moro), Daju, Tulishi, Keiga, Miri, Kadugli, Korongo, Talodi-Mesakin, Lafofa, and "Hill Nubians"
    D. Nubian (3%)
    E. West African (fallata) (6%): Fulani, Hausa, Kanuri, Songhai (Zabarma)

Sources: Table adapted from Dunstan M. Wai, *The African-Arab Conflict in the Sudan* (New York: Africana, 1981), 17, 21, 22. Percentages adapted from John O. Voll and Sarah P. Voll, *The Sudan* (Boulder: Westview, 1985), 8-13. Additional information from Catherine Miller, 13 June 1997; R. C. Stevenson, *The Nuba Peoples* (Khartoum: University of Khartoum, 1984), 12-15; and Benaiah Nyaing Duku, "The Kuku," *A Concise Study of Some Ethnic Groups in Sudan* (Cairo: Sudan Cultural Digest Project, 1996), 35 fn 3.

their languages and special customs, but they are linked culturally to their Arab neighbors through Islam and particularly through membership in influential *sufi* religious orders.

    Nuba peoples are localized in the west in the Nuba Mountains of southern Kordofan. They have several distinct languages and adhere to various religions, ranging from traditional African beliefs to Islam and Christianity. The names for their groups are based on the isolated hills on which these villagers lived. Only recently have enhanced communications, tensions with neighboring Arab peoples, and a growing sense that they remain second-class citizens even if they are Muslims and relatively Arabized intensified their politicization and self-awareness. They have reappropriated the term "Nuba," which was used in the nineteenth century by Arabs to mean black people who could be enslaved, using it now as a nationalist term to denote their common and distinct identity.[45]

Nubian peoples traditionally lived along the upper reaches of the Nile River, extending into Egypt. Nubia comprised independent Christian kingdoms prior to the Muslim conquest of Egypt in 641 A.D. Later, Nubians converted to Islam and some became Arabized in language and self-identification. In the 1960s many Nubians suffered physical dislocation, when the construction of the Aswan High Dam flooded their villages. But their educated elite has been better integrated into the dominant Arab political and economic systems than most of the other African peoples.

The Fur, who live in the far west in the area centered on the mountains of Jabal Marra, have a strong tradition of independence. The Fur sultanate lasted—virtually continuously—from the fifteenth century until 1916, nearly twenty years after Britain occupied Sudan. The sedentary Fur controlled major desert trade routes, and intermingled for centuries with migrants from west Africa, Arab traders and holy men from the Nile Valley, and other indigenous peoples.[46] Pride in their special history and culture remains strong among the Fur.

The south has a greater variety of peoples than the north, but "they are all racially akin to tropical Africa and identify culturally with Africanism."[47] Dinka, who are the largest African group in the country as a whole, comprise 40 percent of southern residents. They traditionally herd cattle in Bahr al-Ghazal or along the eastern bank of the White Nile, living in relatively small units that lack an integrated political structure. The Nuer, another Nilotic people, also have a decentralized society whose peoples were frequently in conflict among themselves and with contiguous Dinka groups. The Nilotic Shilluk, in contrast, had a centralized system and claim to have founded the Funj kingdom, based in Sennar, in the sixteenth century. Shilluk controlled territory as far north as Aba Island on the White Nile until the mid-nineteenth century, when they were pushed south by the better-armed Turko-Egyptian forces. In the southernmost province of Equatoria, there are a wide variety of peoples, many of whom are closely related to peoples across the border in Zaire, Uganda, and Kenya.

Fragmentation in the south is greater than in the north, where Arabized peoples comprise the central core and African peoples are located on the geographic periphery. There are also nonindigenous communities that occasionally have political significance, such as the small Coptic (Christian) community in Khartoum that originated in Egypt and Muslim migrants from West Africa who settled in the Nile Valley on their way to or from the pilgrimage to Mecca. Some joined the Mahdist religio-political movement in the late nineteenth century. Subsequently, the British encouraged West Africans to labor on agricultural schemes along the Nile, but they were denied citizenship and therefore the right to own land. Known pejoratively as *fallata*, they have varying origins and differing degrees of Arabization. Estimates of their numbers range from one to six million, with 6 percent being their probable share of the total population.[48]

These ethnic distinctions should not be seen as permanent or primordial. Ethnic designations shift over time and the movement of peoples across the Sudan resulted in transformations in self-identity. Fertit, for example, was the word for pagans used to encompass a wide range of small groups in western Bahr al-Ghazal. Those largely Arabized and Muslim sedentary peoples only recently began to use the word Fertit in political discourse.[49] Many peoples have created new histories and genealogies to suit their new identities. For example, the Ja'aliyyin are Arabized Nubians who claim to be descended from Ja'al, a descendant of Abbas, the uncle of the Prophet Muhammad: they thereby acquired an impeccable Arab and Muslim lineage.[50]

In some ways the extreme diversity creates a tolerance for others, since peoples of differing customs, languages, and beliefs must interact with each other. For example, Arab pastoralists who move their camels and cattle into Dinka and Nuba territory in search of pasturage in the summer require access to the Dinka and Nuba fields for grazing after the farmers harvest their crops. Considerable intermarriage also takes place among those peoples. However, interaction also fosters intolerance and mutual stereotyping as well as clashes over limited resources and raids for cattle and grain. Arab-Islamic Baqqara nomads consider themselves superior culturally to the "pagan" Dinka, whereas Dinka have imprinted the image of those Arabs as slavers who seized their wives and children.[51]

LINES OF DEMARCATION

In sum, two crucial lines of cultural demarcation in the Sudan involve language and religion. Just over half of the Sudanese speak Arabic as their native tongue. In the north, Arabic is the principal language at home as well as in education, commerce, and government. But in the south a hundred indigenous languages are spoken and English has been the preferred language (rather than Arabic) for the educated elite. Nonetheless, a linguistic profile of the Sudan in the 1970s underlined the linguistic diversity within both parts of the country.[52] In the south the researchers found that whereas 87 percent of the residents of Bahr al-Ghazal spoke Dinka languages, 52 percent of the residents of Upper Nile spoke Nuer, 25 percent Dinka, and 14 percent Shilluk. In Equatoria, the language map was even more complex: 24 percent spoke Zande, 19 percent Teso, 18.4 percent Bari, and 13 percent Latuko, with smaller numbers speaking other distinct languages. In none of the three regions was Arabic the indigenous language of more than 1.7 percent of the residents.

In the north, the greatest contrast was between Khartoum province, which was 96 percent Arabic speaking and Kassala, where 36 percent spoke Arabic as their indigenous language, 50 percent spoke Beja, and 11 percent spoke West African languages. In Dar Fur, 55 percent spoke Arabic, 21 percent Fur, and others spoke Masalit, Zaghawa, and west African languages. In Kordofan, two-thirds spoke Arabic and 27 percent Nuba languages. In the Northern province, 81 percent spoke Arabic and 19 percent Nubian dialects. Thus, even in the north, regional languages competed with Arabic.

Moreover, the linguistic map in Khartoum would be different today: with the influx of migrants from the west and the south, African languages and cultures have a marked impact on the capital city. By 1989, 40 percent of its population identified themselves as African, including many Muslims who came from Dar Fur or Kordofan.[53] Thus, the linguistic bifurcation between the north and south needs to be qualified. Nonetheless, Arabic is decidedly the lingua franca in the north, whereas that status is still contested in the south and the lack of Arabic has important implications for the relative power of the south.

Religion also serves as a significant distinguishing mark which overlaps with language in the south. Although precise figures are impossible to obtain, approximately 70 percent of the Sudanese people are Muslim, 25 percent follow indigenous beliefs, and 5 percent are Christian. The north is overwhelmingly Muslim, with pockets of Christians in the Nuba Mountains as well as Christian communities in the towns. The latter include some Christians whose ancestors immigrated to Sudan from the Arab provinces of the Ottoman Empire in the nineteenth century, but most are southerners who migrated north. Most southern peoples adhere to indigenous beliefs, although about 20 percent have converted to Christianity since the early twentieth century. Perhaps 10 percent converted to Islam, mostly since independence.

Religious communities are not homogeneous. Indigenous beliefs are rooted in local customs and histories. The majority of Christians are Roman Catholic, but there are also Protestant, Coptic, and Greek Orthodox communities. Muslims belong to a wide variety of *turuq* (brotherhoods), which originally were formed around revered preachers but in time became complex and far-flung organizations. Brotherhoods cut across ethnic lines: for example, many Beja are members of the Khatmiyya order (led by the Mirghani family), while other Beja are members of the Ansar movement (led by the Mahdi family). Many West Africans also adhere to the Ansar movement.

Despite the diversity of the Sudanese people, the fact that some 70 percent of the population is Muslim and half comes from Arabic-speaking peoples has a major impact on its political culture. It is especially important that Arabic is the language of the Quran: Arabic culture is automatically linked to faith in the minds of most Sudanese. Issues involving the national language and the role of Islam as the majority's religion have been vitally important in its political life—and have been highly divisive. The assertion of an Arab-Islamic identity by the northern majority has alienated African and non-Muslim peoples. That divide has had enduring political ramifications and has embittered political life.

THE CONTESTED SUDANESE NATION-STATE

In the Sudan, there is acute tension between the proponents of ethnic nationalism, whose Arab-Islamic paradigm has dominated political life since independence, and the proponents of territorial nationalism, who seek to restructure the system to respect minority rights and create an overarching common political identity. That tension has been exacerbated by the frequent imposition of a control model, rather than a pluralist model, under which the ruling ethnic nationalists maintain that the majority religion and most widespread language should define the country's identity and be expressed in its legal and political system. In that sense, they insist, the country is Muslim and Arab in character. They note that Arabic is studied by most young people in school and used as the lingua franca in commerce and the central government. In their view, minority peoples who speak locally based languages or subscribe to Christianity or indigenous belief systems must either assimilate culturally to the Arab-Islamic majority or remain in separate territorial enclaves in which they can be exempted from the application of certain religious laws or linguistic requirements. This perspective sees any compromise of that Arab-Islamic identity as impossible, since that would require relinquishing the image of a country that seeks to be homogeneous in language and religion and intrinsically linked to Arab-Islamic civilization.

This strongly assimilationist version of the ethnic nation-state model defines the lines of political cleavage throughout the country. In the north, for example, Fur and Beja seek to maintain their distinctive cultural systems: they want to retain their indigenous languages and the special characteristics of their Islamic rituals. They adopt varying modes of accommodation, assimilation, and resistance to the dominant system. The conflict is most stark in the south, whose African peoples have cultural, linguistic, and religious traditions that are completely distinct from the Arab-Islamic north. Ethnic nationalists view the south and Nuba Mountains as fertile fields for conversion to Islam. They also press for the use of Arabic as the sole language in administration and instruction throughout the country.

Such pressures date back to the Turkiyya and Mahdiyya periods in the nineteenth century, when Muslim traders and slavers coupled economic dominance in the south with the assumption that their own culture was superior to that of the southern peoples. When the British kept the two parts of the country separate in the 1930s and early 1940s, many politicians in the north considered the peoples of the south "the lost brother" snatched away by the British; they maintained that, without that artificial separation, the diffusion of Arabic and Islam would have led to the disappearance of southern cultural specificity.[54] With independence, adherents of ethnic nationalism sought to promote the country's Muslim-Arab identity. General Ibrahim Abbud (1958-1964) Arabized administrative and educational systems in the south and expelled foreign Christian missionaries. Parties based in Islamic religious movements renewed that homogenizing drive in the mid-1960s as did Ja'far Numairi (1969-1985), when he instituted Islamic penal, commercial, and tax codes in 1983. Prime Minister al-Sadiq al-Mahdi (1986-1989) sought to retain Islamic laws, while exempting non-Muslims in the south. The current president, Umar Hasan Ahmad al-Bashir, who seized power on 30 June 1989, argues that he is fighting for Sudan's Arab-Islamic existence: "We believe that what we now apply in Sudan is God's will."[55] Only minor exemptions from Islamic punishments for non-Muslims are possible, under that absolutist paradigm, and cultural Arabization must be pursued comprehensively.

That assertion of ethnic nationalism has led to divergent reactions on the part of the other peoples inside the Sudan. Those reactions comprise, basically, demands to secede or demands to restructure the political system. Proponents of the secessionist approach assert that they have the right to self-determination, which can enable them to choose to secede and form an independent state. They reject assimilation into the majority culture and reject being accorded a special, limited status as a minority group. Some spokespersons of this approach stress that the initial formation of the country was illegitimate and coerced. Others view separation as the necessary outcome after years of discrimination and civil war, which have eliminated the possibility of gaining equal rights and political status. Secessionist demands were strong in the south in the 1960s, and they resumed after Islamic laws were promulgated in 1983. One political leader stated bluntly: "if one of the nationalities [in a multi-national state] imposes itself as the state nationality, where do the other nationalities go?"[56] He argued, after Bashir's coup in 1989, that creating a theocratic state would result not in assimilation but in disintegration and partition of the country.[57] This call for secession became increasingly insistent during the 1990s and remains the favored option among southerners. Even some Islamists have concluded that the north-south polarization is so intense that the only solution is to divide the territory into two states, thereby ending the "illusion" of a united, homogeneous country.[58]

Those who call for restructuring the political system argue that a territorial nation-state can be achieved so long as it is based on the ethnic pluralist model. Their approach seeks to set aside definitions of majority and minority and to create, instead, an inclusive identity that accords all citizens equal rights. The status of citizens should be defined not by religion, language, or culture but rather by birth and residence in the territory that comprises the Sudan. The political system should incorporate that diversity into both central and regional institutions. The approach would place substantial power in the hands of the marginalized peoples living in outlying provinces and would reduce the control by (and benefits that accrue to) the Muslim Arab elite living along the central Nile River. Perceived economic, social, and political imbalances would be redressed through programs to transfer resources from the center to the periphery. Ethnic diversity would be built into the political system in a way that does not privilege any one group but rather enables all the Sudanese peoples to gain a stake in the system. Those who adhere to this approach maintain that a decentralized polity will limit centrifugal pressures rather than exacerbate them: ethnic groups will want to remain within one country if they find room for self-expression and self-rule instead of being pressured to assimilate and being denied their distinctive identities.

This ethnic pluralist approach was endorsed in the Addis Ababa Accord of 1972, which acknowledged the rights and individuality of the southern peoples. During the rest of the 1970s, the constitution prohibited discrimination on the basis of religion, race, language, or gender; stressed Sudan's dual Arab and African identity; and called for respect for Islam, Christianity, and "noble spiritual beliefs." When Numairi unilaterally abrogated the Addis Ababa Accord and the constitution in 1983, the Sudan Peoples' Liberation Movement (SPLM), which led the renewed rebellion in the south, retained that call for a pluralist political system.[59] The SPLM rejected the concept of fixed religious, linguistic, or ethnic majorities and minorities, arguing that the concept of a permanent Muslim majority automatically "isolates large segments of the population from the political process and thereby denies them their legitimate basic rights."[60] SPLM's proposed "New Sudan" would blend the various languages and cultures into a unique pattern in which no single element would have hegemony and the specificities of each culture would be respected by all. This approach was endorsed by many political activists in the north, particularly in the Koka Dam Accord of 1986 and the SPLM's agreement with the Democratic Unionist Party in 1988. It was reaffirmed, after the military coup in 1989, by the opposition National Democratic Alliance (NDA). In particular, the SPLM and NDA agreed at Asmara in 1995 that the Sudan must be a country for all its citizens and that the political system must be based on democracy and religious pluralism.

Moreover, the Asmara accord endorsed holding a referendum in the south on self-determination. That provision was particularly important for southern participants and provided a way for northern political forces to acknowledge southern fears. Indeed, a leader of an Islamic-oriented party stressed that according the right of self-determination was a way to bolster unity: if the north does not abide by the agreed-upon program during the transitional period, he declared, then the south can exercise its right of self-determination and can terminate the union.[61] Recognition of the conditionality of unity is an important component of the ethnic pluralist model.

The ethnic and territorial nationalist approaches are bitterly contested in the Sudan. Strict adherence to the concept of an ethnic nation-state has generated an equally strong and violent backlash among the marginalized peoples. The long-term civil war has displaced much of the population in the south and Nuba Mountains and has spread to the Fur in the far west and the Beja in the east. Since the NIF-military coup in 1989, civil society has been dramatically restricted as NIF leaders have rejected all dissenting perspectives and sought to mold the society in their Islamist image. The ethnic pluralist approach inherent in the Addis Ababa Accord served to reduce strife from 1972 to 1983. Today, the NDA and SPLM offer a more comprehensive formula that is also based on a pluralist nationalism. Nonetheless, the possibility of constructing such a system remains remote. The "war of visions" depicted by former ambassador Francis Deng[62] continues to tear the country apart. The analysis of the intensification of that struggle since 1983 forms the core of this book.

2

Historical Legacies

GIVEN THE DEPTH of the conflict over the identity of the Sudan, it is important to place the current tensions in historical perspective. Although that history establishes a framework for the struggle, the historical experience itself is contested by the parties. They read conclusions about the present into the past and cast blame on various actors, according to their own assumptions and beliefs. Conflict among ethnic groups is partly based on their contested histories. In the Sudanese case, the peoples have written different histories about their interaction, especially in the nineteenth century and during British colonial rule. Moreover, over time ethnic identities that were relatively fluid hardened and became politicized; contrasting perspectives became entrenched. Contested images of the Sudan were held firmly by elites of the varying groups by the 1960s.

The boundaries of the contemporary Sudanese state were established by the British in the wake of their conquest in 1898. Before the nineteenth century, the territory was the eastern reaches of what medieval Arabs called *bilad al-sudan* (the land of the black people), a broad band that extended through central Africa. Independent kingdoms and sultanates controlled varying amounts of territory and engaged in trade, cultural interchange, and military conflict. Christian kingdoms in Nubia lasted until the fourteenth century, but gave way to gradual Islamization and Arabization through immigrants from Egypt. Eventually many Arabized Nubian groups even claimed descent from the prophet's uncle Abbas. Some of the northern riverine peoples traveled west in response to political pressure or economic opportunity. They then married Nuba and Beja women, engaged in cattle and camel breeding, and journeyed up the White Nile and into Bahr al-Ghazal in search of ivory and slaves. In a somewhat similar process, the "black sultanate" of Funj (1504-1821) at Sennar contributed to the Arabization and Islamization of the indigenous peoples. Moreover, the Beja in the Red Sea hills maintained a distinct culture even as they converted to Islam and intermarried with Arab immigrants. Some descendants claimed Arab pedigree through such "adoptive ancestors."[1] The assimilationist thrust assumed that Arabic and Islam were superior to indigenous beliefs and languages and therefore should be emulated and even adopted genealogically. Nonetheless, non-Arab enclaves remained in the north. The scattered villagers in the Nuba Mountains had difficulty fending off slave raids from the nomadic Baqqara Arabs. In contrast, the powerful Muslim sultanate in Dar Fur lasted from the mid-1600s until 1874, staking out a key role in trans-African trade. Ali Dinar restored the sultanate in 1898 and warded off British control until 1916. Meanwhile, Islamic religious preachers (*faqis*) from Arabia and North Africa established sufi brotherhoods (*turuq*, sing. *tariqa*), some of which acquired substantial economic power and political influence. The turuq were often exempted from paying taxes and were granted land from which they could derive revenue. The last politically significant tariqa to emerge was the Khatmiyya, which originated with Muhammad Uthman al-Mirghani (1793-1853) and was closely identified with Turko-Egyptian rule.

Despite a general perception that the swamps of the *Sudd* (barrier) blocked contact between north and south, considerable trade, cultural exchange, and military clashes took place between the peoples living in those territories. Within the south peoples' sources of livelihood consisted of cattle herding, fishing, subsistence farming, and trade in ivory and gold. As noted earlier, they had diverse languages, religious beliefs, and political structures. Although the south was subject to sporadic slave raids from the north, the exchange was relatively equal until the nineteenth century. Indeed, the Shilluk, who lived north of the Sudd, had military prowess that equalled the Arabs' until the latter acquired firearms and armed river steamers in the nineteenth century.

Today politicians argue over the origins of the northern and southern Sudanese. Some southern intellectuals argue that Shilluk, Dinka, and Nuer all originated in the north and migrated south relatively recently.[2] They maintain that self-defined Arabs are really African genetically, with only minute traces of Arab blood. In contrast, northerners tend to emphasize their own Arab lineage. They often argue that some southern peoples originated in East Africa and came after Arab tribes settled in the north. These arguments present one group as authentic and seek to delegitimize the lineage and territorial claims of other groups. If nationalism is rooted in ethnicity, then the most "authentic" people have primacy. If, instead, all the peoples have equal claims to the land—as in territorial nationalism—then such distinctions are immaterial.

TURKIYYA (1821-1885)

The Turko-Egyptian invasion of 1821 brought the first attempts to form a centralized administration.[3] The Turkiyya established military garrisons, constructed telegraph lines, and collected taxes in the north. Although the Funj king surrendered without any resistance, other groups fought off the invasion. Moreover, people revolted in various localities against the heavy taxes that had to be paid in cattle or in slaves for Muhammad Ali's army in Egypt. Over time, the government developed administrative structures, established schools, improved communications and security, and dammed seasonal rivers, all of which encouraged economic growth and both internal and external commerce in the north.

However, for the non-Muslim peoples the Turkiyya caused disastrous dislocations, initially due to the seizure of men to replenish the army in Egypt.[4] Dinka, Shilluk, Ingessana, and Beja (in the east) resisted the initial expeditions, whereas the scattered groups in the Nuba Mountains could not fend off the raids. Private Arab armies also organized periodic *ghazwa*s (slave hunts) in which they seized ivory, slaves, and cattle. Ottoman, Sudanese, and European traders established fortified stations (*zaribas*) in which slaves were held until they could be transported to the north as well as Libya, Egypt, and Arabia. Slave-owning increased substantially within northern Sudan, where slaves began to be used not only as agricultural laborers and servants but also as cooks, blacksmiths, and construction workers.

From the perspective of peoples in the south, *jallaba* (Muslim Arab merchants from the north), European traders, and Ottoman officials were all part of the Turkiyya that devastated their societies. Despite sporadic efforts by the government to stop the slave trade, "the Upper Nile and Bahr al-Ghazal had thus been opened to a predatory commerce and over large areas the traditional tribal structure was in dissolution."[5] Slave raids uprooted people and undermined social units. Conscription into the armed forces was similarly perceived as a form of enslavement and social dislocation, since soldiers rarely returned home.[6] Southern peoples also opposed government efforts to monopolize the trade in ivory, which was one of the few sources of cash income in the south, and they opposed paying taxes and being forced to provide labor (*corvée*) for infrastructural projects. Moreover, their cultures and beliefs clashed with those prevalent in the north. Although individuals converted to Islam and traders learned Arabic for practical purposes, particularly in western Bahr al-Ghazal, most peoples resisted conversion to Islam. This disinterest in conversion was based on their sense of the inherent value and superiority of their own religions and cultures. It grew into active resistance, since Islam and Arabic entered the south transmitted by an alien army and slave-raiding merchants.

These southern perspectives differed sharply from the version of history presented by contemporary Islamists in the north. The latter argue that slavery was commercialized and promoted by Europeans, not by northern Sudanese.[7] They note that slavery was practiced within the south and southerners captured other southerners to sell to merchants in the zaribas. Islamists also assume that the people in the south would have naturally adopted Islam (with Arabic as its linguistic vehicle) through the gradually expanding contact. In time, southern peoples would have recognized the superiority of Islam over their primitive religious beliefs and would have preferred Arabic as the lingua franca. In the meantime, as peoples who were not monotheists, they could be raided and compelled to convert to Islam. Assimilation would benefit the southern peoples as, they assumed, it had benefited other non-Arab peoples in the north.

MAHDIYYA (1885-1898)

The schism intensified during the Mahdiyya, the indigenous politico-religious movement that overthrew the Turkiyya in 1885.[8] In 1881 Muhammad Ahmad Ibn Abdallah proclaimed himself the Mahdi, who would purify and guide the believers and uproot the corrupt, oppressive Turks. Mahdist forces won what seemed like miraculous victories against the well-armed Egyptian troops and brought together a diverse mix of pious disciples, merchants, and nomads. In 1883 the governors of Kordofan and Dar Fur surrendered to the Mahdiyya and, in the east, Beja rose in revolt under Uthman Diqna. The governor of Bahr al-Ghazal surrendered in April 1884 and Khartoum fell in January 1885. Sawakin, the port on the Red Sea, remained under joint British-Egyptian control. European administrators in Equatoria, to the far south, also stayed at their isolated posts. Although the Mahdi died in the summer of 1885, his successor Khalifa Abdallahi institutionalized the Mahdist state that controlled the north until the British conquest in 1898.

At the time, the Mahdiyya was viewed as a religio-political movement that roused the Muslim peoples to a spirit of martyrdom and sought to return the society to the practices of a pure Islam. But, to today's northern nationalists, the Mahdiyya was the key "national liberation movement"[9] that forged the Sudan into one nation, transcending tribal and sectarian allegiances. The perspective from the south was starkly different. Although some peoples in the south cooperated with the Mahdi in order to expel the Turkish garrisons, they did so to free themselves from foreign control and from predatory raids. They, therefore, turned against the Mahdist troops when they imposed centralized rule, collected taxes, and resumed slave raids. The messianic Mahdiyya linked slaveholding with the religious and cultural transformation of slaves from unbelievers to believers. Equally important, many leading Mahdists came from merchant families whose livelihood was threatened by the Turkiyya's efforts to end slavery.[10]

Thus, the Mahdiyya was reconstructed in the national imagination of the north as a period of liberation and assertion of cultural values. It showed that the Sudanese were equal to Europe and able to defeat the once-mighty Ottoman Empire. The Mahdiyya invigorated their national image and held positive symbolic significance as a golden age. In contrast, within the south, the Mahdiyya was seen as the culmination of the depredations of the Turkiyya. Although the Mahdist forces could not consolidate their control over the south, their frequent raids further destabilized its society and economy. Dunstan Wai emphasizes that the "scars of the brutality inflicted on the Southern Sudanese still remain."[11] This period fixed a collective memory that the northerner was the primary source of danger. Those polarized images remain potent today.

ANGLO-EGYPTIAN CONDOMINIUM

Britain sought control over the Sudan for imperial strategic reasons that were largely related to preventing other European powers from seizing the sources of the Nile and gaining footholds along the Red Sea from which they could threaten the sea route to India. But the official justification presented by London, which had been the de facto ruler of Egypt since 1882, was the restoration of Turko-Egyptian sovereignty. Therefore, when it defeated the Mahdiyya in 1898, Britain established a joint regime known as the Anglo-Egyptian Condominium.

In practice, Britain instituted its own legal codes and administrative systems and ruled through British officials in the central administration and provinces. In rural areas the British sought to build up the authority of tribal leaders, through often contradictory policies by which the shaikhs were paid salaries, placed in charge of tribal courts, and accorded enhanced power. In some cases, already influential families consolidated their influence, but in other cases this led to the artificial search for "lost tribes and vanished chiefs."[12] Historian Martin W. Daly views the approach as frequently "an anomalous attempt to 'tribalize' people who had no memory of tribal authority or desire to recall it."[13]

British officials cultivated close relations with the leaders of the principal Islamic religious orders. The most important were Sayyid Ali al-Mirghani, leader of the Khatmiyya, whose leaders had been closely aligned with the Turkiyya and who opposed the Mahdiyya; al-Sharif Yusuf al-Hindi, head of the Hindiyya tariqa; and the posthumous son of the Mahdi, Sayyid Abd al-Rahman al-Mahdi, who was wooed by the British during World War I.[14] They subsequently allowed al-Mahdi to collect *zakat* (Islamic tithes) from the *Ansar* (followers of the Mahdi) and to develop lucrative pump-irrigated cotton schemes on Aba Island and in the Gezira district. Many Ansar laborers were west African migrants who were paid in grain and clothing. The economic power accumulated by the turuq leaders enabled the Ansar and the Khatmiyya to establish political movements that commanded the allegiance of millions of believers in the rural areas of the north and dominated political life in the capital.

The British were wary of the small but vocal urban educated class, which was influenced by Egyptian nationalism in the 1920s and pressed the government to place Sudanese citizens in responsible administrative positions as well as to move toward self-rule. An early manifestation of those protests was the

White Flag League, which the British suppressed in 1924. The league was founded by Ali Abd al-Latif, an Egyptian-born Muslim whose Dinka parents were originally slaves. The members of the league, enthusiastic about the Egyptian revolution of 1919 and Egypt's gaining nominal independence in 1922, called for political unity of the Nile Valley and encouraged anti-British demonstrations in Sudanese towns. The movement attracted Arab and Dinka officers, government clerks, artisans, and workers. Some workers were employed by the railway headquarters at Atbara, which was the first industrial complex in the country. Although the league's members were few in number, they included persons from the new urban lower-middle class that opposed the traditional tribal and sectarian elites. Today, the repression of the White Flag League is viewed as the crushing of the first modern struggle for freedom in the Sudan. Such analyses, however, often omit Abd al-Latif's Dinka heritage and his parents' slave background, as that would imply that a southerner of slave origin could be the authentic leader of an interethnic Sudanese national movement. Moreover, analyses sometimes omit the fact that Mahdi and Mirghani—along with other religious and tribal elites—viewed Abd al-Latif as a "dangerous upstart."[15] Since the White Flag League threatened the established social order, that elite welcomed its repression.

British officials concluded that they should restrict schooling in order to prevent an educated class from emerging that would be discontented with the condominium. An important exception was Gordon Memorial College, which developed several professional schools by 1936 and brought together the brightest youths from the north. The students and graduates of that college confirmed British fears by quickly becoming active politically. In 1931 students protested against cuts in the starting civil service salaries, since that would directly affect their careers. Some teachers, such as Ismail al-Azhari,[16] had been educated in Beirut and returned with pan-Arab and secular nationalist beliefs that they promoted at the college. Most importantly, Abd al-Rahman al-Mahdi supported cultural societies for secondary school and college graduates and underwrote a publishing house that printed literature, political writings, and a newspaper.

The graduates of post-elementary schools and colleges, who totalled 5,000 in 1938,[17] joined together that year to form the Graduates' General Congress (GGC). The GGC was established to press for political rights as well as to serve their professional interests. The GGC, led by Azhari, modeled itself on the Indian National Congress and aimed to have enlightened northern Sudanese take the lead in defining and achieving clear political goals. The growing politicization of the GGC was evident in April 1942 when its leaders submitted a memorandum to the governor-general that requested self-determination, a representative Sudanese body, a Higher Education Council, judicial reform, and educational and economic development at the end of the war. GGC's internal tensions, which grew as Mahdi and Mirghani jockeyed for influence among the graduates, resulted in a schism the next year. Azhari founded Ashiqqa (blood brothers) in 1943, with the tacit support of Ali al-Mirghani, who talked of unity of the Nile Valley in order to maintain the support of Egypt. Abd al-Rahman al-Mahdi founded the Umma Party in 1945, on a platform that called for complete independence. The split in the northern nationalist movement between the two religio-political leaders and their success in linking secularist intellectuals to their sectarian camps had a debilitating impact on pre-independence political life. It also colored postindependence political maneuverings that became locked into "sterile feuds of sectarianism."[18]

SOUTHERN POLICY

Southern political life developed along a different trajectory from the north. Although Anglo-Egyptian troops made incursions into the south in 1898 and established outposts there by World War I, thirty years passed before the many uprisings were subdued. Religious figures and tribal chiefs led local (and uncoordinated) efforts to resist the new rulers. The motivations for resistance remained similar to those of the nineteenth century, with the exception that slave raids had ended. Those motivations included the outsiders'

> destruction of social values; forced labor; taxation irrespective of individual wealth and without provisions of equivalent return in social services; [and] forced reduction of . . . group freedom.[19]

The British pursued their "pacification" program with greater determination than the Turkiyya and Mahdiyya. The British shared the perception of previous conquerors that the peoples in the south were primitive and pagan. Southern peoples required moral guidance that could be provided by Christian missionaries from Europe. The British appointed and dismissed chiefs, despite their avowed support for indirect rule, and established courts which applied British rather than indigenous codes of procedure and which frequently deviated from customary law and its punishments.[20] The British raided cattle camps to collect taxes, continued the corvée system that forced people to work without pay to construct roads, and resumed the Turkiyya's state monopoly on the sale of ivory, which had been an important source of income for indigenous peoples. Overall, the historian Robert O. Collins concludes, there was an "inherent contradiction between British intervention to promote Native Administration and its erosion of tribal custom and authority."[21]

Subsequently, the British attempted to seal the south off from the north in order to "protect" the south from Muslim influence. The ostensible reason for this policy of isolation was to end northern pressure on and dominance of the south and Nuba Mountains. The orders were intended to stop Arab tribes from seizing slaves, cattle, and grain from the south, and to end the alleged pressure to convert to Islam. Missionaries and many government officials were hostile toward Islam. More broadly, British officials sought to keep Arab and Islamic influences out of East Africa, which should fall under the sway of English values and Christianity.[22] As initially articulated through the Closed District Order of 1922, which applied to Kordofan, Dar Fur, and parts of Kassala and the White Nile provinces as well as the south, Sudanese who lived outside those areas could travel to or live there only if they obtained a special permit. The Permits to Trade Ordinance of 1925 allowed the authorities to exclude northern traders (*jallaba*), who had dominated commerce in the countryside. Egyptian officials were removed after 1924 and some northern Sudanese officials were replaced by British officials. Arab-style dress (such as the *jallabiyya*) was prohibited as were names that the British deemed nonindigenous. In practice, however, large numbers of northern traders and officials remained in and even moved to the south.[23]

The British formalized a language policy in 1928 according to which vernacular languages were taught in primary schools, English was designated the official language, and Arabic was excluded from schools and government offices. Although residents in trading towns spoke varying Arabic patois, this policy created linguistic barriers with the north.[24] Catholic and Protestant missionaries opened schools, whereas Muslim schools, mosques, and preachers were banned. The policy was particularly disruptive for western Bahr al-Ghazal, where British officials expelled indigenous Muslim, Arabic-speaking groups into the no-man's-land bordering Kordofan and Dar Fur in 1930, in an extreme interpretation of orders to prevent contact between Arab and southern peoples.[25] In those areas, the Arabic language, Islam, and Arab customs had been prevalent for the past century and were stamped out unnaturally.

British policy was also problematic since it did not foster economic and social development in the south or Nuba Mountains and thereby widened the already substantial gap with the north.[26] The limited number of missionary schools did not meet the population's need to train technicians, soldiers, teachers, and clerks. There were no government secondary schools in the entire south until after World War II. Key British officials blocked government and private development efforts, arguing that the indigenous population had no desire to improve its economic welfare. Private economic investment and production were discouraged by the difficulty of transporting goods within the south and the high cost of railway transport from the railhead in Al-Ubayyid to Port Sudan. Trade with the north relied on the river system. There were no organized markets for handling cattle and animal products, and fishermen lacked transportation, storage, and credit facilities that might have enabled them to expand into commercially viable operations. The government refused to allow projects to grow tobacco and coffee in the south, in order to protect customs revenues earned on the import of cigarettes and coffee from abroad. The only serious development scheme was an integrated cotton-growing and processing project for the Azande people, which began in 1945 and soon suffered economic difficulties. Economic and social development in the south, therefore, lagged significantly behind the north by the time the Sudan gained independence in 1956. The gap can be illustrated by the contrast in per capita gross domestic product in 1956: 119 Sudanese pounds (SL) in greater Khartoum and SL71 in the Gezira area; the level fell to SL27-28 in the rainfed clay plains and sand dunes of the western and central parts of the country. From there it dropped to a mere SL12 in the three southern provinces.[27]

NORTHERN RESENTMENT

Northern Sudanese resented deeply the British separation of the south. A northern historian even declared that "the harm done by the fanatical and arbitrary policy of the Condominium regime in the Southern Sudan far outweighs that of memories of the slave trade."[28] Islamists argue today that British and missionaries' biases against Islam and Arabic culture made the educated southern elite hate the north. They maintain that the British aimed to create an anti-Islamic culture. Islamist leader Hasan al-Turabi asserts that without the forced separation southern ethnic groups would have disappeared through intermarriage and the gradual diffusion of Arabic and Islam. An Islamist intellectual commented that some northern Sudanese[29]

> exhibited a romantic attachment to the South, "the lost brother" snatched away by the aliens, and long due back. . . . There was a general feeling of a need to make up for lost time by spreading the "national" (Arab-Islamic) culture in the South as a basis for unity. This conception presupposed that the South would act as an inert mass, waiting to be reshaped anew.

That intellectual conceded that this northern conception ignored the fact that tensions predated British rule and ignored the reality of strong indigenous cultures that would withstand or selectively incorporate northern cultural and religious values. Finally, it ignored the Sudan's demographic composition: at independence, barely 40 percent of the country's population claimed Arab descent and a slim majority of 51 percent spoke Arabic as their indigenous language.[30] The perception of a dominant Arab Islamic culture belied the reality of heterogeneity.

JUBA CONFERENCE

British policy would have made sense if it had led to the separation of the south from the north, then either turning it into an independent state or attaching it to a neighboring African country. Although an occasional British official suggested those solutions, they were never considered seriously.[31] In 1946 the British formally acceded to pressure from northern politicians and the Egyptian government to keep the south within a united Sudan. Egypt wanted the Nile Valley to remain united under its monarchy. Britain had formed an advisory council in 1944, whose Sudanese members were all from the north. Those members insisted that the council's jurisdiction include the south and argued that the south need not be represented by southerners.[32] Without consulting the south, the British and the advisory council agreed to establish a legislative assembly whose jurisdiction would encompass the entire country.

To diffuse criticism, the British convened a conference in Juba in 1947. Its agenda did not include the principles of unity or separation. Rather, conferees discussed how the south should be represented in the legislature and special safeguards for the south. The British government selected the seventeen southern delegates to the conference, who were virtually all on its payroll as tribal chiefs, junior officials, or police officers. Despite those inhibitions, some of them expressed their fears that northern politicians would outmaneuver them and that they would be underrepresented in the assembly, with only 14 percent of the seats. They argued that the south needed to strengthen its educational and economic systems before joining with the north and therefore required the protections inherent in a federal system. They cited the history of slavery to indicate that "it would take time to develop mutual respect and promote [a] genuine sense of equality."[33] The most senior chief from the south articulated the fear that a hurried union would result in a violent divorce, if northerners reverted to their ancestors' rapacious behavior. Nonetheless, British officials joined the three northern participants in insisting on a unitary system and persuaded most of the southern delegates to support that concept on the grounds that the south would benefit tangibly: the region's isolation would end and the south would gain its fair share of civil service posts.

By the next year the government cancelled trade and travel restrictions between the north and south, allowed a mosque to be built in Juba, and permitted large numbers of northern civil servants and teachers to transfer south. Overall, the preparations for independence marginalized southerners.[34] The legislative assembly seated in December 1948 allocated 14 percent of the seats to the south; those MPs comprised an easily outvoted minority. The one southern MP appointed to the thirteen-member Constitutional Amendment Commission in 1951 resigned when he lost the vote to create a federal system and establish a ministry for southern affairs under a southern minister. Similarly, southern MPs could not stop the ministry of education from decreeing that Arabic would be the only official language and that all intermediary and secondary schools would teach in Arabic. The first Sudanese minister of education considered that the best way to achieve national integration was to assimilate the south into the northern educational system. The south's exclusion from decision-making was further emphasized by the fact that no southerners participated in the delegations sent to Cairo in 1952 and 1953 to decide whether the country should become independent or should merge with Egypt. Finally, the program to Sudanize the civil service, announced at the end of 1954, appointed only six southerners to 800 senior administrative posts. No southerners became governors, deputy governors, or district commissioners; northern officials ruled the south. The all-northern Sudanization commission claimed that southerners lacked seniority, experience, and academic degrees; their lack of fluency in Arabic was an important, though unstated, factor. Collins terms that the "single worst act of folly in the south," since southerners had expected a quarter of the posts and this action confirmed their suspicions of northern intentions.[35] Northern politicians stressed the rights of the numerical majority and formal equality for all citizens. In contrast, southern leaders stressed the need to protect the minority and the need to achieve equitable opportunities and access to economic and political goods. Each side felt it upheld a moral principle; the polarized perspectives deepened the conflict.

In 1953, the Khatmiyya-Ashiqqa alliance [renamed the National Unionist Party (NUP)] contested a second round of parliamentary elections and won 51 of the 97 seats, reducing Umma's share to 22. NUP leader Azhari became the first Sudanese prime minister. A member of the Sudanese Communist Party (SCP) was elected to one of the five graduates seats. The Southern Party (later renamed the Liberal Party) gained nine seats and was supported by three independent MPs. The proclamation of self-government on 9 January 1954 called for a referendum in which the public would choose between independence and union with Egypt. But in August 1955, the assembly voted to evacuate foreign troops immediately. In October NUP and Umma agreed to move to immediate independence, bypassing the referendum. Parliament passed the transitional constitution on 31 December 1955 and Sudan became independent the next day. For such politicians as Abd al-Rahman al-Mahdi this was a deeply emotional moment that symbolized Sudan's resurrection seventy years after the Mahdiyya.[36]

The accelerated move to independence shocked southern politicians. Marginalized politically and excluded from decision-making in Khartoum, the southern MPs announced in November 1955 that they would not endorse the independence proclamation unless the south gained federal status. They called for a plebiscite in the south under UN auspices to determine the region's relations with the north. However, they finally settled for a vague promise that "the claims . . . for federal government in the three southern provinces [will] be given full consideration" after independence.[37] They realized too late that "full consideration" did not guarantee a favorable outcome and later cited this as a prime example of the tricks played on them by northern politicians. To them, "independence" meant that they exchanged one foreign ruler for another.

VIOLENCE IN YAMBIO AND TORIT

The transition to independence proved violent.[38] In July 1955 police shot at Zande demonstrators who protested the arrest of a Zande member of parliament after he supported the concept of federation at a political rally. Southern fears of economic displacement intensified when, soon after northern managers arrived in June 1955 to run the cotton and textile scheme in Yambio, they dismissed 300 southern workers. When the workers petitioned for increased wages, threatened to strike, and attacked northerners in Nzara town, the manager called in police and soldiers to quell the protests.

Soon after, a unit of the Southern Defence Corps stationed at Torit (East Equatoria) was ordered to go to Khartoum for the independence celebration. Southern soldiers were already irritated that northern officers had taken over from the British and feared that the order was a plot to disband and kill them. The soldiers refused to get into trucks to travel to Juba on 18 August 1955 and then killed more than 300 northern officials and civilians (including women and children) in Torit. Attacks on northerners spread to a dozen other towns in Equatoria. The government airlifted Arab troops to Juba and declared a state of emergency. Although the soldiers laid down their arms when the British pledged to treat them fairly, they fled into the bush when they realized that northern troops (rather than British) would supervise their surrender. The four persons who remained to meet the northern soldiers were summarily executed, along with numerous southern policemen. Northern troops also burned houses and destroyed crops and livestock in neighboring villages.

What was perceived as a mutiny by the government in Khartoum, necessitating a firm crackdown, was viewed as justified resistance in the south. Northern politicians blamed the uprising on outsiders: some claimed that Catholic missionaries brainwashed the soldiers to hate Islam and northerners.[39] Alternatively, they claimed that Egypt instigated the mutiny to try to block Sudanese independence.[40] Those perspectives did not comprehend that the suppression of the Torit uprising—coming on the heels of the south's political and economic marginalization—confirmed southerners' worst fears. It had a far-reaching impact on the north-south relationship.

Thus, as Sudan gained independence, assimilationist tendencies came to the fore that sought to undo decades of separation and integrate the south on the basis of the Arab-Islamic paradigm. The northern politicians took full advantage of their automatic majority in the legislative and executive institutions. No serious consideration was given to an alternative paradigm that would posit the independent Sudan as a multiethnic country in which due consideration should be given to the culture and economic interests of its varying peoples. In the wave of enthusiasm for independence in the north, southern protests seemed illegitimate and even treasonous. They did not perceive those protests as statements by people who were distressed by a political transformation from which they were virtually excluded. The situation provided a clear case of one ethnic group imposing its values and symbols as the country's ethnic-nationalism rather than embracing an inclusive territorial nationalism that would encompass the country's diverse peoples.

UNSTABLE GOVERNMENTS AFTER INDEPENDENCE

Although Sudanese political life was dominated by northern parties, those political forces were not united. Within six months of independence, the alliance between Azhari's secularists and the Khatmiyya broke up. A new coalition government brought together the parties of the two sayyids, who rejected federalism on the grounds that it would encourage secession and sought a constitution that would enshrine Islam as the official religion and shari'a as a basic source of legislation. Since the forty-six-member National Constitutional Committee formed in September 1956 had only three southern members, the committee recommended a centralized, unitary system, with shari'a the source of law and Arabic the official national language.[41]

Those recommendations increased instability in the south. A new degree of self-assertion by educated southerners was evident when their Federal Party won 40 of the 46 southern seats in elections to the 173-seat parliament in 1958. The party platform demanded federation, equal status for English with Arabic and for Christianity with Islam, an orientation toward Africa rather than the Arab world, and a separate military force in the south consisting exclusively of southern troops and officers.[42] The southern MPs walked out of parliament on June 1958 when the government rejected all their demands and insisted on adhering to a unitary system. Beja, Fur, and Nuba politicians also sought a decentralized political system and inclusion in decision-making. But they could be contained or co-opted more easily, in part because of their smaller numbers and limited representation in the parliament and in part because the government could invoke Islamic solidarity to win over Beja and Fur and some of the Nuba.[43]

The parliamentary system assumed that participants agreed on the rules of the political game and adhered to a basic national consensus. In Sudan, however, support for political parties was based on ethnicity, religion, and personal allegiance. Non-Arab and secular-oriented groups were automatically and permanently in the minority. Given the lack of national consensus, those who were outvoted had limited incentives to remain inside the political system. Conversely, the Islamic- and Arab-oriented political parties were assured control over the parliament and cabinet and could ignore other perspectives. Assimilation and marginalization could be carried out by ostensibly democratic means. The existence of some elected representation and freedom of speech put brakes on repression but did not check efforts to institute the ethno-national vision of one part of the population at the expense of the rest.

ABBUD REGIME

In this context of deflated legitimacy for parliamentary rule and heightened regional and religious tension, the high command of the armed forces seized power. Commander-in-chief Major General Ibrahim Abbud had the tacit support of the prime minister, who feared that he was being marginalized politically. The coup d'état on 16/17 November 1958 occurred hours before parliament was scheduled to convene to vote on the contentious issues of an Islamic constitution and federalism. On the day of the coup, a mass meeting was scheduled by Fur politicians to endorse the southern-sponsored demand for federation.

Abbud opposed secularism and the devolution of power to marginalized groups.[44] Instead, he sympathized with the Islamic-oriented Khatmiyya and Ansar, while being fed up with their factionalism and preoccupation with personal rivalries. Abbud appointed himself prime minister and surrounded himself with military officers. He suspended the constitution, closed parliament, and banned political parties. His actions were challenged in 1959 by members of the armed forces, including a group with ties to Nubians who were furious that they would be removed from their ancestral homes when that area would be flooded by the construction of the Aswan High Dam. During the next two years, politicians—especially from the Umma, National Unionist, and Communist parties— lobbied to restore parliament, which propelled Abbud to intern a dozen leading politicians for seven months in 1961. Railway strikes, protests at the Mahdi's tomb, and student demonstrations induced Abbud to release the politicians and conduct elections for local councils in 1963. However, he did not let the parties field candidates, which resulted in a widespread boycott. When the government forbade elections for the Gezira tenants union in 1963, the communist-organized tenants struck at the height of the picking season and compelled the government to capitulate, enabling the Communist Party to sweep those elections. But power remained concentrated in the hands of Abbud and his narrowly based regime.

Meanwhile, the south exploded when Abbud tried to stamp out unrest, impose Arabic, and limit the rights of Christian churches. He argued that cultural homogenization was essential to Sudan's unity and believed that Christianity was an alien religion that foreign missionaries had imposed on the south. He expressed contempt for African religions and disparaged indigenous languages and customs. Abbud pressured Zande and Toposa chiefs in Equatoria to convert to Islam and to order their people to also convert. The government required Arabic in southern schools in order to achieve national integration and religious unity. It constructed many Muslim religious schools and mosques and changed the weekly holiday in the south from Sunday to Friday, the Muslim day of rest. Those measures provoked strikes throughout the southern school system in April 1960 and October 1962.[45] Since northern Sudanese tended to blame foreign missionaries for southerners' resistance to Arab-Islamic culture, Abbud restricted their medical, relief, and educational operations. That culminated in the Missionary Societies Act of May 1962, which regulated churches and nationalized missionary schools. In February 1964 the government expelled all 300 foreign missionaries, blaming them for fomenting separatism and encouraging the widespread armed revolt. The government also transferred north many southern officials and teachers, ostensibly to promote national integration but probably because they were potential leaders within the south. No economic development or infrastructure projects were undertaken in the south except for the extension of the railway to Wau, whose aim was to ensure military control rather than to enhance economic growth. No southerners were recruited into the armed forces and few entered the police or prison services, ostensibly because they were not fluent in Arabic. For example, from 1956 to 1964 the army commissioned 589 officers of whom twenty came from the south.[46]

Abbud's policies revived memories of the military and slave raids of the Turkiyya and Mahdiyya, with the accompanying pressure to convert to Islam and adopt Arabic culture. His approach was a crude assertion of the dominant paradigm of a homogeneous country with one national religion and national language. Moreover, the restraints on government action during the parliamentary period vanished under military rule. As unrest spread, the armed forces bombed and burned villages to the extent that half a million southerners fled into exile. The core of the southern guerrilla forces that combined into the Anya-Nya comprised soldiers who had mutinied at Torit in 1955 and others from the pre-independence Southern Corps.[47] The guerrillas coalesced politically in 1960 into a movement that became known as the Sudan African National Union (SANU). At its national convention in Kampala (Uganda) in November 1964, SANU proclaimed the goal of independence for the south.

Meanwhile, mounting military casualties compelled the government to establish a commission of enquiry in September 1964 to investigate the causes of southern discontent.[48] Northern political activists used that investigation as an excuse to air a wide range of grievances and argue that the civil war could not end while the military remained in power. When a communist student leader was killed in a clash with security forces, 30,000 people attended his funeral. On

24 October, the chief justice persuaded Abbud to meet representatives of professional groups, who formed the Professional Front and galvanized a general strike
in Khartoum that was joined by trade unions and politicians. Significantly, young
army officers refused to fire on the demonstrators. Senior officers then intervened to mediate an agreement whereby Abbud resigned and a civilian transitional government was formed on 30 October. That October Revolution acquired
mythic proportions for democratic forces in the north as an exemplary use of
moral power by unarmed civilians to overthrow an unjust regime. Opposition to
Abbud, however, did not mean that most northern political forces had stopped
supporting the concept of an Arab-Islamic nation. Nonetheless, the short-lived
transitional government that followed the October Revolution displayed an un-
usual sensitivity to southern perspectives and concerns.

ROUND-TABLE CONFERENCE

The transitional civilian government, headed by the educator Sirr al-
Khatim al-Khalifa, was composed of representatives of five northern parties, the
Professional Front, and three southern politicians selected by the new Southern
Front (SF). Leaders of the ideologically opposed Sudanese Communist Party
(SCP) and Islamic Charter Front (ICF) served in the cabinet, for the first time.
Significantly, a southerner became minister of interior, a highly sensitive post
that had always been held by a northerner. However, the leaders of the powerful
traditional Islamic parties resented being relegated to one portfolio each in the
cabinet.[49] The Ansar mounted a massive demonstration in February 1965 that
compelled Khalifa to restructure the cabinet so that the majority fell to Umma,
NUP, and ICF, with SCP reduced to one portfolio and the Professional Front
curtailed.

The transitional government was mandated to prepare parliamentary elections, but Khalifa also sought to use the opportunity to end the civil war. Khalifa
had gained the respect of southerners when he was director of education in the
south. He authorized southern ministers and politicians to contact Anya-Nya
leaders in exile, and then made important gestures such as granting them amnesty, welcoming a delegation from SANU to Khartoum in February 1965, and
promulgating a cease-fire before convening a Round-Table Conference in the
capital in March 1965.[50] All the northern parties and southern groups were represented at the conference, but they were far too divided to reach any agreement.
Northern parties were preoccupied with the campaign leading up to parliamentary elections the next month and feared that they would lose votes in the north
if they made political concessions to the south. They rejected the idea of establishing a federation and viewed even the discussion of secession as treasonous. At

most, the south could gain local self-rule and an accelerated economic development program.

The south did not speak with one voice at the conference. Aggrey Jaden, representing the majority in SANU, argued that the conference should discuss only how to facilitate the south's transition to independence. William Deng, speaking for the breakaway faction of SANU, endorsed federation between the south and the north. Southern Front delegates called for a referendum that would include all possible options—secession, federation, local government, and unity. While SF preferred federation, this approach would enable the south to have a free choice; their approach embodied the concept of self-determination in its fullest sense.

The Round-Table Conference was an important face-to-face meeting at which northern and southern politicians spoke as equals and southern politicians gave full voice to their grievances. Nonetheless, neither side trusted the other enough to reach an agreement. Memories of Torit made the Anya-Nya fear giving up their arms, whereas fears of southern secession made northerners demand that the guerrillas disarm. The delegates accepted the proposal by African observers to establish a twelve-person committee composed of six southerners and six northerners to draft a working paper that would be considered when the conference reconvened. Meanwhile, the government should institute immediate reforms, such as resettling southern refugees; hiring southerners in the police, armed forces, and civil administration; equalizing wages in the south and north; guaranteeing freedom of religion and missionary activity for Sudanese nationals; establishing a university in the south as well as a girls' secondary school and agricultural training programs; and creating a southern development agency. Those measures would be difficult to implement, however, without an overall peace accord.

POLARIZATION UNDER CIVILIAN GOVERNMENTS

The committee spent more than a year preparing its recommendations. By then, the sectarian parties regained power through elections in April 1965 and further elections in April 1968.[51] Fighting prevented voting from taking place in the south in 1965, which meant that the south had no representation in parliament for three crucial years. The fragmentation in the legislature was intensified by the behavior of the traditional politicians, who resumed their pre-Abbud pattern of wrangling over ministerial posts rather than developing coherent policies. The wrangling was exacerbated by the division of the Umma party between factions headed by Imam al-Hadi and the youthful al-Sadiq al-Mahdi, who had just returned from studies at Oxford University to claim the leadership of the movement in his capacity as great-grandson of the Mahdi.[52] The 1968 elections also skewed representation toward the traditional Islamic parties, although an outspoken contingent of southern MPs was elected and, for the first time, northern non-Arab regional groups gained seats.

During the second democratic period (1965-1969), three key policy steps involved expelling the SCP from parliament, renewing discussion of an Islamic constitution, and intensifying the war in the south. Competitive overbidding among northern Islamic forces fostered the assertion of the assimilationist control model that ignored the interests of other ethnic groups and ideological tendencies. Given their parliamentary majority, they could use democratic devices to achieve nondemocratic ends. In particular, the Islamic Charter Front (ICF) had gained five MPs in 1965 under the newly invigorated leadership of Dr. Hasan al-Turabi, a law professor who had graduated from the Sorbonne. He had restructured the Islamist movement to appeal to young intellectuals and had gained wider support by his activism during the October Revolution. Turabi succeeded in persuading the assembly to ban the Communist Party on the grounds that the party was atheist and thereby antithetical to the country's religious values.[53] This action placed ideological restrictions on the inclusiveness of the parliamentary process. By touching on the sensitive issue of religious faith, Turabi pressured the traditional Muslim politicians into following his ideological lead.

Overall, the governments continued Abbud's policies that promoted Arabization and Islamization. For example, al-Sadiq al-Mahdi strongly reasserted the Arab-Islamic ethic when he became prime minister in 1966:[54]

> The dominant feature of our nation is an Islamic one and its overpowering expression is Arab, and this nation will not have . . . its prestige and pride preserved except under an Islamic revival.

In line with this perspective, the draft constitution of 1968 termed Islam the official religion and Arabic the official language. Shari'a would serve as the basic source of civil and criminal law and communism and all atheist ideologies would be banned. Regions would not select their own governors or control their own security forces. State discrimination against non-Muslims would thereby be legalized. The draft constitution enshrined the values and assumptions of ethnic nationalism: the elevating of one group's language and religion and the denial of even minority group rights to those of different languages and faiths. Rather than finding a way to include them, its terms definitively excluded them. As a result, southern MPs, who maintained that the constitution "would deprive some citizens of their basic political and civil rights,"[55] walked out of the constitutional committee. They joined other secular and regional political forces to found the Front for the Protection of Liberties. Growing discontent among Beja, Nuba, and Fur indicated their concern that, as Africans with distinctive cultures, their particular cultural traditions would not be respected in a narrowly shari'a-based and Arabizing political system.

The civil war intensified during this period. In June 1965 the all-northern parliament resolved unanimously to give the security forces a "free hand" to "restore law and order."[56] Soldiers killed unarmed demonstrators in Juba in July 1965 and razed half of its residential areas. A few days later, the army cordoned off the cathedral in Wau during a wedding and killed 76 persons, including 49 southern government officials. Then the army killed 187 civilians in August near Malakal. The editors of SF's newspaper went on trial for publicizing those killings, which southerners viewed as a concerted campaign to eliminate their educated leadership. Two years later, the army killed fifteen tribal chiefs while they were detained in the Bor garrison.[57] Pledges made at the Round-Table Conference to expand education and development, resettle refugees, and guarantee religious freedom remained unfulfilled, and the government reverted to the view that Anya-Nya were treasonous rebels.

Meanwhile, the committee appointed by the Round-Table Conference recommended the decentralization of power to the regions, short of federation or secession.[58] Each region would elect a regional assembly that would, in turn, elect a regional government. Police and district officers would be recruited locally, and each region would craft its own economic plans. Southern residents would be permitted to preserve their indigenous cultures and to teach indigenous languages in school. But the exact relationship between the regional and central governments remained unresolved, and the committee did not agree as to whether the south should remain three separate provinces or constitute one large region, as southerners preferred. Northerners were particularly fearful that a southern home-guard responsible to the regional government could serve as the nucleus of a secessionist army.

Nonetheless, the recommendations modified the assimilationist approach to national unity and contained important concepts embodying ethnic pluralism. Those recommendations contradicted the assimilationist approach that was being developed in the parliamentary discussion of a draft constitution. Therefore, none of the governments took steps to implement the committee's recommendations. In fact, al-Sadiq al-Mahdi avoided reconvening the Round-Table Conference by assembling an All Party Conference instead, which excluded the external southern parties and the (banned) SCP.[59] In that inauspicious political climate, the Anya-Nya's convention of August 1967 set up the Southern Sudan Provisional Government in areas controlled by Anya-Nya, in line with the movement's emphasis on secession. Nonetheless, another convention of March 1969 reserved the option of establishing a federation if acceptable terms could be negotiated.

Overall, the second period of parliamentary rule proved disastrous. By 1969 the political system had even less legitimacy than its predecessor in 1956-1958. The south was seriously alienated; the left chafed at its restricted status; professionals and students resented being pushed aside after they had led the October revolution; and non-Arab groups pressed for federation. Nuba officers and politicians apparently began to plot a coup d'état. Before they could act, a group of secularist, pan-Arab Free Officers seized power in May 1969. They included some of the junior officers who had welcomed the overthrow of Abbud in 1964 but were now sharply disillusioned with democracy.

This capsule history indicates that the political thrust was clearly toward domination by Arab-Islamic peoples of the north. They assumed the right to rule and to define Sudan's national identity according to their own ethnicity. They assumed that non-Arab and non-Muslim peoples lacked cultural—much less national—identities of their own and should be absorbed and assimilated into the Arab-Islamic ethos. Those who objected must be suppressed as illegitimate.

This expression of the assimilationist model not surprisingly led marginalized peoples to call for secession. First they objected to the terms of the union and then they rebelled when even moderate demands were brushed aside. Knowing that the international community was unlikely to recognize and support a secessionist movement, they were willing to consider the option of a federation based on ethnic pluralism. But that option was not taken seriously in Khartoum. Only the Round-Table Conference discussed decentralization as a real option. Otherwise most northern politicians viewed self-determination for the south as a threat to the country's territorial integrity, not as a way to ensure the continuation of the Sudan as a territorial nation-state in which all the peoples would have a stake.

3

The Contradictory Policies of Numairi, 1969-1985

THE COUP D'ÉTAT IN 1969 opened up the possibility of a shift from an assimilationist approach toward a more inclusive formula of national identity, given Ja'far Numairi's criticism of sectarian politics. However, the change came in the context of a reversion to authoritarian rule and a strong assertion of pan-Arabism. Military regimes were the least likely to tolerate criticism or divergent viewpoints and the most likely to try to impose a consensus. Democracies at least needed public support and parliamentary votes to legitimize their authority. In practice, Numairi's drive for total control led to drastic shifts in policy. In 1972 he endorsed a form of ethnic pluralism in the Addis Ababa Accord, thereby ending the war in the south. But in 1977 he began to shift toward an assimilationist approach that culminated in full Islamization. That extreme version of the control model alienated the south and led to the resumption of civil war. Simultaneously, northern politicians were alienated by Numairi's authoritarianism, which bordered on a totalitarian intrusion into citizens' personal lives. That galvanized a wide range of groups to overthrow Numairi, with the tacit support of the armed forces.

Numairi and his Revolutionary Command Council (RCC) identified themselves as secular, socialist, and pan-Arab, modeled on the Nasirite revolution in Egypt. They wanted to sweep aside the religion-based political groups and embark on government-directed development programs. They argued that state-led industrialization and the expansion of capital-intensive agricultural schemes would boost the economy. They initially won support from the trade union movement, led by the Communist Party (SCP), and several communists joined the cabinet.[1] Some other politicians and professionals who were weary of the machinations of the political parties also supported the RCC, including southerners who welcomed Numairi's statement on 9 June (discussed below).

The RCC outlawed political parties and purged the senior ranks of the civil service, police, and armed forces of supporters of the previous regime. Troops stormed the Ansar headquarters on Aba island in March 1970 and leaders of Umma, PDP, NUP, and ICF went into exile to escape the crackdown. Once the religious right was suppressed, Numairi turned against his allies on the left. The

45

showdown with the SCP came in July 1971, after three communists whom Numairi had expelled from the RCC attempted to unseat him. Numairi gained popular support for "saving" Sudan from the "communist menace."[2] Numairi then wielded absolute power, although he did try to establish a popular base by setting up the Sudanese Socialist Union (SSU) as the only party that could contest elections for the Peoples' Assembly.

NEW APPROACHES TOWARD THE SOUTH

Numairi initially spoke of increasing military pressure on the "mutiny" in the south. Nonetheless, on 9 June, only two weeks after the coup, he articulated a sharply different approach that was urged on him by Abel Alier, one of two southern cabinet members. Alier, a former judge, had written the Southern Front's keynote address for the Round-Table Conference. Numairi pledged that the new regime was "determined to arrive at a lasting solution" on the basis of "the right of the southern people to Regional Autonomy within a United Sudan." Furthermore, the government[3]

> recognizes the historic and cultural differences between the North and South and firmly believes that the unity of our country must be built on these objective realities. The Southern people have the right to develop their respective cultures and traditions within a united socialist Sudan.

Numairi did not act decisively until he crushed the traditional Islamic parties and suppressed the left, all of which opposed ideological concessions to the south. The new policy was, however, supported by centrist technocrats who sought economic stability. Numairi made Alier minister for southern affairs and then second vice president, and appointed, for the first time, southern commissioners for the three southern provinces. Meanwhile, Colonel Joseph Lagu, who seized control of the Anya-Nya in July 1970, recognized that even though the guerrillas could prevent the government from controlling the south, they could never achieve a decisive military victory. The military stalemate helped to induce both sides to search for a political accord.

The peace agreement negotiated in February 1972 in Addis Ababa (Ethiopia) resulted in the Regional Self-Government Act for the Southern Provinces.[4] The south became one region, whose regional assembly would elect a High Executive Council (HEC). The regional government was responsible for internal security and local administration in the social, cultural, and economic fields. It had an independent budget, whose revenue came from local taxes and fees as well as from a special fund from the central government to help narrow the gap with the north. Although Arabic remained the country's official language, English was designated the principal language in the south and southern schools could teach indigenous languages. The southern region was represented in the national assembly in proportion to its population. The label "federal" was avoided, since that term was anathema to the north, but a de facto federal system was created.

The Addis Ababa Agreement and the Regional Self-Government Act were incorporated into the permanent constitution of 1973, which specified that they could be amended only by a three-quarters vote in the national assembly and a two-thirds vote in a referendum of the southern electorate. That double safeguard would prevent the northern majority from making arbitrary changes. The constitution stressed the dual Arab and African identity of the Sudan; respect for Islam, Christianity, and "noble spiritual beliefs"; the equality of all persons before the law; and the prohibition of any form of discrimination on the basis of religion, race, language, or gender.

The Addis Ababa Agreement and constitution articulated the ethnic pluralist model, since they included both equality before the law for all citizens and special protections for minorities. Territorial decentralization was combined with proportional representation at the center. The accord recognized that both components were essential. In the past, legal equality for individual citizens at the center had translated into permanent minority status for the south in the legislative and executive bodies and discriminatory measures in the minorities' geographical area. Conversely, regional self-government alone could lead to ghettoization and an inability to impact national-level policies that were critically important to the minority. Practice diverged markedly from theory, however. Implementation of the Addis Ababa accord was hampered by Numairi's effort to manipulate southern politics and control its economy, and by jealousies among southern politicians. In 1983 Numairi unilaterally abrogated the accord when he redivided the south into three regions and instituted Islamic law. Those divisive issues are detailed in the following sections.

ECONOMIC DEVELOPMENT AND NATURAL RESOURCES

When the civil war ended, the south's economy was in shambles. Colonial-era agricultural projects had been abandoned; the infrastructure was destroyed; and a million people had fled abroad or into the bush. The regional government was "starved" for funds to undertake reconstruction and rehabilitation and failed to receive development funds from Khartoum.[5] Southerners were keenly disappointed, since the north-south socioeconomic gap continued to widen. Controversies over the Jonglei Canal and natural resources therefore arose in the context of grievances about inadequate development financing and economic discrimination.

The Jonglei Canal project in Upper Nile province would drain 20 percent of

the huge Sudd swamp through which the White Nile flows and dramatically reduce water loss through evaporation, according to the Egypt-Sudan accord of
1974.[6] The project was received with suspicion and anxiety in the south. Many
people felt Egypt would be the primary beneficiary; rumors that two million
Egyptian peasants would settle along the canal triggered riots in Juba on 10 October 1974. Moreover, the project would quickly destroy pasturage for cattle and
dry up fish ponds, whereas studies for future development projects remained incomplete and none were implemented, even though the canal was more than
two-thirds dug by 1984. At a deeper political and psychological level, many
feared that draining the Sudd would remove the protective barrier separating
the south from the north.

   Oil was equally contentious. The Chevron Oil Company discovered oil in
Muglad (southern Kordofan) and Bentiu (Upper Nile) in 1979. Southerners' fear
that the north would steal their oil crystallized in November 1980, when Attorney General Hasan al-Turabi submitted a new map to the Peoples Assembly that
shifted the northern part of Bentiu into the Kordofan region. Although Numairi
diffused tensions by withdrawing the proposed boundary change, he soon replaced southern troops with northern forces at Bentiu; pocketed the proceeds
from the Chevron license, which the Addis Ababa Agreement stated should go to
the regional government; and decided to shift the site of the oil refinery from
Bentiu to Kosti, a major rail and river junction in the north. Southerners were
furious: a refinery at Bentiu would improve the infrastructure, catalyze economic development, and provide jobs for southern workers. Southern politicians
later argued that the contest over oil was a key reason for Numairi to abrogate
the Addis Ababa Agreement in 1983; Numairi could not accept its provision that
revenues from natural resources would accrue to the regional government. "If
the central government was to retain control of the new found wealth in the
South, [Numairi] must swiftly end what was left of southern autonomy once and
for all."[7]

   The controversy over Bentiu was not the only problematic resource-cum-
boundary issue. The Addis Ababa Agreement provided for the reversion to the
south of certain areas that were part of the south before independence. This
meant that the districts of Hufrat al-Nahas and Kafia Kingi returned to Bahr
al-Ghazal province. But Hufrat al-Nahas contained copper and Kafia Kingi contained uranium. When Numairi tried to transfer Hufrat al-Nahas back to Dar
Fur in 1978, the move was blocked by widespread protests. The Addis Ababa
Agreement also stated that residents of border areas who had ethnic ties to the
south could decide by referendum whether to merge with the south. Abyei district in Kordofan and Kurmuk and Chali el-Fil districts in the Blue Nile thereby
became eligible to hold referenda. But they were never allowed to vote. The un-

resolved issue contributed to the widening sense of grievance against Numairi's manipulations.

Such tensions were typical of problems that arise in an incomplete ethnic pluralist system. Even though arrangements for control over and revenue from resources and development efforts are spelled out in formal agreements, a tug-of-war emerges. The central government uses its power to withhold funds and withdraw rights. Minority groups lack enough power in the center to retain (much less augment) those rights. Autonomy is eroded and changes are not due to negotiations but to the arbitrary assertion of power by the center. This undermines the balances essential to the ethnic pluralist system and promotes a return to the control model, based on dominance by one ethnic group.

ABSORPTION OF THE ANYA-NYA

The undermining of autonomy was particularly visible in the arena of internal security. The Addis Ababa accord specified that half of the troops stationed in the south would be drawn from Anya-Nya, and police and prison guards would be recruited entirely from the south. Intake into the national army would be proportional to population, in order to gradually redress the fact that southerners comprised only 12 percent of the armed forces at that time. Anya-Nya were incorporated as separate units within the armed forces with the intent to integrate the troops fully by 1977. Many Anya-Nya were suspicious of integration and resisted transfer north for training or military duty. The transition was difficult for both sides since they suddenly had to serve alongside their enemies. Former Anya-Nya officers resented their inability to rise in rank and there was anger that no additional southerners were recruited into the officer corps.[8]

Violent incidents broke out in Juba (1974), Akobo (1975), and Wau (1976) when southern troops feared that they would be attacked by northern soldiers or would be transferred north. The government did compel the battalion at Aweil to transfer to Dar Fur in December 1982 and, as noted above, replaced southern troops at Bentiu with northern soldiers to ensure Khartoum's control over the oil fields. The turning point came in January 1983 when Dinka soldiers in the Bor and Pibor garrisons in Jonglei (Upper Nile) refused orders to move north.[9] When northern troops attacked on 16 May, several hundred southern commanders and soldiers evacuated Bor and Pibor and regrouped in Ethiopia. Soon, thousands of soldiers took to the bush, some supporting the reconstituted Anya-Nya II but most joining the new Sudan Peoples' Liberation Army (SPLA), which was led by Colonel John Garang de Mabior, an officer from the absorbed forces who deserted to join the rebels. The results of the Bor standoff bore an eerie resemblance to the outcome of the Torit mutiny in 1955, which triggered seventeen years of civil war.

The military terms for ending a civil war and constructing a regional system are particularly sensitive. The aggrieved ethnic group wants to ensure its own security whereas the central government wants to guarantee that the group will not secede. As power shifted from Anya-Nya and southern politicians to the central government from 1972 to 1982, Khartoum's actions to undermine southern autonomy intensified. Those measures led to renewed warfare, galvanized by many of the same southern officers who had fought before 1972. The security system is particularly difficult to stabilize in an emerging ethnic pluralist system. When the control model is reimposed, security structures are the first to disintegrate.

MANIPULATION OF SOUTHERN POLITICS

Numairi's manipulation of political life in the south enabled him to carry out those economic and military measures. He established "a pattern of presidential interventions which were to make dangerous and eventually destabilizing inroads on the rudimentary, often chaotic but nevertheless still working system in the south."[10]

Elections for the southern regional assembly in 1973, 1978, 1980, and 1982 were contested vigorously, but Numairi intervened each time in the decision on who would be elected president of the High Executive Council (HEC). He also arbitrarily dissolved the HEC and regional assembly in 1980. He played off against each other Alier and Lagu, who had become a major general in the army and head of the Southern Military Command. This meant, as a prominent southern politician concluded bitterly, that "the South was no longer in charge of its own political process."[11] Numairi also played on Equatorian perceptions that Dinkas dominated the regional government, even though the capital was located in Juba and many Equatorians had prominent roles in the regional executive. At the administrative levels, however, Dinka bureaucrats did tend to favor fellow Dinka in the provision of services. Numairi thereby encouraged Lagu (an Equatorian) to demand that the south be redivided into its three original provinces in order to end Dinka domination. Some other politicians agreed that the south was too large and its communications systems too weak to administer effectively from one center. Nonetheless, the southern regional assembly rejected redivision in March 1981 on the grounds that it violated the Self-Government Act and the constitution.

Even when Numairi dissolved that assembly and appointed Major General Gismalla Abdallah Rassas interim president of the HEC in October 1981, Rassas refused to hold a referendum on the issue of redivision prior to electing a new regional assembly. When the assembly was elected in 1982, Numairi demanded that the new regional government formed by Lagu's Equatorian ally Joseph John Tambura, submit a plan in February 1983 to dissolve the regional assembly and transform the HEC into an appointed council whose three members would administer each province. Tambura, the descendant of a prominent Azande family, recognized that most people in Upper Nile and Bahr al-Ghazal opposed redivision, and did not act on that request.

On 5 June 1983 Numairi abruptly decreed redivision of the south into three provinces.[12] He claimed this did not violate the spirit of the Addis Ababa Agreement even though no constitutional guarantee was employed: there was no vote by the regional assembly, no endorsement by the national assembly, and no referendum in the south. Numairi had just been reelected unopposed for a third term as president. "Naked power" ruled. And Numairi immediately disbanded the HEC and regional assembly and replaced them with three governors for Equatoria, Upper Nile, and Bahr al-Ghazal. Those politicians, who were all allies of Lagu, did not realize that the three regions would not retain the powers of the united region. Instead, the president appointed the governors, cancelled direct elections for the regional assemblies, and withdrew their control over revenue derived from trade and natural resources. Military officers in the south answered directly to the defense minister in Khartoum, rather than to the Southern Command in Juba.

Overall, the principle underlying the Addis Ababa Agreement was that the Sudan could remain one country only if the multiplicity of its peoples was recognized and used as the basis on which to build the political system. That respect for diversity was undermined soon after it came into force. Part of the problem lay in the inherent tension between center and periphery. Despite the effort to define the relationship in the constitution, the central government sought to alter the terms so that it could control and allocate all natural resources. Southerners, in contrast, argued that the south, as the poorest region in the country as well as the one in which minerals had been discovered, should receive a major share of anticipated revenues and use the projects to catalyze local development. Control over resources was essential for preserving genuine self-rule. Moreover, tension derived from the nondemocratic political system, in which overwhelming power resided with the president. He could intervene blatantly in regional affairs and undermine nascent democratic processes. Admittedly, southern politicians contributed to that political erosion: they let Numairi intervene when it benefited them personally and discovered too late that their vital interests were damaged by his manipulation.

The north-south accord was further undermined by the growing power of the Islamic trends in the north. Groups such as the Islamic Charter Front, which had been in exile at the time of the Addis Ababa Agreement, rejected that accord as the basis for a national consensus. They sought Islamization and Arabization throughout the country, reviving arguments that, in the short run, non-Muslim peoples must not block the wishes of the Muslim majority and, in the long run, they must assimilate into the dominant community. That renewed Islamist drive is analyzed next. It was ironic that Numairi, who engineered a reconciliation based on respect for the diversity of the Sudanese peoples, later espoused a hegemonic religious formula that contradicted those tenets and deepened divisions during the renewed civil war.

RECONCILIATION WITH NORTHERN POLITICAL FORCES

Numairi ruled until 1977 without the participation or support of any significant northern political groups.[13] Although he formed the one-party Sudanese Socialist Union (SSU) in 1972 to mobilize the public behind the regime, the SSU functioned primarily as a bureaucracy parallel to the government, and Numairi restrained political debate. During the mid-1970s he removed from the cabinet outspoken members such as Foreign Minister Mansour Khalid and the leading southerners.[14] Although Numairi instituted ambitious agro-industrial programs in the north to transform the country into the breadbasket of the Middle East, cost overruns, corruption, and the escalating cost of imported oil derailed those plans. Cotton remained the main export, but exports covered only a third of the import bill and the foreign debt soared. The regime therefore faced unrest among workers and students and weathered serious coup attempts in January 1973, September 1975, and July 1976. The latter was galvanized by the National Front, a coalition of exiles headed by al-Sharif Hussain al-Hindi, former finance minister and leader of the late Azhari's NUP. The National Front included the Umma Party under al-Sadiq al-Mahdi, the Islamic Charter Front led by Turabi, the pan-Arab Ba'th Party, some members of the Khatmiyya-affiliated Peoples' Democratic Party, and regional organizations such as the Nuba Mountains Group led by Rev. Philip Abbas Ghabboush. They smuggled arms and men into the Sudan from Libya, but Numairi crushed the uprising and executed hundreds of people in its aftermath.

This fierce confrontation seemed to shock both sides into realizing that they could not destroy each other. A year later, Numairi reached a secret accord with al-Sadiq al-Mahdi that called for the release from detention and amnesty of opposition politicians and restructuring the SSU so that the opposition could participate fully. Al-Mahdi understood that Numairi agreed to repeal the State Security Act and revise the constitution so as to protect individual liberties and democratic processes.[15] In practice, about 3,000 political prisoners were released and leading politicians returned, including al-Mahdi, Turabi, and Ghabboush. But the reconciliation between Numairi and al-Mahdi was short-lived. Al-

Mahdi sought a fundamental reorientation in policy and institutions whereas Numairi would not allow the politicians to dilute his power. Numairi was shocked that opposition groups, campaigning under the SSU banner, won nearly 40 percent of the seats in the people's assembly in 1978.[16] Although Al-Mahdi was appointed to SSU's Political Bureau and joined the assembly, he soon resigned from the SSU and Umma boycotted the elections in 1980 on the grounds that Numairi had violated his commitments. In 1981 Umma called for the end to one-man rule and the election of leaders who would be accountable to the people.

In contrast, al-Mahdi's brother-in-law Turabi cooperated fully with the regime. Turabi became attorney general and a member of the parliamentary committee that was charged with adapting the legal system to conform to Islamic law, taking advantage of the provision in the constitution that Islamic principles should form a basis for legislation. ICF participated in the SSU and People's Assembly and placed members in key posts in the administration, schools, and unions. It infiltrated the armed forces by encouraging its members to serve in the medical and technical corps and by instituting lecture programs on Islam for the officer corps. Those programs provided "a cover for the [ICF]'s infiltration of, and recruitment from" the armed forces.[17] The movement acquired economic power, particularly through Islamic banks that opened after 1978. Through those multifaceted efforts Turabi implemented a coherent strategy to gain economic and political power.

Southerners viewed this reconciliation with alarm since it could undermine the rights they had acquired in 1972. Indeed, as noted above, Turabi and the ICF minister of interior played key roles in trying to alter the boundaries between north and south to transfer resources northward. Alier argues that Numairi promised the Islamists that he would review virtually all the provisions of the Addis Ababa Agreement: security, language, culture, and religion—all the most sensitive points.[18] By November 1981 there were no southerners left in the cabinet to protest those moves.

Despite Numairi's efforts to mollify religious forces in the north, discontent increased when the regime's economic promises failed to materialize. Drought and famine in Dar Fur, Kordofan, and the Beja-populated Red Sea hills directly affected more than two million people who were primarily non-Arab Muslims.[19] When thousands migrated to Khartoum, Numairi tried to force them to go home. In 1982 the Gross Domestic Product shrank by 3.6 percent and the foreign debt soared.[20] Under pressure from the International Monetary Fund (IMF), Numairi imposed austerity measures that sharply devalued the Sudanese currency and dramatically increased the prices of food and gasoline. Those measures bought time for the government with its creditors but alienated the public. Civil servants, professionals, students, and workers became increasingly restive.

Judges won a strike in February 1981 after a bitter struggle, but Numairi crushed efforts by professionals and workers to improve their conditions. In March 1981 he fired more than a thousand civil servants and in June 1981 the army smashed the powerful Union of Sudanese Railway Workers, which had struck over wage issues and in sympathy for the fired civil servants. A further austerity program in November 1981 reduced or ended many food subsidies and increased the price of gasoline. Numairi deployed the army to quell riots at the University of Khartoum and in the market places. Riots on 1 January 1982 were triggered by additional price increases. The armed forces again restored order.

The military high command resented playing that role. On 12 January 1982, Defense Minister and First Vice President Abd al-Majid Hamid Khalil led a high-ranking military delegation to meet with Numairi.[21] General Khalil, who opposed Numairi's dictatorial and corrupt rule, criticized the harsh measures against rioters, objected to shooting at students and closing universities, and decried the expulsion of western Sudanese from Khartoum. The officers demanded that Numairi restructure the SSU, relinquish some of his personal power, and undertake economic reform. Numairi immediately dismissed General Khalil and twenty-three senior officers, and made the head of the security service, Umar al-Tayib, vice president. Those moves shattered the military command and consolidated the power of the security services.

ISLAMIZATION

By then the Islamic Charter Front provided the sole public support for the regime, as Turabi stated frankly:[22]

> We have decided to collaborate with the government in the hope of reforming the system from within. . . . President [Numairi] knows that there can be no real plot against the government if we stand by it. Nothing can be done in this country without the Muslim Brotherhood [ICF].

There is disagreement as to why Numairi shifted from secularism to Islamization. Some say he experienced a personal religious awakening that persuaded him to stop drinking and require government ministers to abstain from alcohol and gambling. Moreover, it was soon after Numairi's heart operation that he published pamphlets that endorsed Islamic social and political codes: he maintained that the Sudan was "backward" because the people had ceased to be good Muslims and that Islam would unify the country and ensure economic prosperity.[23] Nonetheless, a personal conversion was not essential for these steps. For Numairi, Islamization was valuable politically as a means to checkmate independent Islamic political forces embodied in the Ansar and Khatmiyya and even the ICF, to reduce his dependence on the south, and to create a new basis for his legitimacy, now that economic development had failed. Once Numairi became the infallible *imam*, he could claim the automatic allegiance of the Muslim citizens and could outlaw all dissent.

Carolyn Fluehr-Lobban argues that Numairi paved the way for Islamization by decreeing the unification of the civil and shari'a courts in 1980, which required all judges to apply both sets of legal codes. He followed this on 8 September 1983 with his presidential order that shari'a "be the sole guiding force behind the law of the Sudan."[24] The new Islamic penal and commercial codes were partly based on statutes drafted by Turabi's committee to revise the legal system, but were basically drafted in secret by a small group of advisors.[25] The code instituted the *hudud* punishments specified in shari'a for such crimes as murder, theft, drinking, adultery, and prostitution. In October 1983, twenty-six men convicted of liquor offenses were each lashed forty times before a crowd in the Khartoum market. Two young men had their right hands cut off on 9 December in Kober prison for stealing a car.[26] The first cross-limb amputations were performed on 22 May 1984. Soon after, an adulterer was hanged and a thief was executed. Overall, more than fifty people had one or more limbs amputated and thousands were sentenced to flogging for theft, brewing or drinking alcohol, adultery, prostitution, and political crimes such as agitation and spreading false rumors. Special courts tried the cases in the absence of defense lawyers and carried out the sentences immediately, without time or opportunity for appeal. Hudud penalties applied to Christians and adherents of African religions as well as to Muslims. An Italian priest was flogged for storing communion wine in his home.

The new penal code—known generally as the September decrees—was denounced by a wide range of political and religious leaders as a violation of constitutional provisions for equality and nondiscrimination. A petition by the heads of the Episcopal, Presbyterian, and Evangelical churches and the Sudan Council of Churches stressed the importance of respecting religious and cultural differences and denounced the Islamization that turned non-Muslims into second-class citizens. Underground communist and Ba'th activists rejected the decrees as did Muslim intellectuals. Numairi detained al-Sadiq al-Mahdi and thirty followers in September 1983 after he denounced the decrees during prayers at the Mahdi's tomb. Umma Party leaflets asserted that the decrees transformed Islam into a punitive religion that protected an unjust regime. Muhammad Uthman al-Mirghani, spiritual head of the Khatmiyya tariqa, agreed that the September decrees perverted Islam. Many members of the SSU were disaffected and there were rumblings of discontent within the army.

In the spring of 1984, there was a brief attempt to unseat the regime by mass action. Three thousand doctors resigned on 27 March 1984 to protest the deteriorating economy and poor conditions in the hospitals as well as to denounce amputations on ethical grounds. The teachers' union struck in sympathy, but the strike failed to spread to other major unions. The doctors themselves were divided, since those who were affiliated with the ICF opposed the union's political demands. Numairi dissolved the doctors' union, jailed its leaders, closed the University of Khartoum, and imposed a state of emergency on 29 April 1984. He banned strikes, detained suspects without charge, and allowed security personnel to enter private houses without search warrants.

Only the ICF continued to support Numairi. Although Turabi claimed that he was surprised by the timing of the Islamization and critical of some of the decrees, ICF provided most of the judges for the special courts and welcomed the additional decrees that Islamized banking and *zakat* (alms), which became a government tax. ICF was the only party to support Numairi's additional moves in the summer of 1984 to compel military and civilian officials to swear *baya* (allegiance) to him as the infallible Imam and to amend the constitution to make him president for life and "leader of the faithful."[27] The proposed amendments would replace the elected assembly with a largely-appointed *shura* (consultative) council whose members would lack parliamentary immunity and would not have the right to question government policy, request a referendum, or impeach the president. Shari'a would be the sole source of legislation, and the Islamic penal code and *zakat* would be enforced on non-Muslims as well as Muslims. The draft deleted all references in the constitution to nondiscrimination on grounds of religious faith and barred non-Muslims from becoming president.

The proposed amendments caused an outcry. On 11 July, 105 of the 151 members of the people's assembly insisted on postponing debate, particularly since the changes would strip them of their power. Southern MPs, religious leaders, students at Juba University, and members of the three southern regional governments protested vigorously. Lagu and Alier set aside their rivalry long enough to protest that the proposed amendments violated the constitution, undermined human rights, and ended respect for religious diversity.[28] Faced with such broad opposition, Numairi withdrew the amendments and cancelled the state of emergency in September 1984. Military courts became "prompt justice" courts under the same judges and with the same penalties, but searches on the street and inside houses ceased and lawyers were allowed to defend their clients in court.

Meanwhile, Numairi accelerated his efforts to silence political opposition. He targeted small ideological and regional groups such as the communists, Nuba Mountains Group, Republican Brothers, and Ba'thists. In June 1984, Numairi charged with treason the prominent communist and women's rights leader Fatima Ahmad Ibrahim. But the judge avoided jailing her by ruling that she was "insane" and should be referred to a medical board for treatment. In October 1984, security forces arrested the elderly Rev. Ghabboush and 207 members of the Nuba Mountains Group on charges of preparing to foment disturbances. Judge Al-Mikashfi Taha al-Kabashi wanted to press charges of treason against them, but Numairi feared an uprising by Nuba soldiers and granted them clemency. The Republican Brothers presented a more complex problem. Founded by Ustaz Mahmud Muhammad Taha in the 1940s, that pacifist movement advocated a radical reinterpretation of Islam based on egalitarianism, socialism, and democracy. Taha and about fifty supporters were detained in June 1983 and again at the end of 1984 for leafleting against the September decrees as distortions of Islam that jeopardized the country's unity by making Christians unequal to Muslims. Taha and four leading disciples were charged with inciting disturbances, but Judge al-Mikashfi sentenced them to death as apostates and traitors. Numairi ordered Taha executed on 18 January, calling him the "greatest heretic of this age."[29] Hanging the seventy-six-year-old theologian triggered a sense of revulsion among people who did not otherwise agree with Taha's interpretation of Islam. Finally, al-Mikashfi charged four members of the Ba'th Party with sedition and apostasy on the basis of leaflets that called for the overthrow of the regime. Ultimately, al-Mikashfi could not prove that Ba'thist ideology was anti-Islamic. Although al-Mikashfi was a professor of Islamic studies and a key member of the committee that had drafted the September laws, his courtroom behavior and predilection for altering charges in the midst of trials embarrassed other Islamist judges and led ICF cadres to distance themselves from him, at least temporarily.

Meanwhile, Turabi and ICF celebrated the first anniversary of the shari'a decrees on 25 September 1984 by organizing a march of nearly one million people in the streets of Khartoum. That display of mass strength scared Numairi. The SSU and secret police warned him that ICF aimed to displace him. Soon after, Numairi accused ICF members of overzealous enforcement of shari'a and claimed that they plotted to replace the "fighting imam" (Numairi) with the "scholarly imam" (Turabi).[30] Numairi blamed ICF students for clashes with left-wing, secular, and southern students at the University of Khartoum in February 1985, and arrested more than a hundred members of ICF during the night of 10-11 March 1985, including Turabi, several judges, lawyers, SSU officials, and military officers. Judge al-Mikashfi was jailed in the same prison in which Taha had been hanged. Numairi thereby tried to make ICF the scapegoat for his harsh and unpopular policies.

His attempt to deflect criticism was not credible, but ICF was dangerous to alienate since its militant cadres were the last on whom Numairi could rely. The allegiance of the military and security forces was in doubt. Army officers recognized the futility of fighting in the south, resented the frequent purges in the officer ranks, and disliked suppressing student demonstrations. Nonetheless, the high command of the armed forces hesitated to act against the president, having given him the religious oath of allegiance. Security personnel knew that the September laws had alienated the public and their head, Vice President al-Tayib, had ambitions of his own to replace Numairi. Tayib's 45,000-person security services outnumbered the armed forces garrisoned in Khartoum.

During that final year, Numairi's policies aggravated the renewed war in the south, which he initially termed a minor mutiny that he could end by appointing John Garang vice president. Only on 3 March 1985 did Numairi set up a High Committee for Peace, announce a unilateral cease-fire, and declare an amnesty for the rebels.[31] By then SPLA and Anya-Nya II forces had compelled the French company to stop digging the Jonglei Canal and had forced Chevron to suspend drilling for oil at Bentiu. Guerrilla forces, spread across nearly half of the south, caused extensive casualties among the armed forces and drained the country's financial resources.

Numairi's authoritarianism undermined any possibility of establishing a pluralist political system in which citizens would have equal rights. Instead of sharing power, he played the south off against the northern Islamists, favoring the former in the first half of his rule and then shifting to the latter. His opportunistic ideological shifts left an indelible mark on the country. He took the Islamist perspective to its logical extreme by excluding non-Muslims and silencing Muslims who differed with him. His policies ensured that the south would react by resuming the civil war. After his overthrow, it was difficult to undo his policies. Since Muslim politicians were committed in principle to an Islamic state, they became immobilized, fearful of annulling his laws even though they criticized their content. Northern politicians became trapped in the image of Sudan as a Muslim country. They could not find a way to create a national consensus that would embrace all the Sudanese people.

PART TWO

The Democratic Period, 1985-1989

4

The Transition to Democracy

IN HIS DRIVE to dominate, Numairi suppressed all political opposition and reimposed ethnic assimilationist policies on the diverse Sudanese citizenry. Repression peaked in 1983-1985, generating a rebellion in the south and protests in the north. Numairi's overthrow in April 1985 resulted from that groundswell of dissent and from rising discontent within the armed forces. However, the groups that coalesced to remove him from power did not agree on an alternative constitutional system or on the principles that should guide interethnic relations. During the four years of democracy that followed, polarization was acute between those who endorsed a secular system that would respect diversity and the militant Islamists who insisted on a comprehensive religious system. The pluralist and assimilationist approaches to the nation-state were contested bitterly. The clash threatened to undermine the nascent democracy.

POPULAR UPRISING

The National Alliance for National Salvation that was formed on 18 January 1985, immediately after the execution of Mahmud Muhammad Taha, represented professional and trade unions that sought to remove Numairi from power by a campaign of civil disobedience.[1] The alliance's charter had been in the process of development since June 1984, when Sudanese professionals living in the Gulf initiated an effort to conceptualize a new political vision. They worked closely with counterparts inside the country and met in London with the Sudan Peoples' Liberation Movement (SPLM), Umma Party, Democratic Unionist Party (DUP), and the Sudanese Communist Party (SCP). Their Charter of National Salvation called for a democratic system of government based on the provisional constitution promulgated at independence in 1956. The charter affirmed freedom of organization, expression, and belief, the rule of law, and independence of the judiciary, but did not specifically call for cancelling the Islamic decrees of September 1983. The charter was finalized once the uprising was under way and endorsed by Umma, DUP, and SCP on 4 April.

Public protests began on 26 March 1985, a day before Numairi flew to the United States for consultations. Prices for bread, petrol, and public transport had just doubled and there was an acute shortage of soap and edible oils. Most public schools in the capital were closed because buses lacked the fuel to transport students. A quarter of the population was affected directly by drought and thousands had died in the countryside for lack of food and water. When leaders of the SSU complained to Numairi about those conditions, he callously blamed "destructive consumption habits"[2] and criticized people for spending their income on luxuries. Daily protests galvanized university students, union activists, and townspeople, who stoned shop windows, burned cars, and trashed gas stations. An outpouring of 50,000 people on 3 April called for "bread and liberty." By then, the physicians' union led the professional unions into a general strike that demanded Numairi's ouster. On 4 April strikers cut all water, electricity, and telecommunications in the Khartoum area, closed the airport, and silenced the radio station. Although the security forces arrested some 2,000 demonstrators and union leaders, Vice President and security chief Umar al-Tayib sought to impose a state of emergency so that he could crack down decisively.

However, military officers increasingly leaned toward the strike. Deputy Commander-in-Chief General Taj al-Din Abdallah Fadl endorsed the protests and apparently informed al-Sadiq al-Mahdi that the armed forces would not confront the public in the streets. But his superior, Defense Minister and Commander-in-Chief General Abd al-Rahman Suwar al-Dhahab, insisted to soldiers and officers in the Khartoum barracks and the military academy that they honor their religious oath of allegiance to Numairi. Meanwhile, most officers supported the popular demand to remove Numairi and they reportedly brought a religious dignitary to Suwar al-Dhahab, who convinced him that his oath was no longer valid since Numairi's harmful policies had caused the people to withdraw their support.[3] Officers presented Suwar al-Dhahab with a virtual ultimatum on 5 April, since they were anxious to remove Numairi before he could return to Khartoum.

During the night of 5-6 April, the armed forces sealed off the city center and seized power for "a limited transitional period."[4] Acting as commander-in-chief, Suwar al-Dhahab suspended the 1973 constitution, relieved Numairi and his top officials of their posts, and dissolved the SSU and peoples assembly. The army arrested Vice President al-Tayib and disarmed the security forces. Residents celebrated in the city streets and stormed Kober prison, where they lifted the detainees onto their shoulders and swarmed over the scaffold on which Mahmud Taha and other prisoners had been hanged. By the time Numairi landed in Cairo that morning, for a stopover on his way home, the takeover was complete.

TRANSITIONAL GOVERNMENT

The high command filled the legal vacuum by forming a Transitional Military Council (TMC) on 9 April, chaired by Suwar al-Dhahab [See Appendix 1]. The TMC consisted of the top-ranking officers and the commanders of the barracks in the capital city. Only two of the fifteen members came from the south. All previous laws remained valid until rescinded or amended. The activists who had galvanized the uprising were disturbed by the TMC's quick consolidation of power, since they wanted a civilian transitional government based on the non-religious constitution of 1956. Even though members of the National Alliance gained leading roles in the council of ministers that was installed on 25 April, that cabinet was subordinate to the TMC. The alliance was partly reassured when the TMC agreed to hold elections to a constituent assembly within a year.

Eleven of the sixteen cabinet ministers were chosen by the National Alliance [See Appendix 2]. The TMC selected the minister of defense and the police chose the interior minister. Three seats were allocated to southerners, one representing each province. The head of the new Southern Sudanese Political Association (SSPA), Samuel Aru Bol, became deputy prime minister. Southern activists in Khartoum were disappointed that they had not obtained a larger number of and more influential ministries and had not insisted that the September decrees be annulled. Furthermore, although Prime Minister al-Jazouli Dafallah claimed that none of the cabinet members had cooperated with Numairi or had partisan affiliation,[5] several ministers had strongly Islamist perspectives. For example, the minister of education proposed that all teachers be devout believers. Dafallah and Suwar al-Dhahab displayed their sympathies for the Islamist movement by agreeing to chair NIF's two principal Islamic relief organizations at the end of their terms in office. Similarly, the minister of health later joined the Islamist-supported military regime in 1989.

The Sudan Peoples' Liberation Movement (SPLM) stood outside the political arena in Khartoum but had a powerful impact upon it. As a fighting force, the SPLA presented a serious challenge to the military establishment in the south. As a political force, SPLM rejected the TMC and saw itself as the springboard for a new revolution that would establish a secular, socialist system. As will be discussed in chapter 6, although the SPLM lacked the power to transform the country in its image, a settlement in the south required the SPLM's agreement.

TRANSITIONAL CONSTITUTION

The most important legal issue tackled in 1985 involved the constitution for the transitional period, whose terms would set the tone for the emerging democracy. Would it be an inclusive document to which all citizens could subscribe or would it enshrine the values of only one part of the citizenry? The assimilationist-pluralist tensions were evident in this debate.

The council of ministers submitted a draft constitution to the TMC on 28 July, but several months of delicate negotiations were required until the constitution was promulgated on 10 October 1985.[6] The constitution specified that the provisional constitution of 1956, as amended in 1964, would serve as the basis for the transitional period. It was updated to take into account the establishment of self-rule for the south in 1972 and the regionalization of the north in 1980. The constitution established the independence of the judiciary and included a Bill of Rights.

The transitional constitution stated that *shari'a* (Islamic law) and *urf* (customary law) were the bases of the legal system, as had been the case in the 1973 constitution. Constitutional lawyer Peter Nyot Kok noted three difficulties with this approach. First, urf was not an alternative legal code and, therefore, could not modify or balance shari'a. Second, there was no explicit reference to respecting indigenous African beliefs, in contrast to the constitution of 1973. Third, retaining shari'a made it difficult to repeal the September decrees. Overall, the constitution did not satisfy those in the alliance and the south who wanted to revoke the September decrees and reinstitute secular civil, criminal, and commercial codes. However, it reflected the views of the majority in the TMC and council of ministers. Suwar al-Dhahab believed that, although the September decrees could be "amended" or "modified" to eliminate "incorrect and excessive" punishments, the popular majority prefered to live under Islamic law.[7] Prime Minister Dafallah also wanted merely to correct those aspects of the decrees that "do not conform with Islam."[8] Suwar al-Dhahab and Dafallah believed that cancelling the laws was blasphemous.

Hasan al-Turabi, leader of the Islamic Charter Front, which was renamed the National Islamic Front (NIF), warned the TMC against cancelling "God's laws."[9] He and his followers had been released from jail during the uprising even though they opposed the National Alliance's charter. At a rally in Khartoum on 7 April, Turabi called for strengthening Islamic law, rejected the secular emphasis in the charter, and refused to cooperate with the SCP. NIF views were echoed by Ahmad al-Mahdi, an Ansar leader and uncle of al-Sadiq al-Mahdi, and by a conference of *ulama* (men learned in Islamic law) in July 1985 that endorsed maintaining a reformed Islamic law. DUP leaders and al-Sadiq al-Mahdi, while calling the September decrees un-Islamic, supported the promulgation of alternative Islamic laws. Even the secularist attorney general talked of amending rather than annulling the September laws. Kok commented that these views reflected "the deep ambivalence" of most northern Sudanese toward shari'a and their difficulty in countenancing the abrogation of shari'a once it was in place.

Indeed, the cabinet decided in December 1985 to retain shari'a as the basis of the penal code and to maintain hudud punishments for major crimes although, in practice, no amputations or executions were carried out during the transitional period.[10] Those persons remained in prison, pending final resolution of the status of hudud. This ambiguous outcome was discomforting to secularists and non-Muslims, who wanted a definitive end to the Islamic penal code.

Overall, the uprising of April 1985 represented an important broad-based popular movement that uprooted a bitterly hated regime. The transitional government created a climate sufficiently stable for foreign donors to provide vital food and petroleum aid that staved off economic collapse. They encouraged free public debate and investigated key officials of the Numairi regime.[11] However, criticism mounted from the public that the regime lacked a sense of direction: the *intifada* (shaking off—the Arabic term for the April uprising) had become *inti fadiya* (you are empty). The government was easily pressured by the unions that had brought it to power and thus could not meet the stringent conditions set by the IMF. Price hikes and reductions in subsidies were undermined by worker strikes and demonstrations. There was no clarity in economic policy and no resolution of fundamental political issues. The continuation of the Islamic legal system was a crucial decision. Set alongside the failure to negotiate with the SPLM, which is discussed in chapter 6, it indicated that the assimilationist approach to national identity remained paramount. Parliamentary democracy was being restored in the image of an Arab-Islamic Sudan into which other ethnic groups must fit. The idea that those ethnicities should be accommodated by altering the overarching framework remained incomprehensible to the political elites in Khartoum.

POLITICAL PARTIES

The assimilative approach of the dominant political groups had complicated and ultimately helped to undermine democracy in the 1950s and 1960s. Moreover, the multiple cleavages in Sudanese society seemed to ensure that any political system would be fragile. Ethnic heterogeneity and a geographically dispersed population, coupled with the concentration of political and economic power in the hands of the people living in the center, reinforced inequalities and bred resentment on the part of the marginalized peoples.

The fragility of democracy was compounded by the weak commitment to pluralist values on the part of many political forces. NIF, in particular, viewed democracy as a means to establish an Islamic state and to mold Sudanese society according to its particular vision, and stressed that it could never compromise on the issue of shari'a. Even al-Sadiq al-Mahdi, who frequently emphasized that "what is more important . . . is adherence by consent to democratic decision-making, even if the decision is in conflict with the ideology of this or that party,"[12] argued that shari'a could be applied if the majority supported it. Minorities must accept that outcome. Politicians such as al-Mahdi felt secure in upholding majority rule, since their core religious and cultural values could not be challenged. Conversely, African, Christian, and secular political forces comprised permanent minorities that were always outvoted in parliament and marginalized in the executive branch, and therefore had few incentives to support the political system or view democracy as a means to address their needs and grievances. Some southern politicians tried to restructure the political system in order to end the automatic Arab-Islamic majority. Others exited the system, seeking to secede and leave the north as a relatively homogeneous Arab-Islamic territory. Violence, nonparticipation, and alienation resulted from their disadvantaged position.

Thus, the dominant political forces adhered to an assimilationist model that assumed that national identity was predominantly Muslim and Arab. Minorities sought an ethnic pluralist system based on territorial nationalism in which they would share power in Khartoum, have equal legal rights, and regain regional autonomy. The nature of the nation-state was still contested as they reentered the political arena to compete in the elections in 1986.

Umma Party

The Umma Party had been led by al-Sadiq al-Mahdi since the mid-1960s, when he served briefly as prime minister. Despite the reconciliation with Numairi in 1977, Umma called for popular elections and sharpened its criticism after Numairi instituted the September decrees. Umma's election program was announced within days of the uprising in 1985. Al-Mahdi sought to revitalize the party, adding young intellectuals while retaining core support among the three-million strong Ansar religious movement. The program called for a modern democratic Islamic society that would guarantee human dignity and freedom. Public freedoms and freedom of religion should be guaranteed in the context of a legal code that should consist of the Quran, the Sunna, and "all the other sources of legislation unless they contradict" those codes.[13] Strong regional governments would ensure an equitable distribution of investment and development among the different sectors and regions.

Al-Mahdi wanted Umma to serve as an umbrella party, attracting political allies from professional unions that spearheaded the uprising in 1985 and from adherents of regional movements such as the Beja, Nuba, and even southerners. Al-Mahdi blamed his brother-in-law Hasan al-Turabi for the most harsh aspects of Numairi's Islamist program. He was concerned that the transitional regime did not annul the September decrees, formulate a new penal code, convene the national constitutional conference, or even develop a coherent economic strategy. Such delays exacerbated internal problems and hardened lines of conflict, thereby complicating the task of the elected government. Thus, al-Mahdi positioned himself as a democratic pluralist who would accommodate the perspectives of a wide range of groups. He distanced himself from the exclusivist version of religious assimilationism. Nonetheless, he took for granted Sudan's predominantly Arab-Islamic ethos.

Democratic Unionist Party

The Khatmiyya tariqa formed the base of support for the Democratic Unionist Party (DUP), whose religious leader Muhammad Uthman al-Mirghani generally remained aloof from politics. After the uprising, Mirghani indicated that shari'a should be the only source of law, the September decrees should be revised but not annulled, and the shari'a-based draft constitution of 1968 should be promulgated.[14] DUP did not hold a party conference or publish a comprehensive program and therefore had no organized way to select candidates. Individuals nominated themselves with the support of their family, tribe, village, or religious order. As a result, the DUP often ran more than one candidate in the same constituency, which cancelled out each other's votes. DUP candidates adopted varying stances on current issues, although in general the party supported the parliamentary system based on Islamic principles and sought a mixed economy that would allow private enterprise to flourish. That reflected the support for DUP among large merchants, industrialists, and farmers in the Khatmiyya strongholds of the north and east. DUP's concept of national identity was unself-consciously assimilationist. Its leaders took for granted that Sudan was a Muslim country that should be ruled by Islamic law. They also assumed that Sudan was Arab, despite the inclusion of Beja and Nubians in responsible posts within the party.

The National Islamic Front

The National Islamic Front (NIF) had gained substantial power since 1977 through the executive, legislature, armed forces, student movement, and professions. Through the Faisal Islamic Bank, Islamic *Dawa* (Propagation) Organization, and Islamic African Relief Agency, NIF dispensed patronage, promoted Quranic schools, established health clinics, and built mosques. Its associations for students, teachers, and women had branches in the major towns. NIF convened a party conference in May 1985, just a month after the uprising. Its election program maintained that Islam was the official religion of the state and Arabic the official language.[15] Shari'a must guide all matters of life and be the source of all laws. The economy, educational system, and social programs must be based on Islamic principles and must promote religious faith. Nevertheless, the Islamic principles of *shura* (consultation) and equality meant that religious freedom and the rights of minorities would be guaranteed through a federal system in which regions with non-Muslim majorities could exempt themselves from the penal provisions of shari'a. However, all other laws—including trading and banking—must follow shari'a throughout the country. NIF therefore represented the self-consciously maximalist position in favor of assimilation on the basis of a cohesive Arab-Islamic national identity.

The Sudanese Communist Party and Other Parties on the Left

The Sudanese Communist Party (SCP) had been active among students and workers since the 1940s, but was decimated in July 1971. Secretary General Muhammad Ibrahim Nuqud and other leaders emerged from underground after the uprising. They voiced strong opposition to the September laws and sought a secular, democratic constitution. Nuqud adopted a low-keyed approach to the election, since the party needed time to regroup its supporters and feared that a high-profile campaign might generate a religious backlash, as had occurred in the 1960s.[16]

Although none of the other ideological parties on the left could expect to win seats, they pamphleted vigorously and plastered walls with posters. The Iraqi-backed Arab Ba'th Socialist Party focussed on attacking NIF.[17] Libya supported Revolutionary Committees, which called for direct democracy through popular committees at the grassroots level.[18] Some of the parties joined in a National Progressive Front that included Nasirites, pro-Syrian Ba'thists, Marxists, and the Socialist Labor Organization.[19] Their small size, foreign support, and mutual competition meant they had little prospect of winning seats. These parties tended to be pan-Arab and thereby privileged Arab identity in their nationalist discourse.

Sudan National Party and Other Northern Regional Parties

The Sudan National Party (SNP) was led by Reverend Philip Abbas Ghabboush, a fiery Nuba politician who first stood for election from Al-Ubayyid (Kordofan) in 1965 and lived in exile from 1969 to 1978. When he subsequently joined Numairi's peoples assembly, he pressed for regionalization and development aid to the Nuba Mountains. As a Christian cleric, he denounced the September decrees for making non-Muslims second-class citizens. The SNP election charter stressed the importance of democracy and unity in the context of a secular federal system that would distribute opportunities equally throughout the country.[20] Marginalized regions would be assured representation in the central institutions, diplomatic corps, higher educational bodies, and medical services. Freedom of belief and religion would be guaranteed under a secular constitution. SNP's perspective on national identity was strongly pluralist and adamant on safeguarding minority rights in both the central government and the regions. Ghabboush envisioned Sudan as heterogeneous with a primarily African identity. However, he made an informal agreement with Umma so that Umma did not challenge SNP candidates in the Nuba Mountains and in Ghabboush's district in Omdurman.

Beja, another important ethnic group in the north, were divided between supporters of DUP and the Beja Congress. Many Beja adhered to the Khatmiyya order, led by DUP's patron Mirghani, but others supported rival religious orders. The Beja Congress was led by educated professionals who emphasized the marginalization of the Beja by the central government. Parties that sought to represent Fur and other western peoples also mounted campaigns, although they had little prospect of gaining seats. Thirteen northern and southern regional parties coalesced to form Sudan Rural Solidarity (SRS), which stressed the rights of ethnic minorities and the need for balanced economic development.[21] Its platform criticized holding elections before ending the civil war since the fighting would prevent most southerners from voting. SRS members soft-pedaled the issue of secularism, since they feared alienating potential Muslim voters among ethnic minorities in the north.

Southern Regional Parties

The six parties that competed in the south all supported a secular constitution, but disagreed on the issue of reuniting the south: the two parties based in Equatoria strongly opposed reunification, whereas the four parties based largely in Bahr al-Ghazal and Upper Nile sought to restore the Addis Ababa Accord's structures. Northern politicians played on Equatorians' fear of Dinka predominance to keep the southern parties from coalescing. Personal, political, and ethnic rivalries also divided them.

The two parties active in Equatoria—the Peoples Progressive Party (PPP) and Sudan African Peoples Congress Organization (SAPCO)—were primarily concerned to maintain Equatoria as a separate region. They sought to convene a constitutional conference, with or without the SPLM, which they criticized as a Marxist movement dominated by Ethiopia and the Dinka people. Disagreements between PPP and SAPCO derived in part from their tribal bases, since PPP obtained its core support from Bari-speaking peoples, who comprised nearly 20 percent of the population of Equatoria, and SAPCO attracted Zande speakers, who totalled 25 percent. That division personalized and heightened tribal and intra-regional fragmentation.[22] Tensions also arose because SAPCO leaders had worked closely with Numairi and Tambura's regional government (1983-1985) whereas PPP, led by the former Reverend Eliaba James Surur, was linked to the transitional government in Equatoria.

Political groups based largely in Bahr al-Ghazal and Upper Nile—the Southern Sudanese Political Association (SSPA), Sudan African Congress (SAC), and Sudan African National Union (SANU)—criticized the TMC for holding partial elections, since most of the voting was canceled in their districts. If SSPA, SANU, and SAC could have contested all the districts, they could form a significant bloc of MPs who would argue in favor of negotiations with the SPLM, for the repeal of the September decrees, and for reunification of the south. Lacking those seats, they lost their leverage vis-à-vis the north and Equatoria. The SSPA was formed in April 1985 by transitional government ministers Samuel Aru Bol and Peter Gatkuoth. SANU, headed by former minister Andrew Wieu Riak, had been central during the Anya-Nya rebellion, but was a spent political force, out of touch with conditions in the south and discredited by the failure of the Addis Ababa Agreement. SAC was led by Khartoum-based intellectuals and activists such as Dr. Walter Kuni Jwok, a Shilluk political science professor at Khartoum University, and Dr. Lam Akol, an engineering professor at Khartoum University who subsequently joined the SPLM in late 1986. SAC adopted the most radical positions, demanding the restructuring of power in Khartoum and stressing Sudan's African identity.

The fourth party in Upper Nile was the Sudanese Peoples Federal Party (SPFP), formed by Joshua Dai Wal, a Nuer regional MP (1981-1983) and former assistant commissioner for education. Dai Wal had connections to Anya-Nya II[23] and denounced the SPLA and Dinka political power. SPFP was the only party in the south to suggest that the September decrees might be frozen rather than annulled.

PARLIAMENTARY ELECTION OF 1986

The fact that elections could be held in a reasonably fair and nonviolent manner after so many years of repression was significant.[24] They permitted the open and frank expression of widely varying views and introduced a healthy competition among political forces. However, four structural and political problems risked preventing the institutionalization of an effective system of representation. First, parties had inadequate time to regroup, as the new electoral system and reemergence of political parties took place in less than one year. That gave the advantage to well-organized NIF and also privileged Umma and DUP, which could count on networks of religious adherents in the countryside. Regional ethnic parties lacked the means to communicate with and mobilize their potential constituencies. Other parties had no structure and funds with which they could campaign on such short notice.

Second, the multiplicity of parties and weak internal organization of the DUP distorted the outcome. A candidate could win with significantly less than half of the votes in the district. In addition, DUP—and Umma to a lesser extent—ran more than one candidate in many districts, thereby splitting party votes and generally benefiting the NIF candidate. In the few cases where parties arranged informal electoral alliances, they proved highly effective, for example, in blocking the election of two senior leaders of NIF, Hasan al-Turabi and General Secretary Yasin Umar al-Imam, and ensuring the election of Nuba leader Ghabboush and SCP leader Nuqud.[25]

Third, nearly 10 percent of the seats were set aside for graduates of postsecondary institutes and universities, who could select the district in which they would vote. NIF mounted a coherent strategy to capture those seats. For example, NIF won two graduates seats in the south that it would not have won if voting had been confined to residents of those districts.[26] The strong showing in the graduates' constituencies compensated for NIF's weakness in geographic districts.

Fourth, elections could not be held in most of the south, due to the intense fighting in those areas and SPLM's election boycott. Balloting was postponed indefinitely in 41 of the 68 geographic constituencies: 24 in Bahr al-Ghazal, 15 in Upper Nile, and 2 in eastern Equatoria. Fewer people registered to vote in the entire south than in greater Khartoum, the capital city. Southern politicians feared that if they boycotted the elections, the assembly would function without them and adopt policies starkly inimical to southern interests, as had occurred in 1965. As a result, they contested the elections wherever possible, even though the south gained only 11 percent of the assembly seats.[27] Representation was also lopsided within the south, since two-thirds of the MPs came from Equatoria. The south's numerical weakness was compounded by fragmentation among the parties, which reduced their ability to present a common front against Islamic-oriented political forces.

MANEUVERING TO FORM A GOVERNMENT

A complex picture emerged from the elections. Umma won 39 percent of the seats, which was not enough to form a cabinet on its own. DUP gained 24 percent of the MPs, far less than its leaders had anticipated. NIF won a solid 20 percent, but southern, Nuba, Beja, and Communist parties together totalled barely 17 percent of the seats.

Al-Sadiq al-Mahdi had assumed that Umma would win enough seats to

Table 2. Election Results

I. *Geographic Constituencies plus Graduate Seats*

Party:	Khartoum	East	North	Central	Kor-dofan	Dar Fur	Upper Nile	Bahr al-Ghazal	Equa-toria	Grad-uate
Umma	6	7	2	29	20	34	1	1	0	0
DUP	9	17	11	15	9	2	0	0	0	0
NIF	13	2	4	4	3	2	0	0	0	23
SNP	1	0	0	0	7	0	0	0	0	0
SCP	2	0	0	0	0	0	0	0	0	1
Beja	0	1	0	0	0	0	0	0	0	0
PPP	0	0	0	0	0	0	0	0	8	2
SSPA	0	0	0	0	0	0	3	2	2	1
SAPCO	0	0	0	0	0	0	0	0	7	0
SAC	0	0	0	0	0	0	1	0	0	1
SPFP	0	0	0	0	0	0	1	0	0	0
Indep.	0	1	1	2	0	1	0	0	1	0

II. *Total Votes by Political Party*

UMMA	100	PPP	10
DUP	63	SSPA	8
NIF	51	SAPCO	7
SNP	8	SAC	2
SCP	3	SPFP	1
Beja	1	Indep.	6

TOTAL   260

III. *Graduates Districts* (28 seats)

	All Northern districts	Upper Nile	Bahr al-Ghazal	Equatoria	TOTAL
NIF	21	1	1	0	23
SCP	0	0	1	0	1
PPP	0	0	0	2	2
SSPA	0	0	1	0	1
SAC	0	1	0	0	1

Source: SUNA election booklet (Arabic), 25 May 1986; James Chiriyankandath, "The 1986 Elections," *Sudan after Nimeiri*, ed. Peter Woodward (London: Routledge, 1991), 81; and Lesch, "Party Politics in the Sudan," *UFSI Report* # 9 (1986), 11, which contains typographical errors.

provide him with flexibility in selecting coalition partners. He apparently intended to form a government of "national unity" that would exclude NIF and
base its rule on a combination of the National Alliance charter (April 1985), the
Charter for the Defense of Democracy (November 1985, to be discussed in chapter 6), the Koka Dam Declaration (March 1986, to be discussed in chapter 6), and
the Umma Party program.[28] Al-Mahdi would use the anticipated constitutional
conference to formulate a new legal code to replace the September decrees with
a formula acceptable to both sectarian Muslim movements and African political forces. However, overrepresentation of NIF and underrepresentation of the
south precluded that strategy and meant that al-Mahdi had to include DUP
and/or NIF in the cabinet in order to gain a majority. NIF's declarations that it
was blasphemous to annul the September decrees led al-Mahdi to make defensive statements that he would merely modify the Islamic codes. DUP used its leverage to gain the key ministries of foreign affairs and interior, which left the African (Nuba and southern) parties with merely residual posts.

Furthermore, DUP leaders insisted that Umma and DUP formulate a governing agreement based on Islamic principles.[29] This twelve-point Charter of
National Unity, finalized on 4 May, proposed applying the Islamic draft constitution of 1968 that DUP had authored until the constituent assembly could decide on a permanent constitution. The charter noted that the September decrees
should be abolished, because they provided an improper formulation of shari'a;
they would be replaced by correct Islamic laws, not by a secular formula.

Meanwhile, NIF issued its own charter that called for a national government
that would include all the political parties except the communists, whose views
NIF vehemently opposed.[30] NIF supported the draft constitution of 1968 and argued that, until a permanent constitution could be promulgated, "the 1983 Islamic laws shall remain in force." Moreover, "new laws [must be] derived from
the holy Quran and the Sunna" and must be more comprehensive than Numairi's
system. Non-Muslims should have special minority status rather than the rights
of fully integrated citizens.

The African parties criticized the Umma-DUP and NIF charters for mar-
ginalizing their peoples and issued their own Charter of National Unity on
5 May 1986.[31] Drafted by the Nuba SNP, the charter rejected the draft constitution of 1968, insisted that the September decrees be totally abrogated, and supported a secular constitution that would recognize the Sudan's multiple cultures,
languages, and religions. The charter demanded that the south have a third of the
representation in all national institutions and supported a federal system as the
only way to end Arab hegemony and ensure an equitable distribution of national
resources. The charter reflected their bitterness at the concentration of power in
the hands of the Mahdi and Mirghani oligarchs and their anger that al-Mahdi
offered only three residual cabinet posts to the south and one to SNP, whereas

they had expected to receive six portfolios, including the important interior and housing ministries. In a statement that accompanied the charter, the African parties denounced "the unilateral attitude of the major parties in assuming the absolute right to form an imposed national government in a paternalistic spirit."

Umma leaders were taken aback by this attack, having expected that their meeting with the African politicians on 4 May would simply review the names of potential cabinet members. They met again on 5 May—until dawn of 6 May— but failed to agree on the terms for a governing coalition.[32] Despite that, the assembly convened a few hours later to elect the speaker of the assembly, the members of the council of state, and the prime minister. When the provisional speaker of the assembly refused to let the leaders of SNP and PPP express their criticisms of the proceedings, the African MPs walked out of the hall as soon as he opened the floor for nominations. Nuba leader Ghabboush shouted, "democracy is now nailed to a coffin and buried!" PPP's Eliaba Surur warned: "We tolerated the Arabs for all these years and called this an Afro-Arab country, but from now on, it is African only."[33] The rest of the MPs ignored the African walkout and proceeded with the elections as though nothing had happened. Umma's candidate for speaker was easily elected[34] and later al-Sadiq al-Mahdi was handily elected prime minister.[35] The five members of the council of state, which served as the sovereignty body to guarantee the constitution, were also elected despite the absence of most African MPs. [See Appendix 3.] Those northern politicians did not seem concerned that voting in the absence of important ethnic and regional political forces could weaken their legitimacy. Al-Mahdi even called the African walkout "a deceptive rather than a genuine move" that proved that the boycotters "hate democracy and attempt to distort its image."[36]

The dignity and symbolism of the exchange of power from the transitional regime to the first elected government in eighteen years was all but lost in that acrimony, which continued during the week-long negotiations to form the cabinet. Al-Mahdi made no concessions on portfolios or policies in order to attract African politicians to the cabinet. [See Appendix 4.] He insisted that the south could have only 22 percent of the cabinet posts, which he claimed was their proportion of the population.[37] Al-Mahdi personally decided which southern politicians would be selected for the cabinet, based on a list of names provided by the parties. When he met with Ghabboush on 12 May, the Nuba leader rejected the animal resources portfolio as a poor substitute for the interior and housing ministries. Moreover, in line with the DUP-Umma charter, al-Mahdi asked the attorney general to formulate "alternative" laws to replace the September decrees. Al-Mahdi thereby set aside his campaign pledge to provide a political umbrella under which non-Arabs and non-Muslims could stand. His dismissive manner in dealing with African political forces was an inauspicious way to launch the new parliamentary system.

The war of charters among Umma, DUP, NIF, and the African parties and the haste with which the assembly selected the executive officers epitomized the assimilationist approach. The numerical majority could ignore the wishes of the minorities. There were no safeguards to ensure the rights of those ethnic and religious groups. The clear statement of ethnic pluralism in the African parties' charter was summarily dismissed. Those machinations set the stage for increased polarization in the coming years.

5

Polarization during the
Parliamentary Period

MUTUAL SUSPICION and polarization became acute during the three years following the election of the constituent assembly. These tensions included bickering between Umma and DUP, the sectarian parties that shared executive power, but the most deep-set conflict pitted NIF against the African parties. The vision of exclusivist Islamic-Arab ethnic nationalism confronted the ideal of territorial nationalism that encompasses all the peoples. The tensions underlined the problem of institutionalizing a liberal pluralist system in a country that lacked a national consensus on basic identity issues.

The incoherence of the coalition government's policies can be illustrated in several arenas: foreign policy, economic performance, plans to restructure the administrative systems in the south, and efforts to amend shari'a law and the transitional constitution. In each case, the lack of a clear vision resulted in contradictions and immobility.

Governments were unable to craft a consistent foreign policy.[1] During the first two years, for example, the DUP foreign minister tried to improve relations with Egypt, Iraq, and the United States, whereas Prime Minister al-Mahdi courted Libya, Iran, and the USSR, and criticized the IMF. Those actions sent contradictory signals since Iraq and Iran were at war, Egypt and Libya were at odds, and the U.S.-Soviet rivalry was still intense. Foreign relations also impacted on national identity, as al-Mahdi's effort to unify with Libya displayed. Al-Mahdi hoped that allying with Libya would make him less dependent on other political parties by enhancing his financial and military resources. But the idea of unity was widely opposed, since DUP preferred to ally with Egypt and Saudi Arabia; NIF denounced Muammar al-Qaddafi's unorthodox religious views and his suppression of the Libyan Islamist movement; and Fur politicians resented the militarization of Dar Fur by Chad militias, armed by Libya. Southern and Nuba politicians feared that the government would use more Libyan fighter planes to crush the SPLA and also feared that unity would make Sudan more Arab ethnically, tilting the population balance away from the African and non-Muslim citizens. Thus, even foreign policy concerns had ramifications for the issue of national identity.

76

In its economic policy, the government contended with ongoing protests against escalating prices and shortages of food, fuel, and electricity while seeking to respond to demands from the IMF to reduce public expenditure and privatize public sector corporations. The DUP minister of information criticized the government for failing to define its economic policy, which left it open to pressure from trade unions to increase wages and lower prices.[2] NIF criticized the government for contradictory economic policies that increased the cost of living but did not resolve economic problems or even map a clear negotiating strategy with the IMF and other foreign lenders.[3] NIF itself induced some of the economic difficulties, since the NIF-linked Faisal Islamic Bank controlled half of Sudan's sorghum exports and thereby manipulated the price and availability of that basic food. NIF cadres organized demonstrations against electricity and water shortages, high prices, and negotiations with the IMF. NIF-orchestrated protests against shortages in electricity and water shortages in the capital and the lack of equipment in schools led to hundreds of arrests and the declaration of a state of emergency on 25 July 1987. Parliament endorsed that clampdown on 6 October 1987, in the midst of another wave of NIF-supported protests.

NIF benefited from the public's antipathy to the IMF and its fear of economic chaos, and used the protests to spread its own political views. Demonstrations by NIF students and trade unions in October 1987, for example, combined calls for economic self-reliance with condemnation of the SPLA and demands for comprehensive Islamic laws. The government closed the schools in Khartoum as well as Khartoum University after NIF students clashed with student supporters of Umma and southern movements.

The question of restructuring the administration in the south exacerbated differences among southern politicians and deepened their distrust of the government in Khartoum. Al-Mahdi inherited a system that consisted of three separate regions ruled by military governors, alongside an ineffective Higher Executive Council (HEC). On 1 January 1987 al-Mahdi announced that he would replace the HEC by a Council for the South, headed by Mathew Obur, a discredited former official under Numairi. The three regional governors and five politicians (one from each party) would serve on the council, which would coordinate policy and advise the governors. At that time the southern political parties were divided on the issue of how the south should be ruled. Equatorian PPP and SAPCO and Nuer SPFP opposed reunification, whereas SSPA and SAC strongly supported the reestablishment of one large region for the south. This discord left al-Mahdi free to act as he wished.[4]

Southern politicians denounced al-Mahdi's unilateral action, criticized the choice of Obur, and argued that southerners alone should select the council members and governors. Even though the prime minister responded by saying he would let the southern politicians devise an alternative formula, he finalized the

Council for the South in March 1987 without taking into consideration the southern politicians' preferences. SAC and SSPA withdrew from the cabinet in protest, which precipitated a split inside the SSPA and left only three southerners in the cabinet. Divide-and-rule tactics weakened the voice of the south in Khartoum.

Islamic law continued to be the most contentious issue. Al-Mahdi's inability to alter the September decrees epitomized the incoherence of government policy and the conflicting pressures on the political system. The prime minister sent to the assembly on 10 November 1986 a set of amendments to the transitional constitution that modified the use of shari'a and hudud and increased the powers of the executive vis-à-vis parliament.[5] Even those slight modifications in shari'a were protested by NIF for going too far and by secularist African parties and the bar association for not going far enough. The prime minister tried to deflect NIF's criticism by convening a meeting of Muslim experts from abroad in December 1986, at which NIF MPs heckled al-Mahdi when he argued that the September decrees should be replaced by humane and progressive Islamic laws that would uphold democracy and freedom of expression.

DUP leaders were suspicious of other proposed amendments, such as reducing the quorum for assembly sessions to 30 percent, since that would enable MPs from Umma—who constituted 38 percent of the representatives—to pass legislation without any other MPs being present. Moreover, giving the assembly the power to unseat MPs who changed their party affiliation might be used against the loosely structured DUP. The DUP member on the council of state also noted African politicians' fear of being second-class citizens in a shari'a-based political system. His views were an early indication of the change taking place inside DUP on that sensitive issue.

The version approved by the assembly on 1 April 1987 dropped the right to unseat MPs, required a 60 percent vote for constitutional amendments (instead of the proposed simple majority), and qualified the government's right to legislate when parliament was not in session.[6] The government did not take practical steps to alter the September decrees until December 1987 when it abolished administrative detention and set the maximum number of lashes at ten.[7] NIF denounced those modifications and mounted high-pressure tactics against the government. Its cadres led thousands of demonstrators into the streets to protest that backsliding on shari'a. The prime minister capitulated when he issued draft laws in February 1988 that asserted that shari'a should be followed wherever possible and that non-Muslims in the south should only be temporarily exempt from hudud.[8] A Muslim living in the south would have the option of requesting a trial under Islamic laws but a non-Muslim living in the north must follow shari'a.

Al-Mahdi underlined that territorial duality when he presented the government program to the assembly on 15 March 1988. He claimed the program would ensure Muslims their right to "practice their religion and its tenets to the full" while ridding "ourselves of the distortions to Islam which the September 1983 laws represent."[9] Once again, the prime minister failed to satisfy anyone, since NIF sought a comprehensive Islamic system and secularists sought the abrogation of shari'a.

THE SECOND CABINET:
STALEMATE BETWEEN UMMA AND DUP

Tensions escalated within DUP and between al-Mahdi and his DUP partners. Sharif Zain al-Abdin al-Hindi, the DUP secretary general who served as deputy prime minister and foreign minister, quit the government and threatened to resign from the DUP because Muhammad Uthman al-Mirghani had not convened a party convention and al-Mahdi had failed to craft effective policies. The prime minister responded by calling al-Hindi and the DUP commerce minister uncooperative, the latter having alienated the entire cabinet when he denounced corruption within DUP and criticized al-Mahdi for high-handed actions.[10] Then al-Mahdi angered al-Mirghani when he justified dissolving the cabinet on 13 May 1987 by claiming that the ministers were incompetent, while installing a new council of ministers on 3 June 1987 with all the same persons except the outspoken DUP ministers of foreign affairs and commerce. [See Appendix 5.] That maneuver demonstrated al-Mahdi's leverage over the DUP, as the junior coalition partner.

Relations deteriorated further that month when DUP's Muhammad al-Hasan Yassin resigned from both the Council of State and the DUP politburo, after criticizing nepotism by the council's chair, who was al-Mirghani's brother.[11] When DUP nominated another politburo member to replace Yassin, al-Mahdi rejected that choice because he was ineligible for the post since he had been a minister under Numairi. When DUP refused to nominate anyone else, al-Mahdi selected Mirghani Nasri, head of the bar association, whom the assembly confirmed in August over DUP's objections. DUP then went into "executive opposition," which meant that its ministers remained in their offices but opposed their Umma partners. Al-Mahdi and al-Mirghani failed to restore the coalition accord.

Due to their cavalier treatment by al-Mahdi, DUP leaders sought an alternative coalition. Bitter competition with NIF precluded a NIF-DUP alliance and so DUP began to make a surprising shift toward the African parties. Al-Mirghani claimed that NIF's positions had "aggravated" matters over the past year and its presence in the government would prevent any policy consensus from emerging.[12] DUP's pragmatic shift became evident in January 1988 when it supported the African parties' call for negotiations with the SPLM, a delay in deciding on the role of religion in politics until the planned national constitutional conference, and the formation of a broad-based government of national reconciliation that would exclude NIF.[13]

THE THIRD CABINET: EMPOWERING NIF

The assembly reelected al-Mahdi prime minister on 28 April 1988 on the basis of a new national charter that was supported by all the parties except NIF and SCP.[14] The charter called for "substitute Islamic laws" and "an Islamic economic system," but angered NIF by emphasizing guarantees of "full rights to the non-Muslims," not setting a deadline for the legal changes, and calling for negotiations with the SPLM. Al-Mahdi, however, opposed having any constraints placed on his personal power, as the charter implied. Therefore, he abruptly undermined the charter and checkmated DUP and the African parties in May 1988 by adding NIF to the governing coalition and supporting the NIF candidate for speaker of the assembly.[15] [See Appendix 6.]

Moreover, al-Mahdi appointed NIF's Hasan al-Turabi attorney general. Turabi emphasized that NIF would "salvage the country" from the personal rivalries that bedeviled Umma-DUP coalitions. When he threatened to pull out of the government unless it promulgated a comprehensive Islamic code within sixty days, al-Mahdi caved in. The prime minister stated that new Islamic laws would be implemented "before the end of the rainy season"—a time limit that coincided with NIF's deadline.[16] Turabi was not perturbed by the criticism of secularists, since his draft laws "might stir up a controversy, but eventually the assembly is likely to endorse them by a large majority."[17] To him,

> The Sudanese people have longed for [Islamic law] since independence. The embodiment of Islamic values in Sudanese society was the objective of independence. Promises were made to the Sudanese people regarding the application of the shari'a but these were never fulfilled. . . . We are not talking about a period of two months, we have waited for the shari'a to be applied for 32 years. . . . Sudan has been so late in liberating itself from western pressures and it must now ask for forgiveness by returning to God's laws.

NIF second-in-command Ali Uthman Muhammad Taha also welcomed the opportunity to build Sudanese society on clear Islamist foundations now that those members of Umma and DUP who objected to the Islamist course had been removed from the cabinet. Turabi and Taha declared that the two southern cabinet members supported Islamic law so long as residents in the south would be partially exempt; southerners living in Khartoum would not be exempt since Khartoum had a Muslim majority.

In contrast to NIF's enthusiastic support for shari'a, DUP leaders became wary of Islamization. They were not only concerned about their marginalization in the new government but were also disturbed by the government's hard-line policy toward the civil war. DUP's Sid Ahmad Hussain—whom al-Mahdi and Turabi had excluded from the cabinet—warned that forming an anti-southern and anti-Nuba government would fracture the country.[18] When al-Mahdi capitulated to NIF's deadline for new Islamic laws, DUP protested that the government could not be bound by that timetable. Similarly, members of SSPA and SNP who had defected from their parties to join the government were dismayed by al-Mahdi's about-face, since they had thought that the issue of religion would be deferred until the constitutional conference.[19]

PPP's Eliaba Surur, the first African head of the opposition in the parliament, criticized the "mechanical majority" of Arab-Islamic politicians that could ram Islamist legislation through the assembly.[20] He lamented the government's determination to create a national identity based on one race and one religion, denounced the prime minister's divide-and-rule tactics toward the south, and warned al-Mahdi that he was exacerbating deep ideological, religious, and racial divisions. Surur said he felt comfortable as "an African who wants to be a Sudanese." He regretted that the prime minister was "uncomfortable with being just an African or a Sudanese" and sought an allegedly "superior" identity as an Arab and Muslim. Turabi and Surur's perspectives—along with Sid Ahmad Hussain's warning—expressed succinctly the polarized concepts of national identity. The contest became increasingly acute as Turabi implemented his vision of a monolithic Sudan.

CONFRONTATION BETWEEN DUP AND NIF

In early September 1988, when the two-month deadline passed, NIF urged an end to the "unreasonable delay" in reinforcing shari'a and successfully pressed the council of ministers to endorse its draft laws on 11 September 1988.[21] When the bill was tabled in the assembly on 19 September, African MPs walked out, declaring that the measure would split the Sudanese nation in half. Faced with the automatic majority in favor of some form of shari'a, they did not want to legitimize the debate. Those southern MPs who were members of the governing coalition threatened to withdraw their support should the bill be passed. The Sudan Council of Churches denounced the bill on the grounds that it "jeopardizes the unity of the country," denies "the equality of all citizens before the law," and imposes "degrading" hudud punishments on non-Muslims.[22] Even the president of the Council of the South, handpicked by al-Mahdi, argued that the time was not ripe for shari'a and that its application should at least be excluded from the south and Khartoum.[23]

African MPs could not shift the political balance on their own. But they gained support from the DUP, whose leaders feared the economic and social cost of the war as well as NIF's enhanced power. DUP therefore signed a pathbreaking agreement with the SPLM on 16 November 1988 (detailed in Chapter 6) that called for freezing Islamic laws and convening the constitutional conference by the end of December.[24] DUP thereby placed the value of including all the Sudanese peoples in the constitutional consensus above its long-held value of creating an Islamic state. Before taking that step, al-Mirghani had consulted extensively with other politicians and gained overwhelming support. Even a leader of the government-funded Anya-Nya II militia underlined the importance of separating religion and state:[25]

> We will not agree to use religion as a force to subjugate the Sudanese minorities and the undecided Sudanese who do not believe in any religion. God created us equal and therefore service to God is an individual decision. . . . Peace is a must.

In contrast, al-Mahdi and NIF fiercely opposed the accord. Although the Umma party endorsed its terms, al-Mahdi focussed on its challenge to his personal authority and insisted that the parliament grant him exclusive personal authority to negotiate with the SPLM and organize a constitutional conference.[26] NIF, however, invoked "higher national interests" that required comprehensive shari'a laws, and threatened to leave the government if it froze hudud. When al-Mahdi blocked a formal endorsement of the accord, he once again checkmated the DUP, whose ministers resigned from the cabinet on 28 December 1988.

Both sides used public demonstrations to pressure the government. The DUP-SPLM accord was supported by protesters who invoked the slogan "against hunger . . . against war" to denounce al-Mahdi and NIF political and economic policies.[27] Al-Mirghani had already been greeted with an outpouring of public support when he returned from concluding the accord with the SPLM in Addis Ababa. NIF's protests, in contrast, quickly became violent. Shots were fired outside al-Mirghani's home the night before he left for Addis Ababa. On 17 November a SAM-7 missile hit the military transport plane carrying Defense Minister General Abd al-Majid Khalil and Commander-in-Chief Lieutenant General Fathi Ahmad Ali as it took off from Wau in Bahr al-Ghazal. Although al-Mahdi blamed the SPLA, evidence pointed to dissident northern commanders who opposed the defense minister's endorsement of the accord.[28] A NIF demonstration on 22 November attacked southern residents in Khartoum. And rumors of coup plots by mid-rank officers circulated in the capital.[29]

When the DUP resigned, al-Mahdi quickly formed an Umma-NIF government in which Turabi became foreign minister. [See Appendix 7.] Turabi wielded his enhanced power to dismiss career diplomats, recognize the Afghan guerrilla government based in Peshawar, step up arms purchases, intensify fighting in the south, and consolidate Islamic law.[30] Turabi had already precipitated a crisis within the judiciary when he ordered the courts to drop charges of embezzlement and misuse of funds against several of Numairi's officials.[31] Judges, magistrates, and legal advisors to the attorney general struck in protest against this politically motivated interference with the legal process.

COUNTER-PRESSURE BY THE HIGH COMMAND

Those actions generated strong reactions. Al-Mahdi and Turabi labeled as traitors the leaders of the DUP, African parties, trade unions, and professional associations who met with the SPLM in Ethiopia to call for "a government of national salvation composed of all political forces committed to peace, including the SPLA-SPLM."[32]

Most significantly, Defense Minister Khalil resigned on 20 February 1989.[33] General Khalil opposed NIF's dominance of the government and argued that negotiations with the SPLM were essential, in part because foreign governments would no longer arm the Sudanese armed forces. Khalil strongly implied that a government of national reconciliation should negotiate with the SPLM on the basis of the DUP-SPLM accord. His action did not occur in a vacuum. Numairi had fired him in 1982 for protesting against the politicization of the armed forces and the use of the army to quell civilian protests. In recent months Khalil had decried al-Mahdi's use of Umma-supported militias in the west and south to fight the SPLA and al-Mahdi's appointment as chief of staff in August 1988 of his cousin Major General Mahdi Babu Nimr, son of the Baqqara Arab chief, Babu Nimr. That move signalled that al-Mahdi might build up the militias to rival or surplant the army.[34] Khalil opposed al-Mahdi's proposal to combine the militias into a Popular Defense Force (PDF) that would serve under the army's command. NIF endorsed this idea, but the military command wanted to dissolve—rather than reinforce—the militias. Moreover, Khalil objected when al-Mahdi replaced the politically neutral minister of interior with his cousin Mubarak al-Fadhil al-Mahdi on 1 February 1989, a move that signaled potential party interference in the security services as well as the armed forces. Khalil had already been denounced by NIF for endorsing the DUP-SPLM accord, thereby triggering the apparent attempt to shoot down his plane. Thus, Khalil had professional, political, and personal reasons to stand up to the prime minister and NIF.

The next day three hundred senior officers signed an ultimatum that gave al-Mahdi one week to either supply the armed forces adequately or negotiate a peace agreement.[35] The memorandum, signed by Commander-in-Chief General

Fathi Ahmad Ali, declared that the armed forces were safeguarding the popular uprising of April 1985. DUP, SCP, several southern parties, and the alliance of trade and professional unions endorsed the memorandum and called for a broad-based government to negotiate a comprehensive peace. Al-Mahdi rejected the ultimatum as an illegitimate intrusion by the armed forces into the political arena. The Council of State was divided and unable to act effectively. The officers then submitted a second memorandum on 28 February in which they insisted that al-Mahdi implement all the provisions of the memorandum of 21 February.

Al-Mahdi gave in on 5 March when he agreed to broaden the government on the basis of the seven-point program that the leaders of thirty-eight political parties and two dozen unions signed on 3 March that called for implementing the DUP-SPLM accord.[36] NIF rejected the program, since it did not mention retaining Shari'a. Nonetheless, al-Mahdi delayed asking his Umma-NIF cabinet to resign until the high command of the armed forces sent a third memorandum on 10 March 1989 that demanded immediate steps to reconfigure the government and insisted that al-Mahdi accelerate negotiations with opposition parties and unions.[37] The new government, installed on 25 March, included not only Umma, DUP, and SNP but also a member of the SCP and two representatives of unions. [See Appendix 8.] The African parties won the right to select the southern cabinet members and the members of the Council of the South.[38] A nonpartisan general became minister of defense, but al-Mahdi's relative remained minister of interior. As a sign of the dramatic change, DUP's Sid Ahmad Hussain replaced Turabi as foreign minister and chaired the ministerial committee charged with negotiating with the SPLM. That DUP politician had been ousted from the cabinet a year earlier and had played a key role in DUP-SPLM negotiations.

The council of ministers met for the first time on 26 March to approve the phased program, which was approved by the assembly on 3 April by a vote of 128 to 23.[39] However, when the assembly voted on 10 April to shelve debate on shari'a until the constitutional conference, NIF MPs stormed out and al-Mahdi and two of his relatives did not attend the session, claiming that as spiritual leaders of the Ansar they could not participate in such a vote.[40] Nonetheless, al-Mahdi initialled on 29 June the bill to suspend Numairi's Islamic decrees.

NIF PLOTS A COUP D'ÉTAT

NIF did not accept its sudden loss of power, which had demonstrated that its basic ideological approach had been rejected by the high command of the armed forces and by all the other political forces. NIF was suddenly marginalized just when it had expected to consolidate its leadership and complete the establishment of an Islamic constitutional system. Therefore, as soon as al-Mahdi acceded to the ultimatum, NIF's executive bureau resolved not to participate in any government based on the phased program, since that did not uphold shari'a.[41] Turabi stated that NIF would not join a government that included leftwing parties and unions. The seven NIF ministers resigned in mid-March, the speaker of parliament resigned on 10 April, and the Khartoum commissioner resigned soon after. Nonetheless, Turabi declared, we "will be back soon, by the wish of the people." He added that freedom and stability must be in balance: in certain circumstances, "you must forego some freedom." The NIF executive committee reportedly decided to overthrow the government in a meeting on 31 March 1989.[42]

The movement then followed a two-pronged strategy that galvanized protests in the streets and simultaneously plotted with like-minded officers in the armed forces. NIF demonstrations began in March, using the occasion of Ayatollah Khomeini's *fatwa* (religious edict) that declared the writer Salman Rushdie an apostate.[43] Marches by NIF student unions in Khartoum's secondary schools and universities started on 9 April and continued virtually nonstop into June. Pro-NIF unions organized demonstrations that linked popular complaints about the economy to the deteriorating security situation that NIF itself was fostering. The government failed to contain the demonstrations, which the new Khartoum commissioner denounced as cynical efforts by enemies of democracy to undermine law and order.

NIF stressed that the protests would continue until the government applied shari'a or was overthrown. NIF's former commissioner of Khartoum, for example, declared that Islamists battled the government in the streets because the government had lost its legitimacy by freezing hudud and surrendering to the SPLM. He asserted that NIF was appealing to citizens to escalate opposition "until [the government] falls or amends its decision to obstruct the shari'a."[44] Similarly, NIF Secretary General Yasin Umar al-Imam maintained that NIF was working to oust the government because the party would "not haggle over something that is the foundation of our orientation."[45] NIF's second-in-command Ali Uthman Muhammad Taha detailed NIF's strategy:[46]

the [National Islamic] Front called on the citizens to stage demonstrations and protest against the capitulation pursued by the government. The citizens' response was overwhelming. The slogans were both specific and disciplined: Rejecting capitulation, welcoming peace, calling for readiness to defend the homeland, and emphasizing the masses' adherence to the religion and the faith. So the accusation that the Front is stirring up or promoting religious sedition is baseless.... The *jihad* we have launched embodies the meaning of defence and military resistance to aggression by demanding the acceleration of the popular defense [militias] law and the revival of compulsory military conscription.... [It also embodies] political *jihad* against the present government through demonstrations, professional and unionist pressures and other means in order to force it to retreat and not to surrender to the rebels' conditions....

> We are seeking to oust the government in the same way as it assumed power.... I confirm that a sizeable section of the Armed Forces share our concept and view of the nature of the rebel movement and its objectives and of the preparedness needed to confront it.

Such threats alarmed the government. The ambiguous reference to ousting the government "in the same way as it assumed power" could refer to the 1986 elections but more likely meant that NIF would organize a new version of the 1985 popular uprising, this time based on the Islamist movement and sympathetic members of the armed forces. Taha toured army barracks in the south during June, where he contacted like-minded officers.

A coup attempt was discovered on 18 June. The prime minister said its organizers had planned to attack the parliament while he was speaking and then arrest all the MPs, cabinet members, and the military high command.[47] The plot appeared to be orchestrated by Numairi; later it was evident that NIF-army contacts were behind the scheme. In this tense atmosphere, the interior minister asserted that although[48]

> democracy is getting stronger and firmer in the face of the conspiracies, ... a coup is not based on large numbers of people.... Specific groups create a vacuum [and] destroy political and military leaders.... It is always carried out by pockets of military and civilians conspiring to obstruct the legitimate leadership.

The coup occurred on 30 June, hours before the cabinet and parliament were expected to vote to freeze shari'a and final steps were to be taken to arrange the constitutional conference. By then, although al-Mahdi's personal commitment to suspending Islamic law and negotiating with the SPLM remained in doubt, he had been boxed in by the political forces that supported negotiations. The coup d'état dismantled the entire democratic edifice overnight and destroyed the possibility of creating a constitutional structure that would represent Sudan's diversity.

DEMOCRATIZATION IN A POLARIZED SOCIETY

The sharp cleavage over shari'a brought down the third democratic government in the Sudan. For NIF, democracy was a vehicle through which it could carry out its ideological agenda. When the majority rejected that agenda, NIF decided to impose its ideology by force.

Al-Mahdi also played a major role in weakening the nascent democracy by his preoccupation with his personal power and his reluctance to create a constitutional system. Similarly, al-Mahdi's inability to think of African politicians as equals—rather than as clients—reinforced instability. His apparently opportunistic shifts in policy made the public cynical about the democratic system.

The politicization of ethnicity and religion and the divergent definitions of the nation exacerbated that instability. Questions of majority and minority rights split the political forces. NIF, Umma, and DUP (until 1988) argued that, since most citizens were Muslim, they had the right to institute Islamic law and need only ensure freedom of worship for the religious minority. African and secularist political forces retorted that imposing the majority's views on the entire country denied the minority basic political rights. It took three years of debate before the government took steps to resolve that core issue in a way that could include all religious groups in a new national consensus. Over time, those steps might have moved the country away from ethnic nationalism and toward a territorial nationalism based on ethnic pluralism and decentralized authority.

The failure underlined the difficulty of instituting an enduring democracy in a country in which national identity was still contested and acceptance of pluralism and democratic rules remained tenuous. Governing institutions and political processes would be fragile so long as no consensus was achieved on national identity.

6

Efforts to Resolve the Civil War

THE CIVIL WAR that raged throughout the south provided the sharpest proof that there was no consensus on national identity. The stark contrast in the definition of the Sudan was evident in the polarized views of most northern political forces and the SPLM. The former assumed that Sudanese identity was defined by a cohesive Arab-Islamic heritage, whereas the SPLM sought to transform the Sudan into a territorial nation-state in which all its diverse peoples would have a role and a way to express their particular identity. Despite this polarization, the very intensity of the fighting compelled some politicians in the north to reconsider their positions and to begin to work toward an accommodation that would define national identity in more inclusive ways.

THE SUDAN PEOPLES' LIBERATION MOVEMENT

Colonel John Garang de Mabior articulated comprehensive goals for the SPLM when it was established in July 1983: the creation of "a united Sudan under a socialist system that affords democracy and human rights to all nationalities and guarantees freedom to all religions, beliefs and outlooks."[1] Garang stressed that the SPLM was not a southern movement, focused on regional issues, but was concerned about the Sudan as a whole and merely happened to emerge in the region where exploitation was most intense: "the marginal cost of rebellion in the south became very small, zero or negative; that is, in the south, it pays to rebel." As such, the SPLM was the "vanguard movement for the liberation of the whole Sudanese people." Garang declared that this democratic New Sudan would guarantee equality, freedom, economic and social justice, and would end the monopoly of power by any one group, whether the "gang of generals" in the Transitional Military Council, the family dynasties of al-Mahdi and al-Mirghani, or the ideological sectarian NIF. The SPLM also rejected tribalism and racial distinctions as bases of rule. Although "the emergence of regional political groups [is] a natural revolt against the appalling conditions in which the masses live in those areas," those conditions cannot be overcome by viewing each region and group in isolation and "the root causes of Sudan's chronic social and political instability are essentially national. As such, they should be tackled nationally." Once power was restructured in Khartoum, marginalized areas and peoples would acquire a stake in the economy and a guaranteed position in the central government. Overall, Garang considered that the Sudan was still undergoing a process of "national formation" that would fuse the many ethnic groups into one nation. He asserted: "Our major problem is that the Sudan . . . is still looking for its soul, for its true identity. Failing to find it . . . some take refuge in Arabism, and failing in this, they find refuge in Islam as a uniting factor."[2] Others opt for separatism, since they are neither Arab nor Muslim. Instead, just as the African kingdoms of Funj and Fur fostered Arab-Islamic culture while maintaining their special characteristics, so can a New Sudan blend the languages and cultures into a unique pattern in which no single element has hegemony and the specificities of each culture are respected by all. This articulation of goals was squarely within the ethnic pluralist, territorial nationalist framework: the search for a national identity that would embrace all citizens irrespective of their ethnicity.

Garang's own background indicated the complexity of southern Sudanese identity.[3] Born in 1945 in Bor (Upper Nile) of Dinka parents, he was educated in Bahr al-Ghazal and in Tanzania. After studying for his BA at Grinnell College (Iowa), Garang fought with the Anya-Nya in 1971-1972. He reportedly opposed the Addis Ababa Accord and the absorption of the Anya-Nya into the armed forces, but he became a captain and later a colonel in that army and received military training at Fort Benning in 1974. He then gained a PhD in agricultural economics from Iowa State University in 1981, writing on development issues related to the controversial Jonglei Canal. When Garang returned to the Sudan in 1981, he directed research at the army headquarters in Khartoum and taught agricultural economics at Khartoum University. He gained an acute awareness of the political and economic problems facing the south as well as familiarity with the intricacies of politics in Khartoum and within the military elite.

The SPLM's aims were all-encompassing and highly political, but it was structured along military lines with the SPLM/SPLA high command dominated by commanders in the field. Garang's leadership was challenged by other southern military officers and civilian politicians who felt they had equal or greater credentials for running the movement. Personal rivals included Major Kerubino Kuanyin Bol, former commander at Bor whom Garang detained in 1987, and Lt. Colonel William Nyuon Bany Deng, former commander at Ayod, who defected in 1992. They chafed at serving under Garang, and Kerubino may have also disagreed with the movement's dependence on Ethiopia. Some politicians such as the elder statesman Joseph Oduho objected to Garang's opposition to secession and his insistence that the military wing of the SPLA control civilian operations.[4] Garang also suppressed challenges from Anya-Nya, reconstituted as

Anya-Nya II in 1983, but gained the support of its Nuer commander, Gordon Kong Chuol, in January 1988, who brought with him two-thirds of the Anya-Nya II fighters.[5]

Until May 1991 SPLM's political headquarters was located in Addis Ababa, which provided a crucial sanctuary as well as material assistance and diplomatic support.[6] Mengistu Haile Mariam allowed the SPLA to operate a radio station that served as a vital means for the SPLM to transmit its message directly to the Sudanese public. Ethiopia provided transport planes, helicopters, and trucks, airlifted supplies into the south, and let the SPLA set up training camps, logistical centers, and a prison and POW camp on its soil. By 1991, 400,000 southern Sudanese crowded into refugee camps in western Ethiopia. Reliance on Ethiopia, however, opened up the SPLM to charges of manipulation by that Marxist government, including participating in that regime's combat against insurgencies inside Ethiopia. In fact, assistance from other countries was limited, especially when Libya's Mu'ammar al-Qaddafi shifted his support from the SPLA to the government after Numairi was overthrown. The SPLM maintained offices in Nairobi and Kampala, which handled diplomatic and relief operations and may have served as conduits for some arms. Only after Yoweri Museveni came to power in Uganda in January 1986 and resumed his longstanding friendship with Garang did the SPLA and the Ugandan army cooperate along their common border, including fending off attacks by Khartoum-supported Ugandan dissidents.[7]

The SPLA developed a four-pronged strategy to undermine the government and defeat the armed forces in the south, which focussed on mounting protracted operations that would wear down the armed forces. First, the SPLA destroyed internationally funded development projects, forcing a French company to stop digging the Jonglei Canal in November 1983 and Chevron to suspend drilling for oil at Bentiu in February 1984. Garang said those operations were designed "to achieve maximum shock and embarrassment" while Numairi was negotiating with creditors in Paris.[8] Later attacks closed down oil exploration at Bor, construction of the international airport in Juba, and tea plantation operations near Torit.

Second, the SPLA blocked communication routes within the south and between the north and the south by blowing up railway bridges, ambushing truck and rail convoys, mining roads, and sinking river barges. The army virtually gave up trying to protect communications routes and vital installations during the summer rains, aside from such essential locales as Juba and Wau. Even airdrops of supplies to garrisons were vulnerable to SPLA's SAM-7 missiles, which also downed civilian and military planes and helicopters.[9]

Third, the SPLA isolated strategically located towns and army garrisons and seized populated towns once it established secure lines of communication into Ethiopia. The SPLA was strongest in eastern Bahr al-Ghazal and Upper Nile by 1986-1987, and did not move into Equatoria until December 1984, partly for logistical reasons but also because many Equatorians were suspicious that the SPLA was a Dinka-dominated movement.[10] In the winter of 1987-1988, SPLA captured the strategic town of Kapoeta (Eastern Equatoria), astride the only land route from Juba and Torit to Kenya, and the following winter SPLA overran a dozen towns and outposts in all three regions.[11] That was crowned by the capture of Garang's hometown of Bor (Upper Nile), where the 1983 mutiny had touched off the uprising. The 40,000-strong SPLA controlled half of the rural south in 1985-1986, two-thirds in 1987, and nearly 90 percent by 1989.

Fourth, the SPLA moved into the north through southern Blue Nile and southern Kordofan. The seizure of Kurmuk in the Ingessana Hills of southern Blue Nile province in November 1987 put at risk that province's vital hydroelectric installations and agro-industrial areas. African residents of Kurmuk district had long-standing grievances against Khartoum, having been denied the right to vote on whether they wanted to join the south after the Addis Ababa Agreement. Moreover, those Ingessana people were angry at the government and private Arab businessmen for driving them off their traditional lands in order to establish large-scale sugar and cotton-growing projects, and therefore welcomed SPLM's call to redress the grievances of the marginalized peoples.

The SPLA also capitalized on grievances among the peoples in the Nuba Mountains of southern Kordofan, where ongoing tensions between Nuba and Arab tribes over water and grazing rights were exacerbated by the alienation of land to private mechanized agricultural schemes and by drought, which forced Arab herdsmen to move into the Nuba-populated hills.[12] Nuba political groups supported the SPLM's aim of restructuring the central political system and empowering the marginalized ethnic groups. The SPLA entered the Nuba Mountains in 1985 when its forces killed a hundred unarmed Arab residents of Gardud village in a sudden surprise raid. In 1987 the SPLA mounted a sustained campaign and in 1989 formed a division under Commander Yusif Kuwa that operated near the provincial capital of Kadugli. The government responded by arming Baqqara Arab militias to raid Nuba villages as well as Dinka, Shilluk, and Nuer areas in Bahr al-Ghazal and Upper Nile. Militias captured cattle, sheep, and slaves, thereby depleting the human and material wealth of those areas. Relief workers estimated that 52,000 Nuba villagers were displaced by early 1988.

In the westernmost region of Dar Fur, many peoples resented control from Khartoum, and tension between Fur farmers and Rizaiqat Arab cattle herders escalated in 1984-1985 as drought forced the nomads to encroach upon cultivated land.[13] Fur were angry that the central government let Libyan troops deploy in northwest Dar Fur and permitted rebels from Chad to camp inside Dar Fur, where they joined with Zaghawa tribesmen to raid Fur villages. The SPLA claimed that 6,500 foreign troops were camped in Dar Fur by mid-1988, a number that grew as Libya and the rebels prepared to overthrow the Ndjamena government in December 1990. The extent of destruction was indicated in a report in January 1989 that 57 villages had been burned in the Wadi Saleh agricultural district, where nearly 400 had died, 42,000 were displaced, and 12,000 tons of food were destroyed. Further attacks by 3,000 *murahiliin* (Arab militias) on Jabal Marra in May 1989 burned 40 villages and left 80,000 homeless. Those government-armed murahiliin also attacked displaced persons from the south. In March 1987, in apparent revenge for the SPLA's killing of 150 Rizaiqat militiamen while they raided Dinka villages in western Bahr al-Ghazal, Rizaiqat murahiliin and Arab townspeople killed 1,000 destitute Dinka displaced persons in the largely Arab town of al-Da'ien. When police tried to shelter the Dinka women and children in the police station and on railway cars, the Rizaiqat torched the wagons and stormed the police station. The SPLA played no direct role in these conflicts, since the vast distance prevented the SPLA from aiding Fur groups or protecting displaced persons.

While fighting in the fringes of the north remained tangential militarily for the SPLA, it symbolized the idea that the SPLM was not only a movement of southerners but had national aspirations and a potential base among other deprived peoples. It reinforced the message that the SPLM sought fundamental transformations in the country's identity and political structures, not merely cosmetic changes and token concessions.

PERSPECTIVES IN KHARTOUM

Government officials and politicians in Khartoum reacted to the challenge presented by the renewed uprising according to their own perceptions of political reality. The dominant triad of Umma, DUP, and NIF viewed the Sudan as predominantly Arab and Muslim, within which the south comprised a discrete entity and southern politicians could be relegated to unimportant portfolios in Khartoum. Political life revolved around the needs and perspectives of the Nile Valley core, which would co-opt or contain African Muslims in the west, far north, and east. They assumed that the Muslim majority had the right to institute Islamic legal codes covering not only personal status within the Muslim community but also political, economic, and social regulations pertaining to the entire country. Non-Muslim minorities would have to accept that Islamic framework, within which they would retain freedom of worship and certain other legal protections. This perspective was embodied in Numairi's Islamic codes and NIF's insistence on a comprehensive Islamic system. It was also intrinsic to the visions of al-Mahdi and al-Mirghani, although they believed that tolerant governments would respect the rights of minorities.

From those perspectives, the SPLM's goals were a clear threat. Nonetheless, northern leaders tried to discount the importance of the uprising. Some asserted that the rebellion was merely "Garang's movement" and therefore would end if his personal ambitions were satisfied by a high-level post in Khartoum. Others saw the SPLM as an extension of the secessionist Anya-Nya movement and hoped to placate it by restoring the Addis Ababa Accord. Still others argued that the SPLM was not the sole voice in the south, since five southern parties won seats in the 1986 elections. Divide-and-rule tactics could be used to isolate the SPLM. Moreover, governments called Garang a puppet of Mengistu, who sought to impose a Marxist regime on Sudan,[14] and claimed that the SPLA would collapse without support from Ethiopia, the Soviet Union, and Cuba.

However, northern politicians primarily viewed SPLM's challenge to the structure of power in Khartoum as proof that the movement was anti-Arab and anti-Muslim. That threat galvanized them to uphold the dominant paradigm of a Muslim Arab Sudan at all costs. The chairman of the TMC appealed to Libya, Iran, and the Gulf states for financial and military aid on the grounds that Garang would impose an African identity on the Muslim Arab majority in Sudan. When the SPLA captured Kurmuk, al-Mahdi's officials exclaimed fearfully that Africans were poised to overrun the north. When the SPLA penetrated the Nuba Mountains, the government armed Arab tribes as the first line of defense against African forces. SPLM's insistence on a secular constitution seemed proof of its anti-Muslim orientation. NIF blamed western Christian churches for seeking to thwart the natural spread of Islam southwards into the heart of Africa and "instigating" southerners to demand secular laws and support the "outlaws."[15] Those powerful negative images "proved" that negotiations were impossible. They reinforced the conclusion that the government and the SPLM were engaged in a zero-sum struggle.

Nevertheless, some politicians in Khartoum addressed Sudan's problems from perspectives that were compatible with the SPLM and thereby prevented the conflict from becoming entirely zero-sum. After all, the Addis Ababa Accord and the constitution of 1973 had not simply made the south an isolated enclave but had incorporated proportional representation in the central government and acknowledged the validity of Christianity and traditional beliefs alongside Islam. Those inclusive principles gained acceptance among secularists in the north and were compatible with the tolerance and flexibility in *sufi* movements. For example, the charter of the 1985 uprising rejected Numairi's September decrees and endorsed the nonreligious constitution of 1956. But the political parties that endorsed that approach had barely 17 percent of the MPs and, on their own, could not resolve the conflict.

Ultimately, economic collapse—more than a change in ideology—compelled politicians to find a way out. By mid-1989, the war cost $3 million daily and the government owed $13 billion to foreign creditors, who no longer supplied aid.[16] The fighting wrecked plans to augment Nile waters and end the country's reliance on oil from abroad. Nearly 5,000 members of the armed forces had died in the south, more than 300,000 soldiers were wounded, and at least 250,000 civilians had died from famine or disease. As early as 1987 the Umma finance minister pointed out that, since the war consumed most of the general budget, neither balanced budgets nor economic reforms were possible so long as the war continued. And DUP's al-Mirghani stated bluntly: "the war is exhausting Sudan's resources, lives, and wealth." Thus, even politicians who strongly supported the Muslim and Arab identity of Sudan came to see a political accommodation with the SPLM as necessary to restore economic stability.

In view of the polarity between the dominant political forces in Khartoum and the SPLM, creating mechanisms to overcome the mutual distrust and resolve the conflict was a laborious process. Nonetheless, over the course of four years, political leaders overcame major obstacles to negotiations. The *coup d'état* in 1989 cancelled those efforts and deepened the divide.

TRANSITIONAL PERIOD

The basic way by which Garang sought to end the civil war was to convene a constitutional conference to resolve all the outstanding political and legal issues besetting the country. He first proposed this just before Numairi was overthrown, suggesting "a national congress to be organized by the SPLA, progressive and patriotic elements in the Sudanese Army, and other democratic forces in the country to discuss the essence and programme for the formation of a New Sudan and its New Army consistent with its particularity."[17] That concept was not incorporated into the charter of the National Alliance, however, which referred merely to solving "the problem of the south within a framework of regional self-government based on democratic principles" in which the SPLM was considered one of several voices in the south.[18]

Moreover, members of the Transitional Military Council (TMC) and cabinet were angry that the SPLA did not stop fighting when Numairi was ousted. They were annoyed that Garang called on the TMC to relinquish power and criticized the generals' previous behavior. Garang recalled, for example, that TMC chair Suwar al-Dhahab had urged Numairi to suppress the Bor mutiny in 1983 and that Defense Minister Abdallah had labelled the SPLM "foreign-inspired infidel insurgents" when he was Numairi's chief of military operations.[19]

Although the cabinet was taken aback by Garang's criticism, its members resolved at their first meeting on 25 April to open a dialogue with the SPLM. The next day, the TMC urged Garang to come to Khartoum to talk, decreed a general amnesty for all rebels, and ordered a unilateral cease-fire. The National Alliance

Map 3. THE SOUTHERN SUDAN, 1989
Source: Abel Alier, *Southern Sudan: Too Many Agreements Dishonored.*
(Exeter: Ithaca, 1990).

sent a delegation from its committee for national reconciliation to Addis Ababa in June that met Garang on 12 June. He viewed that as a way to open a dialogue with the progressive forces in Khartoum. In contrast, despite declarations by TMC head Suwar al-Dhahab and Prime Minister Dafallah that they had sent emissaries to Garang,[20] no one in the TMC or cabinet sent any diplomatic messages to the SPLM until June, whereas the TMC rushed its diplomats to Ethiopia and Libya to convince them to stop supporting the SPLM.

In June 1985 Dafallah and Defense Minister Abdallah both wrote to Garang, sending uncoordinated letters with divergent messages.[21] Dafallah focussed exclusively on the south. He downplayed SPLA's role in toppling Numairi, described the SPLM as one of many actors in the south, and claimed that the transitional government had already taken significant steps by reaffirming its commitment to the Addis Ababa Agreement, recognizing the south's unique cultural and ethnic characteristics, and preparing to send relief aid and development assistance to that region. Dafallah avoided the fundamental issues of power sharing in the center and Islamic law by arguing that religious laws need not be divisive and that it was possible to preserve the September decrees while meeting the concerns of non-Muslims. SPLM's most prominent northern member, former Foreign Minister Mansour Khalid, commented sarcastically that the letter reflected the "myopia of the ruling elite."[22]

The defense minister adopted a more forthcoming tone in his letter, reiterating his earlier call for a wide-ranging dialogue with Garang and stressing the national orientation of the SPLM:

> I am well aware, my friend [Garang], that you are not fighting as a rebel or secessionist but you are striving with honour for the achievement of national unity and to improve the lot of the Sudanese, northerners and southerners. . . . [I hope you can return to Khartoum] to participate in establishing the new direction of the Sudan.

Although Abdallah's conciliatory language indicated that the SPLM leadership could play an equal role in the post-Numairi regime, Garang and his officers doubted that was the real intent. They believed the offer was designed to bring Garang to Khartoum, where he could be tempted by a position in the new government and cut off from his military base in the south. Such a move—if carried out prior to agreement on the content of the New Sudan—would marginalize the SPLM rather than transform the governing system.

The SPLM received mixed messages from the two letters which, in any event, were private communications rather than authoritative statements by the TMC and Council of Ministers. The SPLM's suspicions were aroused further by their timing. The letters reached Garang in late June, just as the army initiated a

military offensive in the south and just before Abdallah signed a military proto-
col with Libya that significantly enhanced the fighting capacity of the armed
forces.[23]

The SPLM was still preparing its response to the letters when the Council
of Ministers announced on 24 August 1985 its terms of reference for a national
conference.[24] That declaration stated that the reasons for fighting had ended with
Numairi's defeat but also affirmed that "our people" are

> a mixture of diverse cultural and religious components. . . . The Southern
> Question cannot be resolved except within the frame of the wider question—
> the question of emphasizing national unity.

Although the declaration stressed that "cultural and religious diversities [were]
important challenges confronting our national unity" and therefore some of the
September decrees must "be revised to remove whatever provisions discriminate
against citizens," it nonetheless wanted the proposed conference to focus on "the
southern question." Overall, the declaration gave lip service to ethnic pluralism
while reaffirming the Muslim essence of Sudanese society.

SPLM leaders were disappointed with the government's declaration, but responded positively by announcing a temporary cease-fire and endorsing the
principle of a constitutional conference. The SPLM stressed that the conference
must be national in scope rather than focussed on one region, and must draft
a constitution acceptable to all the Sudanese people. On 1 September 1985 the
SPLM-SPLA high command issued its response to the prime minister's letter, which also constituted a preliminary answer to the Council of Ministers. The
SPLM outlined steps that "the government of the day in Khartoum . . . [must do]
to ensure the necessary favourable conditions for national dialogue."[25] Those five
preconditions for convening a national constitutional conference remained the
core of the SPLM position, to which it adhered throughout the subsequent years:

> First, the agenda must comprise "the Problem of the Sudan, not the so-called
> Problem of Southern Sudan," e.g. the system of government in Khartoum,
> equitable distribution of resources, and the structure of regional governments
> "as reflections of the structure of power at the center, in Khartoum."
> Second, the September decrees must be cancelled rather than modified. Ar-
> rangements to exempt "the south or any other region from national [Septem-
> ber] laws [were also unacceptable]. . . . It is pointless for the SPLM/SPLA to
> participate in a conference of national dialogue within the context of shari'a
> laws."
> Third, the government must cancel the defense pact with Egypt and the mili-
> tary protocol with Libya, since they impinge on national sovereignty.
> Fourth, just before the constitutional conference, the state of emergency must
> be lifted and then a cease-fire would be instituted.

Fifth, the TMC and council of ministers can remain in office during the constitutional conference, but must commit themselves to step down afterwards in favor of a government of national unity that would include all political forces as well as the two "warring armies" (the SPLA and the armed forces).

In sum, the SPLM wanted to cancel the Islamic decrees and military pacts prior to the constitutional conference, which would usher in a cease-fire and a new government.

The Council of Ministers responded officially on 10 November 1985, agreeing that the agenda for the constitutional conference should encompass "*all* major national issues" rather than just the south and agreeing to lift the state of emergency before that conference.[26] However, the Council of Ministers rejected all the other preconditions demanded by the SPLM: the conference itself would decide on shari'a, defense pacts, and political structures. Existing laws would be applied in the meantime so as not to prejudge those issues.

Khartoum had not received the text of the SPLM reply until 24 October, due to complications related to its delivery. By then tensions had risen, partly because the government claimed that the SPLA had supported an alleged attempt by Nuba and southern soldiers to mount a coup d'état on 26 September. The prime minister denounced this "racist" sedition which, by supposedly inciting non-Arab Sudanese against northerners, intended first to assassinate members of the TMC, the cabinet, and leading northern politicians and then to bring Garang to power.[27] The arrest of prominent southern and Nuba politicians on charges of treason infuriated southern and secularist politicians. The SPLM denied complicity, stressing that it opposed military coups and any form of racism. The SPLM spokesman argued that the TMC itself fanned religious and racial feelings by letting the chief of staff address a NIF demonstration of 10,000 persons on 21 September that clashed violently with southern residents in Khartoum. The SPLM charged the TMC with whipping up anti-southern feelings because the army had suffered reverses in the field. SPLM leaders were also irritated by the transitional constitution (discussed in chapter 4), which retained the September decrees.

In this inflamed atmosphere, emissaries from the National Alliance urgently discussed with Garang the need to hold an unofficial dialogue in the north that would include all the political forces and would clarify central questions concerning the rule of law.[28] The alliance convened that conference in Wad Medani in December 1985, where all the members except the DUP endorsed its Democratic Protection Charter.[29] DUP leaders rejected the clause that advocated abrogating the September decrees and insisted that issue be postponed until the constitutional conference. (NIF, which was not a member of the alliance, did not send representatives to the meeting and categorically rejected the Democratic Protection Charter.) Garang did not attend, largely due to the difficulty of guaranteeing his security, but the SPLM praised the charter as a major step toward addressing the fundamental issues and fostering democracy.

The Democratic Protection Charter paved the way for a meeting between the National Alliance and the SPLM in Ethiopia in March 1986. By then Garang had met with leaders of several constituent organizations within the National Alliance, including the Sudanese Communist Party (SCP) and regional groups representing southern, Nuba, and Fur peoples.[30] The SCP-SPLM statement on 1 January 1986 urged the Sudanese people to shed racist and separatist sentiments and to root out religious fanaticism. The joint communique by the SPLM and the Nuba SNP called for a new nonracial Sudan and opposed oppression by dictators and sectarian parties. The joint statement by the SPLM and the Southern Sudanese Political Association (SSPA) stressed that the roots of regional problems lay at the national level and that the government must repeal the September decrees.

The SPLM remained suspicious of the TMC and concerned at the government's rejection of its preconditions. The transitional authorities were equally suspicious of the SPLM, doubting that it really sought peace. The government's contradictory words and actions culminated in March 1986.[31] On the one hand, officials admitted that they faced a dire military situation in the south, declared that the government's only precondition for a peace conference with the SPLM was a cease-fire, and welcomed the alliance's plans to meet with the SPLM. On the other hand, the TMC rushed emissaries to Libya to obtain bombers to strike SPLA-held towns on the eve of that same meeting. The government may have feared that the army's poor performance would enable Garang to dictate the terms of peace, but aerial bombardments undermined conciliatory statements and deepened the SPLM's mistrust.

THE KOKA DAM DECLARATION

The National Alliance and the SPLM had hoped to convene the national reconciliation conference in January 1986 to draft a new constitution and end the fighting before the elections in April 1986. That timetable proved too optimistic. The conference did not convene until 20 March in Koka Dam (Ethiopia) and members of the government and the TMC did not participate. Although Umma sent a delegation, DUP and NIF refused to attend.[32] The Koka Dam Declaration, issued on 24 March, called for the creation of a New Sudan "free from racism, tribalism, sectarianism, and all causes of discrimination and disparity." Its terms included the five preconditions articulated by the SPLM in September 1985, since the national constitutional conference must convene in an "atmosphere conducive" to achieving results. The parties should agree beforehand that the agenda would cover "basic problems of Sudan and not the so-called problem of southern Sudan." The government must repeal the September laws, adopt the constitution of 1956 (as amended in 1964), and annul military pacts that "impinge on Sudan's National Sovereignty." The government must lift the state of emergency and both sides must enforce a cease-fire. The constitutional conference should be held in Khartoum in June 1986, after meeting the preconditions and finalizing arrangements based on the agreed-upon agenda.

The liaison committee quickly began follow-up discussions[33] and participants pledged to approach DUP and NIF to sign the declaration. Although the conferees agreed on basic issues, they differed on the advisability of holding parliamentary elections in April. The National Alliance viewed elections as an important step toward democracy after seventeen years of autocratic rule, whereas Garang considered them illegitimate since a new constitution had not been drafted and SPLM could not participate. In fact, the elections did derail the plans for the constitutional conference outlined at Koka Dam, in part because NIF and DUP's refusal to participate at Koka Dam was "a serious blow to the peace process ... NIF [in particular] held both parties [Umma and DUP] hostage on the issue of sharia."[34] And even though the Umma party endorsed its conclusions, the new prime minister ignored them. Al-Sadiq al-Mahdi's room for maneuver was limited by the Ansar movement, by his DUP coalition partners, by the strongly ideological NIF, and by his own ego, which prevented him from sharing the diplomatic spotlight with anyone else.

AL-MAHDI'S CONTRADICTORY STANCES

As a result, the momentum was lost and the constitutional conference did not convene in June. Al-Mahdi merely sent an emissary to Addis Ababa to ask if the SPLM would join the government, elucidate Garang's ideas on a governing system, clarify the movement's preconditions for the constitutional conference, and request a personal meeting with Garang.[35] Garang welcomed that initiative but declined to join the government or comment on its composition, since he had objected to holding elections without agreement beforehand on the constitution. He insisted that the Koka Dam Declaration provided the only legitimate framework for negotiations and that al-Mahdi should empower its liaison committee to arrange the constitutional conference. Nonetheless, he was willing to meet with the prime minister.

The two leaders met for nine hours on 31 July 1986 in Addis Ababa.[36] Al-Mahdi, who technically met Garang as head of the Umma party rather than prime minister, would not commit himself to a secular code but offered to annul the September decrees within thirty days and replace them with alternative laws that would not hurt the political and civil rights of non-Muslims. He agreed that

Sudan's problems were national, rather than confined to the south; that the government should abrogate the defense accords with Egypt and Libya; and that the state of emergency should be lifted in tandem with implementing a cease-fire. Al-Mahdi sought to form a new committee, rather than use the liaison committee established at Koka Dam.

Al-Mahdi viewed the discussion as relatively successful, but Garang concluded that peace was impossible since the prime minister rejected the Koka Dam Declaration as the sole basis for agreement and would not promise a secular constitution or "commit himself to specifics."[37] Garang wondered why al-Mahdi wanted to bypass the liaison committee and feared that a new committee would make unacceptable changes in order to win over DUP and NIF and would delay the conference in anticipation of weakening the SPLA militarily. SPLM advisor Mansour Khalid noted that Garang did not consider al-Mahdi "a recalcitrant war horse" but rather "a self-absorbed politician . . . [who] wanted to renegotiate Koka Dam so that he might be the one to define the agenda and determine the action."[38] Garang challenged al-Mahdi to announce the immediate implementation of the prerequisites for the constitutional conference, in return for which Garang would declare a cease-fire.

Later, each accused the other of bad faith. Al-Mahdi said that, since Garang labored "under illusions," the government must step up its military pressure. He flew to Libya to obtain more bombers. Al-Mahdi denounced Garang after the SPLA shot down a civilian airplane in Malakal on 16 August, killing the sixty people on board. He stated he would not meet with Garang, who was not only the puppet of Ethiopia but also a terrorist who held the southern people hostage.[39] The prime minister declared that the constitutional conference could be held even without the SPLM. Garang then criticized the prime minister for shooting down "the whole peace process," not merely one plane.[40] SPLA radio denounced the "semifeudal sectarian parties, dominated by two [Mahdi and Mirghani] families" that aborted the plans laid at Koka Dam. Nonetheless, Garang continued to appeal to al-Mahdi to support those peace efforts, promising that the SPLA would then promptly stop fighting.

Nine months later, both sides resumed their tentative contact, after the armed forces failed to regain any territory, the constitutional conference remained on hold, and differences among political groups in Khartoum over a new constitution became increasingly acrimonious.[41] In April 1987 Garang expressed disappointment that the overthrow of Numairi had not led to peace negotiations and stressed that dialogue was essential since neither side could win militarily. He hinted that the government could demonstrate its good intentions by lifting the state of emergency in the north, since he recognized that the fighting made it difficult to lift in the south.[42] Garang encouraged nonofficial contacts: in April and May 1987, he met with former Deputy Prime Minister Samuel Aru Bol, head of SSPA, and with DUP's MP Abd al-Hakim Taifur, as well as with popular delegations from the Nuba Mountains and Kordofan.

Al-Mahdi welcomed Garang's comments and sent him a proposal that suggested that the Koka Dam Declaration has "objective bases which will pave the way to the national constitutional conference."[43] Nonetheless, the prime minister repeated his arguments that modifications were needed since DUP and NIF had not signed it and that "September laws . . . [should] be replaced by a legal position based on diversity in a way which satisfies the aspirations of the Muslims in areas of Muslim majority and the aspirations of non-Muslims in other areas." Al-Mahdi again proposed lifting the state of emergency as soon as a cease-fire was enforced and suggested that they agree to a cease-fire for two weeks in April so that relief aid could reach civilians in the south. Finally, he suggested that a national popular committee discuss the agenda, composition, and date of the constitutional conference. He concluded:

> We urge you to accept the peaceful solution . . . [in order to participate] in the democratic march of the new Sudan, a Sudan which tackles its problems by free dialogue and safeguards for all its citizens' basic freedom and human rights.

The SPLM reacted sharply to the letter, which SPLA radio declared "devoid of the slightest hint that the al-Sadiq government is really serious about peace and dialogue."[44] Al-Mahdi's view that Sudanese society was defined by its Muslim majority "isolates large segments of the population from the political process and thereby denies them their legitimate basic rights." In Sudan's context, "there is no one single definition of a majority." The broadcast categorically opposed retaining shari'a:

> The tenacious adherence by the Khartoum government and the opposition NIF to Islamic shari'a laws is a traumatic political experience for Sudan. The ongoing efforts to reinforce rather than scrap the shari'a laws of 1983 . . . have dealt a mortal blow to prospects for peace in Sudan. . . . [The SPLM] will only accept strictly secular laws.

The broadcast criticized the prime minister for ignoring the Koka Dam liaison committee and disregarding that committee's invitation to DUP and NIF to join its deliberations. The fact that those parties did not yet participate in the liaison committee did not warrant the establishment of an entirely new body to plan the constitutional conference. The commentary concluded that al-Mahdi really sought a cease-fire so he could resupply army garrisons before the rains began in May. In fact, the army launched a military offensive two weeks after the prime minister sent the letter.

The SPLM's official response, issued on 27 July 1987, emphasized the gap between the two sides. Sudan must be "a secular, multiracial united state," not a system with a Muslim majority and a non-Muslim minority. SPLM already accepted the idea of linking a cease-fire to lifting the state of emergency, as the final step before convening the constitutional conference: the cease-fire should not be the first step but should be the culmination of the diplomatic process.

By then the National Alliance had dispersed and could not press to implement the Koka Dam Declaration. Nuba and southern MPs took the lead in organizing popular dialogues with the SPLM, under the umbrella of the Union of Sudan African Parties (USAP).[45] Led by Eliaba Surur, head of Equatoria's Peoples Progressive Party (PPP), those MPs met three times with the SPLM in August and September 1987 to reaffirm support for the Koka Dam Declaration and allay mutual suspicions. The meetings were particularly significant since the PPP had previously denounced the SPLM, criticized Dinka control of the movement, and refused to attend Koka Dam. The participants strongly supported SPLM's call for a secular state. Islam does not need protection, Surur argued, since Muslims are the majority; rather, minorities require safeguards.

Al-Mahdi denounced those dialogues since they challenged his personal control over policy toward the civil war. When the SPLA seized Kurmuk (Southern Blue Nile) in November 1987 and Kapoeta (Eastern Equatoria) in January 1988, al-Mahdi declared that anyone who met with the SPLM was a traitor. Nonetheless, he allowed four senior military officers to meet secretly with SPLM officials in London just after the SPLA captured Kurmuk, ostensibly to explore terms for a cease-fire and the passage of relief convoys through the south.[46] They discussed—and differed over—the thorny issue of Islamic laws.

Meanwhile, the African politicians insisted that they were acting as loyal patriots when they sought to tackle the central ideological issues and enable the SPLM to participate in the constitutional conference. They did manage to draft a Transitional Sudan Charter, which Umma and DUP signed on 10 January 1988 and only NIF and SCP refused to endorse. That charter declared that Sudan had a dual Arab and African identity and that power and resources must be shared equitably.[47] Since "Islam is the religion of the majority," laws to substitute for the September decrees could apply until the national constitutional conference would resolve "the issue of religion in politics." The charter thereby tried to mollify the traditional Muslim politicians while keeping open the possibility of a significant transformation.

Even so, al-Mahdi rejected the constraints the charter placed on his personal authority, for example by designating an Umma dignatory on the Council of State to head a Muslim-Christian delegation to Addis Ababa to arrange with the SPLM to distribute food and medical aid in the south. Al-Mahdi abruptly halted those talks, using the excuse that the SPLA had captured another garrison town a month earlier. He again hinted that contacts with the SPLM were treasonous. Al-Mahdi's stance hardened further when he discarded the concept of a government of national reconciliation based on that charter and joined forces with NIF in May, even though NIF opposed negotiating with the SPLM.

Garang called that coalition an "unholy trinity" of "the warmongering sectarian bigots in Khartoum, who masquerade as national leaders."[48] He attacked NIF Attorney General Turabi for drafting new Islamic codes and denounced al-Mahdi's claim that the army would defeat the SPLA by midsummer. In contrast, Garang praised the new Minister of Defense Abd al-Majid Khalil as a respected officer who had stood up to Numairi and might prevent al-Mahdi from politicizing the armed forces. Furthermore, Garang made two diplomatic gestures. To appeal to the armed forces, he offered to release a lieutenant colonel captured in southern Kordofan and to exchange POWs through the International Committee of the Red Cross. To facilitate negotiations, he suggested convening a "Koka Dam II" conference to include DUP and NIF so that a national consensus would emerge prior to the long-awaited constitutional conference. When he did not receive any official response to these proposals, representatives of the SPLM and the African parties met again in July 1988 to assess the bleak situation.[49] They reasserted their support for the Koka Dam Declaration, their commitment to a secular state, and their determination to hold the constitutional conference. Nonetheless, the prospects for a constitutional conference and a secular state appeared remote.

THE DUP-SPLM ACCORD

The previous chapter noted the surprising shift in DUP's position, which broke the diplomatic impasse. DUP leaders had refused to attend the Koka Dam conference and consistently insisted on an Islamic constitution, but they felt severely constrained by the Umma-NIF alliance, concerned about the impact of the war on the country's economy, and believed that a pragmatic accommodation was essential, given the country's complex social forces. Whether the shift was purely expedient or represented the start of serious rethinking of the country's national identity was unclear.

A member of the DUP political bureau had held exploratory talks with the SPLM officials in May 1987, but the crucial meetings took place in mid-1988 when high-level delegations under Sid Ahmad Hussain and retired General Yusuf Ahmad Yusuf met with SPLM officials in Addis Ababa.[50] Hussain, DUP's deputy secretary general, had just been removed as minister of interior in the cabinet reshuffle, and Yusuf was respected by the SPLM for opposing Numairi's policies in the south in 1983. DUP leaders felt a special urgency since Umma signed an agreement to unite with Libya in August 1988 and the cabinet approved Turabi's draft Islamic laws on 11 September. Those measures risked fracturing the country even further. Under those compelling pressures, the two sides quickly agreed on steps to convene the constitutional conference. After they signed an agreement in principle on 17 October, DUP gained the support of all the political parties and professional and trade unions except NIF. Therefore, when DUP's political and spiritual leader al-Mirghani met with Garang, he could state that "we came to this meeting only after ascertaining that the majority of the Sudanese people support this effort and want peace."[51] At the end of four days, they finalized the accord on 16 November 1988.

The joint statement mentioned the peoples' sufferings, their belief in territorial unity, and their wish to reject worn-out policies that promoted war and caused divisions. In order to enrich democracy, they must not delay a true peace:

> We believe that, because our national problems are of ethnic origin, they can only be solved through a serious, continuing and clear-cut dialogue among all the Sudanese political forces, on an equal footing within the framework of the forthcoming national constitutional conference.

Al-Mirghani agreed to the SPLM's preconditions, including the end to Islamic punishments and laws until the conference could resolve that issue. For the SPLM, it represented a concession to "freeze" Islamic laws rather than cancel them:

> We hereby agree with the DUP ... to freeze all the clauses related to the *hudud* and other pertinent clauses included in the September 1983 laws. No laws with clauses that refer to the above clauses shall be enacted until the national constitutional conference is convened and the issue of the laws is finally settled.

DUP and SPLM also agreed to abrogate military pacts that limited national sovereignty, end the state of emergency, and declare a cease-fire. A national preparatory committee would fix the date, venue, and agenda of the constitutional conference, which they hoped would open on 31 December 1988 and which would enable the SPLM, in Garang's words, to become "part and parcel of the Sudanese political process."

They agreed to reserve their substantive differences until that conference. Garang insisted that the SPLM would demand a secular constitution: the SPLM "has not relaxed or abandoned its position.... We are committed to a nonreligious or nontheocratic state. We are for a secular state ... [but] we are willing to tolerate a freeze and wait for the scrapping at the national constitutional conference." But, since DUP accepted a freeze, "it would be unreasonable for us" to insist on annulling the laws immediately. Garang warned that the call for an Islamic state promoted secessionism: "if one of the nationalities [in a multinational state] imposes itself as the state nationality, where do the other nationalities go?" This hinted that an effort to force an Islamic constitution on the country could lead the SPLM to revive the call for a separate southern state.

Nonetheless, Garang said he was willing to discuss shari'a at the conference and to let Islamist parties try to convince the SPLM delegates otherwise. His dream remained to "create a New Sudan in which all the main nationalities exist and contribute amicably" and whose people would be comfortable as both Africans and Arabs.

Al-Mirghani carefully placed the accord within a framework acceptable to his party and the Khatmiyya tariqa. He emphasized DUP's "Islamic and nationalist" orientation while stressing that:

> Sudan embraces differing views and different nationalities, but all people must live in amity and peace. The majority must have its status in matters affecting it but without making an impact on the rights of the minorities. This will lead us to a long debate and a great deal of argument at the national constitutional conference, but in the end we believe in the democratic course. . . . Through dialogue and democratic practice we shall be able to build a modern Sudan.

The two leaders also differed on the relevance of the Koka Dam Declaration. Garang placed the new accord within its parameters, whereas al-Mirghani claimed that their accord "transcended" Koka Dam, adding: "whatever the DUP's view was then at Koka Dam, we now have a definite date for the National Constitutional Conference. . . . There will be no going back to the past."

SPLA radio then called on al-Mahdi and Turabi to shift "from the high gear of intransigence and war hysteria to the low gear of tolerance and peace," since the SPLM was willing "to tolerate the freeze [of hudud] and wait for the scrapping of the laws at the national constitutional conference. . . . [That provided] evidence of the seriousness of the SPLM/A in the search for a just peace."[52] However, al-Mahdi and Turabi quickly blocked the DUP-SPLM accord since it threatened their rule and demonstrated the limited appeal of their hardline policies. NIF-sponsored protests against the accord degenerated into violent clashes with southern residents. Al-Mahdi was furious that al-Mirghani had one-upped him so effectively. When the prime minister had learned about the first round of talks in August, he had pressed the Ugandan president to arrange a tête-à-tête with Garang that would divert attention from the DUP meetings.[53] Then, when al-Mirghani met with al-Mahdi on 20 November to discuss the steps that needed to be taken to freeze hudud, abolish military accords, and set the date for the constitutional conference, al-Mahdi tried to convince him that the SPLM could not be trusted. He further insisted that parliament confer on him a *personal* delegation of power to negotiate with the SPLM and refused to submit the text of the accord to the cabinet and the assembly for formal endorsement.[54]

Garang criticized the prime minister's maneuvers, insisting that parliament endorse the accord since it was the appropriate constitutional body. Then a preparatory committee should organize the conference. The prime minister should not try to renegotiate its terms and delay implementation.[55] Garang contacted al-Mirghani on 12 December, worried about the delay and about al-Mahdi's un-anticipated hostility. When Umma and NIF blocked a DUP motion to approve the accord, the DUP felt compelled to resign from the government on 28 December. With Turabi elevated to foreign minister in the narrow Umma-NIF government, Turabi quickly stated that the accord was no longer relevant, urged the army to accelerate its military offensive in the south, and renewed his insistence on comprehensive Islamic laws.[56] Although he said that he would formulate a new peace plan, he did not reveal its contents.

Meanwhile, DUP, African parties, unions, and independent intellectuals frantically tried to salvage the situation. USAP's Surur and a DUP delegation conferred with Garang in Addis Ababa in early February and met with the SPLM in Ambo (Ethiopia) on 9-11 February 1989 to reaffirm the DUP-SPLM accord. The Ambo resolutions proposed that the democratic forces unite "to bring about a government of national salvation composed of all political forces committed to peace, including the SPLM/SPLA."[57] Al-Mahdi claimed that amounted to a call for revolution. Security agents at the Khartoum airport interrogated the participants as they flew home.

The Umma-NIF government moved rapidly toward confrontation as it sought to destroy the SPLA and silence critics in the north. Despite their efforts, a dozen garrison towns fell to the SPLA in January and February and the military balance shifted decisively in the SPLA's favor. The crisis broke in February 1989 when Defense Minister Khalil resigned and nearly 300 officers issued an ultimatum to force the prime minister to either obtain the arms needed to fight or negotiate with the SPLM. The officers detailed the failure of their efforts to beg and buy arms from abroad, criticized the political dependence on Libya and Iran created by those arms deals, and indicated that military losses made the situation untenable. They pressed al-Mahdi to implement the steps necessary to convene the constitutional conference.

As discussed in the previous chapter, al-Mahdi capitulated to the officers and established a broad-based government whose program included the terms of the DUP-SPLM accord. Hussain, DUP's chief negotiator with the SPLM, replaced Turabi as foreign minister and was charged with finalizing arrangements for the constitutional conference. The government and then the assembly endorsed the DUP-SPLM accord on 3 April, just as government and SPLM negotiators met in Addis Ababa. The Council of Ministers also began legal proceedings to cancel the defense accord with Egypt. Next, the assembly voted to shelve debate on Islamic laws until the constitutional conference. SPLM welcomed that vote but stated that the assembly still needed to freeze hudud, since the September decrees remained in the statute books, and needed to guarantee that no similar laws would be passed before the constitutional conference.[58] As a conciliatory gesture, the SPLA began a cease-fire on 1 May for the month of Ramadan, which it later extended through June. As the government began to prepare draft bills to freeze hudud, the foreign minister met again with the SPLM in Addis Ababa from 10 to 12 June.[59] By the end of June, parliament would freeze the September decrees and annul the military accords, paving the way for a formal meeting in Addis Ababa on 4 July between al-Mahdi and Garang. Then, shortly before the constitutional conference would open on 18 September, the state of emergency would end and the permanent cease-fire would begin.

For NIF the situation was urgent, since they had been booted out of the government and were isolated in the assembly. The agreements destroyed their dream of an Islamic state. Mid-level army officers with close ties to NIF agreed that negotiating with the SPLM was treasonous. Garang commented bitterly later: "the peace process was at an advanced stage when the fifteen army officers seized power"[60] on 30 June.

The attempts to negotiate indicated not only the complexity of the issues but also the political and personal obstacles blocking their resolution. Nonetheless, it was also evident that important groups and politicians sought to surmount the divide. The SPLM's aim of establishing a nonreligious, nonethnic government in which all the diverse peoples of Sudan would have an equal share threatened the essence of a Muslim and Arab-oriented country. The SPLM platform was fundamentally unacceptable to the head of the TMC and the prime minister of the transitional government as well as to Prime Minister al-Mahdi and NIF. The leaders of the DUP were the only traditional politicians who tried to bridge the gap; even so, their accord papered over substantive differences on the role of religion in the political system. Resolution of those differences was postponed until the constitutional conference.

The major incentive for a resolution was the heavy cost of the war, which drained the government's financial reserves and undermined the economy. Even though the fighting was primarily in the south, the strife destabilized parts of the west and risked disrupting vital economic installations along the Blue Nile. Fighting postponed indefinitely the benefits anticipated from oil and water resources. Most importantly, the senior commanders of the armed forces recognized that they could not win the war. Military and economic reasons combined to propel the DUP and army officers to press for peace.

There were also objective grounds for a political agreement, in that there had already been widespread popular opposition to the Islamist measures adopted by Numairi, which catalyzed the formation of SPLM/SPLA in 1983 and then the uprising in April 1985. There was also growing recognition of the need to redress the imbalance of power within the country by establishing a decentralized system that would give meaningful autonomy at the regional level. A wide range of political groups thereby found common ground with the SPLM long before the government negotiated an accord.

Nonetheless, al-Mahdi opposed the accord and continued to seek ways to extricate himself from its terms. Moreover, the well-organized NIF adamantly opposed negotiations with the SPLM that would dilute or revoke Islamic laws and thereby crush its own political ambitions and ideological aspirations. NIF had sufficient support in the middle ranks of the armed forces to underwrite a coup d'état that blocked negotiations.

PART THREE

Polarization under the Islamist Government

7

The Evolving Political System

THE MILITARY OFFICERS and politicians who seized power on 30 June 1989 held a monolithic vision of the identity of the Sudan. They maintained that Islam, the majority religion, and Arabic, the language of the Quran, represented the essential bases for the country's nationalism and should define its legal, political, and economic systems. Arabic should supercede indigenous languages as well as English, the colonizer's language. Minorities must either merge into that Islamic culture or be exempt from a few religious punishments. Christians could practice their faith, but adherents of traditional African faiths could be compelled to convert, since they were not monotheist "people of the book." The regime sought to compel the public to follow its rigidly defined social code, cultural norms, and religious forms.

Lt. General Umar Hasan Ahmad al-Bashir, chair of the Revolutionary Command Council (RCC) of the Salvation Revolution, underlined the aim of creating an Islamic state and emphasized the officers' close relationship with NIF:[1]

> We upheld the Islamic trend from the beginning. An Islamic organization was created in the Armed Forces when the Communists tried to overthrow the Numairi regime in 1971. When the revolution began [in July 1989] . . . the leadership of the NIF met and decided to . . . join the authorities. We needed a number of their cadres. . . . We are trying to apply the [Islamic] texts gradually and intend to establish an Islamic state in Sudan. . . . We have programs for comprehensive Islamic *daw'a* [call].

The coup d'état enabled NIF to implement its ideology without facing any constraints from traditional Islamic parties or secular groups. NIF purged the government, civil service, and unions of non-Islamists and replaced them with NIF cadres, and then worked to transform public attitudes and behavior. Turabi believed that the government must use law and public policy to reform society, operating within limits set by Islamic law and "public opinion . . . [which] enjoins what is right and forbids what is wrong."[2] In practice, carrying out NIF's policies required a high degree of repression. The more people resisted, the more NIF insisted on imposing an exclusive identity. Turabi stated bluntly in 1995 that he would have preferred a peaceful transformation, "but if you are blocked completely . . . then through jihad. Just fight it out."[3]

This chapter analyzes the evolving political system and the control structures that ensured public acquiescence. The following chapters stress the effort to destroy opposition groups and the struggle by those groups to confront the regime.

RESTRUCTURING THE POLITICAL SYSTEM

The military officers established a fifteen-man Revolutionary Command Council (RCC) in which Bashir consolidated power in his hands as RCC chair, prime minister, and defense minister [See Appendix 9]. The RCC appointed a largely civilian Council of Ministers, which operated under instructions from the RCC [See Appendix 10]. On its first day in power the RCC annulled the constitution, abolished the elected assembly, banned political parties and unions, and closed the newspapers.

The initial justifications were typical of most coup d'états. RCC members argued that the armed forces should guard the society and fight corruption.[4] They asserted that the multiparty system threatened national unity by promoting dangerous divisions and leading to anarchy.[5] The parliamentary system was an alien import from Britain—"a seed that cannot germinate in Sudanese soil."[6] Instead, through indigenous forms of democracy, people would "elect genuine representatives without any trusteeship or tutelage by any sectarian group."[7]

Nonetheless, NIF had been talking about the need for a "salvation revolution" for several years and had prepared for the coup once it was excluded from the government in March 1989. The dream of an Islamist political system would not be realized if the national constitutional conference convened in September 1989. Moreover, NIF was likely to perform poorly in the next elections, scheduled for early 1990.

Military intelligence had identified Bashir since late 1985 as a potential organizer of a NIF-led coup and, therefore, transferred him to outlying garrisons, such as Bentiu and Muglad, the latter being a launching point for fighting in the south and the Nuba Mountains. He was already sympathetic to NIF when he was a student at the military academy and his fighting in the south solidified his views. Bashir was a commander in the last army convoy to take the overland route from Kosti to Juba, and he criticized al-Mahdi for failing to equip the army sufficiently, with the result that many garrisons fell to the SPLA in 1988-1989. Since he was posted in the field, he did not sign the high command's February 1989 ultimatum. However, he later indicated that he supported its demand to purchase more weapons but opposed its call for a peace accord with the SPLM. Bashir had returned to Khartoum two weeks before the coup to prepare to travel to Cairo for a training course, which was "a sure sign that he was not trusted by senior officers."[8] Bashir used that time to prepare the takeover with a small core of military confidants and key NIF cadres such as Ali Uthman Muhammad Taha, with whom he had just met in Muglad. On the night of 30 June, the officers misled soldiers stationed in Khartoum by claiming they were seizing power upon orders from the high command. As a result, no one resisted the takeover. NIF was deeply involved, but its leaders waited to reveal their stake in the new regime.

REVOLUTIONARY COMMAND COUNCIL

The members of the RCC were middle-rank officers, whose Islamist core co-opted colleagues from other branches of the armed forces, including three from the south. The cabinet consisted of civilians associated with NIF and technocrats who endorsed Bashir's anticorruption goals. The RCC dominated policy by making its members rapporteurs of nine policymaking committees. However, their powers were limited by their NIF security aides, who could overrule those ministers and countermand RCC members who were not Islamist.

Behind the official bodies, a shadowy Council of Forty set the regime's strategy.[9] Turabi chaired that secret group of NIF military and civilian leaders, preferring to remain behind the scenes: "I advise our politicians, who want to rule Sudan on the basis of Islamic principles. I do my best so that the Islamic movement fully permeates our society."[10] He added: "I guide and direct [NIF] because I have knowledge of the activities in all the departments." Under NIF's constitution, this *shura* (consultative) body directed the party's operations. Its members included Taha, the second most senior member of NIF and former MP, who handled NIF-military relations before the coup and became friends with Bashir when they attended the military academy. The Council of Forty also included the pivotal secretary of the RCC, Brigadier General Abd al-Rahim Muhammad Hussain, who was NIF's covert head in the armed forces prior to the coup and became minister of interior in January 1993. Medical Staff Counsel Dr. al-Tayyib Ibrahim Khair, known as "al-sikka" (iron bar) for his violence as a NIF student activist, was minister of presidential affairs, through which he controlled Bashir's agenda and oversaw the implementation of RCC and cabinet decisions.

DISAFFECTION WITHIN THE REGIME

By the time the RCC dissolved in October 1993, it had lost a quarter of its members. Aside from Colonel Pio Yukwan Deng, who died in 1991, and Lt. Colonel Muhammad al-Amin Khalifa, who became speaker of the appointed

Transitional National Assembly in 1992, the RCC purged four members for disagreeing with government policy:

- Major General Faisal Ali Abu Salih (interior minister) and Brigadier Uthman Ahmad Hasan (minister of state for defense) opposed the execution of twenty military officers in April 1991.
- Brigadier Martin Malwal Arup, the only Dinka member, was removed from the RCC and lost his position as political superviser of Bahr al-Ghazal on 11 March 1992 for passing intelligence and political information to opposition groups in exile. He had apparently written letters to friends abroad that criticized the appointment of the legislative assembly and the conduct of the war in the south. Malwal had wanted to resign in April 1991, but Bashir had persuaded him to remain since he came from a prominent Dinka family in Rumbek (Bahr al-Ghazal).
- Flight Brigadier Faisal Madani Mukhtar, governor of Kordofan (April 1990 to February 1992) and then minister of health, was removed on 19 January 1993 after he publicly opposed the government's foreign policy, NIF's influence, and the ineffective appointed legislature.[11]

Some other RCC members displayed their disaffection with NIF's power by ceasing to perform their official functions.[12] For example, Brigadier Ibrahim Nayil Idam, chief of security in the initial months of the RCC and the only Nuba member of the RCC, was marginalized after he upheld the concerns of Nuba peoples. When he arranged for Nuba leaders to meet Bashir on 19 December 1989, they asked Bashir to dismantle Arab tribal militias and conduct official investigations into Nuba deaths and disappearances. Instead, Idam was removed as head of security and relegated to minor positions in the cabinet.

Brigadier Tijani Adam Tahir from Dar Fur, who was not a member of NIF, negotiated a reconciliation among the Arab and African peoples in that region. But the accord was undermined by government policies that supported Chad rebels and stirred up Islamist Arab revivalism. Information Minister Colonel Sulaiman Muhammad Sulaiman criticized NIF's political dominance and control over the media.

The strongly Islamist core of the RCC included one military officer from the south, the Equatorian Brigadier Dominique Kassiano. He had led the army attack on the Bor garrison in May 1983 that triggered the formation of SPLM/SPLA. Kassiano remained a staunch supporter of government policy in the south.

NIF also tightened its grip over the cabinet. In April 1990 Islamists became ministers of finance, education, housing, and information and culture. The new finance minister Abd al-Rahim Hamdi had headed the London office of Baraka Islamic Bank and was a founder of Faisal Islamic Bank, both of which had close ties to NIF. In the next reshuffles in January and August 1991, Islamists added the portfolios of higher education, industry, commerce, energy, and mining.[13] Colonel al-Tayyib Khair moved from the presidency to become governor of Dar Fur in 1992, where he crushed the Fur rebellion led by Da'ud Bolad, a former NIF student activist who turned against the party due to its intolerance of African cultures.

In a move that signaled disillusionment among the few southerners who supported the regime, the Equatorian minister of labor and social security resigned in July 1992, not long after Brigadier Malwal was ousted.[14] Father George Kungwoko Kinga—leader of the Toposa people, former Catholic priest, and member of the Council of the South before the coup—accused the government of Islamizing the south, including forcibly circumcizing young boys. He charged that its peace initiatives were insincere: they were intended to gain time to defeat the SPLA and complete that Islamization process.

NIF'S BID FOR POWER

NIF activists became impatient with the military facade, since they wanted to rule directly. When Islamic legal codes were promulgated in 1991, NIF leaflets claimed that "the zero hour is near and the Islamic Republic will be declared in Sudan."[15] In January 1993 Turabi predicted that "Sudan's military rulers will step down in the coming weeks or months" since they have been superceded by the cabinet and the appointed assembly.[16] Turabi hinted at a popular Islamist uprising if the military refused to resign. Bashir retorted that the RCC would not step down until elected officials and institutions were in place at all levels of the political system.[17] In fact, however, even though Turabi did not hold an official position, he played a central role in reshuffling the cabinet on 18 January 1993 and 8 July 1993 to consolidate NIF control over economic and social policy as well as security. The changes marginalized non-Arab Islamists such as Nuba RCC member Nayil Idam and the southern Muslim Abdullah Deng Nhial, who was shifted from the ministry of religious affairs to the new ministry of peace and rehabilitation, with the nominal task of reconstructing the south. Key cabinet appointments comprised:

- Ali Uthman Muhammad Taha became minister of social planning in July 1993.[18] Second only to Turabi in NIF and a leader of NIF's Council of Forty, Taha wanted NIF to rule alone, supported by NIF military leaders. His new super-ministry merged Islamic charities, religious affairs (which included relations with Christian churches and societies), youth, sports, women, and relief activities. His ministry incorporated parts of the information, education, and local government portfolios. Taha sought to mobilize the public behind the ideological goals of the revolution in order to create a cohesive society conforming to the Islamist code of behavior.

- RCC secretary Brigadier Abd al-Rahim Muhammad Hussain, NIF's shadow head of the armed forces before the coup, became interior minister in January 1993.[19]
- Dr. Ali al-Hajj Muhammad, a Fur member of NIF who originally immigrated from Chad, became minister of economic planning and investment in January 1993.[20] Al-Hajj was deputy governor and then regional minister in Dar Fur under Numairi (1980-1982) and minister of internal trade in the coalition government (May 1988-March 1989). In his new position he promoted Islamic banks, facilitated NIF businessmen's purchase of privatized public-sector corporations, and strove to resume oil exploration in the south. Al-Hajj became minister of federal government affairs in July 1993, which enabled him to shape that emerging system, coordinate NIF cadres in the state and local governments, and divide the SPLA by manipulating southern dissidents.

The cabinet changes tried to disguise NIF's dominance by adding two high-profile ministers who were not members of NIF: Abd al-Aziz Shiddu as minister of justice and attorney general and Dr. Hussain Sulaiman Abu Salih as foreign minister. Bashir hoped their presence would encourage opposition leaders to return home.[21] Shiddu, a former judge on the high court, sought to improve the country's human rights image.[22] Abu Salih, a former member of DUP who had already been minister of social welfare, contacted members of DUP living in Cairo and London.[23] But their efforts were ineffective and could not disguise NIF's control. The remaining step was to disband the RCC.

DISSOLUTION OF THE RCC

The dissolution of the RCC on 15 October 1993 and formation of a new council of ministers on 30 October 1993 completed NIF's takeover.[24] [See Appendix 11.] Before dissolving, the RCC appointed Bashir president. However, he was now a civilian president and therefore did not retain the RCC's power to issue decrees, declare war, impose a state of emergency, and abolish the state legislatures. Those powers were transferred to the appointed assembly (discussed below). In its final declaration, the RCC made shari'a the guiding principle behind public law and state policy.

General al-Zubair Muhammad Salih, former deputy chair of the RCC, became first vice president in the new council of ministers and therefore Bashir's successor. Police Major General George Kongor Arop became second vice president, a post traditionally allocated to a southerner but outside the line of succession to the presidency.[25] Disaffected RCC members Sulaiman and al-Tahir were removed and Minister of Finance Hamdi was also replaced, since he was the lightning-conductor for criticism of economic policies.[26] Bashir tried to woo DUP and Umma to join the cabinet, allegedly offering 60 percent of the seats to them as against 40 percent for NIF; but they did not respond.[27] NIF therefore retained all the economic and social portfolios, with Ali Uthman Taha remaining minister of social planning. NIF's control over security was enhanced when the hawkish Dr. al-Tayyib Khair became minister of interior on 13 July 1994.[28] Khair established a central operations room to coordinate civil defense and set up civil defense committees in each state, chaired by the governors. Those measures ensured that NIF would retain control should a serious challenge arise from the armed forces or opposition groups.

Dr. Abu Salih, the increasingly isolated foreign minister, kept arguing that NIF had disbanded and Turabi and Taha did not encroach on foreign policy-making.[29] When Turabi hosted an international conference on Christian-Muslim relations in 1994, Abu Salih called it an "academic exercise" without foreign policy implications. He downplayed Turabi's meeting with the Kenyan president in September 1994 to discuss negotiations with the SPLM and tried to ignore Turabi's trips to Paris to arrange deals to explore for oil, purchase Airbuses, and acquire military intelligence useful for fighting in the south. Abu Salih also tried to ignore Taha when he orchestrated demonstrations protesting the UN International Conference on Population and Development as anti-Islamic. Abu Salih even tried to improve relations with Egypt, although his actions were continually contradicted by the pronouncements of NIF presidential advisor Ghazi Salah al-Din Atabani and by security forces' harassment of Egyptian diplomats and seizure of Egyptian property in Khartoum. During that time the tension between Egypt and Sudan escalated to a virtual war along the border, while Abu Salih anxiously sought to downplay bilateral differences. By the winter of 1994-1995, Abu Salih reportedly had dug in his heels, refusing to resign until he was expelled.

The full consolidation of NIF control took place on 9 February 1995 when Taha replaced Abu Salih as foreign minister. Taha's ally Salah al-Din moved from the presidency to minister of state for foreign affairs. Taha stated that his team would develop a comprehensive strategy based solely on the Quran and Sunna, and would coordinate with other government ministries to ensure harmony in policy and rapid decision-making. In other words, Taha would dominate both the foreign and domestic arenas. In a slap at Abu Salih, Taha remarked that Sudanese diplomats could now "express without hesitation or embarrassment the cultural change that is taking place in Sudan."[30] Those not fully committed to the Islamist course no longer had a role in the government. By then Turabi commented with satisfaction: "El-Beshir's regime has fulfilled all my political aspirations."[31]

However, some of the ministers and advisors overplayed their hand. In June 1995 NIF members of the security apparatus apparently aided Egyptian militants who tried to assassinate Egyptian president Husni Mubarak near the Addis Ababa airport. As evidence mounted of Sudanese involvement, Bashir reshuffled security portfolios.[32] He removed al-Tayyib Khair as minister of interior (barely one year after his appointment), making him minister of public service. He re-assigned both Naf'i Ali Naf'i, who had been director of foreign security, and presidential security advisor Brigadier General Fatih Urwah, since they were implicated in the assault. He elevated two former RCC colleagues: Colonel Bakri Salih to minister of interior and Brigadier Salah al-Din Karrar to the presidential council. Significantly, however, Bashir lacked the power to remove Khair, Naf'i, and Urwah entirely. They were protected by Turabi and could acti-vate loyal security forces against Bashir. In fact, NIF security personnel may have sought to embarrass Bashir on 29 July 1995 when student protests erupted during the speech he delivered at Khartoum University at the invitation of the NIF-controlled student union.[33] When students shouted anti-regime slogans, protested harsh living conditions, and smashed the windows of the interior min-ister's car, security forces teargassed them and rushed the president out of the auditorium. Observers wondered whether the student union had deliberately embarrassed Bashir in order to remind him that he lacked popular support and depended on NIF security agents to remain in power.

TRANSITIONAL NATIONAL ASSEMBLY

Bashir argued that pluralist democracy based on political parties was too divisive, and criticized Numairi's one-party system as totalitarian. He wanted unmediated "popular participation" to manage, build, and secure the country.[34] A mobilized public would fight corruption and promote economic production. NIF members argued that the people could be welded into a harmonious unity to promote virtue and prohibit vice, as required by Islam. These concepts meshed with Turabi's criticism of European democracy for dividing people artificially through political parties and fostering amoral political behavior. An Islamic sys-tem would uphold the equality of all citizens and require the ruler to consult (*shura*) the believers. Moral limits would be placed on the ruler's actions by the binding contracts between the believers and the ruler (*bay'a*).

The RCC set up "popular salvation committees" in October 1989 to help distribute food and maintain security in their localities.[35] Based loosely on the Libyan model, they were trumpeted as a crucial step toward a democracy-without-parties that would rely on volunteer effort to "save" the country. This approach was systematized during the Conference for National Dialogue on the Political System (July to October 1990), which decided that those 9,000 local committees would select representatives for district-level committees and town assemblies, who would then form a regional parliament. At the apex, two people from each region would comprise the central Peoples' Parliament. A conference of 1,636 handpicked delegates endorsed that proposal in the spring of 1991 and, the following fall, a national strategy conference established a ten-year plan to guide the congresses' efforts. Later, Bashir stated that some delegates would be elected by direct elections while others would be selected indirectly by economic congresses and societies for women and youths.[36] But elections kept being delayed, apparently because NIF leaders resisted this formula. NIF feared that opposition politicians would infiltrate base-level committees and therefore sought a tightly controlled system. In some cases, however, the peoples committees enabled the local political-economic elite to tighten its dominance over village political institutions, the distribution of economic goods, and representation at the regional-level.[37]

Despite the talk of elections, the RCC suddenly announced in January 1992 the establishment of a 330-member Transitional National Assembly (TNA). This was the first all-appointed parliament in the Sudan's history. The TNA was instituted before any of the local committees had been elected. Instead of building the legislative system from the ground up, the process was reversed. TNA members included many ex officio members of the RCC, federal ministries, state governments, and state level popular committees.[38] Leaders of the major tribal groups were appointed to the TNA to simultaneously co-opt them and bolster its own legitimacy. Bashir assigned the TNA limited advisory tasks: it would endorse national plans and programs, including federal laws, treaties, and budgets; give advice to the RCC; and mobilize the public.

RCC members Malwal and Mukhtar criticized that appointed system. Malwal claimed that 80 percent of the TNA members were NIF cadres and the rest sympathized with NIF or were technocrats. Security forces scrutinized all the names before their selection. Mukhtar argued that an elected parliament was preferable as the means to express the views of the people.[39]

Despite limited information on the internal workings of the TNA, one can glean examples of dissent within its committees. Most government bills were passed without serious debate, but some members expressed concern that drafts were introduced by NIF task forces without the knowledge of either the attorney general or the relevant TNA committee. Attorney General Shiddu was "acutely embarrassed" that he had not seen many of the bills that he had to defend.[40]

Members were also annoyed that the government ignored legislation passed by the TNA. The chair of the economic affairs committee, Badr al-Din Sulaiman, a former minister of finance under Numairi, developed serious critiques of economic policies.[41] His committee suggested ways to curtail speculation in foreign currency, shield lower-income groups from the escalating cost of living, and modify criminalization for possession of foreign currency. In 1994, TNA members were furious that the government increased electricity rates even though the TNA had rejected that increase.[42] They criticized the unrealistic exchange rate to transfer remittances of Sudanese working abroad, which one member charged violated Islamic law and committee chair Sulaiman termed "the worst law made by this government." His committee excoriated the government for inaccurate figures on exports and money supply, unrealistic projections concerning inflation, and ill-considered agricultural policies that made the economy "a mess." Nonetheless, the TNA passed the budget and government policies remained unchanged.

Similarly, in March 1995, a TNA committee found evidence of serious malpractices and corruption in the sale of public sector companies to private interests, including failure to pay in foreign currency, to advertise and open for bidding, and to state the companies' true value.[43] Those malpractices enabled NIF associates to buy state corporations at low prices. The minister of trade dismissed the committee report on the grounds that TNA members were "employees" and therefore had no right to investigate him.

In December 1993 the TNA suffered a dramatic defection when the deputy speaker—and the highest-rank southern politician—denounced the government and applied for political asylum in London.[44] Aldo Ajo Deng, a long-term Dinka politician who served in al-Mahdi's cabinets and headed the TNA's human rights committee, announced that he opposed the regime's Islamist tenets and discriminatory policies. He criticized the dismissal of 40,000 civil servants and military and security personnel, who were replaced by NIF cadres, and decried the transformation of the judiciary into "a partisan body." Deng denounced the government's effort "to Islamize the south" through military *jihad* and drafting teenagers into militias in which they were compelled to convert to Islam. Deng's defection stunned the regime, which quickly revoked his membership in the TNA and denounced his "betrayal."

ATTEMPTS TO HOLD ELECTIONS

Since the appointed TNA lacked credibility and legitimacy, the government continued to talk about elections. Bashir claimed to favor elections that would be "open to all citizens in all areas,"[45] whereas Turabi viewed elections as premature since "absolute freedom in the Sudan breeds a lot of chaos." If local elections succeeded, then it might be "safe" to attempt regional and federal elections. NIF really feared that its cadres would lose if elections were free and fair.

The government began electing 9,000 basic level committees in May 1992,[46] and instructed governors to convene local level *mu'tamarat* (conferences) in June and regional level conferences in July. The central government prepared their agendas, guided by its ten-year strategic plan for a development *jihad*. The limited information available indicates that few elections were actually held in 1992, due to NIF opposition, and that NIF fared poorly. In Banat district (Omdurman), for example, voters snubbed their noses at the Islamists by electing a well-known beer brewer to the local committee. The initial plan was for government appointees to hold a quarter of the seats on the popular committees. But when NIF leaders realized they were losing the popular vote, the NIF official who headed the committee system arbitrarily increased the official share of seats to 50 percent plus one. As a result, NIF appointees could always outnumber the elected members.

During 1993 officials claimed that 1,600 basic congresses were held in villages and districts, in which more than five million citizens participated.[47] No political parties were allowed since the government argued that congresses provided the best way to express the pluralism of opinions. When local elections were finally held in fall 1994, turnout was minimal and, in some cases, opponents of the government defeated NIF candidates. For example, in Atbara—the main industrial and railway city, which had a history of politicized trade unionism—most NIF candidates lost to members of the (illegal) Communist and Democratic Unionist parties. Security forces then arrested nearly two hundred persons, including the successful candidates, and the government voided the election results.[48] Regional-level elections in the spring of 1995 were also problematic, even though the government tried to avoid the previous fiasco by requiring candidates to support the government credo. Bashir declared that those elected would "uphold justice" and proclaim "There is No God but Allah:"[49]

> We want deputies who will struggle for Islam and are ready to sacrifice their lives and wealth for the sake of shari'a.... The office of a deputy ... is a trust to which one will be answerable on the day of judgment. It is an oath taken before God and allegiance to God the most high and not for selfish gains but for service to the faith and the adherents of the faith.

Ghazi Salah al-Din spelled out NIF's approach: "we must unify the country through a divine Islamic policy open to all.... Elections are being held ... not on the basis of the party system but on the basis that the entire Muslim society belongs to one party, the party of God."[50]

Problems in registering voters delayed elections until 8 March, following Ramadan. By mid-March the chair of the elections commission admitted that elections might fail because of lack of funds and weak voter registration.[51] In fact, turnout was less than 10 percent. In Khartoum state, the government conceded that only 29,000 persons voted, out of a potential 1.5 million; outside observers said the turnout was 12,000. Some polls closed after only two of the allotted ten days had passed, due to the paucity of voters. A foreign correspondent noted that people usually vote in order to avoid trouble: the virtual boycott signalled the public's lack of support for the regime. The six Catholic bishops even issued a daring pastoral letter that called on parishioners to boycott the polls since the elections were imposed on the people, parties were banned, and all candidates had to support a predefined Islamist orientation. Outside Khartoum, however, there were apparently greater efforts to ensure that representation on local and regional councils reflected the area's ethnic and tribal composition and therefore would acquire legitimacy. Through its power to appoint 10 percent of the members, the government also guaranteed that even fractions of ethnic groups would be represented.[52] This won the favor of small groups that had previously been too small to win seats and, in addition, provided an avenue for local elites to attempt to manipulate and benefit from the political system.

PRESIDENTIAL AND PARLIAMENTARY ELECTIONS

Long-delayed elections for the 400-member national assembly and the presidency were held from 6 to 17 March 1996. According to Constitutional Decree #13 (24 December 1995) MPs were selected in two stages: 125 were chosen by the national congress that NIF stage-managed in January 1996, for which NIF stalwart Ghazi Salah al-Din served as secretary general. That congress, which was composed of thousands of representatives from regional committees and professional groups, set the guidelines for government policy. Civilian leaders of NIF thereby ensured their control over a third of the seats in the assembly. The remaining 275 seats were open to direct election, of which fifty were filled by NIF cadres who ran unopposed. According to the constitutional decree, the electoral committee could "persuade" a nominee to withdraw due to moral or educational shortcomings or inadequate commitment to the regime's national charter and policies.[53] At the last minute, all voting was cancelled in the south for "security reasons" and the constitutional decree authorized the president to appoint MPs for those forty-six seats, pending elections.[54] Even if elections had taken place there, results could have been distorted since soldiers could vote in whatever district they were stationed.

Turabi was the only senior NIF official to stand for competitive election, selecting the constituency in which he had been defeated in 1986. Those who ran against him complained that policemen and election officials threatened their supporters, kept their representatives from monitoring inside the polling station, prevented them from placing their wax seals on the ballot boxes, tried to bribe their representatives, and removed names of their supporters from the voting list.[55] Turabi expressed concern that voters might be slow to vote; nonetheless, he reportedly received more votes than were actually cast in his constituency, testimony to the urgency with which his aides sought to ensure his election.

Bashir ran for president against forty-nine other candidates. He had hoped to persuade al-Mahdi, Mirghani, and Garang to compete, but they refused to contest an election run under a one-party system during a state of emergency. Twenty-one of the presidential candidates collectively demanded that elections be cancelled because they were not allowed to hold public meetings, publish manifestos, or have access to the media. The results were hardly surprising: Bashir won 75.7 percent.[56]

Election officials claimed that the turnout was 72 percent whereas opposition politicians argued that 95 percent of the public boycotted the polls. Independent observers concluded that 7-15 percent had voted in Khartoum. NIF security officials could easily rig the elections, since those officials stored the unsealed ballot boxes in their offices every evening and returned the boxes to the polling places the next morning. No record was kept of who voted, what polling station people voted at, or what date they voted. The registration cards were suspect, since they were based on ration cards and therefore included babies and people living abroad. Ballot-box-stuffing and multiple voting were simple to arrange under that system.

The relationship between the assembly and the presidency immediately became contentious. On 1 April Turabi was elected unopposed speaker of the national assembly to cheers of "Allah Akbar" and "La ilaha ila Allah." He articulated an ambitious agenda to "continue the Islamic path."[57] For the first time since 1989, Turabi assumed a central public role. A skillful speaker could use the assembly's power to approve legislation and question ministers to limit presidential authority, thereby isolating Bashir.[58] Bashir recognized that danger and tried to convince opposition figures to join the council of ministers in order to make himself less dependent on NIF. His failure was indicated in the strongly NIF composition of the cabinet, announced on 21 April. Bashir's room for maneuver was also limited since he would not compromise on the government's core tenets:[59]

> The basic Islamic agenda of the regime will not change. Islam is the cornerstone of our policy. . . . There will be no return to multiparty democracy in the country. There will be no reversal of the basic policies of the regime.

The elections sought to put a veneer of legitimacy on the political system. Instead of consolidating the regime's legitimacy, however, the election emphasized its narrowly partisan and ideological nature. The newly elected MPs seemed to feel insecure and isolated. An MP even argued that he presently rode the bus to the national assembly although he feared he would be killed on a public conveyance: with "strong opposition at home and abroad, something should be done to protect our lives and persons as MPs."[60]

FEDERAL SYSTEM

In addition to establishing the facade of a mass base and electoral legitimacy, the rulers sought to create the appearance of geographically decentralized rule. Their federal system was based on NIF's Sudan Charter, which called for the central government to retain authority over national defense and security, foreign policy, nationality and immigration, trans-regional communication, and external and interregional trade. Most importantly, Khartoum controlled the judiciary and legal codes, the financial system, economic planning, natural resources, and education. Decentralization was tightly circumscribed. These views were reflected in the recommendations of conferences on the peace process (October 1989) and the political system (October 1990), which led to the decree of a federal system on 4 February 1991. Each of the nine provinces became a state in which Islamic law would govern all aspects of public and private life, since the Muslim majority should have the right to "practice the values and rules of their religion to their full range — in personal, familial, social or political affairs." (Shari'a laws are detailed in chapter 8.) The three states in the south were exempt from a few Islamic punishments, as articulated in NIF's charter:

> The legislative authority of any region predominantly inhabited by non-Muslims can take exception to the general operation of the national law, with respect to any rule of a criminal or penal nature derived directly and solely from a text in the shari'a contrary to the local culture. The said authority can instead opt for a different rule based on the customs or religion prevailing in the area. . . . The general presumption, otherwise, is for law to be effective country-wide over all persons and regions.

Real power remained concentrated in Khartoum since the national laws prevailed over regional laws and the federal president appointed the governors and state administrators.[61] Bashir frequently shifted them: he replaced most of the military governors with civilians on 16 September 1993, then replaced several of those governors a year later, and decreed additional personnel changes in January 1995. Thus, states lacked any genuine autonomy. In the south, the Christian governors wielded less authority than their Muslim deputy governors and ministers, who controlled finances and set policies for the economy, education, youth activities, information, and culture. Moreover, southern judges, policemen, and prison officers were retired or transferred north to be placed in marginal positions.[62] Posting NIF-affiliated officials in the south and displacing southern officials enabled the government to promote Arabization and Islamization behind a facade of regional self-rule. Similarly, in the north, apolitical bureaucrats served as most of the state ministers, but NIF militants held the crucial positions of *wali* (governor), deputy governor (who was also minister of agriculture), state minister of social planning, head of the general secretariat, and general secretaries for all the provinces and ministries.[63] In the case of Kassala state, the NIF minister of agriculture also headed an Islamic investment shareholding company that sought to dominate the agricultural sector.

When Ali al-Hajj became minister of federal government affairs in July 1993, he even altered several borders to remove valuable resources from the south,[64] e.g., South Kordofan gained control over the oil-rich Pan Thau area of Bentiu, and Dar Fur acquired copper-rich Hufrat al-Nahhas. Thousands of acres of agricultural land and gum arabic forests in Upper Nile were transferred to South Kordofan and White Nile states in 1995, over the protests of southern officials and farmers. All those changes transferred vital economic resources from the south to the north, merely by altering boundary lines.

Al-Hajj transformed federalism by dividing every state into three separate states on 1 February 1994, thereby increasing the total from nine to twenty-six.[65] The sixteen states in the north and ten in the south would each have their own executive and legislature. Nonetheless, Khartoum appointed the governors, ministers, commissioners, civil servants, and members of the judiciary. State judiciaries were abolished. Bashir claimed this change brought the government closer to the people and deployed available development resources more effectively. He asserted that the central administration would shrink, since employees and assets in Khartoum would be reassigned to the new states and the approximately four governates within each state.[66] Bashir conceded there would be short-term financial costs, but insisted that several states would quickly achieve financial self-sufficiency. That was highly unrealistic, since provinces had always relied on Khartoum to cover basic expenses. Indeed, in August 1995 Bashir established a special fund to assist the poorest states, since they could not pay salaries, much less provide services. Moreover, particularly in the south, extreme administrative fragmentation exacerbated ethnic differences, since politicians from each ethnic group sought to control their piece of turf. Similarly, in Kassala state, the government favored one faction of the Hadendowa by creating a separate province for it.[67] The regime intended to foster fragmentation and competition in order to absorb people's energies at the local level and diffuse opposition.

Furthermore, the government reestablished in 1994 the Council of Native Administration in each state, which Numairi had abolished in 1971. This reasserted tribal responsibility for justice and the allocation of resources, but at a diminished level since the councils were merely advisory to the wali. Nonetheless, they brought all of the influential tribes into the local and state governing processes, providing them with a stake in the system. Michael Kevane and Leslie Gray note the irony that this resulted in "having traditional 'tribal' leaders wield authority in the new and modern Islamic state."[68] They comment that, lacking a grassroots power base of its own in the rural areas, NIF needed to gain legitimacy from those local elites, ensure that they would support it, and use them to marginalize the Ansar and Khatmiyya. Given the opportunism of that alliance, one cannot evaluate the rapidity with which support would evaporate should the political winds shift.

Over the course of seven years, the Islamist regime shed its overtly military image and established multitiered political structures that claimed to be rooted in grassroots congresses and direct elections. It also established a federal system that claimed to voice the needs of the diverse peoples who lived far from Khartoum. Those claims were belied by the reality of centralized control under a monolithic ideology. Any potential for liberal or ethnic pluralist systems was stifled by control structures that enforced the regime's assimilationist approach. The content of the Islamist ideology, the mechanisms of control, and the modes by which divergent voices were silenced are analyzed in the next chapter.

8

Indoctrination and Control

CONTROL STRUCTURES WERE based on measures typical of authoritarian governments, with religious justifications provided for silencing critics and legitimizing the indoctrination of citizens. Since the rulers implemented "God's will," critics were not only traitors but apostates. Bashir declared boldly:[1]

> We will gain nothing from relinquishing the shari'a because he who seeks people's satisfaction by causing God's indignation loses everything. . . . Our existence is originally linked to the implementation of this shari'a. Therefore, it is a matter of principle for us. . . . It is better for us to die in the cause of that principle and we are ready for that.

SHARI'A

NIF had struggled for a long time to institute a comprehensive Islamic legal system. Numairi had promulgated an Islamic penal code and partially Islamic commercial and tax codes, but the elected government had not passed NIF's proposed code in 1988 and had stopped enforcing the religiously prescribed punishments (hudud). On the eve of the coup, the government froze the application of Islamic law until the constitutional conference could resolve the thorny issue of the country's basic laws. Those actions triggered NIF's coup d'état.

The legal underpinnings for an Islamist political system were consolidated when the National Founding Conference for the Political System (April–May 1991) adopted a National Charter for Political Action which emphasized that "our intellectual, spiritual and cultural values spring from our subservience to one God and our belief that He is the sole authority in this world and the world after."[2] Adherence to those principles "is the only guarantee for a righteous society" and jihad (holy struggle) against internal and external threats is a religious obligation. Those principles were also embodied in the Islamic Penal Code (March 1991), which restored amputation and flogging. Crimes punishable by death included murder, apostasy from Islam, adultery by married persons, corruption, embezzlement, trafficking in narcotics or black market goods, disregarding currency regulations, and organizing strikes. Public order emergency courts, whose judges were officers in the police or army, flogged illegal vendors on the spot and confiscated or destroyed their equipment. Although Turabi stressed that those punishments would deter theft and misbehavior "in order to morally educate the people,"[3] their severity and the lack of appeal militated against any educational impact.

The civilian government established in October 1993 made commitment to Islam the guiding religion obligatory for citizens. Bashir claimed that God supervised the judiciary, for He is "the all-knowing and all-seeing," and stressed that the permanent constitution would be grounded in Islamic law. Similarly, Turabi declared:[4]

> the country is . . . an Islamic republic for all effective purposes regarding the implementation of Islamic injunctions in the political, economic, social and cultural fields. At present, Islam is ruling in Sudan; Islamic values prevail in society and Islamic injunctions are being implemented in all fields.

The application of shari'a raised the issues of jihad, apostasy, applying Islamic law to non-Muslims, and inculcating Islamic morality. The regime sought to regulate all aspects of citizens' lives and create a homogeneous society.

Ulama (religious scholars) who met in Kordofan in 1992 issued a fatwa (Islamic legal opinion) stating:[5]

> He who is a Muslim among the rebels is an apostate, and non-Muslims a heathen . . . both standing in the face of the Islamic call (*dawa*), and it is the duty of Islam to fight and kill both categories.

Soldiers must kill apostates (Muslims who rebel against the state) and heathens (non-Muslim rebels) who defy the religious-based government. Bashir called the Sudanese people God's *khalifat* (successors to the prophet) on earth, among whom the *mujahidiin* (holy warriors) carried out God's commandments. Soldiers who died in battle were martyrs, who "irrigate the land of the south with their blood so that the land may sprout dignity and honor," and ascend directly to paradise.[6] Bashir required soldiers and police to swear a religious oath of allegiance (*baya*) to him. He let the governor of Kordofan call himself *Amir al-Amura* (prince of the princes) and each Arab tribal chief became an *Amir al-Jihad* (prince of the holy war).[7] Those titles invoked the Mahdist era and earlier struggles of the Islamic conquest. Official military publications termed the rebels *ahl al-harb* (people of war), reflecting the traditional Islamic division of the world between *dar al-Islam* (the abode of Islam) and *dar al-harb* (the abode of war). War booty from ahl al-harb should be divided among soldiers and officers according to strict specifications in the Quran and Sunna. Missionary work was a religious obligation for Muslims among the "heathen" Nuba, Ingessana, and southern peoples. Thus, the war was elevated to a holy struggle to defend dar al-Islam against its enemies and to spread the faith.

The Penal Code (1991) defined an apostate as a Muslim who "advocates abandoning the faith of Islam or declares expressly or by a categorical act that he abandons the faith of Islam."[8] The code mandated the death sentence unless the person recanted. Turabi, however, widened the meaning to include treason: "active subversion of the constitutional order" and "actual insurrection against society" not merely "intellectual apostasy."[9] Thus, political opposition by a devout person could result in a charge of apostasy. In practice, however, when three people were convicted of apostasy in 1994, none were executed.

The application of shari'a to non-Muslims followed NIF's Sudan Charter (1987). Islamic jurisprudence was the general source of law since it

> expresses the will of the democratic majority and conforms to the values of scriptural religions.... [Muslims] have the legitimate right, by virtue of their religious choice, of their democratic weight and of natural justice, to practice the values and rules of their religion to their full range—in personal, familial, social, or political affairs.... [In contrast, adherents of African religions, Christians and Jews] express the value of their religion ... in private, family, or social matters ... [but not political life. Shari'a should] be effective country-wide over all persons and regions ... [except in regions] predominantly inhabited by non-Muslims [who] take exception ... to any rule of a criminal or penal nature derived directly and solely from a text in the shari'a contrary to the local culture. The said authority can instead opt for a different rule based on the customs or religion in the area.

The government rejected applying the concept of *ahl al-dhimma* (protected people), which granted Jews and Christians (but not adherents of traditional African religions) communal legal status with specific obligations and separate communal courts. Instead, shari'a-based commercial and criminal laws applied to all residents.[10] Communal application would mean, for example, that Christians would be exempt from hudud and could drink liquor quietly at home (although they could be punished if they became a public nuisance). The only concession was to exempt residents of the south from five of 186 articles of the Penal Code.[11] Hudud applied to non-Muslims in the north for all crimes except "consuming alcohol [in private], fornication, defamation, and apostasy" from Christianity to Islam. Khartoum courts resumed applying the hudud on 9 December 1989, and executed five men for economic crimes, e.g., smuggling foreign currency out of the country, embezzling public funds, and selling sorghum in the black market. Prominent cases involving Christian citizens sent a strong message that non-Muslims were not exempt. Archangelo Daru was hanged on 17 April 1990 for violating foreign currency regulations and Michael Gassis was sentenced in February 1991 to cross-amputation for breaking into a shop in Port Sudan. (His two Muslim accomplices were not sentenced to amputation.)

Since the regime must reform society and foster the "spiritual development of the individual,"[12] officials insisted that public behavior fit their interpretation of Islamic codes. The Khartoum commissioner closed all public places and businesses at midday on Fridays for prayers, including shops owned by Christians or Jews. The puritanical perspective disapproved of "nakedness," social mixing of men and women, and such customary religious practices as the veneration of saints and the *zar* ceremony to exorcise spirits. The government banned teaching art and music, which spread harmful western and African influences.[13] The ministry of culture threatened to disband the Union of Musicians and Artists, since singing and dancing were perverse and anti-Islamic, and Friday sermons broadcast on official radio stations campaigned against singers and artists for spreading immorality. Khartoum State's public order act (1992) restricted music, dance, and wedding celebrations, and banned men and women from dancing together. Police broke up concerts and wedding parties for violating that act and NIF cadres assaulted female singers and zar drummers. The musicians' union protested in vain that "music and musicians [must be protected] against their enemies, the jaundiced and religious fanatics."[14] Those attacks culminated in the stabbing to death of a singer in the Musicians Club on 10 November 1994. A British journalist commented that the government was "widely blamed for creating the climate of intolerance on which fanaticism thrives" and even an Islamist academic complained that "these people are breeding prejudice and hatred as never before." A TNA member added: "Many in this government understand Islam in a shocking, horrible, ugly, and twisted way. They are putting people like myself, who believe Islam can be humane, in a very difficult situation."[15] Nonetheless, the police continued to raid clubs and private parties in search of liquor, immodest dress, and mixed dancing.

Health care was also affected by the Islamist approach. In February 1995 the ministry of health banned the import of medicines that contained alcohol, arguing that such medicines violated shari'a. The ministry closed the thirteen pharmaceutrical companies that imported those drugs and syrups, and even banned chloroquine, the vital treatment for malaria. Others noted that Islamic law permits the use of alcohol for medicinal purposes and an importer exclaimed: "Our people are dying of malaria. If the decision to ban medicines is implemented, malaria will spread and many more will die."[16] That summer the ministry of health reported a widespread malaria epidemic. By then medical and health services had virtually collapsed, with rehabilitation programs halted and 80 percent of pharmacies closed. The Khartoum hospital discontinued certain complex operations and closed its dialysis unit, due to the lack of medication. Doctors objected to the "popular salvation committees" that ran the hospitals. So many doctors fled abroad that the government banned all travel by medical personnel. In that context, the ban on importing those medicines further undermined the fragile health of citizens.

WOMEN'S STATUS

Bashir stated that the ideal Sudanese woman "should take care of herself, her children, her home, her reputation, and her husband."[17] The family code (1991) not only enshrined shari'a provisions for inheritance, divorce, and child custody but further limited women's rights. For example, shari'a requires four male witnesses to prove adultery, whereas Sudanese courts could convict a woman based on physical evidence (e.g., pregnancy) without eyewitnesses and without the woman testifying in her own defense. This paternalistic morality was upheld by the committee charged with codifying Islamic law, which concluded that women must not go outside after dark without a male companion and men must not work in women's beauty salons. As a result, some towns banned women from selling in street markets after dark, forbade male hairdressers from serving women, and prohibited women from working in cafes. Additional restrictions banned women from traveling abroad without a male companion, riding alone in taxis, and working in offices alongside men, and enabled the husband to decide whether his wife could visit her parents, relatives, and female friends. The regulations peaked in October 1996 when Khartoum state separated men and women in public transportation, theaters, cinemas, weddings, parties, and picnics, enjoined Muslims not to look at members of the opposite sex, and forbade men from watching women playing sports. Those regulations contradicted family traditions that fostered relatively relaxed relations among men and women, frequent visits to relatives' homes, and toleration of a multiplicity of religious practices.

A presidential decree in December 1991 ordered female students and civil servants to adopt the dress code established by an all-male committee, which required a long opaque dress to the ankles and a veil covering the head and forbade trousers, accessories, and perfume.[18] Since women preferred the colorful *thobe*, they ignored the code until NIF's Guardians of Morality and Advocates of the Good and members of neighborhood committees began to flog women in the street. The education minister further decreed in 1994 that female students must cover their body and head and high schools must be segregated by gender.[19]

NIF considered that women should work only if they did not have children, if their income was required by their family, and if the work was an extension of domestic roles, such as teaching girls and providing health care in clinics for mothers and children.[20] NIF attacked as anti-Islamic the informal jobs by poor women in public places. NIF targeted vendors of home-brewed beer (*marisa*)—a staple in the diet in the south and west—but also fined, flogged, and detained women who sold tea and prepared food in the street. Even in a remote village in Kordofan, NIF-appointed district officials flogged women for selling marisa, tea, and groundnuts at truck stops, thereby asserting the power of the Arab male politico-economic elite over socially and economically marginalized Hausa and Burgo women.[21]

The government pensioned off a disproportionate number of women from government jobs, although it was not always clear whether they were fired because of gender or because they criticized NIF.[22] Half of the judges fired in the first wave of dismissals were women, but some pro-NIF women were subsequently appointed to the judiciary and about thirty women were included in the appointed Transitional National Assembly. When several women were dismissed from the diplomatic service in January 1990, the government avoided claiming that the work was inappropriate and, instead, alleged that they had "acquired a taste for wine," insinuating that they had loose morals.

CIVIL, MILITARY, AND SECURITY STRUCTURES

NIF devised a systematic plan to transform the civil service, armed forces, and security structures, according to an official who defected in 1995.[23] By 2003 the Popular Defense Force (PDF) would replace the armed forces, popular police would replace the regular police, NIF would monopolize the civil service, and NIF would control all sovereign and constitutional positions. In actuality, NIF largely completed those transformations by 1997.

Many NIF cadres joined the civil service in the 1980s, accepting low-level posts in remote districts in anticipation of working their way up to policy-making positions. NIF activists entered the armed forces, especially through the medical and engineering corps that required university-educated personnel. NIF also organized courses on Islam for officers, attended by several future members of the RCC, including Bashir. Turabi reflected that[24]

> changes occurred in the Armed Forces and there was a transition . . . to the Islamic way of thinking, which spread to all the enlightened and educated strata. . . . [Therefore] when the Armed Forces took power [in 1989] . . . they declared that they would implement the Islamic laws and tenets.

Once the officers seized power, they purged their opponents. For example, the RCC fired 14,000 civil servants and staff of public sector companies in 1989, many on orders from NIF cadres such as minister of cabinet affairs al-Tayyib Ibrahim Khair. When the government dismissed more than a hundred career diplomats, whom it replaced with young NIF activists, some senior diplomats resigned to protest the politicization of the diplomatic corps. The RCC removed

thousands more civil servants, allegedly on austerity grounds. A foreign journalist described the outcome: senior civil servants cowered before young military
officers and members of the PDF who stalked government offices.[25]

The judiciary was particularly hard hit. By mid-1991, Bashir fired 128 judges
and legal advisors, including fourteen judges from the Supreme Court and twelve
from the Court of Appeals. The judges had struck to protest martial law courts,
the lack of due process in court hearings, and the president's appointing the chief
justice, thereby making the judiciary subservient to the executive branch. Judges
were replaced by "unqualified, fanatic individuals, often with little or no legal
training at all," according to a former leader of the Bar Association.[26]

POPULAR DEFENSE FORCE

The RCC quickly purged the high command of the armed forces, which had
opposed the coup. By October 1993 the RCC fired 1,500 officers and continued
to do so despite the heavy fighting in the south. For example, 227 officers were
fired in early 1995, including fifty-seven brigadiers and generals. Turabi stated
frankly that the army should be "dissolved" into the Popular Defense Force
(PDF) that would mobilize the public behind the jihad.[27] Al-Mahdi had proposed a PDF in 1988, but set aside the idea due to overwhelming opposition from
the military high command. Bashir called the PDF "the legitimate child of the
armed forces," which would be the "school for national and spiritual education."
Through the PDF "the Sudanese citizen's mind can be remolded and his religious consciousness enhanced" and the regime can "restructure and purify society."[28]

The PDF had four distinct components: (1) preexisting Arab tribal militias,
(2) NIF volunteers, (3) drafted students and civil servants, and (4) forcibly en-
rolled teenagers. The first comprised Arab tribal militias and southern units opposed to the SPLA. The PDF commander distributed arms and ammunition to
those cavalry and foot units, called on the Arabs to defend the cultural and religious purity of the north, and coordinated their raids with the army.[29] As un-
paid auxiliaries, they kept their booty, including captured people, cattle, and
grain.

The second category comprised volunteer students and professionals, committed to NIF. Information is primarily available on those who died fighting in
the south, including a former minister of industry and Turabi's youngest brother,
who died with eight PDF recruits when their vehicle hit a land-mine in Western
Equatoria.[30] Those ill-trained volunteers were zealous in their religious commitment. Young people from NIF's "Shabab al-Watan" (The Nation's Youth) also
fought with the PDF.

Third, starting in December 1990, all civil servants, teachers, professors, and students underwent compulsory military training for six-week periods.[31] The first group of 1,500 men sent to al-Qutaina camp, near Khartoum, included diplomats, judges, and professors, who were mostly over fifty years old and were fired if they refused to enroll. Male students entering universities and higher institutes first had to train in PDF camps. Recruits were exposed to harsh living conditions and religious lectures. Conditions were difficult enough that students mutinied at al-Qutaina in December 1991 and evasion remained widespread. In April 1994 the army commander threatened to punish students who failed to join the armed forces or the PDF.[32] By then PDF training was compulsory for students in their final years of basic education and in secondary school, so as to create a responsible, disciplined generation to build the Islamist nation, according to Bashir. Such training could not prepare them for combat, but it indoctrinated inductees and identified refractory individuals.

Fourth, in 1994-1995 every male between the ages of eighteen and thirty became liable for recruitment in the PDF, because of the huge number of casualties in the south and because people failed to volunteer. In one account, when the PDF sent draft notices to 10,000 persons, only eighty-nine responded. An estimated 9,000 had died and 15,000 been wounded in the first half of 1995 alone. Youths were seized off the street and taken to training camps.[33] For example, in January 1993 soldiers stopped all buses in Al-Ubayyid and removed all the teenagers to army trucks. They seized boys on the roads and in the markets, even in the capital city. Governors had to enroll the general public in the PDF,[34] which led to mass military drills in empty lots in city neighborhoods and villages. When Bashir declared that one million Sudanese must be mobilized in 1995, each governor recruited thousands of men, who graduated in batches of 50,000 during 1995-1996.[35] Bashir lauded them as "bold militant" mujahidiin who raised aloft the banner of jihad and resisted imperialist attacks on Islam. The vast expansion of the PDF and its use as cannon fodder in the south were criticized by regular officers in the armed forces, who were also angry that NIF cadres and PDF soldiers replaced career officers and that they were not paid salaries or rations on a regular basis.[36] Bashir arrested some senior officers when they complained privately to him about the government's neglect of the armed forces.[37] Displacement by the PDF peaked in 1997 when the PDF head joined the armed forces' central command.

INTERNAL SECURITY FORCES

The pattern of purges and replacements was duplicated in the police and security services.[38] The RCC immediately fired 400 police officers, and later pensioned off thousands more. Government organs, controlled by NIF cadres, included state security, military intelligence, police security, and foreign security, which monitored exiles. NIF also operated its own units: Revolutionary Security Guards, Guardians of Morality and Advocates of Good, Turabi's private security detachment, and the People's Police.

NIF's Revolutionary Security Guards detained and tortured political dissidents in unofficial prisons outside the control of the prisons' authority.[39] Labeled "ghost houses" by former detainees, those torture centers were located in forty-two buildings in Khartoum by 1993 that, ironically, included the headquarters of the banned Bar Association and of the former Elections Commission. In one instance, a former regional minister of health reported that he searched ghost houses in Sennar for a teenage girl, whom he found unconscious. He took her to a hospital, where medical tests confirmed that she had been repeatedly raped. The minister charged that NIF-supervised security guards used "ugly forms of torture" in ghost houses.[40] Human Rights Watch/Africa reported that torture techniques included immersing the head in cold water, hanging by the hand on the bars of the cell, burning with cigarette ends, electric shock, mock execution, rape, and pulling out fingernails.

The regular security and prison services resented those NIF operations.[41] In 1991 RCC's Faisal Abu Salih resigned as minister of interior because NIF interfered in security matters and even issued passports without consulting his ministry; the police commissioner of Khartoum resigned to protest "security chaos" after a struggle in the airport between police officers and NIF security personnel; and the head of the riot police threatened to march his forces on the Revolutionary Security Guards' headquarters to arrest rogue security officers and denounce ghost houses. After NIF consolidated its control, such protests ended.

NIF's Guardians of Morality and Advocates of Good were formed in 1983 to help Numairi enforce the Islamic penal code and emergency decrees. After the coup the Guardians coordinated the People's Police, an outgrowth of local people's committees that the Civil Defense Act (1991) established supposedly to help cope with natural disasters such as floods and to protect the country from external attack.[42] People's Police, who received only three months' training, patrolled residential areas and markets to combat vice and enforce the public discipline law. They had wide latitude in defining moral offenses and imposing punishments. By 1995 they manned 120 police stations in Khartoum and guarded camps for displaced persons outside the capital. Their security grid on neighborhoods enabled the government to act swiftly at the slightest sign of unrest.

RESTRICTIONS ON INDEPENDENT ASSOCIATIONS

The RCC banned trade union activity and imposed death sentences for strikes and political opposition, since the State of Emergency forbade "showing any political opposition by any means to the regime."[43] The RCC detained the heads of the dissolved trade unions and professional associations after they submitted a petition on 1 August 1989 that asked the RCC to reopen their offices, return their assets, and resume regular union activities. When doctors struck in November 1989, Bashir sought to purge this "fifth column" on the grounds that "anyone who betrays this nation does not deserve the honor of living."[44] However, the RCC adopted a different policy toward religious institutions and student unions, which initially remained open. Overall, since only the Islamist perspective was legitimate, any criticism constituted treason. The regime could not countenance independent groups that fostered alternative cultural visions and challenged its hegemony.

The RCC appointed a new General Union of Sudanese Workers to coordinate the trade and professional unions and redraft their statutes.[45] The Penal Code (1991) decreed three years' imprisonment for medical personnel who struck and also for workers who blocked transportation by sea, land, or air.

Then, the Trade Union Law (1992) restricted sharply the autonomy of unions and denied many workers and employees the right to join or organize unions. The general registrar of trade unions gained the power to inspect all documents, offices, and accounts. Simultaneously, all non-NIF staff were fired from the registrar's office to ensure that those controls would be enforced. When the government held elections for unions that summer, Amnesty International reported that hundreds of union activists could not campaign because they were forced to spend entire days at the security headquarters and because the government threatened them with a "bleak future" if they stood for elections. Despite that intimidation, anti-regime candidates performed sufficiently well that the government decreed that government appointees must hold the majority on each union's board. Just as basic-level committees (discussed in chapter 7) would have 50 percent plus one of their members appointed by the government, similarly the boards of unions and associations would have an official majority of one.

The severity of government controls can be illustrated by the Bar Association, which was active under previous military rulers and outspoken during the parliamentary period, campaigning against Islamic laws and drafting a penal code consonant with internationally recognized standards.[46] The RCC immediately dissolved the Bar Association and detained ten leaders, who had protested the dismissal of judges, dissolution of unions, and establishment of military tribunals. The government then created a new Bar Association managed by an appointed steering committee, which took over the assets of the dissolved association and endorsed the Islamic laws. After the new Trade Union Law came into effect, the government amended the Advocacy Act (1983) in January 1993 to transform the Bar Association into a trade union, subject to the registrar of trade unions and the minister of labor. That undermined its autonomy and meant that security forces could seize case files. Moreover, in March 1993 the registrar suddenly announced elections two days later. Despite urgent appeals to the high court to cancel the elections, they were held and, predictably, won by NIF cadres. Lawyers and judges became tools of the regime, promoting its Islamist image and excluding all other legal traditions and independent perspectives.

CHRISTIAN INSTITUTIONS

Although the regime sought a homogeneous religious culture, the RCC initially exempted Muslim and Christian organizations from the ban on associational life. That enabled sufi turuq, ordinary mosques, and churches to continue functioning.

Christian denominations were already circumscribed by Ottoman regulations and the Missionary Societies Act (1962).[47] Governments often withheld permits to build or repair churches and declared certain geographic areas out of bounds for Christians. Christians reacted with dismay to the Islamic constitutional system. Since non-Muslims would not be allowed to exercise authority over Muslims, they would be excluded from most senior positions. Applicants for government jobs had to provide legal testimonials to prove they were Muslim. The government dismissed hundreds of Christians from the civil service and judiciary, including the Coptic senior judge on the supreme court, Henry Riad. The two key exceptions were Second Vice President George Kongor, appointed to that ceremonial post in February 1994, and Coptic Archbishop Kosmos Filou Saous, Bashir's advisor on Christian affairs.

Non-Muslims faced mounting social and legal discrimination. Christian civil servants had to train in the Popular Defense Force even though its ideology promoted jihad and disparaged Christianity. TV commentators warned viewers they would go to hell if they were not Muslim. The media broadcast Friday prayers but cancelled the Catholic Church's weekly Sunday radio program in 1992. Catholic religious tracts could not be printed. The Anglican Bishop of Khartoum was even lashed on charges of adultery.[48] Christian businessmen had difficulty obtaining and renewing licenses and became frightened when two Copts were executed for violating foreign currency regulations in 1990-1991. One was a Sudanair pilot, son of the Coptic bishop of Khartoum, who was offered a pardon if he would convert to Islam.[49] After he died, thousands of Muslims and Christians expressed solidarity by joining the Coptic community's silent funeral march through Khartoum.

Indeed, by then the government closed more than thirty churches in Khartoum that served displaced persons from the south and west, and suppressed a Catholic society that aided street children.[50] When the government forcibly relocated squatters from the capital to remote sites, it blocked churches from assisting the people and operating schools in those new locations. In contrast, Islamic agencies opened Arabic-language schools and provided social aid, through which they encouraged conversions to Islam. In al-Da'im and Damazin, local authorities prohibited all Christian worship, prevented church agencies from operating in displaced persons camps, expelled priests and nuns from church centers, and destroyed church compounds, thereby eliminating kindergartens and classrooms as well as chapels. Intimidation was most acute in the south, where security forces arrested and expelled Sudanese and foreign priests. When Christian schools were nationalized in 1992, the government Arabized and Islamized their curriculum throughout the country. When Arabization began in Juba (Equatoria), many children tried to flee—soldiers shot them dead and their bodies floated down the Nile, book bags still fastened to their backs.

Church leaders tried to counter these restrictions and changes. For example, in 1991 the general secretariat of the Sudanese Catholic Bishops' Conference, whose members included Archbishop Gabriel Zubair Wako of Khartoum, circulated a pastoral letter protesting shari'a-based discrimination and encouraging resistance against the actions taken against church institutions and clergy.[51] The government, claiming that the pastoral letter violated national security and provoked strife among Sudanese, ordered the bishops to meet with security officials on 15 January 1992 and accelerated actions against church officials. When the Bishop of Al-Ubayyid, Monsignor Macram Max Gassis, went abroad for medical treatment that fall, he remained in exile to call attention to the situation facing Christians in western Sudan. Bishop Gassis testified that officials harassed and arrested priests, nuns, and catechists and hampered church efforts to help displaced persons in Al-Ubayyid. He detailed the "marked deterioration" in human rights since the coup:[52]

> The abuse of human rights in Sudan is so total and complete . . . there is no law and order. This is without doubt the most draconian and arbitrary regime the country has ever known.

Similarly, the general secretariat of the Sudanese Catholic Bishops' Conference wrote on 24 September 1992 to UN Secretary General Boutros Boutros-Ghali, condemning attacks on churches, citing instances of discrimination against Christians, and decrying the "monumental and all pervading security system which controls all aspects of public and personal life."[53] A Catholic leader lamented: "We are at the other end of the bullet. We are the target of Islamic belligerence, the object of this holy war."[54]

The government made cosmetic changes in response to international criticism of its human rights record that culminated in a UN General Assembly resolution on 18 December 1992. That Christmas Eve, the government lifted the nighttime curfew in Khartoum so that Christians could attend midnight mass.

Officials attended church services throughout the country to show solidarity with their "Christian brethren"[55] and the government welcomed Pope John Paul II to Khartoum on 10 February 1993. Nonetheless, in Bashir's presence, the Pope denounced government policies and called for respect for human rights and religious freedom. His open-air mass to a half million persons included many Muslims, so strong was his appeal as a religious authority who might deliver them from their plight. The government subsequently tried to open an embassy in the Vatican and Turabi met briefly with the Pope, but the Vatican remained wary of endorsing the regime.[56]

Despite the effort to present a tolerant image, policies became increasingly restrictive. Turabi took the lead in convening conferences on religious tolerance and peaceful coexistence (April 1993)[57] and on religious dialogue (October 1994), designed to persuade foreign clergy and scholars that the government did not discriminate against non-Muslims. Whereas Bashir stated forthrightly that he planned to transform the Sudan into an Islamic state, by any means, Ghazi Salah al-Din of the foreign ministry offered as evidence of the lack of discrimination the facts that the second vice president was Christian, non-Muslims could drink alcohol in the north, and Islamic laws were not fully applied to non-Muslims in the south, where Christian politicians were active.[58] Turabi denied that the government destroyed churches and proclaimed that the Catholic Church and Islam form "one front against atheists, materialism, and secularism." However, Sudanese clergy called the conference "a fraud perpetrated against the local Church" and the Catholic Archbishop of Khartoum declaimed: "It is a grave error to believe that we are living in a paradise of religious tolerance. . . . Christians suffer discrimination at school, in their place of work, in the army or when seeking lodging or employment." Trust broke down, he maintained, when those Muslims who opposed dialogue with "the *kuffar*" (non-believer) gained "ascendancy."

Shortly after the conference, the government simultaneously repealed the Church Missionary Societies Act of 1962 and introduced a new law to govern Christian institutions, which amended the Organization of Voluntary Work Act (1994) to transform churches into nongovernmental organizations (NGOs). This was even more restrictive than the Missionary Societies' Act and would completely destroy their autonomy. As NGOs, churches and church societies must register with the state. Their application could be amended or rejected. The government could change their constitutions and bylaws, alter their boards of directors and personnel, investigate their sources of income and expenditures, and confiscate their property. The Catholic bishops protested that churches could not be classified as NGOs and emphasized the importance of freedom of worship, evangelism, and charity, and their connection to an international hierarchy.[59] Since the Church is of divine origin, they maintained, a government bureaucrat could not determine its nature and organization. Subsequently, the government delayed promulgating the new law and the churches' status remained in limbo.

ISLAMIC INSTITUTIONS

The government allowed NIF's charitable associations to expand, since their proselytizing advanced its religious goals. Those agencies included NIF's *al-Da'wa al-Islamiyya* (Islamic Call), chaired by former TMC Head General Suwar al-Dhahab, and the African Islamic Agency, chaired by al-Jazouli Dafallah, prime minister during the transitional period. Those Islamic NGOs and charitable funds, funded through Islamic banks, were also powerful economic actors, since they monopolized certain trade activities and sold food at subsidized prices that undercut local merchants.[60]

In contrast, the government criticized Islamic practices that did not conform to its particular line and especially targeted the Khatmiyya and Ansar movements, linked to the banned Democratic Unionist and Umma parties, respectively.[61] NIF leaders could not forgive Muhammad Uthman al-Mirghani for his accord with the SPLM and his opposition to NIF's policies during the coalition government in 1988. In 1991 the government confiscated the personal property of the Mirghani family, including their financial assets and land and, in 1992, the government formally dissolved the Khatmiyya tariqa. All its property and assets, including mosques and shrines, became the property of the state. The government had already confiscated a large plot of land belonging to the Mahdi family on Aba island, the Ansar stronghold, in 1990, and on the eve of Id al-Adha in 1993 nationalized their complex in Omdurman: the mosque of Khalifa Abdullahi, the office of Imam Muhammad Ahmad al-Mahdi, and the tomb of the Mahdi. Those actions made it difficult for the Khatmiyya and Ansar to congregate and potentially reduced their political and economic power. Nonetheless, the measures also signalled the government's insecurity and failure to rout alternative forms of Islamic expression.

Although many sufi turuq initially welcomed the government's support of Islamic law, they tended to turn against the regime as NIF's power grew. NIF opposed sufism, since its religious rituals did not conform to NIF's doctrinaire approach. Therefore, after curtailing the Ansar and Khatmiyya in 1990-1993, the government tried to suppress the turuq in 1993-1994. For example, security forces attacked a sufi mosque near Khartoum during Ramadan and detained the shaikh for a fortnight.[62] The regime also targeted the Ansar al-Sunna al-Muhammadiyya tariqa, whose two principal shaikhs in Omdurman were detained after they declared the regime un-Islamic and asserted that NIF really aimed to amass political power and economic riches.[63] The Ansar al-Sunna adhered to a Wahhabi-related purism that sought to return to the practices at the time of the prophet. Pressure on the Ansar al-Sunna culminated on 5 February 1994 when five men killed twenty-six worshipers inside the mosque. Although the government attempted to blame anti-regime groups, the gunmen themselves claimed that Turabi ordered the attack.

Bashir allowed the Ansar al-Sunna to resume functioning in November 1994, apparently because he realized that NIF's attack on this respected and rapidly growing religious movement damaged the regime's credibility among pious Muslims. The president let the Ansar al-Sunna transmit Friday prayer services on television and spoke at its mosque after Friday prayers, where he emphasized the importance of Quranic schools (*khalwa*s) to reinforce piety.[64] Promoting the Ansar al-Sunna helped Bashir balance the power of NIF, which opposed alternative Islamic currents that threatened its cultural hegemony and its right to define Sudan's Islamic revival. In fact, in 1994 Bashir convened a conference of Islamic movements that established a formal organization, headed by the minister of social planning, that brought together Islamic turuq, religious institutions, and NIF's NGOs.[65] That body and its affiliates at state and local levels controlled Islamic religious activities throughout the country, bringing sufi and fundamentalist groups into a formal alliance that deliberately marginalized the Khatmiyya and Ansar.

EDUCATIONAL POLICY

Schools and universities were crucial arenas for the struggle to create an Islamic state and a pious society. Through education, NIF could stem the western cultural invasion and foster "true" Muslim citizens.[66] NIF had already worked to Islamize the educational system through NIF teachers in secondary schools who recruited students to their ranks. Moreover, even though only a fifth of the students at Khartoum University were affiliated with NIF, NIF controlled its student union from 1978 to 1984. NIF also developed a sophisticated patronage system that attracted support for careerist reasons by providing scholarships to study abroad, financial credit to establish businesses, and employment for university graduates in Islamic banks and firms.

The government's approach to education resembled its takeover of the civil service and armed forces. The new regime purged the ministry of education, replaced administrators and teachers with NIF adherents, banned the elected faculty unions, and Islamized the curriculum. Conferences on education in September 1990 and February 1991 legitimized those measures. NIF-controlled student unions in the universities continued functioning, since they supported the regime. [The political role of student unions is addressed in chapter 9.]

President Bashir, who was automatically chancellor of the universities, made a NIF activist head of the National Council of Higher Education, dismissed the vice chancellors of ten universities, appointed new administrators sympathetic to NIF, and abolished the election of senior administrative officers at Khartoum University.[67] In 1993 the government ordered the college of nursing at Khartoum University, headed by female deans since the 1960s, to appoint a male dean since women should not run institutes of higher education. The government doubled the number of entrants to the established universities, created nine new universities in provincial capitals,[68] and stopped providing scholarships for study abroad. Arabic became the medium of instruction in all public universities in order to foster a common national identity and "get rid of foreign languages from their vocabularies."[69] Arabization made it difficult for southern students to pass the required entrance examinations. At some universities, the government required all students to study Islam, irrespective of their beliefs. The government also closed the Institute of Music and Drama because it promoted un-Islamic values. (NIF objected to classical Arabic music, not only western and folk music.)

Those measures had a drastic impact on the quality of higher education. The government dismissed or "retired" professors who opposed the regime, and hundreds left for jobs in the Gulf or political asylum in the West. The U.S. ambassador noted in 1992: "Every dean or senior faculty member I knew when I came here has been replaced by a member of the NIF."[70] Even the NIF activist who had enthusiastically promoted Islamization when he served as vice chancellor of Khartoum University conceded that the government was destroying the universities: low salaries, lack of books and laboratories, and huge numbers of students made teaching impossible. He noted that more than a hundred professors left the university from 1992 to 1994, including for example all the professors of accountancy.[71] Denuded of instructors, universities hired unqualified replacements or graduate students to teach undergraduates. The vice chancellor of Gezira University in Wad Madani also complained about the lack of funds and poor conditions facing students in classrooms and dormitories. Conditions were even worse in the new universities, which lacked buildings, books, and teachers. A new minister of higher education instituted a systematic review of the university system in 1996, which found an 80 percent shortage in teaching staff and recommended that most new programs be consolidated or closed.[72] When his committee reported to the national assembly, the government fired the minister and replaced him by his predecessor, the very person who had initiated the policies that the report attacked.

The government brought private education under its control through the General Education Act (1991), which abolished the Private Schools Act (1950) and authorized government supervision of private and foreign schools.[73] In February 1992 the government announced plans to nationalize Christian schools and, the next year, confiscated seventeen Egyptian schools in 1993 as well as the Khartoum branch of Cairo University.[74] The government did allow the American

School and Unity High School to remain autonomous and not Arabize their curricula, but then forbade those students from taking the certifying examination necessary for entering universities in the Sudan.

CONTROL OVER INFORMATION

Bashir emphasized that the media must reflect Islamic values, mobilize the public behind the national goals of the regime, and protect the Sudan from the "western foreign mass invasion." The government controlled and channeled information in the newspapers, radio, and television. And the RCC quickly banned the journalists' union, restricted the import of foreign newspapers, closed all newspapers affiliated with political parties, and shut down nearly all the independent newspapers. The RCC appointed prominent NIF writers and politicians to edit the three government newspapers.[75] Those controls were systematized through the Press and Publications Act (1993) and the Foreign Information Council, chaired by NIF ideologue Ghazi Salah al-Din Atabani. Salah al-Din pushed aside the RCC's minister of information, who wanted diversity in the press. The next minister of information was an NIF leader who claimed the right to tell editors what he thought of their performances, and close newspapers if editors did not respond appropriately. Consequently, the government suspended or closed newspapers that criticized leading politicians, aired opposition views, or seemed to question official policies.

The most significant case involved *al-Sudan al-Duwali* (Sudan international), an independent newspaper published in Beirut by an Islamist member of the TNA, Mahjub Muhammad al-Hassan Urwah.[76] Urwah transferred its operations to Khartoum in January 1994, since he had close ties to the regime through his cousin and brother-in-law Fatih Urwah, head of Bashir's security council. However, on 14 February 1994 security forces arrested the news editor, seized the paper's financial records, and suspended publication for two weeks, apparently prompted by an article on the escape abroad of communist leader Muhammad Ibrahim Nuqud. Despite that warning, the newspaper published articles that argued that the armed forces were suffering heavy losses in the south, Muslim youths were being sacrificed needlessly on the battlefield, and the civil war must end with a political solution. Articles detailed torture by security forces and supported the return to multiparty politics. The last straw was an article that criticized corruption among NIF leaders, with specific references to Minister of Social Planning Ali Uthman Taha and Issam Hasan al-Turabi, a son of Hasan al-Turabi. (The article claimed that Issam al-Turabi was detained for barely one hour on charges of dealing in foreign currency, a crime that warranted the death penalty.) Bashir banned the newspaper on 4 April 1994, seized the printing press, detained two editors, and arrested Urwah at the airport as he returned from abroad. Bashir accused the newspaper of "raising doubts about the purpose and struggle of the armed forces and PDF," insulting Islam, and seeking to "kill respect for the revolution." Although Urwah was also accused of plotting with foreign intelligence services, he received only a six-month sentence and was released after three months, due to his high-level connections. The newspaper never reopened.

The numerous closures of newspapers included, in 1995, *al-Kura* (football), for publishing an article on "superstitious matters" that described the practices of a faith healer, and the cultural weekly *Al-Zilal* (shadows) for interviewing a former member of the RCC, who attacked government policies and the lack of democratization.[77] *Al-Rai al-Akher* (another opinion) was suspended in September 1995, even though its editor was a staunch NIF cadre, since articles criticized the regime's economic failures and called for a UN-supervised referendum in which southerners could choose between federation and independence.[78] The next spring the newspaper was closed after reporting that ninety-five imprisoned officers seized their jail in al-Du'aim. Those actions indicated that the government would not even allow newspapers owned and edited by NIF members to express criticism. By the summer of 1996 restrictions were so tight that only two government-owned daily newspapers remained.

The government harassed correspondents from foreign newspapers, prevented foreign newspapers from entering the country, and banned the import of satellite dishes. Nonetheless, it could not prevent international radio and television programs from penetrating its borders. To counteract that, the government established a television channel to export the Islamic salvation revolution to Africa and the Arab world.[79] The station received eight new transmitters in January 1995 and leased time on Arabsat, apparently funded by an international Islamic group in which Turabi had a share.

In sum, the government restricted access to independent sources of information and compelled the media to promote the official version of the news. That official message fostered a homogeneous cultural and political identity, based on the particular Islamist ideology endorsed by the ruling authorities. The press restrictions prevented the public from debating the critical issues facing the Sudan and covered up abuses of power by officials.

The restrictions constituted an extreme version of the control model. The government eliminated most autonomous institutions, suppressed trade and professional unions, banned independent political parties and newspapers, and sought to restructure social and cultural life to conform to its vision of an Islamist society. Christian and Muslim religious bodies were closely monitored, curtailed, and sometimes closed.

Islamist associations monopolized the political, economic, and social arenas, and NIF cadres dominated the civil service, schools, and diplomatic corps. They controlled the security and military apparatuses and operated parallel intelligence, police, and paramilitary forces. Those policies destroyed the civil society that was emerging from 1985 to 1989, during which a wide range of political, economic, social, and religious organizations expressed diverse views. The NIF regime silenced those debates and reopened the core issue of national identity in an acute form. If the Sudan were defined as a purely Arab-Islamic state, then the African groups would have no place within that nation-state. Territorial nationalism would be a hollow concept. The exclusivist definition of the nation led to renewed calls for secession by residents of the south. Northern politicians who opposed the NIF regime feared that separatism and were thus compelled to offer an alternative vision that would respect the differences among the country's peoples. The efforts by northern and southern politicians to come to grips with their national identity and to build an effective opposition are analyzed in the subsequent chapters.

9

The Fragmented Opposition

WHILE THE MILITARY government silenced dissent and imposed a homogeneous ideological vision on citizens, the rebellion in the south intensified and opposition quickly emerged in the north that demanded the restoration of democracy, the reopening of professional and trade unions, and the end to restraints on religious and associational life. Those critics tried to organize themselves through preexisting political and union institutions that coalesced around the new National Democratic Alliance (NDA). Opposition in the north took four forms:

(1) organizing in October 1989 the NDA to galvanize strikes and nonviolent civil disobedience;
(2) attempts at coups d'état by military officers and forming the Legitimate Command (LC) in exile;
(3) use of the few remaining associations to articulate opposition; and
(4) spontaneous protests over economic hardships, encompassing students and townspeople.

That multifaceted opposition indicated the regime's weak public support, but did not shake its control fundamentally. In the past, attempts at coups d'état and opposition from abroad had never succeeded in overthrowing a military regime. Grassroots protests succeeded only when the military was divided, with a significant number of officers ready to side with the protesters. In Bashir's case, he stated bluntly: "we will not relinquish power unless through the barrel of the gun."[1] By 1993 the northern opposition forces appeared adrift, lacking a strategy to overthrow the regime and preoccupied by personal and factional differences involving Umma and DUP as well as secularists versus traditional religious groups. Moreover, southerners were sharply divided on the issue of unity or secession. Antagonistic to NIF and suspicious of traditional sectarian groups, many southerners reemphasized their own ethnic nationalism. Nonetheless, divisions within the south made attaining independence unlikely. The combined impact of the disorganized northern political movement and the weakened SPLA dimmed the prospect of overthrowing the regime.

THE NATIONAL DEMOCRATIC ALLIANCE

The Charter of the National Alliance (April 1985) and the Charter to Protect Democracy (Wad Medani, December 1985) called for civil disobedience in response to a coup d'état. In addition, the high command of the armed forces pledged to uphold the democratically elected government. The coup d'état was therefore directed against the high command as well as political parties and unions. The RCC jailed senior politicians and military officers; others fled the country.

The first test of the regime's intentions came on 1 August 1989 when the presidents of eight trade unions and professional associations submitted a formal memorandum to a member of the RCC. The memorandum outlined the government's obligations under the conventions of the International Labor Organization (ILO) and the Arab Legal Union, which included the democratic election of union officials. The RCC immediately arrested all eight presidents because they "work[ed] against the revolution."[2] It was noted in chapters 8 and 9 that the RCC canceled the trade union law, detained hundreds of union activists, and arrested the leaders of the banned Bar Association. Meanwhile, the detained activists began to plan the political effort that coalesced into the NDA, comprising the fifty-one banned unions and twelve banned political parties. John Garang also urged urban political forces in the north to rebel, complementing SPLA's fighting in the south.[3]

The NDA was announced on 21 October 1989, the twenty-fifth anniversary of the popular uprising against Abbud. Its charter called for a nonviolent campaign to overthrow the dictatorship, abolish Islamic laws, and form a new transitional government. "Free democratic patriotic [military] officers" and police officers issued supportive leaflets. Civil disobedience began after leaders of the banned professional unions met on 24-25 November and the banned Doctors Union declared a seven-day strike on 27 November 1989.[4] The union submitted a memorandum to the minister of health, demanding improvements in the hospitals and calling for the restoration of constitutional democracy. Although doctors associated with NIF's Islamic Medical Association refused to strike, they conceded that the strike was 80 percent effective in Khartoum's government hospital and 40 percent effective in hospitals in Khartoum North and Omdurman. The RCC dismissed and arrested many doctors, and tried four doctors under the emergency laws, charging them with inciting "opposition against the government."[5] Denied defense counsel, they pleaded guilty and one doctor was sentenced to death by hanging.

NDA planned to follow up the doctors' strike with strikes by the unions of engineers, bank employees, and pharmacists on 3 December that would paralyze public services. The engineers union made a serious mistake, however, by announcing the strike beforehand, which enabled security forces to round up the leaders. Nonetheless, students at Khartoum and Gezira universities mounted protests, which resulted in the death of three students on 8-9 December. Professors held a two-day sympathy strike on 9-10 December, demanding an investigation into the deaths and an apology from the police.

Bashir rescinded the death sentence and released two doctors in May 1990 due to diplomatic pressure by Egypt and international human rights organizations. But it was a long time before the NDA attempted to mount another civil uprising. This was partly because of distrust and competition within the NDA and partly because purges and the flight of political leaders made concerted action difficult. Umma and DUP continued to compete for political primacy, expressed in each party's suspicion that the other might make a deal with the regime and in Umma's emphasis on independent action since DUP's Mirghani presided over the NDA. Al-Sadiq al-Mahdi's views on Islamic law and the civil war were not substantially different from NIF, even though he sought to act within a democratic rather than authoritarian context. The fact that Turabi was his brother-in-law augmented suspicion of his potential moves. Moreover, Umma and DUP mistrusted as a communist secularist the NDA spokesman Faruq Abu Isa, the Cairo-based head of the Arab Bar Association, particularly as he often issued pronouncements that were more radical than the sectarian members of the NDA wanted. Umma and DUP preferred a shari'a-based government to an explicitly secular constitutional system. African and southern parties felt marginalized inside NDA, as they had been in the elected parliament. Thus, the NDA contained many unresolved political contradictions within itself.

Moreover, purges in the civil service, public sector, and unions made strikes increasingly difficult, and the RCC preempted opposition by frequently arresting politicians and union activists. The RCC imprisoned Muhammad Uthman al-Mirghani for more than five months and held former Prime Minister al-Sadiq al-Mahdi for six months, until mid-January 1990. Al-Mirghani, who suffered two heart attacks while jailed, was then allowed to travel abroad for medical treatment, where he remained along with most DUP leaders.[6] Umma's minister of interior, Mubarak al-Fadhil al-Mahdi, escaped to Libya immediately after the coup and became a NDA leader, based in London. Dr. Umar Nur al-Da'im, secretary general of Umma, remained in Khartoum until 1993, when he went into exile. The Ba'ath head, Taisir Muddathir, fled the country, as did SCP's al-Tijani al-Tayib and Muhammad Ibrahim Nuqud. The most prominent northern politicians who remained in Khartoum were al-Sadiq al-Mahdi and Sid Ahmad Hussain, the highest-ranking member of DUP still inside the country, whom NIF hated for his role in negotiating accords with the SPLM. Al-Mahdi and Hussain lived under virtual house arrest, banned from travel outside the capital, and detained frequently for long periods. In fact, NIF welcomed the departure of prominent politicians:[7]

> We opened the borders to [our opponents]. They left and became isolated from the society that we are now restructuring according to our Islamic concept.

In other words, after the initial crackdown the regime let its opponents leave, hoping that their credibility would diminish as their ties with grassroots supporters weakened. That would provide NIF with time to transform the society in its image.

OPPOSITION WITHIN THE ARMED FORCES

When the November uprising failed, the NDA sought to establish relations with the SPLM and to create an organized opposition within the armed forces. SPLM and the Umma party signed a pact on 22 February 1990 to remove the military dictatorship, which was followed by an agreement on 5 March 1990 between the NDA and the SPLM to join forces to topple the junta and NIF.[8] Soon after, military officers began to attempt coups d'état, first in March 1990 by Major General Ali Hamid[9] and then in April 1990 by a group of serving and retired officers.[10] Within hours, the government executed twenty-eight officers and buried them in the desert outside Khartoum. Several of these officers were already detained and therefore could not have participated in the coup attempt. The government claimed they were tried before a military court, but most were apparently executed without even the semblance of a trial.

The executions shocked Sudanese in the north. Clandestine manifestos claimed that NIF sought to destroy the armed forces and replace it by the NIF-run PDF. *Imam*s (preachers) protested that the RCC had damaged the reputation of Islam by executing people during Ramadan. The officers' female relatives demonstrated every year in Khartoum, appealing for proper burials.[11]

By the summer of 1990 discontent spread among low-rank Nuba and southern officers, who protested the Islamization and Arabization drives, the escalation of fighting against the SPLA, and the alleged policy of sending southern and Nuba troops to fight fellow Africans.[12] The death sentences imposed on twelve dissenting officers were not carried out, however.

Meanwhile, senior officers organized themselves as the Legitimate Command (LC) of the Armed Forces under General Fathi Ahmad Ali (former commander in chief), General Abd al-Rahman Sa'id (former deputy chief of staff for operations), and Brigadier al-Hadi Bushra (former deputy director of intelligence).[13] They announced on SPLA radio on 25 September 1990: "ana Sudan" (I am Sudan) and denounced the RCC for violating the armed forces' pledge to uphold democracy. The LC signed an accord with the SPLM, when they met in

SPLA-controlled territory in the south in December 1990. They called on officers to resign and enjoined garrison commanders to negotiate cease-fires with SPLA units in their vicinity. One cannot ascertain the impact of those appeals, especially as the RCC cashiered large numbers of officers that winter. The LC did not command troops inside Sudan and could not form an armed force in exile, since Egypt—which served as its principal base—would not allow armed operations from its soil. Over time, General Ali was increasingly perceived as an arm-chair general, living in Alexandria (Egypt) and lacking a strategy to overthrow the regime. Other exiled officers chafed at his inaction.

Nonetheless, officers attempted at least three more coups in 1991-1992. On 15 April 1991 (the first day of Id al-Fitr), the RCC executed twenty serving officers for attempting a coup on the anniversary of the previous year's executions. The RCC then made more arrests and dismissals.[14] On 20 August 1991 the RCC arrested thirteen serving officers, ten retired officers, and politicians from Umma and DUP, charging that LC-organized armored units planned to attack Khartoum on 28 August when their routine desert exercises finished and while President Bashir was in Libya for Qaddafi's annual celebrations.[15] The government claimed that the attempt was funded by Saudi Arabia and the United Arab Emirates (UAE), which opposed Khartoum for supporting Iraq in the Gulf crisis. In fact, DUP's Mirghani had just traveled to Saudi Arabia and the commander of the armored brigade had recently returned from a tour of service in the UAE. Faced with international protests, Bashir commuted the death sentences against thirteen officers. Then in February 1992 nineteen officers were sacked and forty-one more arrested for planning to bomb the RCC headquarters.[16]

STUDENT UNREST

Meanwhile, the RCC had exempted student associations from the ban on unions. In Bashir's words, student groups "operate, issue their papers and do everything from within Khartoum University. . . . The youth have not opposed the coup and they are a sector which can be put to use and whose capabilities can be touched off."[17] A professor observed that the government "decided to let controversy be aired freely in the vacuum of the campuses so as to avoid having the students tempted to spread outside."[18] Nonetheless, students became active in December 1989 in support of the doctors' strike and in reaction to student council elections on 28 November, in which NIF won all forty seats at Khartoum University and all thirty seats at the Khartoum branch of Cairo University.[19]

Student protests had multiple causes. They protested campus issues, such as the abolition of free lodging and meals, the politicization of financial aid, suspending students, and firing professors.[20] Such protests swept Khartoum University in September 1990 and July 1991 and Gezira University in late 1990. Students joined public demonstrations against deteriorating living conditions, food shortages, and high bread prices. They further objected to compulsory training in the PDF[21] and the Islamization and Arabization of higher education, and commemorated the popular uprising of 1985 and the anniversary of the execution of the twenty-eight officers.[22] Daring protests were mounted at the Khartoum University convocation in 1991, attended by RCC Deputy Chair General al-Zubair Muhammad Salih, where students chanted slogans against the government and a student manifesto blamed the regime for destroying the Sudan's political, economic, and social systems; decried the widespread arrests; denounced the federal system as a fraud; and castigated the government for replacing civil servants with NIF cadres. Two student leaders were arrested.

The government allowed students to express their views on campus so long as NIF controlled the Khartoum University Student Union (KUSU). However, the regime restricted KUSU after NIF lost KUSU elections in autumn 1990 to the National Democratic Forum, which combined students from Umma, DUP, and SCP. The government-appointed Vice Chancellor Muddathir al-Tanjari closed the university to avoid clashes that fall and barred the KUSU president from addressing the graduation ceremony in 1991. Even so, Tanjari criticized security forces for entering the campus without his permission, shooting at random, and chasing students into his own office in July 1991.[23] When NIF students seized the KUSU building in September 1991 after KUSU opposed the Islamist "educational revolution" and dissolved several pro-NIF student groups, security forces stormed the campus.[24] After thirty-six students were injured in clashes, the government dismissed nineteen students, closed the university temporarily, prevented KUSU from using its campus building, blocked KUSU's access to union funds, and banned all politically affiliated student groups. Even though KUSU had to operate off campus, without access to its funds, the anti-NIF student bloc won the KUSU election again in October 1991. Tanjari was replaced by his militant NIF deputy Dr. Ma'mun Muhammad Ali Humaida in February 1992. He forced students to take long-postponed examinations by transporting them at night to testing centers, including some located in military barracks and police stations.[25] More than three hundred students were dismissed, and dozens were arrested.

Tempers flared when KUSU elections were canceled in 1992. When the elections were held a year later, the elections committee announced that NIF won by a narrow margin, defeating the "neutral" list (Umma, SCP, African, Ba'ath, and Nasirite) and the anti-regime Muslim Brotherhood. Student demonstrators occupied Humaida's office and accused NIF of rigging the elections by bussing in outsiders to vote. Security forces used teargas to disperse the demonstrators, who smashed windows and doors, cut telephone and electricity lines, and stoned policemen and university guards. Forty students were injured and some three hundred arrested.

Troubles were not confined to Khartoum University. The government banned the student union at the Sudan University for Science and Technology, after protests against shortages of water and electricity led to clashes with pro-NIF students.[26] When Gezira University students struck, security forces arrested 170 students and lashed several male and female students in front of the vice chancellor and the regional governor. Student protests were difficult to contain, since they arose quickly and with minimal prior organization. The effort to indoctrinate students through the PDF evidently failed as each year witnessed new confrontations on the campuses and in the streets.

PROTESTS BY UNIONS

Although the government silenced the professional unions in the fall of 1989, workers continued to organize work-actions. The Railway Workers Union, headquartered in the industrial city of Atbara, was particularly active, since it could close down that vital transportation system. The arrest of thirteen railway personnel in 1989, for example, led to go-slow actions that spread to railway junctions at Port Sudan, Khartoum, Babanusa, and Kosti, and ended only when the government agreed to release union leaders.[27] A year later army units repressed strikes against the lack of basic foods and the rising cost of living. Thousands of railway workers were fired after they sabotaged rail tracks and paralyzed the system. A detained union leader died on 26 November.

In September 1990 the banned federation of trade unions requested an increase in the minimum wage and criticized government support for Iraq in the Gulf crisis,[28] which deepened the country's economic problems by causing Gulf countries to stop exporting oil to Sudan and to expel Sudanese employees. The banned Sudanese Women's Union also blamed government policies for economic deterioration, price increases, escalating the war in the south, dismantling the public sector, and damaging public education. Although the government arrested nearly fifty union leaders on 15 October 1990, violent protests swept Eastern, Northern, and Kordofan provinces during November, in which at least eight people died.[29] In al-Ubayyid, for example, residents burned the governor's home and ransacked the town market.

Protests subsided during 1991 but erupted again in February 1992, triggered by increases in the price of bread, sugar, and petrol.[30] Some three hundred people were arrested, including numerous high school students. Sustained protests resumed in Khartoum and Omdurman in December 1992, beginning with peaceful demonstrations against the cost of living and high rate of inflation.[31] The arrest of twenty-five women indicated their prominent role in challenging the deepening economic crisis. Demonstrations spread to Atbara, al-Fashir, Niyala, Qadarif, and Kassala. In al-Ubayyid the outcry against tripling the price of sugar caused Bashir to heed the warnings from internal security agents and cut the price of sugar as well as cancel a deal to export 50,000 tons. Student protests at Gezira University on 5 January 1993 swelled as crowds burned two gas stations and the customs office in Wad Medani. When discontent simmered throughout 1993, security officials warned Bashir that spiraling inflation and food shortages might trigger a popular revolt. By October 1993 high school students in Khartoum shouted, "We are ready to die for a new government,"[32] and residents protested deteriorating living conditions and fuel shortages that hampered the harvesting and transport of crops. Once again, protests flared in the capital city, Wad Medani, Atbara, and al-Ubayyid as well as Kassala and Gedaref, Sudan's grain belt and the religious center of the Khatmiyya order. The government arrested numerous activists from the unions and DUP and contained outbursts with security forces, PDF, people's police, and motorcycle-riding NIF militants.[33]

HARASSMENT OF AL-SADIQ AL-MAHDI

The presence of al-Sadiq al-Mahdi and millions of followers of the Ansar enabled its political organs to remain active and central to the political opposition. Al-Mahdi was captured a week after the coup and detained for six months, during which security personnel conducted at least one mock execution. Afterwards, his movements were restricted to the capital city and he was frequently placed under house arrest. Nonetheless, he continually criticized the government and called for the restoration of democracy in interviews published abroad and in sermons to the Ansar. The government generally did not dare to prevent him from delivering sermons, but did stop him from addressing other audiences. For example, when the student union at the private Omdurman Ahlia University invited him to speak in January 1993, security forces held him for questioning for twenty-four hours, thereby making it impossible for him to deliver his lecture.[34]

Al-Mahdi was frequently harassed after his sermons. He was held for twenty-four hours in April 1993, after he defied a ban on leading prayers by addressing on 5 April hundreds of thousands of Ansar at the Mahdi center during Ramadan.[35] Al-Mahdi had attacked the regime for religious extremism, distorting Islam, and denying human rights, which risked leading to intervention by international forces, as in Somalia, and to popular armed resistance. To al-Mahdi, the best solution was neither intervention nor armed resistance but the peaceful return to democracy. Dialogue with the regime was impossible unless it restored democracy and convened the national constitutional conference that would end the civil war by logic and dialogue, not terror and repression. When the Ansar marched in Omdurman four days later, following Friday prayers, several leaders were detained for twenty-four hours. Al-Mahdi was held briefly the next week to prevent him from meeting two British members of parliament. Then on 19 May 1993 (the eve of Id al-Adha) the government seized a key Ansar mosque and the Mahdi's tomb, claiming to have found Umma, NDA, and military documents and weapons inside the mosque complex. The confiscations limited the Ansar's ability to congregate, but also signalled the government's insecurity.

THE EXPLOSIVES CASE

The government looked for ways to charge al-Mahdi's supporters with sedition. From April to June 1993, the RCC arrested nearly seventy Umma leaders and four hundred Ansar on charges of conspiring to topple the regime. Detainees included the imam of Wad Nubawi mosque in Omdurman and the head of the Ansar office of *dawa* (Islamic propagation). Then the government claimed that the Legitimate Command had plotted to topple the regime by training young Sudanese communist graduates of Egyptian universities in handling firearms and explosives.[36] They were said to have trained in Lebanon in 1991 under the auspices of the Communist Action Organization but without the knowledge of the Lebanese government. The Egyptian government supposedly agreed to supply helicopters and weapons to support the LC invasion of Sudan. The unit was allegedly sent to Khartoum to blow up public buildings and assassinate Bashir and other officials. The government claimed that the unit blew up the Jabait bridge on the highway to Port Sudan. (Later, the Beja Congress claimed responsibility for that operation.) The government tried eleven people, sentencing five to two to ten years in jail. If true, this represented the most systematic effort in the early 1990s to undermine the regime from exile.

DIVISIONS INSIDE THE SPLM

Even as sporadic protests continued in the north, the coup caused acute crises within the south. It wrecked prospects for a constitutional conference to restructure political life along ethnic pluralist lines. The regime's intense Islamization drive created an equally intense reaction in the south, expressed in the renewed demand for secession and political independence. Garang had difficulty clinging to the goal of a pluralist Sudan, which seemed unrealistic with NIF in power. Southern politicians were also dubious of northern groups' support for equality since they had endorsed an Arab-Islamic identity when they were in power. The struggle over the country's national identity, therefore, became more complex and conflictual.

At first the SPLA continued to perform well militarily, holding off the army's offensive launched on 16 October 1989 and recapturing Kurmuk and additional garrisons the next month. In 1990-1991 an SPLA offensive moved into Western Equatoria and western Bahr al-Ghazal. By the spring of 1991 the SPLA controlled Upper Nile, Equatoria (except Juba and Yei), and much of Bahr al-Ghazal.

However, the SPLA suffered a nearly fatal blow in May 1991, when the fall of Mengistu Haile Mariam caused the SPLM/A to lose its political and military sanctuary in Ethiopia. SPLA officers stationed in Nasir, on the border, were overwhelmed by thousands of refugees fleeing Ethiopia. The Sudanese air force bombed their temporary camps to prevent food and medical assistance from reaching those remote locations. Since Bashir expected the SPLA to capitulate, he stressed that an Islamic federation would solve the country's problems.[37] But Garang continued to reject an Islamic constitution, insist on the separation of politics and religion, and call for the overthrow of the regime.[38]

In contrast, some of the officers based in Nasir concluded that the goal of a unified, multireligious Sudan was unrealistic since the RCC would never compromise on its ideology. Instead, the SPLM should negotiate to gain the south's independence and let NIF create a homogeneous Muslim state in the north. Lam Akol argued that Khartoum would let the non-Muslim south secede, to ensure its dominance in the north. Akol persuaded Riek Machar, garrison commander at Nasir, to support secession and try to overthrow Garang. Gordon Kong Chuol, another member of the SPLA High Command, completed the triumvirate.[39] Kong had led Anya-Nya II before joining the SPLA and, therefore, always preferred secession. Akol, Machar, and Kong declared on 28 August 1991 that they had removed Garang in order to end his human rights violations and to achieve independence. They accused him of ruling the SPLM autocratically, jailing officers who challenged him, and forcibly recruiting teenagers into the SPLA. Their manifesto focused on the profound differences between the north and south:[40]

> The dominant political forces in the North are determined . . . to impose an Islamic system of government on the country. On the other hand, the South is unanimous in rejecting Islamic laws and calling for a secular state as the only unifying bond in a multireligious and multinational state like the Sudan. . . . With such a gulf separating the two parts of the country, Sudan will be condemned to perpetual war unless some drastic action is taken fairly soon. It is evident that the only feasible course of action to bring about peace is for all to accept the fact that the North and the South need . . . a period of time of separate existence.

The manifesto was timed to coincide with a meeting of the thirteen members of the SPLM/SPLA high command in Kapoeta (Equatoria) to assess the altered military situation and outline a negotiating position for Nigerian-mediated talks with the government (analyzed in chapter 10). The Nasir group—later called SPLM/A-United—refused to attend, fearing that Garang would detain them. Nonetheless, they unrealistically hoped that other SPLA officers would support their appeal and overthrow Garang. Rather, the eight senior commanders endorsed Garang's leadership on 31 August 1991, expressing their concern that "splits or civil war in the SPLA . . . [would] delay peace and is in the interest of no one." Commander Yusif Kuwa supported Garang by radio message from the Nuba Mountains, since Nuba feared that the south's secession would leave them isolated in an overwhelmingly Arab-Islamic north.

Nonetheless, Garang recognized the need to respond to the Nasir group's challenge. He convened a meeting in Torit in early September 1991 to reassess the structures and goals of the SPLM for the first time since its formation in 1983.[41] The High Command set up committees to review issues of control and accountability and to initiate civilian administration. Until then, military officers ruled their areas of operation, which caused tension with indigenous civilian leaders and accusations of arbitrary behavior against the population. The meeting also decided to review the cases of commanders detained by the SPLA. But the most significant decision was to modify the SPLM's political goals. The Torit meeting proposed four options: "a united secular democratic Sudan, confederation, association of sovereign states, or self-determination." For the first time, the SPLM hinted that the south would secede if the government maintained its centralized Arab-Islamic system. That shift sought to undercut the Nasir group by acknowledging the widespread yearning for independence. The idea that Sudan comprised two ethnic nations challenged the elusive goal of territorial nationalism.

GOVERNMENT SUPPORT FOR THE DISSIDENTS

Ironically, the government benefited substantially from the split inside the SPLA. The government had encouraged the split by sending false signals that it might let the south secede. Once the split occurred, the government developed a four-prong strategy that encouraged SPLA factions to fight each other, backed off on offering independence, mounted large-scale offensives against Garang's forces, and used the disintegration of the SPLA to facilitate its repression of African peoples in South Kordofan, Dar Fur, and Southern Blue Nile.

First, the government encouraged SPLA-Nasir to attack SPLA-Torit in Bor and Kongor districts in October-November 1991, the fall of 1992, and February 1993. The largely Nuer forces of SPLA-Nasir—joined by thousands of Nuer tribesmen—devastated Dinka villages, destroyed crops, and seized cattle, children, and women to sell in Malakal, Kosti, and Khartoum. In late 1991 alone, 200,000 Twic Dinka fled their homes, retaining only 50,000 out of 400,000 head of cattle.[42] When SPLA-Mainstream (formerly SPLA-Torit) then attacked SPLA-

United (formerly SPLA-Nasir) at Kongor on 27 March 1993,[43] they killed more than sixty civilian and military leaders of SPLA-United who were meeting to endorse establishing an interim period of self-rule, followed by a referendum to choose between independence and unity. The gathering included Colonel William Nyuon Bany, who had defected to SPLA-United on 6 September 1992, and Commander Kerubino Kuanyin Bol, leader of the 1983 Bor mutiny whom Garang had detained for five years.[44] Although Garang appealed to SPLM-United to rejoin his forces, the mutual killings deeply embittered relations. Despite a U.S.-brokered cease-fire on 28 May 1993 that designated Kongor a demilitarized "famine zone" where international relief agencies could operate, clashes continued.[45]

The intra-SPLA fighting undermined Machar and Akol's credibility. Instead of fighting the government, they accepted the army's logistical support and weapons to attack their rivals. SPLA-United suffered defections because of this collaboration and because supporters were shocked at its devastation of southern villages, which belied its concern for human rights. An aide resigned on 30 October 1992, charging that SPLA-United did not check the Nuer troops who killed and abducted Dinka civilians in Bor and Kongor and thereby destroyed Machar's claim to be morally superior to Garang.[46] After Akol signed a political accord with the government (discussed below), more commanders accused SPLA-United of relinquishing the call for independence and fostering tribal warfare.[47]

THE FRANKFURT ACCORD

Second, the government took advantage of the schism by making SPLM-United dependent politically and militarily on Khartoum. The key government interlocutor, Dr. Ali al-Hajj Muhammad, met Akol in Nairobi in November 1991. Akol claimed that al-Hajj assured him that the government would let the south secede in return for which Akol accepted its financial and military support, including airdrops of ammunition to SPLA-United outposts.[48] Al-Hajj and Akol finalized that accord in Frankfurt (Germany) on 25 January 1992. They agreed to an immediate cease-fire and an interim period of indeterminate length[49]

> during which the Southern Sudan shall enjoy a special Constitutional and Political Status within the united Sudan after which period the people of the South shall exercise their right to freely choose the political and constitutional status that accords with their national aspirations without ruling out any option.

On the surface that permitted secession, but Akol's aides—and later al-Hajj himself—stated that unpublished sections excluded secession. Al-Hajj insisted that the choice of "political and constitutional status" would occur within an Islamic "united Sudan." The strategic difference between SPLA-United and SPLM-Mainstream revolved around the question of secession. Since Akol seemed to discard that option, the credibility of the dissident group was called into question.

SPLM-United resumed separate negotiations with the government in Nairobi from 10 to 26 May, 1993.[50] Although they disagreed on the length of the interim period, on whether the south would comprise one or more geographical units, and on whether the referendum would include the option of separation, they agreed on the allocation of powers between the south and the federal government and on a formula for sharing resources. They further agreed that the national-level constitution would apply laws based on general principles common to the states, provided that "the States shall have the right to enact any complementary legislation to the federal legislation on matters that are peculiar to them." Akol admitted this meant that Islamic law would apply nationally, leaving the south with a partial exemption. In essence, SPLM-United capitulated to NIF's ethnic nationalism, making the African south subservient to the Arab-Islamic north.

The cease-fire signed in Frankfurt in January 1992 was followed by cease-fires with Akol and Kerubino at Fashoda,[51] Bentiu, and Fanjak (Upper Nile) in August, September, and November 1993, respectively. The truce with Kerubino was particularly important, since he operated near the long-closed Bentiu oil fields.[52] Government troops could then freely cross territory held by SPLA-United in order to attack SPLA-Mainstream.

MILITARY OFFENSIVES IN THE SOUTH

Third, the government launched full-scale offensives in the south. The southern dissident officers provided the army with valuable information on the deployment and military strategies of the SPLA. The armed forces mounted a four-pronged drive with 80,000 troops in mid-February 1992, which the government called a jihad against the infidels and traitors in order to consolidate the Islamic state. They captured oil-producing Unity Province, dominated the border with Ethiopia, partially cut SPLA supply lines to Kenya, and relieved the siege on Juba.[53] Nonetheless, they suffered 20,000 casualties in the five-month offensive—10 percent of the troops fighting in the south.[54] Ill-trained recruits to the Popular Defense Force (PDF), placed in isolated garrisons, were cut off from supplies during the summer rains. Some reports indicated that the army had to train 17,000 to 19,000 new recruits before it could resume the offensive the next winter.

The government partially resolved that problem by arming Arab militias, under the umbrella of the PDF, to raid Bahr al-Ghazal and Upper Nile and escort troop trains into the south. Militias looted villages, burned houses and granaries, stole cattle, and killed or captured civilians. A PDF publication specified that, following Quranic injunctions, each foot soldier should obtain one portion of the booty and each member of the cavalry (whose definition was expanded to include members of the air force, mechanized brigades, and artillery) should obtain two portions.[55] Fighters were encouraged to seize women and children as servants or concubines and apparently received bounties if women became pregnant, since the children's identity would be Arab and Muslim. The loss of control over Eastern Equatoria hurt SPLA-Mainstream severely, since that dominated the land routes to Kenya and Uganda and provided income from gold mining, tea plantations, and teak forests. Garang relocated his headquarters to Kajo Kaji in Western Equatoria on the Ugandan border. Although he assaulted Juba in mid-1992 and succeeded in controlling the military headquarters for several hours, nearly 40 percent of the SPLA fighters were wounded or died in the operation. Many SPLA commanders criticized the unacceptably high casualties and predictably heavy government reprisals inside Juba.[56]

Further attacks in the spring and summer of 1993 left SPLA-Mainstream with toeholds along the Kenyan and Ugandan borders.[57] Thousands of civilians fled into Uganda and Kenya, and SPLA forces in the Nuba Mountains were isolated. The army's next offensive, launched in February 1995, continued despite a four-month cease-fire negotiated by Jimmy Carter.[58] The army seized Kajo Kaji on 11 July 1995 and bribed government officials in Zaire and the Central African Republic to let troops enter their territory to attack Western Equatoria. The army also set up a base in Dungu (Zaire) from which Idi Amin's West Bank Nile Front raided northwest Uganda. That escalation propelled Uganda to assist SPLA-Mainstream to expel government troops from the Uganda border in late October 1995. The SPLA also overran bases of the anti-Museveni Lord's Resistance Army (LRA) in Equatoria and recaptured ten garrison towns in Equatoria.[59] Fighting remained at a standoff during the winter: the army used human-wave tactics to try to recapture territory south of Juba, but immense casualties, difficulty reprovisioning garrisons, and the inability to pay soldiers hampered its operations.

CAMPAIGNS AGAINST THE FUR, NUBA, AND INGESSANA PEOPLES

The fourth prong aimed to silence and remove civilians of African heritage from the zones just north of the southern provinces. NIF wanted a cordon sanitaire to protect the cultural and religious purity of the north.[60] Official fatwas, which called a Muslim fighting the regime an apostate and endorsed the conquest and conversion of heathens, legitimized attacks on Nuba, Ingessana, and Fur peoples. There was also an important economic component to the government actions, since the government facilitated the creation of large-scale mechanized farms by Nile Valley Arab entrepreneurs and retired military officers on land from which the indigenous peoples had been displaced.

Attacks in those zones predated the major military drive in 1992. For example, on 30 October 1989 the 3,500-strong Misiriyya Arab militia attacked Nuba and Daju villages in Lagowa (southern Kordofan), after tensions arose when Arab herders pastured on Daju fields before the crops were harvested. Moreover, Arab residents resented the influx of Nuba displaced persons.[61] The PDF-linked militia used its overwhelming firepower to destroy twenty villages, kill 125 civilians, burn crops, and displace 20,000 Nuba and Daju civilians. Similarly, on 28 December 1989 a militia composed of Sabaha Arabs (a subbranch of the Misiriyya) rampaged in Jabalain (White Nile).[62] A Shilluk farmhand had killed his Arab employer, who wanted him to work during the Christmas holiday. In response the militia killed 600-1,000 Shilluk, Dinka, Nuer, and Burun civilians in their homes and in the fields. Ninety-one persons were killed in the police station, where they sought protection. In neither Lagowa nor Jabalain was there any threat from the SPLA.

In the Nuba Mountains, at least 157 extrajudicial executions of Nuba politicians, intellectuals, and trade unionists occurred between 1989 and 1992.[63] By then, most Nuba had been removed from the civil and security services or transferred elsewhere. All senior government positions were held by non-Nuba. The sole Nuba member of the RCC was sidelined when he urged Bashir to dismantle Arab militias and investigate attacks on Nuba villagers.

Dar Fur residents had suffered from battles among forces of the Chad government, Chad rebels allied with the Zaghawa people, and the Libyan army since the mid-1980s, which led to the rebels' seizing power in Ndjamena in December 1990. Despite efforts by a Fur member of the RCC to reduce Arab-Fur tensions, the government incorporated Arab militias into the PDF and signed an integration charter with Libya in 1990 that promoted the Arabic language and culture in Dar Fur.[64] At least ninety Fur chiefs and politicians were arrested in the spring of 1990 after they sought to ward off the Arab militia attacks. The destruction of Fur villages by government-supported militias continued in the early 1990s.

The proclamation of jihad in January 1992 legitimized the forced removal of Nuba and Fur and the conversion to Islam of Ingessana peoples and non-Muslim Nuba. Nuba villages were systematically encircled and destroyed, using helicopter gunships and high-level bombers as well as artillery and foot soldiers.[65] Terrified civilians were first relocated to North Kordofan, where there were virtually no health or relief services and jobs could be found only in Arab farms and homes. Then ninety-one special "peace villages" were established out-side the Nuba Mountains, guarded by PDF militiamen. Those "villages" con-tained 167,000 residents by September 1992, 80 percent of whom were children. Children attended Quranic schools, women's literacy programs inculcated NIF's version of Islamic beliefs and behavior, and men were forcibly circumcised. By 1993, 250,000 Nuba were displaced—nearly a third of the 800,000 Nuba in the mountains. The government sold their land to Arab entrepreneurs or handed it over to government and military officers and leaders of Arab militias.[66]

Similar measures among the Ingessana in Southern Blue Nile sought to stamp out indigenous customs and beliefs. Villagers were grouped in fifty-two sites for comprehensive indoctrination and their homes were turned over to large-scale mechanized farms, owned by Arab entrepreneurs.[67] Those measures took place well after the SPLA had left the province. Similarly, the removal of Nuba continued long after Kuwa's SPLA battalion lost contact with SPLA forces in the south and ceased to mount military operations.

DIVISIONS WITHIN SPLA-UNITED

SPLA-United began to splinter in 1994, after Garang and Machar signed a short-lived accord in Washington in October 1993. Machar admitted that the di-vision in 1991 had benefited the government, which made military gains and be-came "arrogant" in negotiations,[68] but Akol and Nyuon criticized the Washing-ton accord and continued to attack SPLA-Mainstream positions. Machar sacked Akol, Kerubino, and Nyuon since they advocated surrender to the "enemy" NIF regime, and changed the name of his movement to South Sudan Independence Movement (SSIM) in September 1994 to underline the goal of secession through armed struggle.[69] Akol then denounced Machar for military errors and accused him of stirring up ethnic tensions between Shilluk (Akol) and Nuer (Machar). Nuer leader Gordon Kong of Anya-Nya II allied with Akol, who reorganized SPLM-United on 22 December 1994 with the support of Kerubino and Nyuon.[70] Although they denounced Machar's collaboration with Khartoum, Kerubino and Nyuon fought alongside the army in Bahr al-Ghazal and on the Uganda border, respectively.[71] They signed secret political-military accords on 4 Novem-ber and 18 December 1994 that committed them to assist the Lord's Resistance Army (LRA), which Khartoum used to weaken Yoweri Museveni.

SPLM-Mainstream took advantage of those schisms and played the factions off against each other. First it convinced Machar to sign a cease-fire in February 1995 and fight the army — a move that prompted the government to seize Nasir from him on 25 March 1995.[72] Then when Nyuon signed a cease-fire with SPLA-Mainstream on 27 April 1995, SPLA-Mainstream used Nyuon to fight Machar in Ayod-Waat in the fall of 1995.[73] Nyuon was killed in December 1995, apparently

by one of Machar's officers. By then southern politicians desperately tried to reconcile the factions. The first attempt sought to end intra-Nuer fighting in eastern
Upper Nile.[74] The second was led by Eliaba Surur, the respected Equatorian
politician who headed the Union of Sudan African Parties (USAP), and Samuel
Aru Bol, a long-standing Dinka politician from Bahr al-Ghazal who was deputy
premier in 1985-1986. After six months shuttling among the groups, they not
only failed to reconcile the factions but split with each other. Surur sided with
SPLM-Mainstream and headed its National Mobilization Committee, whereas
Aru Bol supported Machar's SSIM and denounced Garang.[75]

THE POLITICAL CHARTER (APRIL 1996)

In the spring of 1996 Machar and Kerubino caved in to the government.
Machar's capitulation was preceded by a cease-fire between the armed forces
and SSIM in March, forced on SSIM by its dire economic and military circumstances. The government had forbidden UN flights to eastern Upper Nile, where
Machar wanted help for civilians who faced severe food shortages. His commanders had no way to get arms except through the army or by rejoining SPLA-
Mainstream, which they would not countenance. Kerubino was also desperate,
his forces having dwindled to 500 men who survived by raiding villages near
Gogrial (Bahr al-Ghazal).

Machar and Kerubino flew to Khartoum, where they signed a Political
Charter on 10 April 1996.[76] That charter pledged to "resolve the conflict in the
Sudan through peaceful and political means" in the context of "the unity of the
Sudan with its known boundaries." The charter recognized the existing Islamic
constitutional and federal systems, stated that "Sharia and Custom shall be the
source of legislation," and accepted the current boundaries between the north
and the south that shifted oil fields, copper mines, and gum arabic plantations
into the north (see chapter 7). The referendum at the end of an interim period
of unspecified duration would be conducted in the context of territorial unity,
and only after the "full establishment of peace, stability, and a reasonable level
of social development in the south." They further pledged to mobilize the south
behind the agreement, which hinted that the government expected them to
fight SPLA-Mainstream and groups led by John Luk and Akol that refused to
sign the charter. Luk lost control over Akobo to Machar on 28 June 1996 and
Akol had already been expelled from Tonga on 22 January 1996.[77] In effect, all
that Machar and Kerubino gained were vague promises of self-rule within an
Islamist Sudan.

Although SSIM spokesmen tried to argue that the south could still choose
between unity and independence, neither Machar nor Kerubino referred to se-

cession in their speeches at the signing ceremony in Khartoum. Machar praised the government's and Turabi's "tireless efforts in the search for peace" that would chart "a new path to peace, stability, and prosperity in the country." Kerubino stated that the charter "secures the unity and territorial integrity of the Sudan," and thanked "President Al-Bashir for giving us this opportunity to call all the Sudanese people to join hands to maintain peace, unity, and prosperity." The charter thus represented the culmination of the Frankfurt accord (1992) and the demise of Machar's dream of independence. It did not even unite southern politicians behind him. Machar hoped to head the coordinating council for the south mentioned in the charter, but soon found himself outwitted by the government, weakened by defections, and stymied by rivals from the south. The government pitted him against Kerubino, hoping to wear them both out in operations against the SPLA and Akol's forces, and produced additional commanders to sign the charter, none of whom had fought against the army.[78] Meanwhile, other southern supporters of the regime criticized the charter: former Vice President Joseph Lagu wanted the Addis Ababa formula restored, Equatorians insisted on retaining their separate status, and they all resented Machar's claim to leadership. The government could relax while southerners squabbled ineffectively among themselves.

Differences within and between the NDA and SPLM and the government's divide-and-rule policies toward the south prevented an effective opposition from emerging to counter the Islamist government. The NDA lacked a common goal beyond overthrowing the government and restoring democracy. Endemic rivalry between Umma and DUP and mutual suspicion between Islamic-based parties and secularist northerners hampered cooperation. The NDA seemed an empty vessel, unable to overthrow the government or develop an alternative vision. Student protests and popular anger at economic hardships were insufficient in themselves to shake the government.

The devastating split within the SPLM further weakened opposition forces. Tensions over Garang's intolerance of dissent burst into the open. More fundamentally, disagreements on ultimate goals could no longer be hidden. The remote prospect of transforming the Sudan into an ethnic pluralist state clashed with the long-standing dream of independence. Given the regime's inflexibility in its vision of the Sudan as a homogeneous Islamic-Arab country, that reaction was inevitable. But the split played into the government's hands and left both southern visions further from realization. The Islamist vision was being imposed by force on both the south and the west.

The stark contrast in views toward national identity was evident in negotiations between the government and the SPLM. Those began in 1989, within months of the coup d'état, and resumed under African states' auspices in 1992. The next chapter outlines the contrasting visions and details the efforts to negotiate a resolution to the bitter civil war. When the mediators' efforts ended in late 1994, the lines of disagreement were clarified and the prospects for an accord were bleak. The war of visions continued, intensified rather than diminished.

10

The Impasse in Negotiations

THE COUP D'ÉTAT of 30 June 1989 was intended to halt the negotiations with the SPLM, which were finalizing arrangements for a constitutional conference in September that might establish legal and political structures to represent the diverse Sudanese peoples. While it remained uncertain whether the traditional Islamic parties could accommodate the perspectives of the African peoples, that possibility was enough to propel NIF to act, since NIF opposed any dilution of Sudan's Islamic-Arab identity and viewed the SPLM as a mortal foe with whom compromise was inconceivable.

THE REGIME'S ATTITUDES TOWARD THE SOUTH

The Revolutionary Command Council's (RCC) initial statements criticized the ousted high command for failing "to force the government to make available the minimum of the troops' requirements."[1] They complained that soldiers were trapped under gunfire in water-filled trenches where they could not bury their comrades while politicians in air-conditioned offices made political deals at their expense. The RCC canceled the previous government's approval of the DUP-SPLM accord on the grounds that the majority's right to shari'a must not be compromised. Bashir sought to start from scratch:[2]

> Each side must formulate its own [peace] scenario and then sit at the table to negotiate every clause and every point. . . . It is like it [the DUP-SPLM accord] never existed to us. It has no place in our efforts to solve the Southern problem. The conditions included in that agreement are inadmissable to us.

Bashir proposed resolving the issue of Islamic law through a popular referendum. If the majority supported Islamic law, as he assumed would happen, the south might be exempt from certain punishments in deference to its non-Muslim population. This echoed NIF's longstanding plan, outlined in its Sudan Charter (1987).

The official negotiating position was worked out at a National Dialogue Conference on Peace, held in Khartoum from 9 September to 21 October 1989 and chaired by RCC's Muhammad al-Amin Khalifa, with the 104 participants selected by the RCC.[3] The RCC handpicked the twenty-three southerners, including former vice president Joseph Lagu, who served as deputy chair of the steering committee. It prevented fifty-seven southern politicians from presenting or publishing their petition protesting discrimination, Arabization, and Islamization. Only Major General Peter Cyrillo, former governor of Equatoria, addressed those issues. Cyrillo specifically debunked the idea of a referendum on shari'a in his speech, which represented the consensus among Juba-based politicians. Not surprisingly, the stage-managed conference recommended applying shari'a through a federal system under which a region could exempt itself from certain Islamic punishments, but non-Muslims living in the north would be fully subject to shari'a. It rejected the Koka Dam and DUP-SPLM accords as bases for negotiations. The RCC and cabinet endorsed those recommendations on 1 November 1989, making them the basis for all subsequent negotiations as well as for the Islamic federal system that the RCC began to implement.

GARANG'S RESPONSE

Garang delivered a lengthy speech on 10 August 1989 that offered the SPLM's first comprehensive critique of the coup d'état.[4] Garang said he delayed reacting in order to give the new government the benefit of the doubt, but he now feared they had a theocratic agenda and intended to abort the peace process. It was presumptuous for the self-appointed RCC to annul agreements negotiated by an elected government and act "as if Sudan came into being on 30 June." Focusing solely on the south reflected a "shallow and distorted perception of the nature of the central problem of the Sudan . . . a crude and reactionary position that can only bring disaster, not peace to the country."

> Omer [al-Bashir] thinks that he is *the* Sudanese nationalist and we in the SPLA are *his* Southerners. . . . Has Brig. Omer el Bashir bothered to ask the question as to what it is that makes him the Sudanese and makes Dr. John Garang his Southerner?

The RCC used "the same language as Turabi" concerning Islamic laws, but that vision was alien to Sudan, where "religion belongs to the individual and the state belongs to all of us collectively." Garang criticized the audacity of "a self-imposed military junta" conducting a referendum on shari'a, "when no referendum has been carried out on the junta's assumption of power." He questioned its support among the public and the armed forces, given its "unprecedented" dismissal of more than six hundred officers and its violations of human rights.

Peace was possible only if the RCC restored democracy and held the constitutional conference. This required four specific steps: First, "establishment of an interim broad-based government of national unity . . . including the two armies (the SPLA and the regular Sudanese army), political parties that believe in de-mocracy and the New Sudan, [and] the trade and professional unions." Second, "the establishment of a national, nonsectarian, nonregional army from both the SPLA and the regular army . . . [which] is capable of restoring internal stability, defending democracy, and safeguarding our country's independence and territo-rial integrity." Third, "the convening of the national constitutional conference by the interim government . . . based on the Koka Dam Agreement and the Sudanese Peace Initiative [DUP-SPLM accord] . . . whose purpose . . . shall be the drafting of a permanent constitution." And fourth, "preparation by the interim government . . . for free elections, . . . the subsequent ratification of the constitution by the constituent assembly, and the establishment of a democracy-based government." The SPLM would discuss with RCC emissaries that four-point plan to restore democracy and achieve peace:

> With respect to whether the Movement will talk with the New Military Junta in Khartoum, the answer is yes. . . . They are the *de facto* government in Khartoum and our policy has always been to talk with anyone who claims to be in power in Khartoum. . . . The government of Suwar al-Dhahab was a military dictatorship, while the government of Sadiq el Mahdi was a sectarian dictatorship . . . , yet we talked to these governments. . . . We have already notified the junta through Mengistu Haile Mariam of Ethiopia of our willing-ness . . . to talk with them. . . . The junta will have to brief the Movement as to why they took over power . . . and presumably . . . present their peace . . . pro-grammes. However, we will not listen passively, we will present . . . the Move-ment's peace programme in the context of the establishment of a democracy and the United New Sudan.

At a minimum, face-to-face talks would clarify the RCC's aims. However, re-taining a shari'a-based system would prevent progress in substantive talks and prove that the RCC had a "hidden agenda to partition the country." Imposing shari'a would cause the nation to disintegrate, which the SPLM opposed. More-over, failing to restore democracy would impel the SPLM to support "a general strike and a popular mass uprising to remove the junta" in the north.

SPLM-RCC NEGOTIATIONS IN 1989

The stark contrast in perspectives was evident in the official meetings in Addis Ababa in August 1989 and in Nairobi in December 1989. Bashir initially proposed that he meet face-to-face with Garang as fellow officers "who know what war is really like."[5] He then sent two non-Arab members of the RCC to Addis Ababa on 11 July 1989, less than two weeks after the coup: Colonel Muhammad al-Amin Khalifa, an Islamist officer of Berti background who later chaired the National Dialogue Conference, and Brigadier Martin Malwal, scion of a distinguished Dinka family. They met President Mengistu and Ethiopian diplomats, but no one in the SPLM would see them since the RCC had not yet stated its goals. The delegation asked Mengistu to mediate and handed him a message for Garang.

The first talks were held on 19 and 20 August with Khalifa heading the government delegation and Dr. Lam Akol heading the SPLM team.[6] Akol, SPLM's chief negotiator with the elected government, had been finalizing arrangements for the constitutional conference when the coup erased his efforts. After the August talks concluded, Khalifa praised them on the grounds that neither side imposed preconditions or was bound by past accords, which were now irrelevant and outdated. Although they disagreed on Islamic law, they began a dialogue that both sides wanted to continue. The next step would be a meeting with various people to achieve concrete results—a hint at the coming National Dialogue Conference for Peace in Khartoum.

Akol differed completely in his assessment. He concurred that shari'a was a key point of disagreement, but emphasized that the talks represented continuity with past negotiations and prior accords. Government delegates tried to "deceive us" by talking about the problem of the south and the Addis Ababa Accord, rejecting the Koka Dam and DUP-SPLM accords, calling for a referendum on shari'a while insisting that shari'a would remain in force, and refusing to end the state of emergency and restore democracy. Khalifa's polemical tone angered Akol, who feared the RCC was pretending to negotiate while consolidating power and preparing to escalate the war. As a result, although the SPLA would continue the cease-fire informally, it would not be formalized until the regime endorsed the DUP-SPLM accord. Since the RCC delegation flatly rejected that accord, the SPLM concluded they should not meet again until the RCC accepted the SPLM's four-point program that Garang had detailed in his speech ten days earlier. Akol, therefore, presented that plan to the RCC, expecting to receive its reactions at the next round of talks. For the SPLM, the meeting ended with an "agreement to disagree." Indeed, one delegate concluded, the "extremely wide gap makes it unlikely that the two sides will agree on anything."

The second meeting was arranged and chaired by former U.S. President Jimmy Carter.[7] It convened in Nairobi on 1 December 1989 during a crackdown on civil disobedience in Khartoum and the army's military offensive in the south. Both sides came geared for confrontation, not compromise. Nonetheless, Carter, who had met with Bashir in August and November 1989, had concluded that Bashir welcomed negotiations. Moreover, Carter believed that solving the issue of shari'a would pave the way for an agreement on the nature of the constitutional system. He therefore raised that thorny question at the start of the talks—and produced an immediate deadlock.

The government presented as its peace plan the *Final Report* of the National

Dialogue Conference, which endorsed an Islamic federal system in which regions with non-Muslim majorities could exempt themselves from certain aspects of the hudud. This replaced the DUP-SPLM accord. Shari'a would only be discussed at the constitutional conference, which would lead to a nationwide popular referendum. Khalifa completely rejected the SPLM's four-point plan but called the talks a "success" since the parties agreed to discuss the RCC's *Final Report* at the next meeting.

In contrast, Akol criticized the government's refusal to cancel shari'a, restore public freedoms, and form a government of national unity, which the SPLM sought as preconditions for the constitutional conference. That conference would address a range of position papers, including the government's *Final Report*, but the latter would not form the sole basis for negotiations. Moreover, the two sides did not agree on who would participate in the conference.

When Carter suggested that the government suspend Islamic law for three months until the constitutional conference could convene, Khalifa accused him of bias and rejected his further mediation. Nonetheless, Carter thought he brought the positions of the protagonists closer than they were willing to admit. He even believed that the SPLM had accepted the RCC's *Final Report* as a basis for negotiations.

THE AMERICAN INITIATIVE

Carter's optimistic conclusions persuaded Washington to respond favorably to Bashir's request in March 1990 that the U.S. government assume the role of mediator. With the military balance tilted in favor of the SPLA, Bashir wanted to take the diplomatic high ground. Moreover, the United States believed that NIF viewed the war as a quagmire, which could be ended by letting the south secede. Therefore, the United States proposed through nonofficial emissaries that the government evacuate the south, hold a constitutional conference, and conduct elections to restore multiparty democracy.[8] This would create a de facto independent territory in the south. Bashir flatly rejected the entire plan, whereas the SPLM hailed it.

When Assistant Secretary of State for African Affairs Herman Cohen modified the proposal to thin out—rather than evacuate—government forces and designate civilian safe havens, SPLM rejected those terms. Khartoum accepted a cease-fire and thinning out of troops, but rejected international supervision and ruled out allowing political parties to participate in elections. Before the United States could reformulate its ideas, the Gulf crisis broke out in August 1990 and U.S.-Sudanese relations deteriorated. By November 1990, Khartoum's negotiator Khalifa declaimed that, since the conflict was "between truth and falsehood," the government would "impose peace by force."[9] In any event, it was doubtful that an initiative oriented toward a military cease-fire and disengagement of forces could succeed without being grounded in a comprehensive political agreement.

REGIONALIZATION OF DIPLOMACY

The situation on the ground changed drastically during the summer of 1991, when the overthrow of Mengistu and the split in the SPLM seriously weakened the movement. Although political positions remained diametrically opposed, government officials did not perceive a need to negotiate since they seemed to be defeating the SPLA militarily. Nonetheless, African leaders became increasingly concerned about the regional implications of the civil war, which affected their own security. The Organization of African Unity (OAU) therefore sought to mediate. The OAU tended to support the SPLM position on secularism, but OAU policy opposed secession. At first, efforts by successive OAU presidents Husni Mubarak of Egypt and Sese Seko Mobutu of Zaire yielded no results. But when Garang expressed willingness to talk, in June 1991,[10] the new OAU head, Nigerian President Ibrahim Babangida, sent emissaries to the government and the SPLM. The emissaries gained the parties' agreement on an agenda for talks in Abuja (Nigeria's capital) starting on 28 October 1991. Bashir could not refuse negotiations, despite his expectation of a victory on the battlefield, but he benefited from the delays caused by the schism within the SPLM. Khartoum also insisted that SPLM-Nasir send a separate delegation, anticipating that it could play the two groups against each other.[11]

ABUJA I, MAY-JUNE 1992

Talks finally convened from 26 May to 4 June 1992, with the government, SPLM-Torit, and SPLM-Nasir attending.[12] Khartoum's negotiator Ali al-Hajj had signed a cease-fire and political accord with SPLM-Nasir on 25 January 1992 in Frankfurt that enabled the army to extend its fighting far into Equatoria. Babangida therefore hoped that the negotiations would at least stave off SPLM-Torit's demise and enable it to gain political standing within the south, if not exclusive control.

Khalifa, who again headed the government delegation, felt no need to compromise. He refused to discuss security issues—a cease-fire, foreign monitors, confidence-building measures, or even stopping negative propaganda. Government delegates cut off the Nigerian mediators when they tried to address those questions, saying that security was an internal matter in which non-Sudanese should not interfere and that the government would handle the security situation itself. They did agree to respect the religious, linguistic, and cultural diversities of Sudan and to leave the constitution silent on the question of an official religion, but they refused to mention that in the conference's final communiqué. Overall, they insisted on the primacy of the principle of majority rights: The Muslim majority could establish whatever constitutional system it desired, including one based on shari'a. Religious diversity would only be expressed by exempting the south from hudud and all commercial and tax laws throughout the country must uniformly follow shari'a. According to the government's assimilationist vision, over time Arabic would become the universal language, Islam would spread, and diversities would thereby become insignificant.

Both SPLM delegations rejected the government position. They argued that the multiethnic essence of the Sudan must be upheld by a secular democratic system based on the principle of equality before the law. Assimilation and marginalization (via exemptions) were equally abhorrent. SPLM-Nasir, whose delegation was led by Akol, maintained that, since the effort to create a system based on equality had failed, the aspirations of the north and the south had proved irreconcilable and they should stop trying to retain their artificial unity. At most, a loose confederation was possible, which would free each half to institute whatever legal system it wanted. In reaction to the government's extreme position, the two SPLM delegations merged on the sixth day of talks, asserting a common stance in support of the south's right to self-determination.

The issue of self-determination was contentious, since the government and Nigeria had deliberately excluded it from the agenda. Given Nigeria's suppression of Biafran secessionists, the mediators stressed that they would not preside over a conference that advocated the dismemberment of the Sudan. Khartoum was willing to discuss a referendum on the federal system or on amending certain laws, but not a referendum that included the option of secession. Akol had hoped that the government would negotiate a territorial division, but Khalifa emphasized that "separation comes from the mouth of the gun," not from debates in Abuja. In contrast, the two SPLM delegations insisted on self-determination, because the south was denied that right in the past and because their support for unity was contingent on a specific sociopolitical environment in which all the Sudanese had the same constitutional rights. The more the government insisted on an Islamic majoritarian state and an assimilationist future, the more the SPLM insisted on self-determination.

When Nigeria convened the negotiations, it thought it could deal with the problems piecemeal by establishing a cease-fire, separating the armed forces, and agreeing on the terms for an interim period. After that, the parties would be ready to tackle core constitutional issues. That approach proved impossible. Even so, Babangida tried to prevent a breakdown by gaining the parties' agreement to reconvene quickly to discuss political, economic, and security structures during an interim period. Khartoum claimed this meant that the SPLM had set aside the issue of secession.[13] In any event, the government sought to delay negotiations, anticipating that it would soon defeat the SPLA.

Garang may have also been surprised by his delegation's swift endorsement of self-determination, since he remained committed to unity as the preferred outcome. That tension was reflected in the defection of the head of SPLM-Torit's delegation to SPLM-Nasir, shortly after Abuja I ended. The new focus on self-determination hurt SPLM-Torit's relations with Nuba allies and the National Democratic Alliance. Nuba fighters were wary of the new SPLM proposal that the peoples of the Nuba Mountains, Abyei (South Kordofan), and Ingessana (Southern Blue Nile) join the southern zone since they preferred having federal status within a democratic secular Sudan.[14] The northern members of the NDA also opposed the south's secession, partly on the basis of national sovereignty and partly because that oil-rich area would be lost. Moreover, that would reduce the ability of secular-oriented northerners to stave off demands for an Islamic constitution. This issue exacerbated tensions within the NDA that were mentioned in the previous chapter and was only resolved by the NDA resolution on 17 April 1993 (detailed in the next chapter) that called for a government based on equal rights for all citizens.

ABUJA II NEGOTIATIONS

Almost a year passed between Abuja I and Abuja II, which convened from 26 April to 18 May 1993. During the interval, Khartoum seized additional territory, including SPLM's headquarters in Torit. As Bashir gained confidence, his statements became more extreme:[15]

> We will not abandon our principles for any reason. . . . What we now apply in Sudan is God's will. We will never satisfy humans to displease the almighty God.

Nonetheless, international pressure for a negotiated settlement mounted. The United States, European Union, Vatican, and United Nations all condemned the regime's human rights record, culminating on 10 March 1993 with the appointment of a Special Rapporteur by the UN Commission for Human Rights and simultaneous congressional hearings on the possibility of humanitarian intervention to establish safe havens in the south.[16] Moreover, the armed forces were overextended in the south and needed the breathing space that a cease-fire would provide.

Although Bashir could not avoid negotiations, he preferred private bilateral talks in which the leaders would cut a deal. He tried to achieve that when al-Hajj and Garang met in Entebbe (Uganda) on 23 February 1993, but Yoweri Museveni supported Garang's view that the meeting should simply reaffirm the agenda agreed on at the end of Abuja I.[17] Then al-Hajj sought substantive negotiations at "pre-talks" once the delegations arrived in Abuja, but Nigeria agreed with the SPLM that those discussions should merely formalize the agenda items related to religion and state, and to the nature of the interim period. Khartoum showed its disinterest in negotiations by sending a low-level delegation, headed by al-Hajj, which was only followed on the fifth day by the senior delegates, headed by Khalifa.

The government and the SPLM each presented Babangida with proposals on the interim period, just before the talks started. Khartoum reiterated its *Final Report*, which the foreign minister stated providing formulae for[18]

(1) power-sharing within a united Sudan, excluding secession,

(2) balanced socioeconomic development, and

(3) applying shari'a, without mentioning Islam as the state religion, and exempting the south from certain shari'a provisions.

The SPLM-Mainstream delegation was headed by Major Salva Kiir Mayardit with Nuba commander Yusif Kuwa as deputy head to reassure the Nuba people. The SPLM program emphasized that the New Sudan remained its "preferred solution" and "principled objective"—a democratic, nonsectarian "Sudanese Commonality that transcends race, tribe, language, or religion."[19] However, so long as the rulers rejected that vision and excluded the marginalized peoples, those peoples had the right to self-determination. Indeed, if the government insisted on a unitary state with an Islamizing and Arabizing agenda, then the south must demand its independence, even if that would be achieved "after a great deal of bloodshed and loss of lives and misery for all." The SPLM viewed a confederation between the north and the "marginalized" south, Nuba (South Kordofan), and Ingessana (Southern Blue Nile) as the best way "to solve the problem of the relationship between state and religion, power and wealth sharing." Khartoum's federal system did not share power but rather increased the domination of the central government and Islamized all public, "economic, cultural, and social life." In a confederation, "each confederal state would be sovereign in its laws and security arrangements."

At the end of the interim period, the marginalized peoples would conduct an internationally supervised referendum to choose between confederation and independence. Over time, a "healthy union" could be built voluntarily between the two parts and the New Sudan would then come into being.

FUNDAMENTAL DIFFERENCES

The parties disagreed on virtually every issue during the three weeks, despite detailed proposals by Nigeria and deliberations by technical committees.

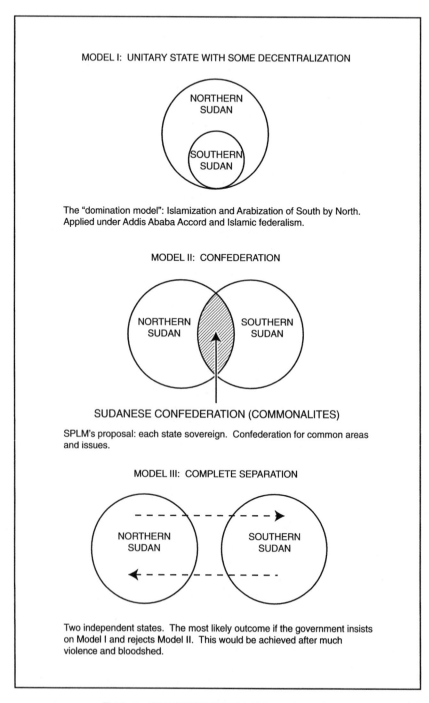

MODEL I: UNITARY STATE WITH SOME DECENTRALIZATION

NORTHERN
SUDAN

SOUTHERN
SUDAN

The "domination model": Islamization and Arabization of South by North.
Applied under Addis Ababa Accord and Islamic federalism.

MODEL II: CONFEDERATION

NORTHERN
SUDAN

SOUTHERN
SUDAN

SUDANESE CONFEDERATION (COMMONALITES)

SPLM's proposal: each state sovereign. Confederation for common areas
and issues.

MODEL III: COMPLETE SEPARATION

NORTHERN
SUDAN

SOUTHERN
SUDAN

Two independent states. The most likely outcome if the government insists
on Model I and rejects Model II. This would be achieved after much
violence and bloodshed.

Table 3. SPLM'S THREE POLITICAL MODELS

The mediator had decided to tackle head-on the issue of religion and state. If that issue could be resolved, then other issues would fall into place; if not, then no accord was possible. That approach led to fierce debates, in which government delegates accused the SPLM of seeking to abolish religion, and declared that abolishing shari'a and hudud as the law of the land would lead to a Muslim uprising. The SPLM, in turn, rejected religious apartheid and stated starkly that the south could be part of an Islamic state only if it were defeated militarily. In brief, the parties deadlocked on:[20]

(1) Religion and state:

(a) The SPLM insisted that a unitary system separate religion from the state. In a confederation, the north could institute shari'a, except in the shared capital city of Khartoum where secular law must apply.

(b) The government insisted that shari'a remain the supreme public law in a unified Sudan. Hudud would not apply to citizens in the south but would apply to non-Muslims in the north. The word "Islamic" would be removed from the official name of the country, in deference to non-Muslims.

(c) Nigeria proposed suspending shari'a during the interim period except as applied to individual Muslims for personal-status issues, as was the case before 1983. The government totally rejected that proposal.

(2) Political system during the interim period:

(a) The SPLM proposed a confederation, with each state establishing its own legal system and foreign policy. Supreme authority would lie with the head of state in Khartoum and the commander in chief of the SPLM (head of the southern government) who would oversee matters of mutual interest, including shared infrastructure.

(b) The government rejected confederation and insisted on its current federal formula, the south's division into several states, and the exclusion of Nuba and Ingessana from the south.

(c) Nigeria proposed that the south have an independent judiciary, its own security forces, and enhanced administrative jurisdiction within a federal formula that accorded more authority to the states than Khartoum's plan, but retained key economic powers at the center and proposed dividing the entire country into many small states to reduce the power of regional blocs.

(3) Socio-economic policies:

(a) The SPLM argued that the southern confederal state would control petroleum exploration and development policy, including import-export trade, banking, mining, agriculture, and international agreements. Each state would control education and religious affairs.

(b) Khartoum insisted the central government control socioeconomic, educational, and religious policies and negotiate international agreements. Since natural resources were common to all Sudanese, the central government should control them.

(c) Nigeria reserved curriculum development, commerce and industry, and fishing to the states. It gained the parties' acceptance of a commission on the allocation of national revenue, as had already been agreed at Abuja I, but they disagreed on the commission's composition and constitutional authority.

(4) Security during the interim period:

(a) The SPLM wanted government troops withdrawn from the south, leaving the SPLA in control, with foreign observers to monitor the cease-fire and disengagement process. It was wary of Nigeria's proposal to leave the army within the south and integrate the SPLA into the national army.

(b) The initial government delegation accepted the idea of a cease-fire commission, without foreign observers. When the high-level delegation arrived, it overruled al-Hajj, emphasized that the current cease-fire was merely temporary, and insisted that the composition of a cease-fire commission could not be discussed until political issues were resolved.

(c) Nigeria proposed a gradual separation of forces, leading to demobilization or encampment, and the creation of a cease-fire commission (including a Nigerian member) with detailed instructions for guaranteeing implementation of the accord.

(5) Referendum on self-determination:

(a) The SPLM proposed that each state hold a referendum during the interim period to choose between confederation and independence.

(b) The government insisted that a referendum not allow the south to secede and not include marginalized peoples living in the north. It could decide only on the preferred form of union.

(c) Nigeria wanted the SPLM to drop its demand for a referendum, since it strongly opposed secession. The national constitutional conference could substitute for that referendum.

The formal negotiations ended after days of bitter mutual recriminations. Toward the end, Khartoum tried to get the SPLM to meet separately in the Sheraton Hotel to reach an agreement without the Nigerians present.[21] Since the talks had broken down, the SPLM agreed to hear the government's position. In that "committee of elders" meeting, Khartoum tried to persuade the SPLM to exclude the northern NDA from politics and relinquish its goal of secession, in return for which the SPLM would control the several southern state governments under the current federal formula. Shari'a would remain intact, the north-south borders would not change, and multipartyism would not be restored. The SPLM delegation unanimously rejected that proposal and ended the off-the-record talks.

When even informal discussions failed, Nigeria sent the conference chair to Khartoum to meet with Bashir, and invited Garang to Abuja. The Nigerian emissary did not manage to meet with Bashir, since the president traveled outside Khartoum to officiate at a PDF ceremony where he announced that the government would not make any concessions at Abuja on shari'a. Al-Hajj added that the Nigerian government had exceeded its mandate as a mediator by pressuring Khartoum to make concessions on shari'a and on security measures. He argued that the real problem lay with the degeneration of the situation into tribal warfare and power struggles among southern commanders. At the time that Garang arrived in Abuja on 17 May, it was apparent that the government was principally responsible for the deadlock.

The Nigerian government then offered a last-ditch proposal to establish safe havens and corridors for relief in the south, leading to the appointment of mutually acceptable civilian administrations as well as a joint military commission. Babangida was concerned that the SPLA was being defeated militarily, and wanted to find an honorable way out. Neither the government nor the SPLM supported that proposal, since the former was preparing another offensive and the latter did not want to freeze the situation at such an unfavorable moment.

In the end, Nigeria issued a press statement as a substitute for a final communiqué. This enumerated the areas of disagreement that were responsible for the failure of the talks. Although the statement described the adjournment as a consultative recess until 19 June, no one had illusions about a return to Abuja. The negotiations illustrated the pitfalls of negotiating in a polarized political context, in which talks heightened mistrust rather than bridged differences. Khartoum quickly broke the cease-fire and launched a large-scale offensive on 24 June 1993. Nigeria, preoccupied with its election campaign, hinted that the circle of mediators should be widened to include Kenya and Uganda, which had immediate interests in the warfare escalating on their borders.

THE IGADD INITIATIVE

The failure at Abuja persuaded African governments active in the Horn of Africa's Intergovernmental Authority on Drought and Desertification (IGADD) to establish on 7 September 1993 a Standing Committee on Peace in Sudan, charged with helping negotiate an end to the civil war.[22] As neighbors, the governments were concerned about the destabilizing impact of the intra-Sudanese conflict. The committee, chaired by Kenyan President Daniel arap Moi, gained Khartoum's approval for its mediation. Presumably the government assumed that Ethiopia and Eritrea were sympathetic since Sudan had assisted them to overthrow Mengistu. The government also contrasted IGADD to the United States, which had placed Khartoum on the list of countries that support terrorism, passed resolutions criticizing the government's human rights violations, and supported reconciliation between Garang and Machar on the basis of self-determination.[23]

During the fall of 1993, IGADD met separately with Bashir, Garang, and Machar, and then set the agenda in January 1994 during separate meetings with delegations from SPLM-Mainstream, SPLM-United, and the government. On 6 January 1994, Garang and Machar agreed on a three-point agenda comprising a cease-fire to facilitate the delivery of relief, that would be observed by neutral monitors; the right of self-determination for the marginalized peoples (southern, Nuba, Ingessana) through a referendum; and the implementation of a comprehensive interim period.[24] Bashir rejected Moi's invitation to come to Nairobi in January and instead sent instead two low-level officials, who agreed to a cease-fire throughout IGADD's mediation. Bashir promptly repudiated their pledge and rejected the draft agenda, stressing that the war would end by military victory, not negotiations.[25] He hoped to complete the occupation of border areas before negotiations could start and, therefore, insisted on postponing the talks, using the excuse that the government could not send a delegation during Ramadan.

The First Meeting: 17-23 March 1994

At the first meeting, held in the Kenyan foreign ministry in March 1994, IGADD tried to bring together Bashir, Garang, and Machar.[26] Bashir refused to meet Garang or even be in the same room when they signed the joint press statement launching the talks. He signed the statement in his residence and flew to Khartoum a half hour before the ceremony, leaving the foreign minister to represent him. Bashir had hoped that Garang would not attend, so he could claim there was no southern movement with which to negotiate. Garang, in contrast, welcomed the opportunity to appear on the same platform as African heads of state. He returned to the south the same evening to counter army raids launched from Juba just as Bashir reached home.

IGADD proposed that the agenda cover the interim arrangements and the constitutional principle underlying resolution of the civil war. However, Khartoum's head delegate al-Hajj insisted that they discuss only the interim period, as that was the issue on which Abuja II had ended. He threatened to leave if self-determination were placed on the agenda. SPLM (United) sided with the government despite its agreement with SPLM (Mainstream) to make self-determination the principal issue. Due to this impasse, the first round never discussed the agenda, failed to agree on a cease-fire, and merely formed a subcommittee on relief aid. That subcommittee agreed to open air corridors to seventy-three sites, create five land passages, and immunize children living in the war zone.[27] SPLM's chief delegate Salva Kiir concluded that, lacking substantive discussions, there was no basis for future talks. But the government achieved its objective of stalling negotiations while it captured additional land. Bashir reemphasized that military victories made the SPLA irrelevant.[28] He said the delegation would attend the second round for only four days. To signal his intent, the air force bombed the Chukudum airstrip on 16 May, shortly before IGADD's plane flew the SPLM delegation from that site to Nairobi.

The Second Meeting: 17-22 May 1994

The start of the second IGADD meeting was delayed by that bombing. The Kenyan foreign minister opened the session with an appeal to take the African initiative seriously and present position papers that would display restraint and sensitivity to the negotiating partners.[29] Khalifa, heading the government team, presented a position paper that did not mention either self-determination or a referendum. Sudan must remain united, and shari'a and custom must be the two main sources of legislation: "States with predominantly non-Muslim populations, where shari'a laws will not apply, can adopt alternative laws." Nonetheless, the paper argued that all citizens were equal, there was freedom of religious practice, and the constitution would be silent on the issue of an official religion. The interim period must be long enough for the authorities to restore confidence, set up governing and administrative institutions, and undertake rehabilitation and reconstruction. The SPLM plan supported a peaceful resolution of the conflict and the right to self-determination by the south, South Kordofan, and Southern Blue Nile. A two-year interim period, in which there would be two confederal states, would lead to an internationally-supervised referendum.

Since the two sides adhered to the same positions they adopted at Abuja II, the meeting adjourned without substantive discussion of these papers or even of a cease-fire. The IGADD mediators then startled the delegates by handing them their own Declaration of Principles (DOP), which they requested be examined confidentially and discussed at the third round of talks in July.[30]

IGADD's Declaration of Principles

The DOP called for a commitment to "a peaceful and just political solution" to the conflict, in which the terms of an interim arrangement and a cease-fire agreement must be "part of the overall settlement of the conflict." "Maintaining [the] unity of the Sudan must be given priority," provided the social and political system is based on "a secular and democratic state" with legal guarantees of "complete political and social equalities of all peoples in the Sudan," "extensive rights of self-administration . . . to the various peoples," the separation of "state and religion," "appropriate and fair sharing of wealth," the incorporation of human rights principles into the constitution, and independence of the judiciary. "In the absence of agreement on the above principles . . . the respective peoples will have the option to determine their future including independence, through a referendum." Specifically, this meant "the right of self-determination of the people of southern Sudan . . . through a referendum."

At Abuja, the Nigerian mediators prioritized the unity of the Sudan and rejected self-determination if that meant secession of the south. In contrast, the IGADD mediators emphasized that unity was conditional on the establishment of a secular state and that, in the absence of such a state, the south had the right to vote for separation. The DOP therefore "enraged" the government, which accused the mediators of bias. Khalifa argued that IGADD governments were beholden to the United States, which he claimed supported the SPLM, and concluded: "we have no option [now] except to continue the war to its finality."[31] In contrast, SPLM-Mainstream found the DOP "even-handed" and a "pleasant surprise."[32] Its newly elected National Liberation Council endorsed the DOP fully as a basis for negotiations.

The Third Meeting: 18-29 July 1994

President Moi opened the third round of meetings on 18 July with a call for a cease-fire and implementation of the agreement to distribute relief supplies.[33] He solicited responses to the DOP, which the IGADD secretariat would review for common principles. The government delegation rejected the DOP completely, on the grounds that mediators should not state their preferred outcome and that the issues of religion and state, secularism, self-determination, and secession were outside IGADD's scope. Khalifa delayed until 22 July presenting a written statement and then indicated the government would only discuss an interim period, based on its known federal formula and focussing on how to share power and wealth within the south. In contrast, the SPLM-Mainstream delegation was joined by SPLM-United (by then called SSIM) in endorsing the DOP and expressing full confidence in the IGADD mediators. They supported the Sudan's unity only in the context of a secular constitution and insisted that a referendum be held at the end of the interim period that would uphold the principle of self-determination. They expressed regret at the lengthy adjournments between IGADD meetings and criticized the lack of a cease-fire.

Once again, views seemed irreconcilable on self-determination and secularism. Government negotiators declared that "self-determination" implied, falsely, that the north was engaged in colonial rule over the south. Khalifa again stated frankly that he would not sanction dismembering the Sudan: "if you want to separate the south from the north it will be done through the barrel of a gun. We will fight for it to the last man."[34] Nonetheless, for the first time, the government spelled out its concept of a referendum, which involved a three-phased process, without any international monitors. The first referendum, at the end of an interim period based on the current federal system, would accept or reject federalism. If the voters rejected federalism, then a second referendum would select among alternative forms of union. A third referendum would include secession as one of the options. On paper, this offered the prospect of independence for the south. In practice, that was unlikely since the government proposed that all the Sudanese vote, not just those residing in the south.

A last-ditch negotiating session on 27 July focussed on self-determination and the transitional period, and established a tripartite committee to specify the points of (dis)agreement. The next day IGADD issued a six-point "non-paper" on self-determination, just before adjourning the talks for two months.[35] IGADD asserted the "inalienable right of the people of South Sudan to freely determine their destiny" by means of "an internationally supervised referendum by the end of the interim period," in which they "shall freely choose from all options including independence." The "interim arrangements shall be within the framework of a united Sudan." The SPLM welcomed the IGADD "non-paper," adding that the right of self-determination should also apply to the Nuba Mountains and Ingessana Hills. The government rejected the words "inalienable" and "self-determination." At most, the people of the south would "freely determine their future status" *within* the Sudan through an internationally supervised referendum.

Even accepting this limited version of self-determination caused Khartoum to rebuke the two senior delegates, Khalifa and al-Hajj, and to accuse them of conniving with fellow Africans to undermine the Arab-Islamic character of Sudan.[36] They were replaced by NIF's Ghazi Salah al-Din Atabani and Naf'i Ali Naf'i.

The parties did agree to a cease-fire, starting at midnight 23 July. Garang at first balked, since there were no international monitors. He feared the army would continue its attacks and would reinforce garrisons, as it had during previous cease-fires.[37]

The Fourth Meeting: 5-7 September 1994

The fourth and final meeting opened on 5 September 1994. By then the government was actively seeking to bypass IGADD and to avoid further discussion of its DOP.[38] Negotiators Salah al-Din and Naf'i criticized IGADD for issuing that DOP and again refused to discuss self-determination and secularism. In his opening speech on 7 September, Salah al-Din stressed that "the problem in the southern Sudan . . . was bred and nurtured by the British colonialists . . . [without any] relation to the question of implementation of Sharia as a source of legislation." He blamed IGADD for instigating the SPLM to raise the issue of self-determination, which was a concept that lacked any legal or moral basis.[39] Khartoum would establish a permanent cease-fire once unity was ensured by force. Shari'a was "irreplaceable" and the partial exemption for non-Muslims in the south was a voluntary concession, not a right. In fact, the government's duty was to Islamize all of Africa, since that task had been interrupted by European colonialism.

The chair abruptly ended the session after that speech, even before SPLM made its opening statement. The SPLM wrote to Moi afterwards that "the Sudanese government delegation unceremoniously brought the talks to a dead end." Moreover, "reneging" on "elements of self-determination" already agreed upon in July proved "Khartoum's unreliability as a negotiating partner and its lack of commitment to negotiate . . . in good faith."[40]

Even though the talks deadlocked, the Kenyan president said he would continue to chair the IGADD committee and he scheduled an IGADD summit meeting for 19 September. That move prompted Khartoum to send Turabi to meet Moi on 17 September. Bashir and Garang also met separately with Moi, at his request, on 18 September. Turabi rejected any compromise on shari'a and self-determination and called the government's version of federation sufficient, especially as the SPLA was defeated militarily. Bashir also refused to alter the government's positions on Islamic law and self-determination. He wanted Moi to mediate alone and to broker a bilateral deal with Garang.

Bashir attended the IGADD summit, whose summation reaffirmed that the DOP provided "a valid basis for the talks" even though the two sides "had reached a deadlock on the vital issues of separation of state and religion and . . . self-determination for Southern Sudan."[41] Bashir concluded that IGADD had reached a dead end, and he resisted further efforts by Moi to resume negotiations.[42] Instead, he intensified his search for alternative mediation mechanisms in Africa, Europe, and the United States in an effort to maintain the image of a peacemaker while completing military operations on the ground and resettling southerners in "peace villages." He also fostered tension on the border with Eritrea, which caused a break in diplomatic relations and enabled him to claim that the mediators were biased.

In contrast, the SPLM hoped IGADD would mobilize additional governments and international organizations behind the DOP, which Moi attempted by extensive travels through Europe and Africa in December 1994. The IGADD committee called on 4 January 1995 for the UN secretary general to station an observer in Nairobi.[43] IGADD mobilized western governments through the Friends of IGADD, which included Australia, Britain, Canada, Italy, Norway, and the United States. IGADD wanted these countries to provide political support and material resources for their mediation effort. More importantly, IGADD wanted them not to assume a role as rival mediators.

CARTER'S CALL FOR A CEASE-FIRE

Meanwhile, Bashir welcomed the cease-fire that Jimmy Carter proposed in March 1995 as part of his Africa-wide campaign against guinea worm and river blindness. His proposed health program in the southern Sudan would also immunize children against polio.[44] Although Garang initially welcomed this program, the government especially benefited by cooperating with a high-profile international humanitarian mission that bypassed IGADD and enabled it to use the two-month cease-fire to prepare a final offensive against the SPLA. Carter facilitated the government's aims by agreeing to exclude international monitors and to let troops continue administrative movements during the cease-fire period.

The armed forces frequently violated the cease-fire, which began on 28 March 1995, and even bombed inside Uganda, thereby prompting Museveni to break diplomatic relations on 23 April. Nonetheless, Carter lauded Khartoum for upholding freedom of religion after he attended church services in government-controlled Juba. He also suggested that IGADD stop discussing self-determination and secularism, since the government would never accept those principles. He called on the SPLA to release seventy-two recently captured soldiers, without requesting a general exchange of POWs. Carter's naive diplomacy complicated the situation just as the Friends of IGADD met in the Hague on 5 April 1995 to strategize on ways to renew IGADD's efforts and contain the regime, which those governments increasingly feared due to its Islamizing zeal and actions to subvert their rule.[45] Carter's cease-fire lasted until 28 July, when the government renewed its military offensive and captured an outpost on the Uganda-Zaire border. When it made incursions into Uganda on 27 August, Museveni supported SPLA's counteroffensive in September.[46] Meanwhile, Carter's immunization program was barely under way. He expressed shock at the government offensive, not comprehending that his efforts had facilitated those military operations rather than enhanced the prospects for a negotiated peace.

What began as an effort by the governments of Kenya, Uganda, Ethiopia, and Eritrea to end the civil war shifted to all-out confrontation with Khartoum when the Sudan rejected the IGADD DOP and continued to destabilize neighboring regimes. Only Kenyan President Moi maintained the effort to mediate.

By 1997 Khartoum faced hostilities on its borders with Eritrea, Ethiopia, and Uganda.

The polarized political context doomed negotiations. With neither side willing to compromise its core beliefs, no solution was possible. The government would not give up its Islamist essence or allow the south to secede. SPLM-Mainstream maintained its preference for a united, secular Sudan, adhering to the fallback position that called for self-determination. Unless one side made an about-face or capitulated, negotiations could not achieve results.

Foreign mediation played a marginal role. Efforts by the OAU and the United States remained peripheral, in part because mediators lacked either credibility or clout with both sides. In the absence of internal political will, foreign mediation was at best irrelevant and at worst damaging, by reinforcing polarity or assisting one party. Carter's conference in Nairobi in December 1989, for example, made each side acutely aware of their differences and led them to redouble their efforts to defeat each other militarily. Carter's cease-fire initiative in 1995 was also damaging since it was not linked to effective negotiations and allowed one side in the conflict to strengthen its military position. The Abuja and IGADD initiatives were crucial in articulating political differences and outlining possible structural resolutions. But the demise of the Nigerian regime made follow-up to Abuja impossible, and the IGADD mediators' views were distinctly more favorable to the SPLM than to Khartoum. Moreover, they lacked mechanisms for carrying out their proposed solutions.

The stark differences evident in the negotiations underlined the two sides' divergent perspectives on national identity. So long as the regime adhered to a strict Islamist conception of the Sudan, there could be no accord with the SPLM. The SPLM's dream of a transformed multiethnic political system remained utopian. The government sought to impose its vision by force. The SPLM could only try to counteract that force by strengthening its alliance with the NDA. The difficulty of overcoming the political differences between the NDA and SPLM are examined in the next chapter. By 1995-1996 those differences had been largely overcome and the NDA emerged as a viable opposition force. Civil upheaval and military force, rather than negotiations, were the likely means by which the national identity crisis would be resolved.

11

The Emerging Consensus within the Opposition Movement

By 1993 THE drive to unseat the regime approached a dead end. The military struggle in the south was in disarray, with secessionists forming paradoxical alliances with the government that enabled the army to pin down the SPLA on the borders with Uganda and Kenya. Negotiations between the regime and the SPLM sponsored by Nigeria and IGADD underscored their diametrically opposed visions of the Sudanese nation. And the government felt no need to accommodate the SPLM politically since the SPLA could not mount a serious military challenge. Meanwhile, the government systematically dislocated Fur and Nuba, uprooted African displaced persons from Khartoum, and fended off sporadic protests in northern towns. NIF's political and security apparati had firm control, stressed by the shift from military to overtly Islamist civilian rule in October 1993 and the 1996 elections that elevated Turabi to speaker of the national assembly.

As the lines of cleavage sharpened and the military situation deteriorated, the opposition's efforts to overthrow the regime became more urgent. Through laborious and wrenching processes of self-criticism and political dialogue, the NDA and SPLM began to coordinate and even reached a consensus on the country's political identity. Since mutual distrust remained strong, they sought to commit each other to specific constitutional principles. The SPLM feared that the major northern political groups within the NDA still wanted to create an Islamic-Arab state which would marginalize Africans and therefore pressed those politicians to adhere to egalitarian norms and support ethnic plurality. Failing that, they must accept the south's right to self-determination and independence. Northern members of the NDA, fearing that the south would secede, made concessions on the issue of religion in political life. Thus, the issues of religion-and-state and self-determination became strongly linked in the NDA-SPLM debate, just as they were linked in government negotiations with the SPLM and were stressed in IGADD's DOP.

SPLM-NDA RELATIONS

SPLM signed an accord with the NDA on 4 March 1990 to unite their efforts to overthrow the regime, restore democracy, and convene the constitutional conference. SPLM and Umma had already pledged on 22 February 1990 "to tirelessly work together with their fellow brothers in the NDA to accelerate the removal of the military dictatorship of the Muslim Brothers [NIF] in Khartoum, the holding of a constitutional conference, and the establishment of a democratic government with the active participation of all members of the NDA."[1] Umma then broadcast appeals on Radio SPLA for Arab militias in Dar Fur and Kordofan to "halt hostilities against the SPLA" and fight against the government instead.[2] The SPLM also let Umma use its clandestine radio station to broadcast political statements, including commemorations for the officers executed after the alleged coup attempt in 1990. Soon after, SPLM endorsed the formation of the exile Legitimate Command and broadcast its declarations on the SPLA radio.

Nonetheless, key issues remained unresolved. Neither the SPLM-Umma communiqué nor the resolutions of the first NDA summit, held in February/ March 1991 in Addis Ababa, specified the content of the future constitution. Leaders of DUP and Umma wanted to delay that decision until the junta was overthrown. They even rejected a proposal to simply support the principles of international human rights conventions.[3] That disturbed the SPLM and northern secularists, who feared that DUP and Umma would revert to past behavior once they regained power.

Northern members of the NDA were, in turn, disconcerted by the schism in the SPLA in 1991 and the Nasir officers' call for secession. NDA condemned that "reactionary, retrograde step" as "a rude and treacherous shock to the aspirations of all Sudanese for the restoration of democracy, peace, and national reconciliation in a united Sudan."[4] NDA members were wary of SPLM-Torit's apparent retreat from unambiguous support for Sudan's territorial unity. Garang's movement suggested that even though "the SPLM/SPLA . . . will actively . . . strengthen the NDA . . . [to] bring about peace within the context of a united secular democratic Sudan," "confederation, association of sovereign states, or self-determination" were legitimate alternatives.[5] Secular political forces in the north particularly feared that territorial partition would fortify NIF's claim that Sudan was a homogeneous Muslim country and would end the only military pressure on the regime, which came from the south. This issue therefore "triggered some combustible issues," serving as a "wake-up call" to signal northern politicians that they faced a stark choice: unity must be based on a nonreligious constitution.[6] A religion-based system would guarantee separation.

Nonetheless, an urgent NDA meeting in Cairo in September 1991 failed to support a secular constitution, since leaders of DUP and Umma feared a backlash from their religious supporters if they agreed to annul Islamic public law.[7] That failure damaged Garang's effort to convince other southerners that unity was preferable to secession and reinforced southern fears that sectarian parties were incapable of undoing the shari'a-based constitutional system.

Similarly, the next NDA meeting in London in January 1992 completed a 260-article constitution, but failed to agree on articles 8 and 9, which dealt with the sources of legislation.[8] At DUP's insistence, and with Umma's tacit support, the summit decided to delay debate on those two articles until the NDA could assume power and hold the constitutional conference. That again deepened southern fears and accelerated SPLM's decision to endorse self-determination in negotiations with the government at Abuja in July 1992. Meeting simultaneously in Cairo, the NDA vigorously opposed secession but still did not resolve the constitutional issue beyond stating that the Sudan should not be a religious-based state.[9] Another urgent NDA meeting in Cairo on 28 October 1992, however, issued a new collective statement that appeared to represent a breakthrough. That statement stressed the dangers posed by NIF's theocratic state and by its transformation of the civil war into a jihad, and concluded:[10]

> The NDA declares ... its full commitment to the establishment of ... a Democratic Sudan based on recognition of cultural and religious multiplicity, respect for religious beliefs, equality between different faiths and beliefs; a Sudan based on the rule of law, independence of the judiciary, and respect for human rights, where no legislation or enactment inconsistent with these principles can be applied; a Sudan where religion cannot be abused for political expediency; religion is a divine concept between God and the individual, the State is for all citizens; a Sudan which does not accept a theocratic state. ...

The manifesto was intended to boost Garang's standing by proving that northern political forces endorsed the separation of religion and state. However, its wording also rebuffed al-Sadiq al-Mahdi, who had written the RCC in August 1992 proposing that it join other political forces in a transitional government that would restore democracy—a gesture that left ambiguous the future role of religion in politics. As a result, Umma representatives refused to sign the new NDA manifesto, and DUP also expressed reservations. Instead of reinforcing the NDA, the declaration nearly sundered the coalition. The crisis underlined the urgency of finding a formula to satisfy both the secularists and the political parties that were based on religious movements.

THE NAIROBI DECLARATION (APRIL 1993)

NDA leaders struggled to find such a formula. Just before the SPLM resumed negotiations with the government in Abuja, Umma joined the other parties for intensive meetings in Nairobi. Garang addressed the NDA conference for the first time, reiterating his vision of a united, democratic, and secular Sudan but warning that, when one group dominates others, those peoples cannot be blamed for seceding. On 17 April 1993 the conferees unanimously upheld the principles of equal rights and nondiscrimination:[11]

(1) International and regional human rights instruments and covenants shall be an integral part of the laws of Sudan and any law contrary thereto shall be considered null and void and unconstitutional.

(2) Laws shall guarantee full equality of citizens on the basis of citizenship, respect for religious beliefs and traditions, and without discrimination on grounds of religion, race, gender, or culture. Any law contrary to the foregoing stipulation shall be null and void and unconstitutional.

That Nairobi Declaration helped to reinvigorate the NDA. Umma and DUP signalled their renewed support for the effort to achieve a consensus by issuing resolutions on the issue of religion and state, from which passages were incorporated into the declaration. This occurred in the context of deepening restrictions against their own religious movements inside Sudan. Moreover, by referring to international conventions without spelling out their content, the wording was more palatable than the blunt October 1992 manifesto. Garang hailed the declaration as a "victory for a unified Sudan" that confirmed that the "pious Sudanese people" did not want to impose their beliefs on others.

The Nairobi declaration did not deal with the related question of self-determination, although Garang had alluded to that issue in his speech at the NDA conference. Therefore, many northern politicians reacted with dismay to the joint resolution of Garang and Machar endorsing self-determination, issued in October 1993. The renewed crisis again threatened to rip apart the NDA.[12] Politicians from DUP, the Sudanese Communist Party (SCP), the Legimate Command, and Nuba Mountains strongly opposed self-determination, which they considered tantamount to secession. Nuba, in particular, feared their vulnerability inside the north if the south became independent. DUP and SPLA's Nuba commander Yusif Kuwa even issued a joint statement on 12 July 1994 that affirmed the primacy of unity in the context of democracy, the equality of all citizens, ethnic and religious diversity, and autonomy for all regions.[13] They did allow an escape clause, however:

In the event that agreements reached at the National Constitutional Conference are broken by one of the parties, the other party is free to exercise its right for self-determination.

HARASSMENT OF POLITICIANS

Meanwhile, the government intensified its surveillance of opposition politicians in Khartoum. Bashir had hoped Umma and DUP would join the civilian government formed in October 1993. Instead they stiffened their opposition once NIF was clearly in charge. When Turabi visited his brother-in-law in January 1994, for example, al-Mahdi did not repeat his earlier call for including the present government in a transitional government. Instead, he warned Turabi that NIF would be held accountable for the harm done to the country. Al-Mahdi declared that dissolving the RCC was "plastic surgery" to "deceive and camouflage" reality:[14]

> The junta promised to release the people from its hardships, end the civil war, and improve international relations. But the economy is ruined, peace in the south is further away than ever, and for the first time Sudan has been isolated by the international community. . . . I do not believe that fundamentalism can put down roots in Sudanese society, where traditionally Muslims have been very tolerant of Christians and Jews.

At that time, security agents interrogated the former prime minister for eight hours after he met with the U.S. ambassador. In December 1993 they confiscated his car, arrested his driver and three Umma leaders, and interrogated his wife Sara al-Fadhil al-Mahdi, after they found in the car a copy of an Umma party study on the issue of self-determination.[15] Security officials frequently questioned other close relatives and activists. Nonetheless, at the end of Ramadan, al-Mahdi led the prayers before an estimated 200,000 adherents and then walked the five miles to his home, surrounded by the immense crowd. Security forces did not dare interfere, but they detained him overnight in April after his sermon on Id al-Fitr and arrested dozens of Ansar demonstrators after Friday prayers on 9 April 1994. Nonetheless, al-Mahdi repeated his call for democratic elections in his sermon for Id al-Adha in May.

The standoff culminated in the arrest of two senior Umma executives—Dr. Hamad Bagadi and Brigadier (Retired) Abd al-Rahman Farah—in May 1994 for allegedly plotting with the Egyptian embassy to assassinate senior NIF leaders and sabotage installations.[16] Bagadi and Farah required medical treatment in the Omdurman military hospital after being tortured. The government broadcast their confessions on national television on 20 June, although they were so weak that they mumbled unintelligibly. The confessions provided the excuse to hold al-Mahdi incommunicado in a ghost house in Khartoum. He and his aides were not released until July, after al-Mahdi publicly condemned assassinations and bombings and stated that his aides might have been lured by a double agent. Although al-Mahdi damaged his credibility by criticizing two long-term aides, his statement demonstrated the fine line he had to tread. If he endorsed violence to overthrow the regime, he could be executed for treason. He had to distance himself from plots hatched by NDA exiles.

The government also harassed the most senior leader of the DUP still in Sudan, Sid Ahmad Hussain, deputy secretary general and a key architect of the DUP-SPLM accord. In 1992 he was tried and acquitted for plotting with the SPLM to overthrow the regime. In July 1993 he was held in a ghost house after participating in a student-organized symposium called Peace in Sudan. On 17 November 1993 he was arrested after he denounced government policies toward the south at a commemoration of the fifth anniversary of the DUP-SPLM accord.[17] Although released on 20 February 1994, he was rearrested a month later. Despite this ongoing intimidation and the confiscation of Khatmiyya properties, thousands of supporters and diplomats attended on 14 May 1994 a commemoration for the late Ali al-Mirghani, the Khatmiyya spiritual leader who had died in 1968.[18]

The government jailed prominent trade unionists and leaders of the Communist Party in the spring of 1994, including the poet Mahjub Sharif and the communist trade union activist Dr. Magdi Mohammedani.[19] As unions pressed the government to pay long-overdue salaries, thirty-six trade union leaders were arrested on 24 April 1994 alone.

Meanwhile, large-scale student demonstrations in al-Ubayyid in February 1994 protested the imposition of a school tax, escalating prices for basic commodities and medical services, the shortage of affordable water, and the scarcity of fuel, which had halted all public transportation and electricity.[20] Protests spread to the main market and residents burned the Islamic cultural center, NIF headquarters, and a *khalwa* (Quranic school). They torched Islamic banks in a nearby town. Army and security forces confronted the students and shut down the market. NIF's Guardians of the Revolution killed five students, and sixty students were detained. Acute shortages of bread, petrol, and other basic necessities sparked further clashes on 19 April 1994. Protesters burned Islamic banks and gasoline stations in Wad Medani and railway maintenance workshops in Atbara, and also occupied the market and main street in Omdurman for two hours before the police and armed forces dispersed them. Three people died in Wad Medani, where the government closed the university and dismissed twenty-nine students. Although the government shrugged off the violence as the acts of *shamasa* (ruffians),[21] the principal participants were workers, civil servants, and students. However, the uncoordinated demonstrations could not lead to a coherent civil uprising. Opposition remained sporadic and ineffective.

SPLM-UMMA ACCORD AT CHUKUDUM

The disagreement within the NDA over self-determination began to be resolved in 1994. Garang, in his first response to the uproar, argued that the right of self-determination was a basic component of democracy and human rights—principles that the NDA upheld.[22] Failure to endorse the right of self-determination would place the NDA on the same plane as the government. He hoped the SPLM and the NDA could soon discuss this issue, reminding the NDA that he had already warned them that the failure to establish a mutually acceptable political system would impel the south to demand independence.

Surprisingly, Umma concurred with Garang's articulation of this principle of conditional unity, although its secretary general Umar Nur al-Da'im expressed concern that the Garang-Machar declaration had been issued before the NDA formulated its own views on self-determination. After a lengthy internal debate, Umma resolved in February 1994 that the south had the right to conduct a referendum on its future and concluded forthrightly: "We accept the future which the peoples of the South freely decide for themselves."[23] Umma hoped the south would opt to remain within the Sudan if the constitutional conference were to institute a democratic government based on territorial decentralization. Umma recognized that a vote for secession would be the outcome not only of current policies, which overwhelmingly alienated African Sudanese, but also of its own prior view that "Sudanese self-consciousness . . . was Islamic-Arabic" and its failure to recognize the grievances of the "African Sudanese ethnic groups."

This frank statement paved the way for the Chukudum Accord of 12 December 1994, which Umma leaders Nur al-Da'im and Mubarak al-Fadhil al-Mahdi signed at the SPLM headquarters in Equatoria. Nur al-Da'im hailed the powerful symbolism of northern politicians entering the south to remove the psychological barriers between the two peoples and strengthen mutual confidence.[24] The trip also entailed risks, since the air force bombed nearby on the third day of the meeting. The Chukudum Accord conceded that unity could not be based on force but must arise from free choice. It endorsed the NDA's Nairobi Declaration of April 1993 and the IGADD DOP, which upheld territorial unity in the context of a secular and democratic state. The accord called for pluralist democracy based on a federation or confederation, and recognized the south's right to hold a referendum on self-determination during the transitional period. The referendum could be held within two years, but would definitely take place within four years. Moreover, the north would not force the south to remain within the Sudan. The declaration acknowledged that whereas SPLM argued that the right of self-determination applied to the peoples of Abyei, Nuba Mountains, and Ingessana Hills, Umma opposed that potential piece-by-piece dismemberment of the country. Since those peoples were not represented at Chukudum, the signers agreed to consult them on this issue.

Al-Sadiq al-Mahdi explicitly endorsed the Chukudum Accord and the south's right to conduct a referendum based on the principle of self-determination in his public sermon at the end of Ramadan.[25] He emphasized that if southerners vote for independence, northerners should not maintain unity by force. This provided the essential imprimateur by the head of the party and the former prime minister. Overall, al-Mahdi became increasingly outspoken in his calls for civil resistance to restore democracy and his declarations that shari'a must not be used to coerce people and bolster dictatorship.[26]

The government cracked down again, arresting al-Mahdi and fourteen Umma leaders on 16 May 1995. Before he went to Kober prison, al-Mahdi issued a press statement intended to express his real views in the event that he should be tortured into making a contrary statement. He reaffirmed his opposition to the government and held it accountable for any hostile actions against himself or the Ansar movement. Al-Mahdi's manifesto was followed by an ultimatum on 20 May 1995, which nine Ansar leaders handed to Bashir at the presidential palace, demanding their leader's release and the restoration of Ansar property. They noted that al-Mahdi had calmed the Ansar, persuading them not to confront the regime violently. The government would be responsible should any harm come to their leader. This ultimatum may have deterred the government from torturing al-Mahdi or accusing him of treason. Nonetheless, he was held incommunicado for a full three months.

THE ASMARA DECLARATION (DECEMBER 1994)

The government was increasingly nervous since the Chukudum Accord had been followed by the NDA's Asmara Declaration of 27 December 1994 and the NDA convention in June 1995, whose militant resolutions the government claimed al-Mahdi helped to prepare. The Asmara Declaration emphasized that the future political system must be grounded in the reality of the multiracial, multiethnic, and multicultural Sudanese society.[27] The declaration endorsed the "non-use of religion in politics" but avoided the word "secular" in deference to Umma and DUP. If those principles were violated, the south would have the right to seek independence by voting in the referendum at the end of the transitional period. The declaration was signed by Garang, Umma's Nur al-Da'im, DUP's Mirghani, and Brigadier Abd al-Aziz Khalid Uthman, head of the new Sudanese Allied Forces (SAF). SAF sought to represent secular northern politicians and intellectuals previously associated with the national alliance of unions as well as military officers who were impatient with the ineffective Legitimate Command. DUP was the most hesitant to sign, but Mirghani recognized that the only way to convince southerners to cooperate was to open the safety valve of a referendum on self-determination.

Nonetheless, the call for the "non-use of religion in politics" and endorsement of self-determination caused tensions inside DUP and Umma. An unsigned critique on 28 January 1995 was apparently authored by DUP Secretary General Sharif Zain al-Abdin al-Hindi and Deputy Secretary General Hussain, who was undergoing medical treatment in London. They wanted unconditional unity, and also criticized al-Mirghani's autocratic management of the party.[28] Mirghani undermined those dissidents when he convened in Cairo on 4 March 1995 the DUP's first party congress since 1967, at which he deflected criticism by emphasizing that territorial unity remained the primary value. Dissent was less effective within Umma. Former assembly speaker Muhammad Ibrahim Khalil, a long-term Ansar living in Washington, D.C., who rejected secularism and criticized self-determination, was joined by Nasr al-Din al-Hadi al-Mahdi, cousin and rival of al-Sadiq al-Mahdi, in a short-lived attempt to form an alternative party and gain Saudi support for an Islamic constitution.[29]

NDA CONFERENCE IN ASMARA

The Chukudum and Asmara principles were endorsed by the conference of all the parties and unions associated with the NDA, held in Asmara from 17 to 23 June 1995.[30] The participants agreed that the political system must be based on democracy and religious pluralism. While again avoiding the word "secular," resolutions upheld the international human rights conventions, called for the abolition of Islamic public law, and prohibited forming political parties on religious bases. The conference called for a confederation in which most powers would devolve on the two regions. The central government would coordinate defense and foreign policies, but the south would maintain its own standing army, at least during the interim period. The south would conduct a referendum at the end of the four-year transitional period. This proposed confederation strikingly resembled the model that Garang had outlined to the NDA in Nairobi in April 1993 and that SPLM had tabled at the Abuja negotiations. Later, NDA secretary general Mubarak al-Fadhil al-Mahdi stressed that self-determination was invoked to end forty years of southern suspicion of the north. If the central government failed to abide by the agreed-upon program, then the south could exercise the right to secede.[31]

The status of the Ngok Dinka of Abyei (South Kordofan), the Ingessana in Southern Blue Nile, and the Nuba in South Kordofan remained contentious.[32] The conferees tried to maneuver around the problem by upholding the principle of self-determination as a basic right of all the peoples in the Sudan. But exercising that right would be tightly circumscribed. The SPLM and the South Kordofan regional government would jointly administer Abyei and the Nuba Mountains during the interim period. Similarly, the SPLM and the Southern Blue Nile regional government would jointly administer the Ingessana Hills. A referendum would then ask the Dinka of Abyei whether they wanted to remain in South Kordofan or join Bahr al-Ghazal. In the Nuba Mountains and Ingessana Hills an initial referendum would ask if they wanted the right to self-determination. Only if they voted in favor would they hold a referendum on the form of self-determination. This complex approach took into account the prevalent northern Arab view that only southerners (including the Abyei Dinka) had the right to secede. Nuba activists, in particular, remained dissatisfied with the Asmara formula, which they feared would undermine their rights.

Secret annexes to the Asmara resolutions endorsed a strategy to topple the regime that would combine guerrilla warfare in the north and south with a civilian uprising in the major northern towns. By then the Legitimate Command was disintegrating, partly because General Fathi Ahmad Ali faced criticism from other officers for failing to undertake military actions. Brigadier Khalid's Sudanese Allied Forces (SAF) stressed the need for military operations in the north in coordination with the SPLA in the south. In 1995 SAF opened training camps in Eritrea, joined by officers cashiered after the coup. The Beja Congress also formed an armed force in eastern Sudan, in response to the targeting of their distinct ethnicity by NIF's narrow Islamization program. The Beja Congress criticized the government for forcing Beja youths into the PDF so as to fight fellow Africans in the south, stamping out their language, suppressing sufi orders, and depriving the region of social services, health care, and basic education.[33] The Beja Congress and SAF trained in camps in Eritrea with the intent of striking the sensitive highway and railway between Port Sudan and Khartoum and destabilizing the grain-growing Kassala-Gedaref area. The Eritrean government insisted that the NDA admit the Beja Congress and SAF, even though DUP wanted to represent Beja (since a third of the Beja were adherents of the Khatmiyya order) and the LC opposed bringing in an alternative group of army officers. The LC crumbled further when its second-in-command, General al-Hadi Bushra, returned to Khartoum on 10 August 1995 because he opposed NDA's endorsing self-determination and separating religion and state.[34] Although the government trumpeted his defection and appointed him minister of roads and communications in April 1996, the LC claimed to welcome his departure, since his negativism and divisiveness may have meant that he was already an agent provocateur.

CIVIL DISOBEDIENCE

The Asmara resolutions positioned the NDA to provide a credible political alternative to the regime and to begin to organize a serious military strategy for the north. The NDA planned a civilian uprising for October 1995, the thirty-first anniversary of the overthrow of Abbud. Al-Sadiq al-Mahdi, speaking at the Ansar mosque in Omdurman shortly after his release on 26 August 1995, endorsed the Asmara resolutions, equal rights for all citizens, and the south's right to self-determination. He emphasized that Sudanese must use peaceful means to change the government. Given his vulnerability, he could not endorse publicly the use of force.[35]

The plan for an October uprising risked being exposed when on 2 September 1995 security forces arrested a dozen communists and students who were then accused of plotting against the government. The organizers hastened to start street protests, even though preparations were not yet in place. On 9 September, when students at Khartoum University denounced the detentions, they were attacked by knife-wielding NIF students. Fifteen students were injured, including one whom a NIF cadre stabbed in the back while he addressed a rally. Protests gained intensity during the next week and continued sporadically until the end of September, joined by students at other universities as well as the general public, angered at a sudden 50 percent increase in the price of bread.[36] Demonstrators chanted "No to peddlers of religion" and "The people are hungry." They smashed the windows of banks and cars, burned the headquarters of the NIF student-aid fund, and tore down Islamist posters. The government mobilized members of NIF mass organizations—*Shabab al-Watan* (Youth of the Homeland or Patriotic Youth) and *Hai'at al-Difa'a an al-Aghida wa al-Watan* (Organization for the Defense of the Faith and the Homeland)—to disperse demonstrators with teargas and live ammunition and to man roadblocks and search cars. NIF security forces closed the bridges from Khartoum to Omdurman and Khartoum North, and blocked traffic from entering or leaving the city, which sealed off the capital from the outside. Nonetheless, protests spread to Wad Madani, Port Sudan, Atbara, and smaller towns.

The government blamed left-wing students and foreign infiltrators for the demonstrations, and even arrested forty Ethiopian and Eritrean refugees on charges of "conspiracy and sabotage."[37] The foreign minister downplayed the significance by arguing that only 3,000 of the country's 750,000 university students joined the riots. The interior minister assembled the state governors to reaffirm their adherence to the Islamic federal system. And Bashir, addressing a rally of NIF's Organization for the Defense of the Faith and the Homeland, attacked the opposition for "hiding behind students": they should "face us with their weapons, because we will not relinquish power unless through the barrel of the gun." The overt use of violence would give the government the excuse to mow down protesters.

REJECTION OF ELECTIONS

Despite the risk of arrest, opposition politicians in Khartoum supported the comprehensive political transformation called for in the Asmara declaration and stressed that they would not be co-opted by pseudo-democratic elections. For example, in November 1995 five prominent southern politicians appealed to Bashir to restore democracy and recognize the south's right to self-determination.[38] Led by the respected Abel Alier, a key architect of the Addis Ababa Accord and a judge on the International Court of Justice in the Hague, they argued that the theocratic state excluded non-Muslims and they explicitly endorsed the Asmara Declaration. Alier later warned that "people in the South, Abyei and other aggrieved communities will probably vote for separation, if the unity option is not made more attractive."[39] Although NIF cadres urged Bashir to detain those petitioners, he hesitated, given Alier's international prominence and their strong support within the large southern community in Khartoum. However, Alier's subsequent speech at the private Omdurman Ahlia University led Bashir to warn that he had crossed a "red line," raising the fear that security forces might charge him with treason.

Opposition politicians endorsed the NDA pledge of 16 January 1996 to boycott the presidential and parliamentary elections scheduled for March. Bashir had hoped to persuade al-Mahdi, Mirghani, and Garang[40] to compete with him for the presidency, but they emphasized the lack of "neutrality or fairness" in elections held "under fanatic party control."[41] Under pressure from mediators, al-Mahdi did meet Turabi on 8 February 1996: after his brother-in-law lectured for an hour, al-Mahdi interrupted to ask if his aim was to keep the government in power. When Turabi said yes, al-Mahdi halted the meeting and left. Al-Mahdi said he would discuss only how power should be handed over to the people, not reconciliation with the regime. In his sermon for Id al-Fitr, al-Mahdi explicitly called on the Ansar to boycott the elections.

Bashir and Turabi evidently worked at cross-purposes. If Bashir should broaden the regime's political base by co-opting leaders of Umma or DUP, he could weaken NIF's grip. NIF tried to torpedo that prospect not only by Turabi's tough stance with al-Mahdi but also by breaking up a breakfast meeting at al-Mahdi's home on 7 March 1996, convened to discuss a meeting Bashir had just held with two DUP leaders.[42] When security forces detained Alier and Umma's former attorney general Abd al-Mahmud al-Hajj Salih, al-Mahdi successfully demanded their immediate release. Later that day al-Mahdi led a delegation of fifty Ansar elders to Alier's home, where they slaughtered a bull as a sign of solidarity and esteem. When Alier invited guests to his home on 22 March, 2,000 people showed up. They included al-Mahdi, with his family and a large contingent of Ansar, and the son of the late DUP leader al-Azhari, leading a substantial DUP delegation. NDA leaders were careful to minimize public activities during this period, which coincided with the national assembly and presidential elections. They did not want the government to blame the opposition for the paltry voting turnout. Despite that low profile, security forces arrested nearly 200 politicians and trade unionists in late February, as a preventive measure. Moreover, a colonel in the military academy attempted a coup d'état in March.[43]

CALL FOR THE GOVERNMENT TO RESIGN

After the elections, which confirmed Bashir as president and elevated Turabi to speaker of the assembly, the NDA renewed its demand that they resign. Al-Mahdi criticized the election "comedy" in his sermons and, when Bashir insisted on meeting him on 3 April 1996, the former prime minister demanded that Bashir relinquish power to a genuinely democratic government.[44] Al-Mahdi refused to participate in further discussions, thereby underlining his rejection of co-optation.

These moves culminated on 10 June 1996 when NDA leaders living in Khartoum wrote Bashir, addressing him as commander in chief of the armed forces, not as president.[45] They condemned the 1989 coup, the regime's undermining of the armed forces and the civil service, the "barbaric and degrading forms of oppression," the "total economic collapse," the loss of lives in the south, and the "spread of corruption." They demanded a democratic transformation based on the principles of the NDA charter and the Asmara resolutions, and called on the "ruling authority to resign" immediately—warning that otherwise "the Sudanese people have legitimate alternatives for realizing their historic rights." Al-Mahdi called the appeal the last chance to reach a settlement without bloodshed in the north, noting however that "it may already be too late" for the regime to change. DUP emphasized that the demands had Mirghani's full support. And NDA's Mubarak al-Fadhil al-Mahdi stressed that this letter made clear that the internal and external opposition articulated a united stance.

Just beforehand, the government arrested numerous doctors, engineers, and trade union activists in Khartoum and confiscated additional Ansar property. Nonetheless, when an Ansar leader warned that the regime should not provoke the Ansar into retrieving their property by force, security forces returned the property intact. The roundup of union activists continued, however, since the letter of 10 June was followed by similar statements in regional capitals and calls by unions for a general strike. University students also protested sporadically,[46] secondary school students demonstrated in late August when classes resumed, and several doctors were arrested after striking against deteriorating medical services. Despite the festering unrest, Bashir downplayed the significance of the NDA letter and the protests, stating that he still hoped to absorb individual politicians into the current system on his own terms and emphasizing that he would neither alter "the basic Islamic agenda of the regime" nor "return to multiparty democracy." [47]

AL-SADIQ AL-MAHDI'S ESCAPE

As the NDA entered into military and political confrontation with the regime, the status of politicians inside the Sudan was increasingly at risk. The warnings to Alier and frequent detentions of al-Sadiq al-Mahdi and Sid Ahmad Hussain underlined their vulnerability. Al-Mahdi's presence in Khartoum, in particular, inhibited the NDA since he would be the first to be silenced should military operations intensify. During the fall of 1996, al-Mahdi's life was threatened and the government mounted an "extensive campaign of arrests of imams of mosques . . . and cadres of the Umma party."[48]

Therefore, on 5 December 1996 al-Mahdi agreed to the Umma leadership's decision that he leave the country and no longer serve as a "hostage and human shield," protecting the regime from all-out confrontation.[49] Pretending that illness prevented him from attending his daughter's wedding, he escaped to Eritrea, reaching Asmara on 9 December. Al-Mahdi left behind a letter to Bashir that detailed the regime's failings and demanded he accede to the popular demand to end "partisan fanaticism" by restoring democracy. Although Bashir responded that al-Mahdi's "joining the so-called opposition would not frighten the revolution," he immediately convened the National Security Council to assess the security lapse and arrested at least fifty security personnel. Turabi was acutely embarrassed, since he had attended his niece's wedding without suspecting the real reason for al-Mahdi's absence. The government quickly arrested numerous Umma party leaders, harassed al-Mahdi's sons, and threatened to confiscate his personal property.

ACCELERATED PRESSURE

The effort to achieve political and military coordination within the NDA intensified after meetings in November 1995 in London and January 1996 in Asmara. Following al-Mahdi's escape, he participated in meetings in Asmara of the leadership council in March and June 1997. He also traveled extensively in the Arab world and the West to convince leaders of the seriousness of the Arab-African alignment in the NDA and its credibility as the democratic alternative to the existing government. Among Arab and Muslim leaders, he especially sought to undermine the government's claim to embody Islamic legitimacy.

During this time, NDA added several more members, which expanded its secular and regional representation: the Sudanese Federal Alliance led by the respected former governor of Kordofan, Ahmad Diraij; the Sudanese Women's Movement, led by Fatima Ahmad Ibrahim, founder of the women's union in the 1950s and the first female member of parliament, representing the SCP; Sudan

National Party, which had elected eight Nuba MPs to the 1986 parliament; and the African Party of Southern Sudan.[50] Over the coming years special working groups debated and refined the draft constitution for the interim period. It was critically important that its terms gain support from all the constituent members, so that it would be perceived as legitimate and so that the SPLM would be reassured that the NDA had not just issued declarations of principle but had agreed upon binding laws.

Differences in perspective persisted, reflecting in part the view of Umma, DUP, and LC that they represented the system elected to office before the coup and therefore had the right to lead the restoration of the political system. Moreover, DUP's Mirghani chaired the NDA, with LC's General Ali as deputy chair,[51] and Umma's al-Fadhil al-Mahdi as NDA secretary general. In contrast, SAF, SPLM, and African regional groups sought to create a new political system in which marginalized groups would gain significant roles. The DUP-Umma-LC triumvirate exerted their weight by excluding representatives of the Beja Congress and SAF from the March 1997 leadership council meeting. But, overall, they had to accommodate those groups, whose fighting forces exceeded those of Umma, DUP, and LC, and which were supported by the Eritrea, NDA's host government.[52] Moreover, their credibility depended upon proving that they had set aside attitudes that took for granted the right of Muslim Arabs to rule.

Meanwhile, the SPLM rebuilt its administrative structures in Equatoria to introduce civilian authority at the grassroots level. The Torit resolutions in September 1991 had stated that military commanders should report to civilian authorities, but no changes occurred until the SPLM convention at Chukudum, which could not be held until April 1994 because of the deteriorating military situation. It was organized by Nuba commander Kuwa, who did not have access to his operational zone in the Nuba Mountains at that time.[53] The thousand delegates, selected at local meetings in the south and Nuba Mountains, reaffirmed Garang as chair and Salva Kiir as deputy of the newly elected National Liberation Council and of its Executive Council, and commander in chief of the SPLA. The convention called for civilian administrative structures, modified the SPLM charter (1983) to include the concept of self-determination, endorsed negotiations through IGADD, and reaffirmed support for the NDA and the common goal of overthrowing the regime. Although implementation was slowed by the lack of resources, the reluctance of some SPLA officers to give up power, and continuing logistical difficulties on the ground, further meetings culminated in forming a Civil Authority for the New Sudan (CANS) in 1996. They used the term "authority" rather than "government" to avoid "sending the wrong signal that we are seceding."[54] The SPLM also convened a conference of indigenous and international nongovernmental organizations in Chukudum in April 1996 to strategize on how to deepen civil society institutions. Civilianization enhanced the influence of Equatorian members of the SPLM, since CANS was initially consolidated in that province. By mid-1996 the SPLA also regained control of enough territory in Bahr al-Ghazal to appoint as governor Commander Nhial Deng Nhial and to place civil commissioners alongside military commanders in many districts.

On the military front, initial agreements at Asmara in 1995 led to a Higher Coordination and Supervisory Committee formed in late 1996 to supervise military operations.[55] The committee was headed by Mirghani, General Ali, and NDA Secretary General al-Fadhil al-Mahdi, even though none of them commanded significant troops. Garang headed the Joint Military Command (JMC), which planned and carried out military operations in both the north and the south. For the first time a southern commander gained operational responsibility over northern troops, including those of SAF, Beja Congress, Umma, DUP, and LC. By mid-1997 the JMC started to play a significant role in allocating specific assignments for each group on each battlefront and enhancing coordination of the newly renamed United Armed Forces.

In the south, an initial push into western and central Equatoria by the SPLA in October 1995 was followed by a major offensive starting in March 1997 that recaptured two-dozen towns and garrisons in eastern Equatoria and encircled Juba.[56] The SPLM established administrative structures throughout the region and struggled to assist the thousands of civilians who trekked home from refuge in Uganda. Anglican bishops associated with the New Sudan Council of Churches also returned to their dioceses and even provided chaplains for SPLA units.

The SPLA reentered Bahr al-Ghazal in the fall of 1995 and launched a serious drive to consolidate its hold in May 1997, which culminated in Garang's first visit to the region since forming the movement in 1983.[57] The SPLA aimed to cut the overland route to Juba, open its own supply routes north to the Nuba Mountains, and ward off raids by former-SPLA commander Kerubino as well as raids by Arab militias from Kordofan. Since Kerubino's troops, based in the Gogrial garrison, attacked fellow Twic Dinka villagers and herdsmen, residents welcomed protection by the SPLA. Moreover, NDA and SPLM jointly sought to reduce the threat of raids by Rizaiqat and Misiriyya Arabs, whose seasonal migration from Dar Fur and Kordofan into the south was manipulated by the government into religious-based attacks on the Dinka.[58] In June 1996, al-Fadhil al-Mahdi led a mission, along with a Misiriyya Arab member of the Umma party and Dinka politician Bona Malwal, to explain that the regime was hostile to the Ansar and especially to the family of the Mahdi, which the tribesmen did not realize. Al-Fadhil al-Mahdi stressed their duty as Ansar to oppose the government as well as their practical self-interest in reaching accords with Dinka over grazing and water rights. In the presence of the mission, Misiriyya and Dinka discussed their grievances and started to establish the basis for a mutual accommodation. This led to months of quiet in northern Bahr al-Ghazal, until PDF units resumed raids along the railway toward Wau in April 1997.[59]

Additional cattle raids by Nuer from Upper Nile were fended off by local Apuk Dinka groups, since the SPLA lacked a real presence in north-east Bahr al-Ghazal. Several government-allied militias controlled sections of Upper Nile, based in largely Nuer territory.[60] Those included Anya Nya II in the oil-producing Bentiu area and Riek Machar at Fangak on Zaraf Island, Bor, and Pachalla on the Ethiopian border. The SPLA's relatively limited presence was centered on Kongor, north of Equatoria, and the territory adjoining the Ingessana Hills. The government was determined above all to secure northern Upper Nile, in order to guarantee the anticipated oil revenues.

Once supply lines reopened to the Nuba Mountains, Kuwa returned in late 1995. Fighting remained difficult given the distance from logistical support in Equatoria and the harassment of its rear by Kerubino's forces. Moreover, the government launched all-out air and land offensives in July 1996 and the winter of 1996-1997, and encouraged PDF raids against Nuba villages.[61] Nonetheless, the exiled bishop of al-Ubayyid, Macram Max Gassis, whose diocese included the Nuba Mountains, celebrated Christmas mass in a Nuba village in December 1996. Moreover, the SPLA presence forced the government to divert troops from the south and east, and helped to reactivate the Sudan National Party, which became a member of the NDA in 1997 in order to assert the Nuba people's regional and secularist interests.

Combined SPLA/NDA forces opened a third front along the Ethiopian border in the Southern Blue Nile. In March 1996 the SPLA's New Sudan Brigade seized the 1,000-soldier Khawr Yabus garrison, overran Pachala a week later, and negotiated the surrender of another nearby garrison. Government forces had not expected an attack, since they were protected to the south by Riek Machar's troops in Upper Nile. Led by local commander Paul Malik Agar, the renamed United Armed Forces then seized the garrisons at Kurmuk, Qeissan, and Keili in January 1997, shortly after al-Mahdi escaped from Khartoum.[62] Agar consolidated SPLM control over nearly all of Southern Blue Nile Province except Damazin and the vital Rusayris dam, twenty miles to the north. NDA forces on the north side of the Blue Nile captured much of Northern Blue Nile Province in coordinated attacks that spring. Local officials who had chafed under the Islamist regime joined the new civil administration based in Kurmuk, which promoted the rights of the Ingessana peoples. The regime blamed the Ethiopian army for the setback, but found itself dangerously exposed. In the past governments had focussed their military resources on recapturing Kurmuk, but this time the government lacked the capacity to mount a counterattack in the Ingessana Hills, although the army did attempt to recapture villages in the Northern

Blue Nile Province. Agar's forces linked up with SPLA Commander James Oath, who controlled a previously isolated enclave in northern Upper Nile, although they were both harassed by Machar's troops.

A fourth front along the Eritrean border, extending from the Red Sea to Kassala, opened on 4 April 1996 with the ambush and killing of six PDF militiamen by Beja Congress guerrillas.[63] That was followed by the destruction of a railway bridge and a road bridge on the route to Khartoum in July 1996. The Beja Congress and Khalid's SAF ran training camps inside Eritrea, from which SAF units raided the grain-producing Kassala region. When the commander of the Kassala garrison defected to SAF, the regime's distrust of the regular army deepened and PDF forces subsequently patrolled the border.[64]

The new level of coordination within NDA was reflected in December 1996 operations by SAF, Beja Congress, SPLA's New Sudan Brigade, and even DUP and Umma, under the umbrella of the United Armed Forces. They ambushed and killed soldiers and PDF units, seized vehicles and arms, and downed a military helicopter, not only along the border but sixty miles deep into Hamesh Koraib province in attacks that were coordinated with the offensive toward Damazin.[65] During the spring the government ordered vehicles to travel from Khartoum to Port Sudan only with military escort and, in the summer, closed the border with Eritrea. According to outside observers, by mid-1997 the NDA controlled a 114 square kilometer area with 29 towns and villages along the Red Sea coast, with 92,000 residents, plus 86 towns and villages in Hamesh Koraib, with 360,000 residents.[66] As in the Ingessana Hills, local officials, police, and teachers switched sides. Notably, even the powerful Bitai family—leaders of an exclusively Beja tariqa, who had participated in elections in 1995 and 1996 and had convinced the Khartoum government to create a separate province for Hamesh Koraib—endorsed NDA rule. The Bitai elders denounced the NIF for emphasizing jihad rather than religious tolerance, called for restoring democracy, and sought recognition of Beja cultural and economic interests.

Military operations in the east, center, and south were therefore the key form of confrontation with the government in 1996-1997. They harassed the regime's communication lines to the Red Sea and threatened the principal source of electric power for the capital city as well as placed substantial territories under an alternative civil administration. These operations were intended to trigger a civil uprising in Khartoum, linked to dissident army and police officers. Indeed, leaflets that circulated in Khartoum in the name of the trade unions and NDA led to demonstrations in Khartoum on 4 to 5 January 1997, and Al-Mahdi explicitly called on the army and police to support the popular uprising and oust the regime.[67] In response, the government tightened surveillance, closed universities, ordered high school graduates to fight in the PDF for at least twelve months, and announced the trial in absentia of NDA leaders for waging war on the state.[68] Nonetheless, the suppression of the attempted uprising in September 1995 showed the overwhelming power of NIF and government security forces in the capital. And purges of army officers made unlikely the success of a military takeover.

GOVERNMENT RESPONSE

The government also responded by accelerating its Islamization program, formalizing its agreements with dissident southern commanders, and suddenly calling for renewed negotiations with the SPLM. Accelerated Islamization reflected NIF's view that an Islamic state could not have a military leader and that a thoroughly Islamic constitution was long overdue. Although Bashir appointed a sixty-member National Constitutional Commission to rewrite the basic laws—and expanded the commission in October 1997 to 377 members—an inner core of NIF members wielded effective authority over its contents.[69] Army officers criticized the provision that the presidentially appointed Supreme Court would safeguard the constitution, replacing the armed forces in that pivotal role. Southern MPs protested that crucial provisions in the southern agreements with the government, signed in April 1996 and renewed in April 1997, were omitted from the draft constitution.[70] For example, the draft placed police forces under the federal government rather than the state and did not mention the commitment to hold a referendum on unity or separation at the end of the four-year interim period.

The issue of restoring a multiparty system proved most contentious. Although the majority within the commission supported the principles of freedom of association and assembly and included those provisions in the draft submitted to President Bashir on 12 February 1998, freedom of political association was omitted from the revised draft that the president presented to the national assembly on 9 March 1998.[71] The powerful parliamentary speaker Hasan al-Turabi, together with Ghazi Salah al-Din, secretary general of the National Congress, insisted that freedom of association must occur only within the National Congress, which would serve as the sole political party. For example, just as professional societies and trade unions were represented inside the National Congress, so could Machar's United Democratic Salvation Front be incorporated into the congress. Turabi argued that a one-party system would enhance the unity of the Sudanese people:[72]

> I am a unitarian calling for unity of the Sudanese people . . . as our faith tells us that our God is one, our party is one, and our path to God is one.

Turabi underlined his determination when he accepted a petition denouncing multipartyism that was handed to him by ulama and imams who burst into the assembly session on 18 March, shouting "No to partisanship, no to sectarianism, 100 percent yes to Islam!"[73] Although that pressure tactic angered many MPs, twenty-six of whom voted against the article in the constitution that limited the formation of political associations, all the other articles of the draft constitution passed unanimously and the draft was submitted to President Bashir on 28 March.[74] The president called for a referendum in early May, in which voters could use a green card to vote "yes" or a red card to vote "no."[75] Bashir announced that he would sign the constitution on 30 June 1998, the ninth anniversary of his seizure of power. By then, the NIF power-brokers firmly controlled the levers of political power: in February 1998 Turabi became secretary general of the National Congress as well as speaker of parliament, shortly after Foreign Minister Taha was elevated to first vice president upon the death of al-Zubair in a plane crash.[76]

Meanwhile, the regime manipulated southern politicians, setting individuals and factions against each other in order to maximize its own control.[77] Vice President al-Zubair had brought together on 15 February 1997 the leaders of the armed groups that had signed the charter in April 1996, together with the ten governors of the states in the south and a half-dozen southern officials in Khartoum. The meeting was intended to reach an agreement on forming a Council for the South, but it ended in disarray since the Muslim governors opposed any such council. Moreover, southern officials who had consistently supported the Islamist regime did not want to come under the authority of the militia leaders who had defected from the SPLA. In any event, those militia leaders failed to assist the armed forces materially: when challenged to fight on behalf of the regime, Machar's Nuer troops fled from Juba and engaged in mere skirmishes near Torit, and Kerubino failed to respond to the request that he send forces to the east to defend Damazin.

The government then pressured the commanders to sign "The Sudan Peace Agreement" on 21 April 1997, which formed a presidentially appointed Council for the South that would include the ten governors and representatives of the militias.[78] Although the south gained the right to self-determination, which would be carried out by a referendum at the end of the interim period, the president could alter the length of the interim period and the terms of the April 1996 accord took precedence, thereby ensuring that unity would remain the primary principle. The accord was weakened further when the national assembly amended the text in ways that ensured northern control over the appointments to the council and when, as noted above, the draft constitution failed to include its key provisions.

"The Sudan Peace Agreement" accentuated rivalries among the southern commanders. When Bashir appointed Machar chair of the Council for the South in August 1997, Kerubino challenged his authority. Kerubino began to negotiate secretly with the SPLM/SPLA to rejoin the opposition forces. Although the regime tried to appease him by appointing him Machar's deputy on the council and the south's minister for local government and public security, he defected on 28 January 1998. Together with nearly 2,500 SPLA officers and soldiers who had pretended to return to the government fold during January, he attacked the army garrisons at Wau and Aweil.[79] Although the government managed to regain control over the vital rail terminus and airport at Wau, the defection stunned the regime and caused its troops to wreak retribution against civilians in Wau and to disarm Kerubino's militiamen stationed in Jebel Awliyya and Khartoum. Al-Zubair was engaged in an urgent mission to shore up support among southern militias when his plane crashed on 12 February 1998; Brigadier Arok Thon Arok and the new governor of Upper Nile also died in the crash.

Ethnic differences were manipulated in the contest for power: Machar (Nuer) was set against other claimants to power who were Dinka (Kerubino, Arok, and Second Vice President Kongor) and Shilluk (Lam Akol). Intra-ethnic tensions also surfaced, with Anya-Nya II leader Paulino Matip asserting his control over the oil-rich Bentiu area against fellow Nuer, Machar, and other Nuer claimants to power. Moreover, the selection of governors exacerbated the rivalries. The system called for Bashir to nominate three candidates for each governorship; the state assemblies, which Bashir appointed on 17 November 1997 upon the recommendation of Machar, then voted for one of those candidates at the end of November.[80] In one bitter contest, Lam Akol lost out to a Nuer rival, Timothy Tong Tut Lam, for the governorship of Upper Nile. Tong subsequently died in the plane crash on 12 February 1998; Akol survived the crash and became minister of transport in the reshuffled cabinet in Khartoum on 9 March 1998, a token position that was distant from his former base in the field. Overall, half of the governors were former militia leaders and half were long-term government officials, thus perpetuating the internal tensions that had complicated the establishment of the Council for the South and had enabled the northern politicians to maintain their policies of divide-and-rule.

Bashir sought to use the April 1996 and 1997 agreements as the basis for negotiations with the SPLM, thereby bypassing the IGADD process and the IGADD DOP, which emphasized secularism and the south's right to self-determination. The government had staunchly rejected that self-determination clause and argued that there was no need to negotiate with the SPLM. However, military setbacks in the south and east in 1996-1997 placed pressure on Bashir. He then called for direct talks with Garang, arranged by Kenyan President Daniel arap Moi or South African President Nelson Mandela, outside of the IGADD framework.[81] Bashir also met with the presidents of Uganda and Ethiopia in a vain attempt to resolve bilateral tensions, woo them away from supporting the NDA and SPLA, and win their support for the April 1996 agreement.[82]

Despite those efforts, the Sudanese government could not bypass IGADD, which had been renamed the Intergovernmental Authority on Development (IGAD). An IGAD meeting that was scheduled for 28 May 1997 was postponed, largely because the SPLM did not want to be pressured into signing a cease-fire just when it was making significant military advances. Nonetheless, both parties attended the IGAD meeting in Nairobi on 8-9 July 1997, at which Bashir finally signed the DOP.[83] IGAD hailed that act as a commitment by the government to restore democracy and guarantee self-determination for the south. In contrast, Bashir stressed that he did not view the DOP as legally binding and that he was committed only to the April 1996 agreement. He continued to try to use Mandela[84] and even Jimmy Carter[85] to bypass IGAD.

IGAD reconvened in Nairobi from 29 October to 7 November 1997. Foreign Minister Taha headed the government delegation and Salva Kiir headed the SPLM team.[86] Machar served as a consultant to the government delegation, and the NDA sent a delegation to Nairobi to support the SPLM and to lobby to gain the right to participate in the negotiations. The government emphasized that "sharia and custom shall be the sources of legislation in the Sudan;" that popular participation would take place "through participatory democracy," an implicit reference to the National Congress system; and that "its adherence to the maintenance of the unity of the Sudan [is] a paramount priority." The SPLM's position paper argued that unity could not be sustained unless religion were excluded from the political realm, insisted on political pluralism, asserted the right of the south and other marginalized peoples to self-determination, and called for a confederal union of a northern state and a southern state during the interim period. In the government's view, secularism and confederation were nonstarters. In the SPLM's view, an Islamic federation with limited political participation was out of the question. The SPLM was annoyed that the Ethiopian chair allowed the government to present its internal peace agreement, which deflected attention from the strongly worded DOP and appeared to put the onus for failure on the SPLM. The terse communiqué issued by IGAD at the close of the talks merely called on the parties to resume negotiations in April 1998.

Subsequently, the government sought to strengthen its position by finalizing the constitution. This would present the SPLM with a fait accompli at the next round of talks.[87] Within the opposition movements, the northern politicians in the NDA became increasingly anxious about their exclusion from IGAD and concerned that IGAD was overly weighted toward Africa. Their anxiety was partly caused by their fear that the SPLM's confederal formula was an implicit recipe for secession and that an SPLM-government deal would enable the SPLM to gain an independent state, while leaving the NDA in the political wilderness.[88] Al-Sadiq al-Mahdi proposed that the range of mediators be extended to include Arab and Muslim countries, such as Egypt, Saudi Arabia, and the United Arab

Emirates. In his view, the NDA would keep up its pressure "until the regime collapses or an uprising explodes or a genuine peaceful transfer of power to a national entity leading up to an elected authority is realized."[89] IGAD could provide the means for that peaceful change, but only if "all the parties to the conflict" were included. Although the IGAD talks reconvened in May, there was no change in their composition, and no substantive progress was achieved. In any event, the IGAD states rejected the inclusion of Egypt as a formal participant in the negotiations.

By 1998 the NDA-SPLM alliance emerged as a serious movement that challenged the regime both politically and militarily. Its inroads into the north and control over extensive areas of the south enabled the coalition to start to create rudimentary political and administrative structures on the ground, asserting a practical alternative to the regime. Moreover, the coalescing of its political position in 1995 and subsequent efforts to deepen its consensus on a national constitution began to establish a credible alternative political vision to the Islamist government.

Those practical and conceptual moves placed the government on the defensive. On the one hand, the Islamists became more strident in asserting their position. On the other hand, some members of the government frantically sought a cease-fire and made at least verbal concessions to southern aspirations and to the negotiating principles articulated by IGAD. However, the contradiction between NDA-SPLM and the government appeared too deep to bridge. The exclusivist Islamist vision by the autocratic government collided with the pluralist vision propounded by the NDA and long articulated by the SPLM. Confrontation, rather than negotiation, appeared the means by which the bitter contest would be resolved.

12

Conclusion

THE IDENTITY OF the Sudanese nation and the cultural boundaries of that nation-state are contested heatedly. The bitter struggle has nearly destroyed the country. The Arab-Islamic image that dominated the drive to achieve independence and was taken for granted in the political debates in Khartoum during the 1950s and 1960s has been increasingly challenged by those peoples whom it excluded. They emphasize that the country has been deeply divided regionally in ways that reinforce the political salience of ethnic and religious cleavages and make those cleavages the markers of political and economic dominance and marginalization.[1] They demand the structural transformation of the political system and of power relations so that they can gain an equal stake in the system and an equitable share in the country's resources and development. Should that prove unattainable, they seek to realize their asserted right to self-determination through an act of secession that will enable them to create their own state.

ENHANCED POLARIZATION

When discussing ethnic and religious differences, one risks reifying them and making them appear unduly rigid and permanent. There can be a core sense of ethnic identity based on linguistic, religious, or racial differences attributed to familial blood lines or group-relations that have endured over a long historical time frame. That identity provides important markers of sameness within the group and difference from others. It can be compounded by differences in religious beliefs and practices.

Those identities need not be sharply distinct, monolithic, or unchanging. Individuals can share characteristics with more than one group. Fur and Beja see themselves both as African culturally and as devout Muslims. Similarly, southerners can use Arabic for commerce without altering their self-identity. A person's regional, racial, religious, linguistic, and gender identities will be more salient and relevant in certain political contexts than others.

Within identifiable groups there are wide variations and frequent internal conflicts. People who consider themselves Beja, Fur, and Nubian speak varying languages that are not always mutually intelligible. Within the Dinka and Nuer peoples, clans war over land and water rights. Moreover, Islam is expressed through a wide array of practices and diverse structures. Several sects of Christianity have taken root, and the beliefs of traditional African religions vary significantly. Peoples' approaches to religion are often syncretic, since indigenous practices have influenced and subtly altered both Islam and Christianity. In fact, one of the most bitter political conflicts today surrounds the practice of Islam: the National Islamic Front seeks to impose its version of orthodoxy on other Muslims and fiercely rejects the beliefs and practices of sufi orders. NIF's homogenizing zeal has caused a strong backlash among Muslims.

Identities are not immutable. The social psychologist T. Abdou Maliqalim Simone observes that identity is a "cultural acquisition that serves a pragmatic function in terms of staking claims for access to resources and opportunities."[2] In that regard, for example, peoples who have virtually no Arab "blood" call themselves Arab by virtue of an adopted lineage that they trace symbolically to the family of the Prophet or to important Arab dynasties and tribes. They thereby acquire, in Simone's words, the "elevated social status" that accompanies that lineage. Individuals and groups become Arab by process of adoption and acculturation. Through quite different historical processes, Nuba, who are divided into numerous linguistic and religious groups, gained a sense of self through the tribulations of attacks from Arab tribes and discrimination by central governments. Over time they came to perceive themselves as a distinct ethnic group with clear cultural boundaries and political needs. Similarly, West Africans come from diverse backgrounds in widely dispersed parts of Africa. As a result of legal classification as foreigners as well as social and economic discrimination, they have constructed an increasingly clear group identity and "play[ed] down their intra-group differences."[3] Thus, as Nelson Kasfir remarks, shifting identities take place in the context of "changing patterns of dominance and subordination of different groups." Nonetheless, to Kasfir "the evolution of attitudes over many years tends to create habits of identification that are difficult to change because they are taken as self-evident."[4]

The manipulation of ethnicity can disrupt patterns of interaction between peoples of varying religions and customs. For example, the seasonal movement of tribes with their herds onto lands cultivated by other peoples has tended to be regulated through custom and local mediation so that neither community is harmed. The deliberate disruption and ideologizing of those relations—notably between Nuer and Dinka and between Arab nomads and southern peoples—has destroyed entire communities within the south. The official decree of jihad even legitimized those attacks as the defense of the faith against the infidel. Creating religio-ethnic militias "unavoidably entrenched ethnic identification as the basis for war and thus the problem for peace."[5] Complex negotiations would be required to undo that damage, as evidenced by the journey of Ansar leaders to Bahr al-Ghazal in 1996 to convince Arab tribesmen that they should oppose the NIF regime, restore the symbiotic relationship with the Dinka, and reestablish customary methods for resolving conflicts.

THE CONCEPTS OF NORTH AND SOUTH

The very concepts "north" and "south" are recent, created by imperial fiat and deepened by post-independence political decisions.[6] Nonetheless, the widely shared sociocultural marker of Islam in the north fosters a vision that differs significantly from the south and that sees a positive value in promoting within the south the universal values embodied in Islam. From the perspective of the south, the north means not merely difference but danger, deriving from "the violence of the original contact" in which northerners seized slaves and subordinated the southern peoples.[7] Southerners also associate the spread of Islam with their own weakness and vulnerability and resent the assumption that they lack complex and vibrant cultures and religions of their own.

As a result, most residents of the north and south have "opposing visions of history."[8] For example, the Mahdiyya may be imagined as the first independent nation-state, embodying the virtues of Islam and Arabic culture, or as a period of Arab attacks on Africans and the return of slavery. The British period is also viewed through different lenses, with many northerners seeing it as an era that blocked an otherwise natural progress of Islam and Arabic into the south. Thus, north and south emerge as not merely geographic concepts but as expressions of unequal relations and divergent historical memories.

Thus, over time ethnic categories can be politicized and hardened, not through a natural, unmediated process but through the manipulation of identity for instrumental purposes by political movements. Politicians enhance their own power and mobilize publics using ethnicity, religion, and regionalism as rallying cries. The assertion of the centrality of Islam and Arabic to Sudanese national identity derived from the Nile riverine elite's automatic assumption that their position, values, and priorities were national, whereas other groups' demands and problems were local and particular. Underneath that ingrained sense of superiority, however, was a feeling and fear of marginality.

FEAR OF MARGINALIZATION

In particular, the increasingly shrill call for Islamization and Arabization of the country arises from a recognition that the Sudan is marginal in the Arab and Muslim worlds. Arabs tend to view northern Sudanese as African, due to their skin color and cultural patterns, and have even used the humiliating term *abid* (slave) to describe them. Similarly, Sudanese are marginal to the Muslim world, lying on the frontiers of Africa and generally adhering to syncretic religious practices that diverge from strict orthodoxy. This marginalization leads many northern Sudanese to cling fiercely to their Arab genealogies and to assert vigorously their Islamic credentials. The National Islamic Front seeks to impose its particular form of orthodoxy on other Sudanese Muslims and to spread Islam throughout Africa, as displayed on an NIF banner: "We will only stop when the forces of Islam have raised the Islamic flag over Capetown and the whole continent of Africa has been Islamified."[9]

The sense of marginalization is compounded by their growing insecurity vis-à-vis their increasingly assertive African compatriots, who comprise at least half the population. As Africans from the south and west pour into Khartoum, its Africanization "intensifies the perceived threat to Islam" and disrupts the alleged "cultural homogeneity of the north."[10] Similarly, SPLA inroads into northern territories are visualized as an invasion by infidel African hordes, determined to efface Islam and destroy Arabs.

Instead of recognizing and accepting the country's religious and linguistic diversity, Islamists react by mounting a counteroffensive to secure dar al-Islam, ward off "the threat to northern cultural identity posed by SPLA,"[11] and forcibly expel Africans from Khartoum, relocating them in remote sites where systematic programs of Arabization and Islamization try to efface their southern and western cultural practices. More broadly, programs to require Arabic in the school system, instill an Islamic curriculum, inculcate Islamic law, and promote Islamist values through the media, civic ceremonies, and cultural events, all aim to create a homogeneous Sudanese nation that will erase cultural particularities and ethnic differences.

The actions taken to enforce uniformity and foster homogeneity have unintentionally resulted in severe backlashes. The normal interethnic competition for political posts, educational benefits, and a stake in the economy is distorted by the unequal power relations and the ideological pressure from the center. The more the government in the north seeks to Arabize and Islamize the country, the more African peoples react against that pressure and deepen their counteridentities.

THE CONTESTED NATION-STATE

The concept of nation-state prevalent in the Sudan has been based on an ethnic nationalism in which the Arab-Islamic majority defines the country's identity according to its image. When coupled with an autocratic political system along the lines of the control model, ethnic nationalism leads to the attempt to eliminate differences by defining them away and/or by instituting structures that marginalize minorities.

In the contrasting model of a territorial nation-state, all the residents have legal equality and share allegiance to the state. The government is based on common political ideals rather than ethnicity or religious adherence. Sudanese have given lip service to this form of civic loyalty, but its content has remained vague and incapable of mobilizing people behind shared objectives and aspirations. To many, the idea of being Sudanese remains "more a hollow abstraction than a confident conviction."[12]

Given the high level of abstraction of civic or territorial nationalism, some have suggested that an ethnic pluralist model would be appropriate for the Sudan. That approach would not suppress or deny ethnic differences but would accommodate them within the political system. It would incorporate two essential safeguards: equal rights under the law for all citizens and special measures to represent the diverse groups. Guaranteed seats in the central parliament, decentralized authority in the regions, and freedom of religious and linguistic expression would provide means to validate and represent the different groups. Both safeguards are essential: in particular, recognition of minority rights in a geographic enclave must not provide the excuse to abandon the principle of nondiscrimination at the countrywide level.

That approach was partially articulated in the Addis Ababa Accord of 1972 and the constitution of 1973, which offered a proportional role for southerners in the central institutions, self-rule in their region, religious freedom, and the option of using English and indigenous languages in the schools and administration within the south. Numairi suggested that a new Sudanese nationalism could emerge that would supersede prior loyalties to tribe or religious movement while recognizing regional diversities. The limits of the approach were evident when Numairi systematically undermined southern autonomy, marginalized its representatives in Khartoum, seized control over its natural resources, and transformed the legal and political systems along Islamist lines. Constitutional guarantees were clearly insufficient to ensure that the ethnic pluralist approach would be institutionalized in a context in which power remained concentrated in Khartoum and easily manipulated by an autocratic ruler.

The SPLM called for an even more radical restructuring of the political system in order to create an inclusive identity and end the privileging of any groups. Equality at the center would be coupled with increased power to the marginalized peoples in the north and south. This would reduce the control by and benefits that accrued to the riverine Arab elite. The SPLM attempted to soften the elite's resistence by proposing a national constitutional conference at which a consensus would be reached among all the political forces: change would not be forced on the elite but would be the product of political bargaining.

This approach was recognized in the negotiated agreements during 1988-1989. Those accords were resisted by some members of Umma and all of NIF precisely because they might transform power relations and end the hegemony of Islamic law. The National Democratic Alliance (NDA) finally underwrote these concepts in April 1993, after nearly four years of wrestling with the issue, emphasizing that a future democratic government should base its laws on the provisions of the international human rights codes and ensure nondiscrimination among its citizens. The NDA stated more precisely at Asmara in June 1995 that religion must not be injected into the constitutional system.

Other Sudanese have suggested that ethnic pluralism is not feasible, given the intensity of the polarization within the Sudan, the commitment of the current regime to a monolithic cultural identity, and the organic link between leading northern political parties and their religious bases. In their view, minorities should have the right to self-determination, enabling them to choose to secede and to form their own state(s). In international law, self-determination has been viewed as a one-time act that permitted ethnic groups to create their own states in Europe in the wake of World War I and that allowed colonized peoples to end foreign rule after World War II. Recently, however, a view has begun to emerge that secession should be endorsed as a conditional right to be invoked in situations where the government fails to uphold equal rights and engages in severe discrimination against ethnic minorities.

The demand for secession was raised by the first Anya Nya revolt and articulated at the Round Table Conference in 1965. It has become particularly insistent under the current regime, given the systematic legal discrimination against non-Muslims. Even some militant Islamists have concluded that partition is the only realistic way to resolve the contradictions between the Islamist and African secularist vision. That would end the illusion of a united country, enabling each part "to preserve what is left" rather than destroy the entire country.[13] Indeed, that can be seen as the logical conclusion of NIF's policies. From southern perspectives, if reconciliation is impossible and marginalized peoples find that justice and freedom are denied, geopolitical union cannot be legitimate and will be resisted by all available military and diplomatic means.

Others see asserting the right to self-determination as a way to contain centrifugal forces, since it places pressure on the government to uphold basic rights and reduce discrimination. Thus, the southern constitutional lawyer Peter Nyot Kok comments that guaranteeing the right to self-determination could be the basis for healthy cooperation and coexistence, rather than a threat to unity.[14] Along those lines, the SPLM position has been that unity is not an end in itself but must be anchored in nonsectarianism: recognition of the multiethnic, multi-religious and multilingual character of the Sudanese people is essential in order to keep the country united.[15] If Khartoum rejects a democratic, nonsectarian, multilingual Sudan, the excluded peoples will choose separation. If Khartoum accepts a just political system, then the south is likely to exercise its right of self-determination by opting, instead, for federation or confederation. That prospect was recognized by the NDA in the Asmara accords of 1994-1995, with northern politicians concluding that granting the marginalized peoples the right of self-determination was the best way to ensure that the central government would be fair and genuinely representative, thereby ensuring that self-determination would result in the continuation of a united country rather than in partition.

REDEFINITION AND REALIGNMENT?

The political forces in the NDA are engaged in a process of redefining the nation and establishing new alignments that could transform relations and restructure power, even though mutual suspicions remain strong. Activists on behalf of the marginalized peoples fear that the riverine elite will reassert its control if the NDA comes to power. Nonetheless, they are attempting to forge a consensus that will lead to the establishment of a democratic system based on the principles of ethnic pluralism.

The reconceptualization was evident in debates that presaged the NDA resolutions in 1995. In often-tense discussions in a symposium in 1993, southerners challenged their northern partners forthrightly.[16] They asked, for example, if the NDA could countenance a southern president; how Islamist politicians could expect southerners to respect their religion if they did not respect the faiths of the people of the south; and why the NDA relied on the SPLA to fight the government alone. They stressed that southerners would need clear guarantees in order to overcome their lack of confidence in any Khartoum-based government. And they emphasized that the only way to overcome their strong aspiration for independence would be to establish a con/federal system that would ensure self-rule and self-expression in their region.

Northern representatives of the NDA as well as independent intellectuals attempted to respond to those fears. The legal scholar Abdullahi an-Na'im agreed that the responsibility lay with northerners to prove to southerners that they would be secure within a united Sudan; otherwise, the south should be allowed to secede. The secularist secretary of NDA, former foreign minister Faruq Abu Isa, argued that the top priority was to cooperate to remove the Islamist regime but recognized that if, at the end of an interim period, the north and south found they could not live together, then the south could secede. And political scientist Taisier Mohamed Ahmed Ali, a key mediator in the 1980s, maintained that secession would be the easy way out: it would be more challenging and ultimately more rewarding for each side to yield ground to the other in order to establish a common nonreligious state. In line with the rethinking within the Umma party, Umar Nur al-Da'im conceded that mistakes made by the north had been greater than those made by the south. He argued that most Sudanese reject an Islamist state that denies others their rights and thereby compromises national unity; instead they seek rights based on citizenship. A key lesson from the years of civil war, he averred, was that "no national group is justified in claiming exclusive authority over the others" and that any groups that are deprived of their rights will resist that injustice.[17] He concluded that there must be a pluralist system in which there will be mutual tolerance, democratic decentralization, and guarantees of human rights for all citizens.

That northern mea culpa was evident in the Umma Party's statement in February 1994 on the controversial issue of self-determination, which declared that "self-searching into the past" led the party to recognize that "modern Sudanese self-consciousness centered . . . on their Islamic-Arabic identity. Sudanese economic development has tended to be in the northern area. They also enjoyed the lion's share in political power. The country's external outlook was governed by Arabic and Islamic horizons."[18] Meanwhile, the party and other northern political forces did not recognize the increasing self-awareness and self-assertion of "African Sudanese ethnic groups." Therefore, those "deprived Sudanese elements expressed protest against the dominant culture." The statement acknowledged that the northern groups only "slowly came to realise the real causes of those protests." The manifesto claimed that they had just reached the point of "making the necessary national adjustments to define and protect those rights" when NIF launched the narrowly partisan coup that alienated most Muslims and Arabs and made other ethnic and religious groups conclude "that there is no place for them in the Sudan." The call for jihad against the south, in particular, was a "bitter seed [that] bred bitter fruit [in] the current call for self-determination." The manifesto expressed the party's realization that, should a referendum take place now, the south would support separation. But the party hoped that a national constitutional conference during a democratic interim period could create the possibility of "unity in a just Sudan" and thereby diminish the pressures within the south for secession. Nonetheless, Umma indicated that the south should have a free choice and that unity should not be coerced.

One might dispute the claim that the Umma prime minister was ready for fundamental "national adjustments" in 1989. Nonetheless, the statement indicates a radical reconceptualization on the part of that strongly Arab-Islamic party, rooted in the Ansar movement and the religious nationalism of the Mahdiyya. That rearticulation helped to achieve the Asmara accords and the renewed sense of common purpose within the NDA.

Appendix:
The Changing Composition
of Governments

1. Transitional Military Council, 1985-1986

1. General Abd al-Rahman Muhammad Suwar al-Dhahab, chair (former minister of defense and commander in chief)
2. General Taj al-Din Abdullah Fadl, deputy chair (former deputy commander in chief and vice president of military staff)
3. Lt. Gen. (Air Force) Muhammad Mirghani Muhammad Tahir; chair, committee on the south
4. Lt. Gen. (Navy) Yusif Hasan Ahmad; chair, elections committee (former director of naval administration)
5. Lt. Gen. (Engineering Corps) Muhammad Tawfiq Khalil, chief of staff; chair, committee to develop the armed forces (former director of logistics)
6. Lt. Gen. (Retired) Yusif Hasan al-Hajj; chair, economic affairs committee
7. Maj. Gen. Fabian Agang Long, commandant of the staff college (Dinka from Bahr al-Ghazal)
8. Maj. Gen. James Loro Sirsio, chair, interim High Executive Committee for the South (Bari from Equatoria; former southern command head)
9. Maj. Gen. Uthman al-Amin al-Sayid
10. Maj. Gen. Ibrahim Yusif al-Awad al-Jaali
11. Maj. Gen. Hamada Abd al-Azim Hamada, armored corps
12. Brig. Uthman Abdullah Muhammad, minister of defense (former director of operations)
13. Brig. Fadlallah Burma Nasir (former commander of Khartoum district; Baqqara Arab)
14. Brig. (Engineering) Abd al-Aziz Muhammad al-Amin (mechanized corps)
15. Brig. Faris Abdallah Husni (former director of military intelligence)

Source: Ann Mosely Lesch, "Transition in the Sudan," *UFSI Report* #20 (1985), 3.

2. Interim Council of Ministers, 1985-1986

1. Al-Jazouli Dafallah, prime minister (former head of the physicians union)
2. Samuel Aru Bol, deputy prime minister and irrigation and water resources

(former vice president of the High Executive Committee in the south; president of Southern Sudanese Political Association; Dinka)
3. Brig. Uthman Abdullah Muhammad, defense (member of TMC)
4. Abbas Madani, interior (former police commissioner)
5. Ibrahim Taha Ayyub, foreign affairs (former ambassador to Kenya; Nubian)
6. Awad Abd al-Majid, finance and economic planning (former director of Barclays Bank in Sudan and earlier governor of the Bank of Sudan); resigned November 1985
7. Umar Abd al-Ati Umar, justice and attorney general (former deputy head of the bar association)
8. Muhammad Bashir Hamid, information, culture, youth, and sports (political science professor, Khartoum University; active in the faculty association)
9. Bashir Hajj al-Tom, education (education professor, Khartoum University; taught in Saudi Arabia, 1970-1985)
10. Sid Ahmad al-Sayid Hamid, trade and commerce (businessman; former director of the budget and undersecretary in finance ministry)
11. Abd al-Aziz Uthman Musa, energy, industry, and mining (former director of Central Electricity Generating Board)
12. Sadiq Abdin, agriculture (former official, Rahad Agricultural Scheme)
13. Hussain Abu Salih, health and social welfare (neurosurgeon; deputy head of the doctors' union)
14. Amin Makki Madani, construction and public works (lawyer; helped draft National Charter; active in National Alliance)
15. Peter Gatkuoth, transport and communications (Nuer politician; vice president of SSPA; deputy minister in Ministry of Southern Affairs in 1971-1972)
16. Oliver Batali Albino, labor (politician from Equatoria; removed on 13 June, charged with embezzlement and smuggling hashish); replaced on 10 September by Dr. Stanley Jimmy Wango (veterinarian; former MP in Equatoria; Peoples Progressive Party)

Source: Lesch, "Transition in the Sudan," *UFSI Report* #20 (1985), 5.

3. Council of State, 1986

1. Ahmad al-Mirghani, president: DUP high committee, Nile Valley Parliament 1982-1985, businessman, brother of Muhammad Uthman al-Mirghani, born in 1941.
2. Muhammad al-Hasan Abdallah Yassin: Member of DUP general secretariat. [resigned June 1987; replaced over DUP objections by Mirghani Nasri, former head of the bar association].
3. Idris Abdallah al-Banna: Umma political bureau.
4. Ali Hasan Taj al-Din: Umma, former banker in Jiddah (Saudi Arabia), from Dar Fur.
5. Pacifico Lado Lolik: SAPCO secretary general, graduate of Khartoum University medical college, former Equatoria minister of health, former speaker of Equatoria regional assembly, detained April-October 1985, lost election bid in 1986, born in Juba in 1938.

Source: Lesch, "Party Politics in the Sudan," *UFSI Report* #9 (1986), 12.

4. First Council of Ministers, May 1986

1. Prime Minister & Defense: al-Sadiq al-Mahdi (Umma head, former prime minister 1966-1967, age 51)
2. Deputy Prime Minister & Foreign Affairs: Sharif Zain al-Abdin al-Hindi (DUP secretary general, brother of the late Sharif al-Hindi, Hindiyya tariqa, age 47)
3. Interior: Sid Ahmad Hussain (DUP political bureau, lawyer from Northern region, MP, age 43)
4. Attorney General & Justice: Abd al-Mahmud al-Hajj Salih (Umma MP, lawyer from White Nile, judge 1967-1974, age 44)
5. Energy & Mining: Addam Musa Madibu (Umma secretary general, defense minister under al-Mahdi 1966-1967, engineer from the west)
6. Agriculture & Natural Resources: Umar Nur al-Da'im (Umma, majority leader in assembly, agriculture PhD, agriculture minister under al-Mahdi 1966-1967, exile 1970-1978, MP 1978-1982 and on SSU central committee, detained 1983-1984, MP from White Nile, age 51)
7. Finance & Economic Planning: Bashir Umar Fadul (Umma assistant secretary general, PhD Manchester University 1978, economics lecturer Khartoum University, MP, age 35)
8. Commerce & Supply: Muhammad Yusif Abu Harira (DUP from Eastern region, professor Khartoum University, MP)
9. Industry: Mubarak Abdullah al-Fadhil al-Mahdi (Umma, al-Sadiq al-Mahdi's cousin)
10. Animal Resources: Ismail Abbaker (Umma, veterinarian, assistant commissioner animal resources Dar Fur, MP Dar Fur, age 39)
11. Irrigation & Hydroelectric Power: Aldo Ajo Deng (SSPA, SANU secretary 1968, deputy speaker peoples assembly 1979, commissioner Bahr al-Ghazal 1980, MP 1982-1983, deputy governor Bahr al-Ghazal 1983-1985, Dinka, age 44) [expelled from SSPA when he refused to resign from the cabinet in February 1987]
12. Labor & Public Service: Walter Kuni Jwok (SAC president, secondary school Uganda, PhD Oxford University 1982, Khartoum University politics lecturer, MP Upper Nile, Shilluk, age 43) [resigned February 1987]
13. Transport & Communications: Seraphino Wani Swaka (MP for PPP, engineer, in Uganda 1965-1972, MP in regional assembly and Equatoria 1978-1985, age 50)
14. Housing, Public Works, & Public Utilities: Muhammad Tahir Jilani (DUP, minister in Eastern region in early 1980s, businessman, Beja, age 42)
15. Culture & Information: Muhammad Tawfiq Ahmad (DUP, owned insurance company, columnist in "al-Sahafa" newspaper, MP from Wadi Halfa, Nubian, age 68)
16. Health & Social Welfare: Hussain Abu Salih (DUP, neurosurgeon, former deputy head physicians' union, minister of health and social welfare in transitional cabinet)
17. Local Government: Joshua Dai Wal (SPFP president, MP, assistant commissioner education Upper Nile 1979-1981, minister of tourism and wildlife in south 1981-1982, age 51)

18. Education: Bakri Ahmad Adil (Umma, postgraduate studies petroleum administration and mining, governor Kordofan 1980s, ex SSU politburo, from Kordofan, age 51)
19. Cabinet Affairs: Salah al-Din Abd al-Salaam al-Khalifa (Umma)
20. Peace & National Constitutional Conference: Muhammad Ahmad Yaji (independent, former diplomat, uncle of Khalid Yaji who chaired the National Alliance)

Source: Lesch, "Party Politics in the Sudan," *UFSI Report* #9 (1986), 13.

5. Second Council of Ministers, June 1987

1. Prime Minister & Defense: al-Sadiq al-Mahdi (Umma)
2. Foreign Affairs: Muhammad Tawfiq Ahmad (DUP MP, former culture and information minister); resigned September 1987, replaced by information minister Sanadah.
3. Deputy Prime Minister & Interior: Sid Ahmad Hussain (DUP)
4. Attorney General & Justice: Abd al-Mahmud al-Hajj Salih (Umma)
5. Energy & Mining: Addam Musa Madibu (Umma)
6. Agriculture & Natural Resources: Umar Nur al-Da'im (Umma)
7. Finance & Economic Planning: Bashir Umar Fadul (Umma)
8. Commerce & Supply:* Ibrahim Hasan Abd al-Jalil (DUP, economics professor at Khartoum University) [replaced DUP's Abu Harira]
9. Industry: Mubarak Abdullah al-Fadhil al-Mahdi (Umma)
10. Animal Resources: Ismail Abbaker (Umma)
11. Irrigation & Hydroelectric Power:* Mahmud Bashir Jamma (Umma MP, engineer, deputy governor Dar Fur 1980-1983)
12. Labor:* Lawrence Modi Tombe (PPP)—Ministry of Public Service was separated from Labor but no minister was named
13. Transport & Communications: Aldo Ajo Deng (SSPA faction, formerly irrigation minister)
14. Housing, Public Works, & Public Utilities: Muhammad Tahir Jilani (DUP)
15. Culture & Information:* Ma'mun Sanadah (DUP), who also became foreign minister 11 October 1987
16. Health: Hussain Abu Salih (DUP)
17. Social Welfare and Zakat [new ministry]:* Ms. Rashida Ibrahim Abd al-Karim (Umma)—the first woman in the cabinet
18. Local Government:* Red Chok Jok (SPFP, later governor of Upper Nile)
19. Education: Bakri Ahmad Adil (Umma)
20. Youth and Sports [new ministry]:* Hasan Muhammad Mustafa (DUP)
21. Cabinet Affairs: Salah al-Din Abd al-Salaam al-Khalifa (Umma)
22. Peace & National Constitutional Conference: Muhammad Ahmad Yaji (independent)
* new ministers [those who merely changed portfolios are not starred]

Sources: SUNA, 3 June 1987 (FBIS 3 June 1987); *Sudan Times*, 5 June 1987.

6. Third Council of Ministers, May 1988

1. Prime Minister: Al-Sadiq al-Mahdi (Umma)
2. Defense:* Ret. (Army) General Abd al-Majid Hamid Khalil (Numairi's defense minister from 1978 and first vice president from 1979, removed in 1982; independent)
3. Foreign Affairs: Hussain Sulaiman Abu Salih (DUP, former health and social welfare minister)
4. Interior:* Abbas Abu Shama (independent)
5. Attorney General & Justice:* Hasan Abdallah al-Turabi (NIF, attorney general 1979-1982, former advisor to Numairi, SSU politburo member 1977-1985)
6. Energy & Mining: Bakri Ahmad Adil (Umma, MP, former education minister)
7. Agriculture & Natural Resources:* Al-Fatih al-Tijani (DUP, minister of finance Kordofan 1982-1985)
8. Finance & Economic Planning: Umar Nur al-Da'im (Umma, former agriculture and natural resources minister)
9. Economy & Foreign Trade: Mubarak Abdallah al-Fadhil al-Mahdi (Umma MP, former minister of industry)
10. Internal Trade, Cooperation, & Supply:* Ali al-Hajj Muhammad Adam (NIF, former deputy governor Dar Fur, regional minister Dar Fur 1980-1982)
11. Industry:* Abd al-Wahhab Uthman (NIF, MP, finance minister in Northern Region 1982-1985, former undersecretary Ministry of Finance and Economy)
12. Animal Resources: Ismail Abbaker (Umma)
13. Irrigation & Water Resources: Mahmud Bashir Jamma (Umma)
14. Labor & Social Security:* Mathew Obur Ayang (former head of Council of the South, speaker regional assembly in south 1982-1983, regional education minister 1978-1979, Anya-Nya II leader)
15. Public Works & Housing:* Uthman Umar Ali al-Muhammi (DUP)
16. Public Service & Administrative Reform:* Fadlallah Ali Fadlallah (NIF MP)
17. Transport: Aldo Ajo Deng (MP, formerly SSPA, irrigation minister 1986-1987, then transport & communications minister)
18. Public Communications:* Taj al-Sirr Mustafa Abd al-Salaam (NIF)
19. Culture & Information:* Abdallah Muhammad Ahmad Hasan (Umma MP, MP 1967-1969)
20. Youth & Sports:* Joshua Dai Wal (SPFP MP, local government minister 1986-1987)
21. Health:* Awhaj Muhammad Musa (DUP, minister in Eastern region 1982-1985)
22. Social Welfare & Zakat:* Ahmad Abd al-Rahman Muhammad (NIF, minister of internal affairs 1980-1985)
23. Local Government & Regional Coordination:* Richard Makobe (former minister in Equatoria)
24. Cabinet Affairs: Salah al-Din Abd al-Salaam al-Khalifa (Umma)
25. Education & Scientific Research:* Al-Shaikh Mahjub Ja'far (Umma)
26. Refugee Affairs & Relief [new ministry]:* Hasan Ali Shabbu (DUP MP)

27. Tourism, Hotels, & Aviation [new ministry]:* Amin Bashir Fallin (SNP MP, Nuba, major in Numairi's SSO)
28. Religious Affairs & Awqaf [new ministry]:* Abd al-Malik Abdalla al-Jaali (DUP, last minister of religious affairs under Numairi)
29. Speaker of Southern Council [cabinet rank new]:* Angelo Beda (speaker, regional assembly in south 1980-1981)

The Ministry of Peace and National Constitutional Conference was abolished.
*   new ministers [those who merely changed portfolios are not starred]

Sources: SUNA, 16 May 1988; *Sudan Times*, 22 May 1988; *Wakh* (Manama), 6 May 1988 in FBIS-NES-88-094 (16 May 1988).

7. Fourth Council of Ministers, December 1988 and February 1989

1. Prime Minister: Al-Sadiq al-Mahdi (Umma)
2. Defense: Ret. General Abd al-Majid Hamid Khalil (resigned February 21; replaced by Salah al-Din Abd al-Salaam al-Khalifa, Umma, previously Minister for Cabinet Affairs)
3. First Deputy Prime Minister and Foreign Affairs: Hasan Abdallah al-Turabi (NIF, also Justice till February 1)
4. Interior:* Mubarak Abdallah al-Fadhil al-Mahdi (Umma, former Economy & Foreign Trade), February 1
5. Attorney General & Justice:* Hafiz al-Shaikh al-Zaki (NIF, February 1, previously minister of state for justice)
6. Energy & Mining:* Habib Sarnub al-Daw, February 1 (Umma, Nuba MP, former general secretary of Nuba General Union)
7. Agriculture & Natural Resources: Umar Nur al-Da'im (Umma, also Finance) till February 1, then Aldo Ajo Deng (also Second Deputy Prime Minister; former transport minister)
8. Finance & Economic Planning: Umar Nur al-Da'im (Umma)
9. Economy & Foreign Trade: Abdallah Muhammad Ahmad Hasan (Umma, also culture and information until February 1)
10. Internal Trade & Supply: Ali al-Hajj Muhammad Adam (NIF)
11. Industry: Abd al-Wahhab Uthman (NIF)
12. Animal Resources: Ismail Abbaker (Umma)
13. Irrigation & Water Resources: Mahmud Bashir Jamma (Umma)
14. Labor: Mathew Obur (Anya-Nya II)
15. Public Works & Housing: Salah Abd al-Salaam al-Khalifa (Umma, also Cabinet Affairs) till February 1, then Hasan Shaikh Idris*
16. Public Service & Administrative Reform: Fadlallah Ali Fadlallah (NIF)
17. Transport & Communications: Taj al-Sirr Mustafa Abd al-Salaam (NIF), February 1
18. Culture & Information:* Bashir Umar Fadul (Umma, February 1; finance minister 1986-1988), government spokesman
19. Youth & Sports: Joshua Dai Wal (SPFP)

20. Health: Taj al-Sirr Mustafa Abd al-Salaam (NIF) till February 1, then Dr. Mamun Yusuf*
21. Social Welfare & Refugees: Ahmad Abd al-Rahman Muhammad (NIF)
22. Local Government & Regional Coordination: Richard Makobe
23. Cabinet Affairs: Salah al-Din Abd al-Salaam al-Khalifa (Umma; Defense Minister from February 21)
24. Education: Al-Shaikh Mahjub Ja'far (Umma)
25. Tourism, Hotels, & Aviation: Amin Bashir Fallin (SNP, Nuba)
26. Speaker of Council of South: Angelo Beda
* new ministers. Public communications, religion, and relief ministries were abolished.

Sources: SUNA, 30 December 1988 (FBIS-NES-88-251, 30 December 1988); MENA, 31 January and 1 February 1989 (FBIS-NES-89-020, 1 February 1989); *Sudan Times*, 2 February 1989.

8. Fifth Council of Ministers, March 1989

1. Prime Minister: Al-Sadiq al-Mahdi (Umma)
2. Defense:* Ret. Army General Mubarak Uthman Rahma (independent)
3. Foreign Affairs & First Deputy Prime Minister:* Sid Ahmad Hussain (DUP, interior minister 1986-1988)
4. Interior: Mubarak Abdallah al-Fadhil al-Mahdi (Umma, interior minister since February 1)
5. Attorney General & Justice:* Uthman Umar al-Sharif (DUP)
6. Energy & Mining: Bashir Umar Fadul (Umma assistant secretary general, former culture and information minister)
7. Agriculture & Second Deputy Prime Minister: Aldo Ajo Deng (SSPA, anti-Aru Bol group)
8. Finance & Economic Planning: Umar Nur al-Da'im (Umma)
9. Commerce, Cooperation, & Supply:* Mirghani Abd al-Rahman Sulaiman (DUP)
10. Industry:* Ibrahim Radwan (DUP)
11. Animal Resources:* Paolino Zizi (SAPCO)
12. Irrigation & Water Resources: Mahmud Bashir Jamma (Umma)
13. Labor and Social Security:* Akasha Babikir (trade unions)
14. Public Works & Environment: Ismail Abbaker (Umma, former animal resources minister)
15. Public Service & Administrative Reform:* Abu Zaid Muhammad Salih (SCP)
16. Culture & Information:* Hussain Sulaiman Abu Salih (DUP, former health and then foreign minister till December 1988)
17. Youth & Sports:* Robert Bendi (south)
18. Health:* Abd al-Rahman Abu al-Kul (medical association), chair of committee to study the election laws
19. Local Government:* Joseph Ukel Abang (SSPA MP, pro-Aru Bol)
20. Cabinet Affairs: Salah al-Din Abd al-Salaam al-Khalifa (Umma)
21. Education: Al-Shaikh Mahjub Ja'far (Umma)

22. Social Welfare, Relief, & Rehabilitation:* Awhaj Muhammad Musa (DUP, health minister till December 1988)
23. Tourism & Hotels:* Muhammad Hamad Kuwa (Nuba, SNP)
24. Transport & Communications: no one named (designated for Umma)
25. Chairman, Southern Council: Angelo Beda (unchanged, but this time he was elected by the southern parties)
* new ministers

Sources: SUNA, 25 March 1989; Khartoum National Unity Radio, 26 March 1989 (FBIS-NES-89-057); *Sudan Times*, 28 March 1989.

9. Revolutionary Command Council, July 1989

1. Lieutenant General Umar Hasan Ahmad al-Bashir: RCC chair; prime minister and defense minister July 1989; minister of culture and information, November 1991-May 1992; president from October 1993.
2. Major General al-Zubair Muhammad Salih: RCC deputy chair; deputy prime minister July 1989; previously nicknamed "the imam" while he studied at the Islamic African Center; interior minister April 1991-January 1993; first vice president from October 1993; died in plane crash near Nasir, Upper Nile, on 12 February 1998.
3. Major Ibrahim Shams al-Din: chair, administrative and legal affairs committee from July 1989; commanded seventh Armored Brigade in Khartoum at the time of the coup; member of the Council of Forty; presidential advisor in October 1993.
4. Colonel Bakri Hasan Salih: chair, security and operations committee from summer 1989; since October 1993, president's advisor for security affairs (supervises and coordinates internal security and foreign security); interior minister as well as presidential advisor, August 1995.
5. Naval Brigadier Salah al-Din Muhammad Ahmad Karrar: chair, economic committee; minister of transport, then minister of energy in January 1993; minister in prime minister's office, August 1995.
6. Brigadier Dominique Kassiano: Zande from west Equatoria; anti-SPLA ever since he led the attack on the Bor mutineers in 1983; former military commander in west Equatoria; political supervisor for Equatoria from July 1989; labor minister from July 1992; minister for environment and tourism in 1995.
7. Lt. Colonel Muhammad al-Amin Khalifa Yunis: Berti from Dar Fur; political supervisor of Eastern region from July 1989; chair, National Peace Dialogue Conference fall 1989 and led negotiations with the SPLM through July 1994; left the RCC in January 1992 to head the Transitional National Assembly.
8. Brigadier Uthman Ahmad Hasan: not NIF but a key conspirator with Bashir before the coup; political supervisor of Northern region from July 1989; chair of political committee from July 1989 and state minister for defense from February 1990 until he was removed in April 1991 after he opposed executing officers.
9. Major General Faisal Ali Abu Salih: not NIF but a key conspirator with Bashir

before the coup; interior minister from July 1989 till he was removed in April 1991 for opposing the execution of officers.

10. Colonel Pio Yukwan Deng: brought in by Bashir as No. 3 in RCC; Shilluk; anti-SPLA; commanded Kapoeta garrison in 1976; commissioner for West Equatoria under the TMC and al-Mahdi; political supervisor of Upper Nile from July 1989; supervisor of Southern Council from August 1989; chair, political committee from April 1991; died on 3 August 1991 from heart attack.

11. Brigadier Martin Malwal Arup: Dinka from Rumbek (Upper Nile), son of the distinguished chief Malwal Arup; colleague of Bashir's in the parachute corps; political supervisor of Bahr al-Ghazal from July 1989; wanted to resign, April 1991, because of the execution of officers; removed 11 March 1992.

12. Flight Brigadier Faysal Madani Mukhtar: not NIF; political supervisor of Kordofan from July 1989; April 1990 became governor of Kordofan, them minister of health in February 1992; removed 19 January 1993.

13. Brigadier Tijani Adam Tahir: from Dar Fur; not NIF; as political supervisor of Dar Fur from July 1989 negotiated Arab-Fur tribal reconciliation; chair of legal and administrative committee, RCC; responsible for investigative committees; rumors by April 1991 that he would be removed from the RCC; removed from the cabinet October 1993.

14. Colonel Sulaiman Muhammad Sulaiman: official spokesman as chair of information committee and political supervisor of Central province from July 1989; April 1990 became governor of Central region, then minister of culture and information from May 1992 to October 1993, when he was removed from the cabinet.

15. Brigadier General Ibrahim Nayil Idam: Nuba from South Kordofan; head of national security, security advisor to Karrar, from January 1990; removed to minister of youth and sports and, after July 1993, minister of communications and tourism till July 1994, when expelled from the cabinet.

Secretary to the RCC: Brigadier (Engineering) Abd al-Rahim Muhammad Hussain: air force engineer; minister of interior January 1993 to July 1994; secretary general of the presidency from October 1993; NIF's covert head in the military prior to the coup d'état; member of the Council of Forty.

10. Council of Ministers, July 1989

1. Prime Minister and Defense Minister: General Umar Hasan Ahmad al-Bashir (RCC).
2. Deputy Prime Minister: Major General al-Zubair Muhammad Salih (RCC).
3. Minister for the Presidency: Staff Col. al-Tayyib ("Sikka") Muhammad Ibrahim Khair (NIF doctor, military medical staff).
4. Foreign Affairs: Ali Sahlul (career diplomat).
5. Interior: General Faisal Ali Abu Salih (RCC).
6. Justice and Attorney General: Hasan Isma'il al-Bili (former judge 1962-1968); replaced in 1992 by Abdullah Idris (former dean, law faculty, Khartoum University) until January 1993.

7. Culture and Information: Ali Muhammad Shammu (minister of culture and information under Numairi; then undersecretary for information in Abu Dhabi), replaced in April 1990 by an Islamist minister; Bashir held the post from November 1991 to May 1992, then Col. Sulaiman Muhammad Sulaiman (RCC) till October 1993.

8. Finance and Economy: Sayyid Ali Zaki (PhD agricultural economics, Michigan State University, 1980; then ministry of planning, including undersecretary, 1983; executive director of Islamic Bank for Development, 1988); replaced in April 1990 by NIF's Abd al-Rahim Hamdi, a founder of the Faisal Islamic Bank and head of the London office of the Baraka Islamic Bank.

9. Agriculture and Natural Resources: Ahmad Ali Qanaif (PhD in genetics, University of California; then coordinated the government's horticultural research; openly pro-NIF).

10. Religious Guidance: Abdullah Deng Nhial (Upper Nile; BA/MA in Arabic language and teaching from al-Azhar University; former schoolteacher), until July 1993 when he headed the new ministry of peace and rehabilitation.

11. Irrigation and Water Resources: Yaqub Abu Shura Musa (PhD in water resources from Colorado State University; chair, water resources research unit in irrigation ministry).

12. Energy and Mining: Abd al-Munim Khawjali; soon replaced by former NIF MP and Industry Minister Abd al-Wahhab Uthman, who was replaced in January 1993 by RCC Brigadier Salah al-Din Muhammad Ahmal Karrar.

13. Industry: Muhammad Umar Abdallah (Kordofan; PhD in engineering; production manager in public sector companies under Numairi; general manager in Abu Dhabi late 1980s; pro-NIF). He left to become chair of the Gum Arabic Company in 1990 and died in the south in 1993, fighting in the Popular Defense Forces; replaced in 1990 by a NIF member.

14. Education: Mahjub al-Badawi Muhammad; replaced in April 1990 by the Islamist Abd al-Basit Sabdarat, who was defense lawyer for the 1969 RCC members who were tried in 1986.

15. Housing, Public Works, and Public Utilities: Major General Engineer (Retired) Muhammad al-Hadi Ma'mun al-Mardi (explosives field engineering; director, military research branch in armed forces; director, College of Defense); replaced by an Islamist in April 1990.

16. Trade, Cooperation, and Supply: Faruq al-Bishri Abd al-Qadir (PhD in urban and regional studies, University of Birmingham; administrator in Dar Fur, Equatoria, North; former head of ministry of local government; pro-NIF).

17. Health and Social Welfare: Muhammad Shakir al-Siraj (health inspector in South Dar Fur; senior physician in Blue Nile, Equatoria, Khartoum; undersecretary, ministry of health; health commissioner for Khartoum; dean, college of medicine, Juba University); replaced in February 1992 by RCC Brigadier Faysal Madani Mukhtar, till removed from RCC and cabinet January 1993; then Lt. Col. Galwak Deng Garang became minister.

18. Relief and Displaced Persons: Peter Orat Ador (southern; former chief of customs at Port Sudan).

19. Transport and Communications: Ali Ahmad Abd al-Rahim (employed in rail-

road authority 1962-1981, including general manager of mechanical transportation administration in 1978; general manager of maritime ports authority, 1981; transferred to ministry of transportation in January 1989); soon replaced by RCC Brigadier Karrar until January 1993.

20. Labor and Social Insurance: Kinga George Dalking (Toposa from Equatoria; minister of agriculture in Council of South, 1986-1989); resigned July 1992, went into exile; replaced by RCC Brigadier Dominique Kassiano.

21. Local Government and Regional Coordination: Natali Bankar Ambu (Bahr al-Ghazal; certificate from University of Birmingham in management science; inspector in Bahr al-Ghazal; assistant governor in Eastern Equatoria; director of prime minister's local government and training office).

22. Youth and Sports (created 1990): RCC Brigadier Nayil Idam.

Sources: MENA, 9 July 1989 (FBIS-NES-89-130 10 July 1989); *al-Quwwat al-Musallaha*, 11 July 1989 (JPRS-NEA-89-057, 28 August 1989).

11. Council of Ministers, October 1993

1. President: General Umar Hasan Ahmad al-Bashir (ex RCC)
2. First Vice President: General al-Zubair Muhammad Salih (ex RCC)
3. Second Vice President: Police Major George Kongor Arop
4. Finance: Abdullahi Hasan Ahmad (former director of Faisal Islamic Bank, NIF) *
5. Information and Culture: Abd al-Basit Sabdarat (lawyer, NIF, former minister of education) *
6. Education: Ibrahim Ahmad Umar *
7. Defense: Major General Hassan Abd al-Rahman Ali *
8. Presidential Affairs: Awadh Ahmad al-Jaz
9. Foreign: Hussain Abu Salih [removed February 1995]
10. Interior: Brigadier Abd al-Rahim Hussain (former RCC secretary). In July 1994 Al-Tayyib Khair became interior minister
11. Justice and Attorney General: Abd al-Aziz Shiddu
12. Labor and Administrative Reform: Brigadier Dominique Kassiano (ex RCC)
13. Communications and Tourism: Brigadier Nayil Idam (ex RCC); In July 1994, replaced by Kashobo Kuku, Nuba former minister of state for social planning
14. Energy and Mining: Brigadier Salah al-Din Muhammad Ahmad Karrar (ex RCC)
15. Social Planning: Ali Uthman Muhammad Taha (NIF No. 2), who became foreign minister in February 1995
16. Agriculture, Natural Resources, Animal Wealth: Ahmad Ali Qanaif (in the position since July 1989)
17. Health: Colonel Galwak Deng Garang
18. Irrigation: Yaqub Abu Shura Musa (in the position since July 1989)
19. Economic Planning and Investment: Ibrahim Ubaydullah al-Hussain
20. Transport: Uthman Abd al-Qadir Abd al-Latif
21. Industry and Trade: Taj al-Sirr Mustafa Abd al-Salaam

22. Bureau of Federal Government: Ali al-Hajj Muhammad
23. Secretary General of Presidency: Brigadier Abd al-Rahim Hussain (also interior minister)

Presidential advisors: Brigadier Bakri Hasan Salih and Colonel Ibrahim Shams al-Din, both formerly of RCC

*   new ministers

Sources: Omdurman radio, 30 October 1993 (FBIS-NES-93-209, 1 November 1993); *Hayat*, 1 November 1993 (*Sudan Update* 4:23, 10 November 1993); Omdurman radio, 13 July 1994 (FBIS-NES-94-129, 6 July 1994).

Glossary

abid	slave
ahl al-dhimma	protected people (Christians, Jews)
ahl al-harb	people living in non-Muslim lands
amir al-amura	"prince of the princes," a Muslim military commander or governor
Ansar	helpers or followers of the Mahdi
Anya-Nya	the general name for the southern guerrilla movement in the 1960s, whose name combines the Madi words "inya nya" (a snake poison) and the Moru "manyanya" (an insect that kills large animals)
baya	religious oath of allegiance in Islam
bilad al-Sudan	medieval Arabic term for central Africa, "the land of the black people"
dar al-harb	"the land of war," lands where non-Muslims live
dar al-Islam	"the land of peace," land where Islamic law is enforced
dawa	call to Islam, propagation of the faith
Fallata	pejorative term for pilgrims who immigrated to Sudan from West Africa
faqi	Muslim holy man, religious preacher, legal expert
fatwa	opinion of an expert on a point of Islamic law
ghazwa	slave hunt
hadd (pl. hudud)	"sacred frontier," the concept of trespassing moral boundaries; religiously prescribed Islamic punishments
Id al-Adha	Feast of the Sacrifice, celebrated on the last day of the Muslim pilgrimage
Id al-Fitr	Feast of Breaking of the Fast, celebrated to mark the end of Ramadan, the Muslim month of fasting
imam	(1) Muslim prayer leader; (2) divinely ordained religious leader of an Islamic state
intifada	"shaking off," popular uprising
jallaba	northern merchants who traveled from the Nile Valley to the south and west of the Sudan
jallabiyya	dress commonly worn by men in north Sudan, consisting of a long, loose garment
jihad	(1) self-exertion in the cause of God, the inner struggle against

	impious temptations; (2) religiously sanctioned warfare by Muslims to defend Islam against non-Muslims
kafir (pl. kuffar)	nonbeliever, infidel
khalifat (pl.)	successors to the prophet Muhammad as leader of the Islamic community
khalwa	Quran school for children
mahdi	the expected deliverer in Messianic times, whose mission is to establish the just rule of Islam
marisa	local fermented beer
mujahidiin (pl.)	holy warriors
murahiliin (pl.)	Arab militia
mu'tamarat (pl.)	conferences
Quran	the holy scripture of Islam, containing the revelations of God transmitted to Muhammad by the Angel Gabriel
sayyid	religious leader, notable
shaikh	title of respect for a tribal leader, learned man, or leader of a Sufi brotherhood
shamasa (pl.)	homeless street children, ruffians
shari'a	the divinely ordained law of Islam, the "path" or "way" that governs all aspects of Muslim behavior
shura	consultation
sikka	iron bar
Sudd	barrier; swamps in southern Sudan
Sufism	the practice of Islamic mysticism
tariqa (pl. turuq)	Sufi religious brotherhood
thobe	women's outer covering commonly worn in north Sudan
ulama (pl.)	persons learned in Islamic law and sciences, official interpreters of shari'a, members of the religious establishment
umma	(1) the world Muslim community; (2) the political party of the Mahdist Ansar movement
urf	customary law
wali	Muslim governor, guardian
zakat	obligatory sharing of wealth with the poor and the community that is one of the pillars of Islam
zar	spirit-possession ceremony
zariba	thorn bushes placed for protection around an encampment, fortified camp, frontier post

Notes

1. The Problem of National Identity

1. This approach was represented most clearly by the late Edward Shils. Critiques are provided by Anthony D. Smith, *The Ethnic Origins of Nations* (New York: Blackwell, 1986), 12 [cited hereafter as Smith (1986)]; Karl W. Deutsch, *Nationalism and Social Communication* (Cambridge: MIT Press, 1966), 17; and Rasma Karklins, *Ethnopolitics and Transition to Democracy: The Collapse of the USSR and Latvia* (Washington: Woodrow Wilson Center Press, and Baltimore: Johns Hopkins University Press, 1994), 5-6.

2. John A. Armstrong, *Nations before Nationalism* (Chapel Hill: University of North Carolina Press, 1982), 282, and 6, 241, 291. The French intellectual Ernst Renan offered comparable views in his "What Is a Nation?" (1882), *Becoming National*, ed. Geoff Eley and Ronald Suny (New York: Oxford University Press, 1996), 47.

3. Karklins, 4, 8; Deutsch, 104.

4. Eley and Suny, 7. They cite (23-24) Elie Kedourie and Jurgen Habermas, who emphasize the conscious cultural production in nation building.

5. "Imagine" is the term coined by Benedict Anderson in *Imagined Communities: Reflections on the Origin and Spread of Nationalism* (London: Verso, 1983). See Smith (1986), 20, for an analysis of Anderson's approach and that of the modernists Fredrick Barth and Ernest Gellner.

6. Smith (1986), 207.

7. Anthony D. Smith, *National Identity* (London: Penguin, 1991), 42 [hereafter cited as Smith (1991)].

8. Smith (1986), 200-201.

9. Armstrong calls that a mythomoteur, i.e., "a coherent, strongly held identity belief" that provides a sense of a common past (292-93). Smith (1986), 15, adopts Armstrong's concept of mythomoteur, which he defines as the "constitutive myth of the ethnic polity" that helps to preserve and transmit identity to future generations.

10. Smith (1986), 15. On religion as a source of solidarity, see ibid., 14, 34-37; Smith (1991), 84; Armstrong, 6, 201, 238-40.

11. Barth, as discussed in Armstrong, 5.

12. Deutsch, 19, 96; Smith (1986), 26.

13. Deutsch, 97, 107, 110.

14. Smith (1986), 30, 55-56, 156, 169.

15. Quotations from Smith (1986), 39.

16. Smith (1991), 82. Hurst Hannum, *Autonomy, Sovereignty, and Self-Determi-*

nation: The Accommodation of Conflicting Rights (Philadelphia: University of Pennsylvania Press, 1996), 24, uses "statism" for Smith's "territorial nationalism" and reserves "nationalism" for "ethnic nationalism." Hannum's terms are less confusing than Smith's, but Smith's are closer to general usage.

17. Eley and Suny, 5; Smith (1991), 76-77, 82-83. The historicist approach to language and culture of Johann Gottfried von Herder (1744-1803) in his *Treatise upon the Origin of Language* (1772) and *Outlines of a Philosophy of the History of Man* (1784-91) influenced the organic nationalism of Johann Gottlieb Fichte (1762-1814). See, for example, Fichte's *Addresses to the German Nation* (Berlin, 1807-1808), trans. R. J. Jones and G. H. Turnbull (Chicago: 1922).

18. Smith (1991), 114, 76; Karklins, 3-4, 144; Hannum, 26.

19. Smith (1991), 82, 108; Karklins, 45 on India; on U.S., see Hedva Ben-Israel, "Nationalism in Historical Perspective," *Journal of International Affairs* 45 (winter 1992), 394.

20. On colonial policies, see Smith (1991), 107; Eley and Smith, 28; and Hannum, 456.

21. Smith (1991), 114.

22. Austin Ranney, "Politics in the United States," *Comparative Politics*, ed. Gabriel A. Almond and G. Bingham Powell, Jr., 6th ed. (New York: HarperCollins College Publishers, 1996), 792.

23. Karklins, 17.

24. Karklins, 16; also 5, 46.

25. Eley and Suny, 12, 19; Hannum, 453-54.

26. Hannum, 9; Smith (1986), 9, 163, 223.

27. Karklins, 18.

28. Hannum, 6.

29. Karklins, 16, and 8, 15, 19, 167.

30. Hannum, 69, 462; Karklins, 15.

31. Saad Z. Nagi, "Ethnic Identification and Nationalist Movements," *Human Organization* 51 (winter 1992), 311.

32. Text in Hannum, 85-87; examples, 8, 74-81, 95-101.

33. Smith (1986), 163.

34. Hannum, 473 and 10, respectively.

35. Hannum, 59. On language: Rupert Emerson, *From Empire to Nation* (Cambridge: Harvard University Press, 1967), 132-34.

36. Hannum, 13; on minority treaties, 50-53.

37. Hannum, 27-36, 41, 44; Smith (1991), 131-33, on ethnic secessionism in post-colonial states.

38. Amitai Etzioni, "The Evils of Self-Determination," *Foreign Policy* 89 (winter 1992-93), 21.

39. Hannum, 35; Finnish case, 471. See also Allen Buchanan, "Self-Determination and the Right to Secede," *The Journal of International Affairs* 45 (winter 1992), 347-65.

40. Michael Lind, "In Defense of Liberal Nationalism," *Foreign Affairs* 73:3 (May-June 1994), 88.

41. Lind, 99.

42. Lind, 97. For another analysis, see Alexis Heraclides, "Secession, Self-Deter-

mination and Nonintervention: In Quest of a Normative Symbiosis," *The Journal of International Affairs* 45 (winter 1992), 407-408.

43. Etzioni, 21. For an analysis partly arising from the Israeli context, see Sammy Smooha and Theodore Hanf, "The Diverse Modes of Conflict-Regulation in Deeply Divided Societies," *International Journal of Comparative Sociology* 33 (January-April 1992), 26-47.

44. John Obert Voll and Sarah Potts Voll, *The Sudan* (Boulder: Westview, 1985), 8-13; P. M. Holt and M. W. Daly, *The History of the Sudan* (Boulder: Westview, 1979), 3-8.

45. R. C. Stevenson, *The Nuba People of Kordofan Province* (Khartoum: Graduate College Publications, Monograph #7, University of Khartoum, 1984), 3, 11; Catherine Miller, comments to the author, Cairo, 13 June 1997.

46. R. S. O'Fahey, *State and Society in Dar Fur* (New York: St. Martin's, 1980), 2-5.

47. Dunstan M. Wai, *The African-Arab Conflict in the Sudan* (New York: Africana, 1981), 19.

48. Voll and Voll, 12; Catherine Miller comments to the author, Cairo, 13 June 1997.

49. Comments by Catherine Miller, 13 June 1997, who notes that by the late nineteenth century the Feroge, Kresch, Linga, Banda, Longo, and Bandala peoples were identified from outside as Fertit. Recently, Balanda (a mixed group of former slaves) have started to call themselves Fertit.

50. Gabriel Warburg, *Islam, Nationalism and Communism in a Traditional Society: The Case of Sudan* (London: Frank Cass, 1978), 1.

51. Francis Deng, *War of Visions* (Washington: Brookings Institution, 1995), argues that Arabs captured by Dinka were incorporated into their families as full relatives whereas Arabs held Dinka slaves in bondage, 74.

52. Robin Thelwall, ed., *Linguistic Profile: Aspects of Language in the Sudan* (1978), cited by Edward Bukulu Mandeson, "Multi-Lingualism and Educational Development in South Sudan," in Mom K. N. Arou and B. Yongo-Bure, *North-South Relations in the Sudan since the Addis Ababa Agreement* (Khartoum: University of Khartoum, 1988), 326.

53. Survey in 1989 by the Department of Geography, University of Khartoum, cited by T. Abdou Maliqalim Simone, *In Whose Image? Political Islam and Urban Practices in Sudan* (Chicago: University of Chicago Press, 1994), 198.

54. Quotation from Abdelwahab El-Affendi, "'Discovering the South': Sudanese Dilemmas for Islam in Africa," *African Affairs*, 89: 356 (July 1990), 372; Hasan al-Turabi, *Islam, Democracy, the State and the West*, Arthur L. Lowrie, ed. (Tampa: WISE Monograph #1, 1993), 64.

55. Interview in *al-Hayat* (London), 5 September 1992.

56. Comment by SPLM leader John Garang at his joint press conference with Muhammad Uthman al-Mirghani, following the signing of the DUP-SPLM accord; SPLA radio, 18 and 19 November 1988. Garang himself *opposed* secession.

57. SPLM's official statement on the new regime, broadcast on SPLA radio 14-15 August 1989, Mansour Khalid, ed. *The Call for Democracy in Sudan* (New York: Kegan Paul International, 1987), 251.

58. Quotations from El-Affendi, "Discovering the South," 371, 383-89.

59. Speeches by SPLM leader John Garang that express this approach can be

found in *John Garang Speaks*, ed. Mansour Khalid (London: Kegan Paul, 1987); for example, 21-23 (speech on 3 March 1984), 26 (speech on 22 March 1984), and 43 (speech on 9 April 1985).

60. SPLM radio, 20 April 1987.

61. Interview with Mubarak al-Fadhil al-Mahdi, an Umma party leader and secretary general of the NDA, in *al-Hayat*, 10 August 1995 (FBIS-NES-95-157, 15 August 1995).

62. *War of Visions*.

2. Historical Legacies

1. P. M. Holt and M. W. Daly, *The History of the Sudan* (Boulder: Westview, 1989), 8 and 3-8, 28-43 for historical background. On the Arabization logic, Francis M. Deng, *War of Visions* (Washington: Brookings Institution, 1995), 401, 413. On Nuba, Martin Daly, *Empire on the Nile* (Cambridge: Cambridge University Press, 1986), 129. On Fur, R. S. O'Fahey, *State and Society in Dar Fur* (New York: St. Martin's, 1980), 12-13. On Khatmiyya, John Obert Voll, *A History of the Khatmiyyah Tariqah in the Sudan* (Harvard University: unpublished dissertation, 1969).

2. Deng, *War of Visions*, 413; Lazarus Leek Mawut, *Dinka Resistance to Condominium Rule, 1902-1932* (Khartoum: University of Khartoum, 1983), 2-3, cites archeological evidence that the population in today's Khartoum was originally similar to Dinka and Nuer. In discussions with the author, Stephanie Beswick concurred with this evidence, but Robert Collins disputed it.

3. Richard Hill, *Egypt in the Sudan, 1820-1881* (London: Oxford University Press, 1959); Holt and Daly, 47-82.

4. On slavery: Abel Alier, *Southern Sudan: Too Many Agreements Dishonored* (Exeter: Ithaca, 1990), 11-12; Hill, 62-64, 101-102, 138; Heather J. Sharkey, "Luxury, Status and the Importance of Slavery in the 19th and early 20th Century Northern Sudan," *Northeast African Studies*, 1:2-3 (1994), 187-206; and Dunstan M. Wai, *The African-Arab Conflict in the Sudan* (New York: Africana, 1981), 27-29.

5. Holt and Daly, 71; Abel Alier, "The Southern Sudan Question," *Southern Sudan*, ed. Dunstan M. Wai (London: Frank Cass, 1973), 13. The slave raids by the Ja'ali trader al-Zubair Rahma Mansur in Bahr al-Ghazal were fictionalized in Francis Deng, *Seed of Redemption* (New York: Lilian Barber, 1986).

6. Daly, 134. On cultural resistance, Stephanie F. Beswick, "Non-Acceptance of Islam in Southern Sudan: The Case of the Dinka from the Pre-Colonial Period to Independence (1956)," *Northeast African Studies*, 1:2-3 (1994), 20.

7. Hassan Makki Mohamed Ahmed, *Sudan: The Christian Design* (London: Islamic Foundation, 1989), 52; Hasan al-Turabi on the natural adoption of Islam in Arthur L. Lowrie, ed., *Islam, Democracy, the State and the West* (Tampa: WISE, 1993), 64. According to Deng, *War of Visions*, 27, intra-Dinka and Dinka-Nuer raids led to the absorption of captured slaves into their new households and their incorporation as full members of the community.

8. Holt and Daly, 85-113; Alier, *Southern Sudan*, 12-13; Mekki Shebeika, *The Independent Sudan* (New York: Robert Speller, 1959), 132, 336-37.

9. Mohamed Ahmed Mahgoub, *Democracy on Trial* (London: Andre Deutsch,

1974), 26, 29, 31. Mahgoub's grandfather, Abd al-Halim Musaad, commanded Mahdist forces that captured Khartoum.

10. The Mahdi's commander in chief, Hamdan Abu Anja, led a private slave raiding force that the Turkiyya armed forces harassed [Gabriel R. Warburg, "National Identity in the Sudan," *Asian and African Studies*, 24 (1990), 154].

11. Wai, *African-Arab Conflict*, 31; Robert O. Collins, *The Southern Sudan, 1883-1898* (New Haven: Yale University Press, 1962), details the "extended raids" that spread "anarchy and fear" in the south and enhanced "the Southerner's hatred and fear of the Northern Sudanese" (177).

12. Criticism by a British education official, quoted in Holt and Daly, 137, which covers this period, 117-58.

13. Daly, 367 and, on indirect rule, 360-78. Shebeika analyzes the condominium agreement, 446-58.

14. Hasan Abdin, *Early Sudanese Nationalism, 1919-1925* (Khartoum: Khartoum University Press, 1985), 19-30, 146-55; Tim Niblock, *Class and Power in Sudan* (Albany: State University of New York Press, 1987), 50-52, on the sayyids' economic power.

15. Holt and Daly, 133; Abdin, 48, and Deng, *War of Visions*, 104-10, stress Abd al-Latif's background, which is downplayed in Muddathir Abdel Rahim, *Imperialism and Nationalism in the Sudan* (Khartoum and London: Khartoum University Press and Ithaca, 1986), 104-108; Afaf Abu Hasabu, *Factional Conflict in the Sudanese Nationalist Movement 1918-48* (Khartoum and London: Khartoum University Press and Ithaca, 1985), 45-48; and Shebeika, 480.

16. Azhari was one of the first Sudanese to receive a BA from the American University of Beirut. He returned to Khartoum in 1930 to teach at Gordon Memorial College (Shebeika, 480). His grandfather was Mufti of Sudan (1924-32) and a member of the delegation to London in 1919. Warburg, *Islam, Nationalism and Communism in a Traditional Society: The Case of Sudan* (London: Frank Cass, 1978), 67-70.

17. Warburg, *Islam, Nationalism*, 26: this totalled only .001 percent of the Sudan's six million population. The demands in the GGC memorandum are listed in Mahgoub, 41.

18. Mahgoub, 42 (an ironic comment, considering that Mahgoub fully participated in those "sterile feuds"). Abu Hasabu details the sayyids' support for graduates and cultural societies and the debilitating impact of factionalism on northern political life.

19. Alier, *Southern Sudan*, 13. He mentions the Atwot leader Awuou Kon, killed in 1907; Dhieu Allam of the Atwot, killed in 1912; Mayen Mathiong of the Agar who rose up against the British administration in Rumbek in 1902 when its officials tried to impose taxes and demanded forced labor to construct roads and government rest houses; and Ariadhdit of the Bor Yol in Aweil, who fought the British from 1912 to 1923. Distinguished chiefs included Gbudwe Basingbi of the Zande, who had already fought the Turkiyya and Mahdiyya but was killed in 1905 when betrayed by another southern leader, King Tambura. That particular event still resonates, since Tambura's grandson supported the division of the south in 1983, an act that many southerners saw as a betrayal of his people (Alier, 16). Alier, 17, mentions that, after the south

gained self-rule in 1972, streets in Juba were named after those leaders. Douglas H. Johnson, "Foretelling Peace and War," *Modernization in the Sudan*, ed. M. W. Daly (New York: Lilian Barber, 1985), 121-34, analyzes how the wars waged by the Lou Nuer in 1917 and 1928-29 with the British were incorporated into their prophetic teachings. See also Mawut on Dinka resistance to British rule and, on the changes in domestic slavery, Ahmad Alawad Sikainga, *Slaves into Workers: Emancipation and Labor in Colonial Sudan* (Austin: University of Texas Press, 1995).

20. On British rule in the south, see Daly, 135-48, 396-418; Robert O. Collins, *Shadows in the Grass: Britain in the Southern Sudan, 1918-1956* (New Haven: Yale University Press, 1983), cf on courts, 162-65; Abdel Rahim, 70, on chiefs' courts (introduced in 1931) and text of Civil Secretary's Memorandum on Southern Policy in 1930 (244-49); for a northern Islamist perspective: Ahmad, 7, 63, 72; southern views include Mawut, 13-14, 18-28, 41; and Deng, *War of Visions*, 77-87. For a lively account of tensions between British officials and missionaries: Lillian Passmore Sanderson and G. N. Sanderson, *Education, Religion and Politics in Southern Sudan, 1899-1964* (London: Ithaca, 1983).

21. Collins, *Shadows*, 157; for example, Upper Nile, 150-53, 160-61.

22. Collins, *Shadows*, 170, cites a 1924 memorandum by the financial secretary.

23. Details in Daly, 412. Northern doctors joined the three new hospitals in the south after the medical school in Khartoum produced its first graduates in 1928: Alexander Cruikshank, "The Golden Age of Tropical Medicine and Its Impact on the Modernization of the Sudan," *Modernization in the Sudan*, ed. M. W. Daly (New York: Lilian Barber, 1985), 92.

24. Abdel Rahim, 77-78, 82-83; Collins, *Shadows*, 166-96, 210, 217-19. In Nuba areas, government schools used Arabic whereas missionary schools emphasized the vernacular: Fund for Peace, *Living on the Margin* (New York: 1995), 12.

25. Collins, *Shadows*, 180-85; Daly, 415.

26. G. N. Sanderson, "The Ghost of Adam Smith," *Modernization in the Sudan*, ed. M. W. Daly (New York: Lilian Barber, 1985), 101, 106-10, 115-16; Daly, 418-19; Alier, *Southern Sudan*, 18; Raphael Koba Badal, *Origins of the Underdevelopment of the Southern Sudan: British Administrative Neglect* (Khartoum: Development Studies and Research Centre, University of Khartoum, 1988). On the Zande scheme, Collins, 314-32.

27. B. Yongo-Bure, "The First Decade of Development in the Southern Sudan," *North-South Relations in the Sudan since the Addis Ababa Agreement*, ed. Mom K. N. Arou and B. Yongo-Bure (Khartoum: University of Khartoum, 1988), 374-77; also 391-92, 398.

28. Letter by Professor Muddathir Abdel Rahim in the *Guardian* (4 June 1964); similar views in Ahmed, 86, 101-102; Turabi, *Islam, Democracy*, 64.

29. Abdelwahab El-Affendi, "Discovering the South," *African Affairs*, 89: 356 (July 1990), 372.

30. Gabriel R. Warburg, "National Identity in the Sudan," *Asian and African Studies* 24 (1990), 152, citing the first population census of the Sudan (1955-56).

31. A rare example was the document prepared for the Milner mission in 1920 that discussed linking the south to "some central African system." (Holt and Daly, 139) Daly, 411, notes that one official proposed in 1905 to cede the south to the Congo. See also Collins, *Shadows*, 169.

32. Comment by Umma's Muhammad Ahmad Mahjub; Collins, *Shadows*, 284.

33. Alier, *Southern Sudan*, 20; Wai, *African-Arab Conflict*, 35-44 (quoting Chief Lolik Lado, 44); Wai, ed. *Southern Sudan*, 194-95; Deng, *War of Visions*, 89-92; Bona Malwal, *People and Power in Sudan* (London: Ithaca, 1981), 24-28; Holt and Daly, 153; Collins, *Shadows*, 286-92, 412-20, 432-56; Abdel Rahim, 166-71 and Civil Secretary's Memo (1946), 253-56.

34. Alier, *Southern Sudan*, 22; Collins, *Shadows*, 436-37; Sanderson and Sanderson, 297-98, 304-305, 312-13; Wai, *African-Arab Conflict*, 45-47. The southern commissioner who resigned was Buth Diu, a Nuer MP.

35. Wai, *African-Arab Conflict*, 56; Collins, *Shadows*, 454, notes that NUP members in the south warned party leaders against this policy and urged that all governors, deputy governors, and district commissioners come from the south.

36. Mahgoub, 23, says al-Mahdi cried during the independence ceremony; on parliament's debates, Mahgoub, 55-57; Warburg, *Islam, Nationalism*, 83-89.

37. Malwal, *People and Power*, 47; Wai, *African-Arab Conflict*, 69; Peter Nyot Kok, *Governance and Conflict in the Sudan, 1985-1995* (Hamburg: Deutsches Orient-Institut, 1996), 13, declares that southern votes for independence were "obtained by fraud" since the northern politicians did not intend to support federalism.

38. Wai, *The African-Arab Conflict*, 57-67 on Zande, Yambio, and Torit; Collins, *Shadows*, 332, 457-58 on Yambio and Torit; Malwal, 33-35, 52-57. The chief justice quashed the conviction of the Zande MP after a Commission of Inquiry ruled that his trial was a farce and indicated abuse of power by the government.

39. Ahmed, 119; Abdel Rahim, 225, on Egyptian involvement.

40. Abdel Rahim, 225. He notes that the mutiny occurred two days after the parliament voted for immediate self-determination and that Egypt urged the British governor general to declare a constitutional emergency after the mutiny. Abdel Rahim does not mention either the order to the troops to go north or the extra-legal execution of the mutineers.

41. Kok, 120; Wai, *African-Arab Conflict*, 70-71. The three southern members soon boycotted committee meetings, since they were always outvoted.

42. Sanderson and Sanderson, 353-56.

43. Wai, *African-Arab Conflict*, 75.

44. Bechtold, 203; Lesch, "Military Disengagement from Politics: The Sudan," *Military Disengagement from Politics*, ed. Constantine P. Danopoulos (New York: Routledge, 1988), 26-30; Mahgoub, 184-86; Warburg, *Islam, Nationalism*, 109-14.

45. Wai, *African-Arab Conflict*, 77, 85-91; Alier, *Southern Sudan*, 24; Sanderson and Sanderson, 358-59, 367-68, 399 and on missionaries 394, 397, 406-407, 451-56 (text of 1962 act).

46. Wai, *African-Arab Conflict*, 89.

47. Anya-Nya combines the Madi words *inya nya* (a snake poison) with the Moru word *manyanya* (a tiny insect that kills large animals by spreading in a mass over their bodies), according to Deng Awur, "The Integration of the Anya-Nya into the National Army," *North-South Relations in the Sudan since the Addis Ababa Agreement* (Khartoum: University of Khartoum, 1988), ed. Mom K. N. Arou and B. Yongo-Bure, 63-64. Elias Nyamlell Wakoson, "The Origin and Development of the Anya-Nya Movement 1955-1972," in Mohamed Omer Beshir, ed., *Southern Sudan: Regionalism and Religion* (Khartoum: University of Khartoum, 1984), 184-88.

48. Bechtold, 212; Mahgoub, 189-90; Wai, *African-Arab Conflict*, 93; and Warburg, *Islam, Nationalism*, 114-15.

49. Warburg, *Islam, Nationalism*, 115; Mahgoub, 197; Bechtold, 218-19.

50. Northern delegates: Umma, National Unionist Party, People's Democratic Party, Sudan Communist Party, Islamic Charter Front, and Professional Front. Southern delegates: SANU-Jaden, SANU-Deng, Southern Front, plus individuals selected by northern politicians. Alier, *Southern Sudan*, 27-32; Wai, *African-Arab Conflict*, 101-104; and Mohamed Omer Beshir [head of the conference secretariat], *The Southern Sudan: Background to Conflict* (London: Hurst, 1968).

51. Bechtold, 220 ff on 1965 election: PDP boycotted; Umma and Azhari's NUP each won about a third of the seats; SCP won 11 seats; ICF won 5 seats; and 21 northerners were seated unopposed to represent the south. Bechtold, 246, 269 and Mahgoub, 201-202 on 1968 election: DUP (PDP and NUP)—101 seats; al-Sadiq's wing of Umma—36 (Sadiq lost); Imam al-Hadi's Umma wing—30 (plus support by 6 independent MPs); SCP (socialist independents)—1; ICF—3 (Turabi lost); Beja and Nuba—5; SANU—15; Southern Front—10; 9 other independents.

52. Imam al-Hadi's Prime Minister Mahgoub (199-201) called al-Sadiq an ambitious upstart, whereas Bechtold (245) claimed that al-Sadiq ran the first competent and professional administration, when he was prime minister from July 1966 to May 1967.

53. Warburg, *Islam, Nationalism*, 116-19; Bechtold, 243.

54. Maiden speech, in Wai, *African-Arab Conflict*, 117.

55. Alier, *Southern Sudan*, 38; Kok, 121.

56. Alier, *Southern Sudan*, 33; Malwal, *People and Power*, 39, 97. Estimates of the deaths in Juba ranged from the official figure of 430 (inquiry by a judge of the court of appeal) to the Southern Front's *Vigilant* report of 1,400, out of 10,000 residents in the city; Mansour Khalid, *The Government They Deserve* (London: Kegan Paul International, 1990), 228. Alier notes, on the Malakal attack, that the court acquitted the editors on the grounds that they should not be punished for revealing governmental atrocities.

57. Malwal, *People and Power*, 42, and Khalid, *Government They Deserve*, 231, state that soon after Prime Minister al-Sadiq al-Mahdi "cried profusely" over the grave of a young northern officer killed by the Anya-Nya, the twenty-four chiefs were shot dead in the garrison. Not coincidentally, a son of one of those chiefs participated in the SPLA attack that overran the Bor garrison in April 1989.

58. Alier, *Southern Sudan*, 35-38.

59. Malwal, *People and Power*, 110-11.

3. The Contradictory Policies of Numairi, 1969-1985

1. Peter K. Bechtold, *Politics in the Sudan* (New York: Praeger, 1976), 259-63; Gabriel Warburg, *Islam, Nationalism and Communism in a Traditional Society* (London: Frank Cass, 1978), 121-22; Mohamed Ahmed Mahgoub, *Democracy on Trial* (London: Andre Deutsch, 1974), 226-27, names the RCC and council of ministers.

2. Bechtold, 261, 268.

3. Quoted in full in *Perspective on the South* (Khartoum: Ministry of Guidance

and National Information, 1983), 21-22; Abel Alier, *Southern Sudan* (Exeter: Ithaca, 1990), 43-51, reviews the steps by which the statement was developed.

4. Dunstan M. Wai, *The African-Arab Conflict in the Sudan* (New York: Africana, 1981), 142ff. on the negotiations and 162-64 on seven mutually reinforcing factors that favored negotiations, of which military stalemate was a key. Hizkias Assefa, *Mediation of Civil Wars* (Boulder: Westview, 1987), 151-65, 183, on Numairi, Alier, Lagu, and mediators' roles in the context of the "hurting stalemate," a term analyzed by I. William Zartman in *Ripe for Resolution: Conflict and Intervention in Africa* (New York: Oxford University Press, 1985). Alier, *Southern Sudan*, 89-99, on the delegations and negotiations: Alier headed the government delegation, along with foreign minister Mansour Khalid and other northern ministers and military officers.

5. Regional minister of mining and industry, Bona Malwal, *Sudan* (New York: Thornton, 1985), 30, 20.

6. Alier, *Southern Sudan*, 193-212; Mohamed Osman El Sammani, *Jonglei Canal* (Khartoum: University of Khartoum Press, 1984); John Waterbury, *Hydropolitics of the Nile Valley* (Syracuse: Syracuse University Press, 1979), 76-77, 90-92, 200-202; Robert O. Collins, *The Waters of the Nile: Hydropolitics and the Jonglei Canal, 1900-1988* (Oxford: Clarendon, 1990).

7. Malwal, *Sudan*, 30, 32; Raphael Koba Badal, *Oil and Regional Sentiment in Southern Sudan* (Syracuse: Department of Geography, Syracuse University, 1983); Alier, *Southern Sudan*, 215-24, which notes that the southern commander who was removed from Bentiu (Captain Silva Kiir) became a senior commander in the SPLA.

8. Alier, *Southern Sudan*, 162, 138-42. Two hundred and seventy southerners entered the army in 1974, but none subsequently; only 5 percent of those accepted in the military college came from the south. Captain John Garang de Mabior (the future head of the SPLM/SPLA) commanded Anya-Nya in Upper Nile at the time of the accord, which he opposed. William Nyuon Bany, a major in Anya-Nya, was demoted to captain; after he filed a complaint, he was demoted to regimental sergeant. He escaped with his troops from Ayod on 6 June 1983 and became a commander in the SPLA until he died in 1995.

9. Alier, *Southern Sudan*, 244-47. Brigadier James Loro Sirsio from First Division (Southern Command) headquarters visited Bor in January 1983 and arranged to delay the transfer; he became a member of the Transitional Military Council (TMC) in 1985-86. The National Defense Council in Khartoum—Vice Presidents Umar al-Tayib and Lagu, Attorney General Turabi, the minister of energy and mining, HEC President Joseph John Tambura, the commander of the First Division, and the three chiefs of staff—ordered the attack. Of the chiefs of staff, General Abd al-Rahman al-Suwar al-Dhahab favored the attack but General Yusuf Ahmad Yusuf opposed the use of force. Subsequently, al-Suwar al-Dhahab headed the TMC in 1985, whereas Yusuf promoted negotiations with the SPLM. The attack was led by Commander Dominic Kassiano, an absorbed officer from western Equatoria who supported the NIF coup d'état in 1989. Bor commander Major Kerubino Kuanyan Bol became an SPLA officer. Colonel John Garang, then director of research in the army headquarters in Khartoum, was sent by Numairi to Bor to restore order but, instead, defected.

10. Mohamed Beshir Hamid, "Devolution and the Problems of National Inte-

gration: A Case Study of the Sudan," *North-South Relations*, ed. Mom K. N. Arou and B. Yongo-Bure (Khartoum: University of Khartoum, 1988), 152.

11. Malwal, *Sudan*, 30-31, which notes that Attorney General Turabi drew up the presidential decrees that gave Numairi the power to dissolve the regional institutions in the south and to institute direct rule there for up to two years without holding elections; Mohammed Beshir Hamid, "Confrontation and Reconciliation within an African Context: The Case of Sudan," *Third World Quarterly*, 5:3 (April 1983), 323-24; Bona Malwal, *People and Power in Sudan* (London: Ithaca, 1981), 205-45.

12. Presidential Decree #1 in *Perspective on the South*, 35-37; background in Malwal, *Sudan*, 33-34; Alier, *Southern Sudan*, 183-92, 231-35. The three governors were Joseph James Tambura, Equatoria, former HEC president; Dr. Lawrence Wol Wol, Bahr al-Ghazal, a former Dinka official; and Daniel Kuot Mathews, Upper Nile, Nuer former regional minister for industry. Tambura justified redivision in *Sudanow* (August 1984) 17 and (March 1985) 14-15.

13. Bechtold, 273, notes that Turabi was released in November 1972; al-Sadiq al-Mahdi was released from house arrest in December 1972 but then went abroad; Ahmad al-Mahdi and former prime minister Muhammad Ahmad Mahjub returned in 1974. The properties of al-Sadiq al-Mahdi and his uncle Ahmad al-Mahdi were desequestrated in May 1974.

14. Bechtold, 279. Removed from office in 1975, Khalid joined the SPLM in 1983 as its northern spokesman.

15. Interview with al-Sadiq al-Mahdi, 18 May 1985.

16. A total of 140 of the 374 seats were won by the opposition, including 30 Umma, 30 NUP, and 20 ICF.

17. Peter Nyot Kok, *Governance and Conflict in the Sudan* (Hamburg: Deutsches Orient-Institut, 1996), 42; Abdullahi an-Na'im and Peter Nyot Kok, *Fundamentalism and Militarism* (New York: Fund for Peace, 1991), 8; Abbashar Jamal, "Funding Fundamentalism," *Middle East Report* 21:5 (September 1991), 16; T. Abdou Maliqalim Simone, *In Whose Image?* (Chicago: University of Chicago Press, 1994), 36-37.

18. Alier, *Southern Sudan*, 175.

19. Tony Barnett and Abbas Abdelkarim, eds., *Sudan: State, Capital and Transformation* (London: Croom Helm, 1988), 2-3 analyze the structural causes and effects of the famine. Some 8,000 were deported in September 1981 alone.

20. The foreign debt reached $9 billion by 1985. In 1982-83, cotton exports were $250 million of the $590 million exported. Imports totalling $1.7 billion consisted of: (1) oil and petroleum products for the railway, trucks, industries, and mechanized farms, (2) goods and supplies for rural development, e.g., fertilizers, pesticides, and farm machinery, (3) manufactured goods, and (4) foodstuffs (grain and sugar). *Economic Trends Report*, U.S. Embassy, Khartoum, 12 January 1984, 1. Oil imports jumped from $13 million (1970) to $400 million (1984), partly due to increased per-barrel cost; *Middle East Reporter*, 5 May 1984.

21. Alier, *Southern Sudan*, 187-89. Khalil was also SSU secretary general and chief of staff. He reemerged as defense minister under al-Sadiq al-Mahdi (1988-89) and led the effort in February 1989 to remove the National Islamic Front from the cabinet and form a government of national unity to negotiate with the SPLM.

22. *Le Monde*, 4 October 1983.

23. *The Islamic Way: Why?* (1980) and subsequent pamphlets may have been

written by Muhammad Mahjub Sulaiman, Numairi's press advisor (SUNA, 24 April 1985).

24. Carolyn Fluehr-Lobban, *Islamic Law and Society in the Sudan* (London: Frank Cass, 1987), 280. She notes that many judges resigned in protest at the 1980 decree.

25. The code was drafted by Professor al-Mikashfi Taha al-Kabashi (see fn 29) and Numairi's young advisors, al-Nayal Abd al-Qadir Abu Gurun and Awad al-Jiid Muhammad Ahmad. Abu Gurun, son of a sufi shaykh in Khartoum, graduated from Khartoum University's law faculty. Numairi met him at a sufi ceremony and appointed him judicial assistant in the presidency and, in March 1985, legal attaché. Observers commented on his braided hair, black turban, and perfumed clothes. Abu Gurun introduced Numairi to al-Jiid, whose great-grandfather founded a sufi order in Ifaina village, Gezira. Numairi appointed him attorney general in March 1985. Mansour Khalid says al-Jiid claimed "telepathic communication with the Prophet Muhammad: al-Jeed told Nimeiri that the Prophet had appeared to him in a dream and told him that Nimeiri was destined to save the Islamic nation." *Nimeiri and the Revolution of Dis-May* (London: Routledge and Kegan Paul, 1985), 277-79.

26. SUNA, 12 November 1983. The men, held in Kober prison, had their right hands severed at the wrist by prison guards, who used knives while they sat blindfolded on chairs with their legs tied. They were then taken to a hospital for treatment, since all the doctors refused to amputate the limbs of prisoners. Later, Numairi altered his views on punishment for embezzlement and announced that prisoners would be amnestied if they repaid the state the sums stolen (SUNA, 17 February 1985). Al-Mikashfi objected to that presidential interference in the judiciary. Numairi protected the rich and punished the poor, according to a Muslim accountant who commented to the author that white collar crimes were not punished by hudud whereas poor people who stole bread to feed their families lost their hands. That person viewed those rulings as perversions of Islam, which required fairness and equity.

27. *Arabia* (London), August 1984, 32-33; *International Herald Tribune*, 9 August 1984; *Middle East Reporter*, 16 June 1984; *Le Monde*, 28 December 1984; Khalid, *Nimeiri*, 277-79.

28. Joint letter to Numairi, 12 June 1984; text in Lesch, "Rebellion in the Southern Sudan," *UFSI Report* #8 (Indianapolis: 1985), 13.

29. SUNA, 24 January 1985. Al-Mikashfi, a former professor of Islamic studies at Omdurman Islamic University, had no courtroom experience before he became a judge under the September decrees. He became a NIF MP in 1986. English translation and analysis of Taha's writings: Abdullahi Ahmed An-Na'im, *Toward an Islamic Reformation* (Syracuse: Syracuse University Press, 1990). Taha advised the disciples to recant to avoid hanging. Instead of letting them submit written petitions, Numairi videotaped their confessions, which he broadcast on television to humiliate them.

30. *Le Monde*, 28 December 1984; Khalid, *Nimeiri*, 390-94.

31. The committee was headed by Sirr Khatim al-Khalifa, head of the transitional government in 1964-65 and host of the Round-Table Conference. Four southerners appointed to it refused to serve: Abel Alier, Dr. Peter Nyot Kok (law professor, Khartoum University), Dr. Lam Akol (engineering professor, Khartoum University), and Isaiah Kulang. Alier, *Southern Sudan*, 238; Kok, 55; SUNA, 4, 14, and 18 March 1985; *Sudanow*, April 1985, 9.

4. The Transition to Democracy

1. Mansour Khalid, *The Government They Deserve* (London: Kegan Paul International, 1990), 336-38, 341; Peter Nyot Kok, *Governance and Conflict in the Sudan* (Hamburg: Deutsches Orient-Institut, 1996), 18, 21.

2. SUNA, 26 March 1985; *International Herald Tribune* (IHT), 1-7, April 1985 on the uprising.

3. Suwar al-Dhahab press conference on 15 April: "I had contacted the troops in my capacity as Commander-in-Chief and Defense Minister and got acquainted with their unity. The citizens had been linked in an oath of allegiance but it was dropped when they withdrew it from the ousted president for logical reasons. So when all the citizens gave up allegiance, the Armed Forces was obliged to follow suit because it is an integral part of the people." (SUNA, 16 April 1985).

Suwar al-Dhahab was born in Al-Ubayyid (Kordofan) in 1935, entered the military college in 1954, joined the army intelligence corps in 1957, and spent 1967 in an infantry course in the United States. He had tours in England and Jordan and was posted to Uganda in 1968 as military attaché. He became a full colonel in 1972 and a brigadier and commander of the southern staff (Juba) in 1975. In 1982 he became commander of operations and a full general. He became chief of staff and deputy minister of defense in 1983, during which he repressed the Bor mutiny. He became commander-in-chief and defense minister in March 1985, just before the uprising.

4. Communiqué #1, 9:30 a.m., 6 April 1985: "The Armed Forces kept watching the deteriorating security situation in the country and the complicated political situation that it has reached. In order to prevent bloodshed and to protect the independence of the nation and the integrity of its territory, the Armed Forces unanimously decided to respond to the will of the people and take over power and hand it back to the people after a limited transitional period." (SUNA, 7 April 1985).

5. *Akher Sa'a* (Cairo), 24 April 1985. Dafallah was born near Wad Medani in 1935, graduated from the Khartoum Medical College in 1959, and conducted research on stomach cancer in London in 1966-69 and in Japan in 1980. He was active in the 1964 revolution and had chaired the physicians' union since 1982.

6. Alliance views in SUNA, 1-4 June 1985; southern views in SUNA, 1 June 1985; also SUNA, 15-16 July, 24 July, and 22 August 1985; *al-Ahram*, 15 September 1985; Kok, 27-28 and interview with Kok, 7 January 1986.

7. *IHT*, 15 April 1985; SUNA, 16 April and 28 May 1985; *al-Siyasa* (Kuwait), 4 July 1985.

8. *New York Times*, 23 April 1985; also SUNA, 1 June and 6 July 1985.

9. Kok, 24-26; Umma Program; *al-Mustaqbal* (Paris), 1 June 1985; attorney general in *al-Sharq al-Awsat* (London), 9 July 1985.

10. Manslaughter, theft, adultery, prostitution, fornication, corruption, and war against Muslim citizens. SUNA, 30 December 1985.

11. Each three-judge state security court was headed by a judge from the supreme court, which had to confirm the sentences. Defendants had legal counsel and were tried under prevailing laws (Kok, 29). The proceedings were broadcast on TV. Cases:

(1) Dr. Baha al-Din Muhammad Idris ("Mr. Ten Percent"), state minister for special affairs at the presidency since 1982, was a former zoology lecturer at Khartoum University, who was dismissed in the 1960s for divulging exam answers to his student girlfriend. He was convicted of treason for corruption involving contracts to purchase helicopters and jet fighters and also projects of the Daiwoo Company (South Korea). SUNA, 26 May, 8 and 31 July, 3 and 5 August 1985; *Egyptian Gazette*, 28 July 1985; *al-Ahram* (Cairo), 28 August 1985.

(2) Umar al-Tayib, convicted of treason for organizing the airlift of Ethiopian Jews to Israel (1984), abuse of power, and misappropriation of public funds: *Observer* (London), 21 April 1985; SUNA, 29 April, 24, 28, and 22 May, 1-5, 15, and 30 June, 8 July 1985.

(3) Members of the 1969 RCC, who received thirty-year sentences for overthrowing the elected government: *Sudan Times*, 12 December 1986. Their defense lawyer Abd al-Basit Sabdarat served as minister of information in the post-1989 government.

(4) Others included former ministers of finance, planning, and energy/mining, the head of the Military Trading Corporation, and Numairi's brother Mustafa [SUNA, 3 and 20 May, 4 and 12 June, 8 July 1985; *al-Ahali* (Cairo), 28 August 1985]. Former energy and mining minister Sharif al-Tuhami was on trial by early 1987, defended by Abd al-Aziz Shiddu, who became attorney general after the 1989 coup and was also Umar al-Tayib's defense lawyer.

The government tried to persuade Egypt to return Numairi to stand trial in Khartoum, but Cairo upheld his right to political asylum so long as he did not engage in political subversion. (MENA, 17 July 1985; *al-Siyasa*, 6 July 1985; *al-Hawadith*, 14 June 1985.)

12. *Al-Ahali* (Cairo), 16 April 1986.

13. Text of Umma program, 6 April 1985 (Arabic). Party conference in February 1986 elected al-Mahdi chair, selected a five-member general secretariat and 360-member central committee, and reestablished regional committees. Interview with al-Mahdi, 18 May 1985; *al-Ahali*, 16 April 1986; *al-Musawwar*, 18 April 1986.

14. *Al-Musawwar*, 18 April 1986. DUP was challenged by NUP, led by lawyer Ali Mahmud Hasanain, who stressed that the multilingual, multiracial, and multireligious Sudan should not be ruled on a sectarian basis. Decentralization would enable outlying regions to obtain their fair share of resources and revenues. NUP helped formulate the Charter for the Defense of Democracy in November 1985 and participated in the Koka Dam conference in March 1986. NUP did not win any seats to the parliament. *Al-Ahram*, 10 April 1986; *Sudanow* (January 1986), 38.

15. Election program and *The Question of the South of the Sudan* (Arabic) in 1986; interviews with Turabi (19 May 1986) and Ali Uthman Muhammad Taha (20 May 1986); *Sudanow* (September 1985), 26-28; *Africa Confidential*, 12 March 1986; *al-Sha'ab*, 15 April 1986; *IHT*, 22 April 1986; SUNA, 1 and 3 May 1986. The 2,200 person conference in May 1985, which included 120 Muslims from the south, reelected Turabi, the political bureau, and the consultative council. The original Muslim Brotherhood (MB), headed by Sadiq Abdallah Abd al-Majid, joined the National Alliance and signed the National Charter in 1985. MB nominated three candidates, none of whom won.

16. *Al-Musawwar*, 11 and 25 April 1986; *al-Ahali*, 9, 16, and 23 April 1986. The

three SCP MPs included Joseph Adisio Madistu, nephew of Joseph Garang, the SCP minister executed in 1971. Madistu wanted to cancel the September decrees, formulate a secular constitution, negotiate with the SPLM, and reunify the south.

17. Headed by brothers Badr al-Din and Taisir Muddathir Amin, it ran 90 candidates (10 in the capital), who won 36,000 votes. *Al-Ahram*, 15 and 24 April 1986; *Arabia*, (May 1986), 29.

18. Led by Abdallah Zakaria; *Sudanow* (February 1986), 2; SUNA, 13 May 1986.

19. *Al-Ahram*, 10 April 1986.

20. Charter of National Work (Arabic), 1986; interviews 27 May 1986 with Ghabboush and Professor al-Amin Hamouda of the General Union of the Nuba Mountains, whose two candidates gained 822 votes.

21. *Sudanow*, February 1986, 40-41. The northern members were Sudan National Party, General Union of the Nuba Mountains, Southern Dar Fur Development Front, General Funj Union (Blue Nile), and the North and South Funj Unions.

22. Kok, 47. Young PPP activists interviewed in January 1987 criticized senior politicians who based their power on their positions as chiefs; they argued that personalities—not policies—divided PPP and SAPCO. SAPCO secretary general Dr. Pacifico Lado Lolik was speaker of the Equatorian assembly and its president, Morris Lawiya, served in the Equatorian regional government. They both lost in the 1986 election, but al-Mahdi named Lolik to the Council of State and made Lawiya governor of Equatoria. PPP's Surur, Secretary General Lawrence Modi Tombe, Transitional Government Minister Jimmy Wango, and three regional commissioners won assembly seats.

23. When interviewed on 8 January 1987, Dai Wal denied ties to Anya-Nya II but noted its "sympathy" for his party.

24. Details on the elections in Lesch, "Party Politics in the Sudan," *UFSI Report* #9 (1986) and "The Parliamentary Election of 1986: Fatally Flawed?" *Northeast African Studies*, I: 2-3 (East Lansing: Michigan State University Press, 1995).

25. Turabi complained that an "unnatural" coalition of DUP, Umma, SCP, and the Ba'th Party "ganged-up" to support the DUP candidate against him; *al-Ahali*, 7 May 1986; *al-Musawwar*, 25 April 1986. SCP's Nuqud defeated al-Imam, with support from Umma and DUP.

26. Ahmad al-Radi Jabir (Upper Nile) and Ali Tamim Fartak (Bahr al-Ghazal). Fartak, a Muslim member of the NIF politburo, headed NIF's Western Bahr al-Ghazal Development Committee.

27. In Upper Nile, voting could be held only in the towns of Malakal, Renk, Kodok, and Nasir; in Bahr al-Ghazal, only in Wau and Aweil. Kok, 42-43, 46, 52.

28. *Al-Musawwar*, 2 May 1986; *al-Ahali*, 23 and 30 April 1986.

29. *Al-Musawwar*, 25 April 1986; *al-Ahram*, 29 April 1986, 2 and 5 May 1986; on the south, *Guiding Star* (Khartoum), 15 May 1986.

30. Charter for a National Government, 29 April 1986 (Arabic and English); SUNA, 30 April 1986.

31. Charter of National Unity and accompanying statement (Arabic mimeo); interview with Ghabboush, 27 May 1986; SUNA, 5 May 1986. SAPCO was the only African party not to support the charter, since it made a deal with al-Mahdi to gain representation on the Council of State. SPFP also hesitated to confront al-Mahdi, since Dai Wal wanted to join the cabinet.

32. Description of 4-6 May 1986 based on an internal memorandum by Laurence Modi Tombe, secretary general of PPP, 6 May 1986; interview with Ghabboush, 27 May 1986; SUNA, 7 May 1986; *al-Ahram*, 7 May 1986. Tombe noted that PPP proposed that each of the nine regions appoint two persons to the cabinet, which would guarantee African political forces 7-9 of eighteen ministries.

33. Both quotations in Tombe's memorandum. SNP, PPP, SSPA, SAC, and SPFP walked out, joined (briefly) by the three southern MPs in NIF and SCP—an indication of the strength of ethnic ties. The walkouts and Ghabboush-Mahdi altercation are detailed in Lesch, "Party Politics," 12-13.

34. Dr. Muhammad Ibrahim Khalil of Umma defeated NIF's Muhammad Yusuf Muhammad. Khalil, who was al-Mahdi's foreign minister in 1966-1967, later was a legal advisor to the Kuwait Development Fund and helped draft the Alliance charter in 1984-1985.

35. Al-Mahdi won 165 votes; NIF's Ali Uthman Muhammad Taha 49; and SCP's Dr. Izz al-Din Ali Amr 3.

36. SUNA, 7 May 1986.

37. SUNA, 14 May 1986; *al-Ahram*, 15 May 1986; interview with Ghabboush, 27 May 1986.

5. Polarization during the Parliamentary Period

1. Lesch, "Sudan's Foreign Policy," *Sudan*, ed. John O. Voll (Bloomington: Indiana University Press, 1991), 59; on Libya: *Al-Sharq al-Awsat*, 3 September 1988 (FBIS-NES-88-175, 9 September 1988) and interview with Turabi, 6 November 1988 (FBIS-NES-88-218, 10 November 1988); and MENA, 2 November 1988 (FBIS-NES-88-213, 3 November 1988).

2. Muhammad Tawfiq, *Al-Tadamun*, 28 March 1987 (FBIS-NES 7 April 1987); Abbashar Jamal, "Funding Fundamentalism: The Political Economy of an Islamist State," *Middle East Report* 172 (September 1991), 15.

3. Turabi, *al-Majallah* (London), 15 April 1987 (FBIS-NES, 23 April 1987); demonstrations and state of emergency in Omdurman radio, 25 July 1987 (FBIS-NES 27 July 1987); MENA, 4 October 1987, and SUNA, 6 October 1987 (FBIS-NES-87-194, 7 October 1987); Kuwait News Agency (KUNA), 19 October 1987 (FBIS-NES-87-202, 20 October 1987).

4. SUNA, 18 January 1987 (FBIS-NES 20 January 1987); parties' views in SUNA, 7 February 1987 (FBIS-NES 9 February 1987); *Sudan Times*, 6 February 1987 (original names for council of the south), 8 February 1987 (southern parties' rejection); al-Mahdi on Omdurman radio, 23 March 1987. In January 1987 the author interviewed southern intellectuals, Equatorian governor Peter Cyrillo, and leaders of SSPA, SPFP, and PPP, who criticized Mahdi's high-handed actions as well as the individuals appointed. SSPA split when its cabinet member Aldo Ajo Deng refused to resign and half of SSPA's eight MPs remained with him. A year later, although al-Mahdi endorsed the Sudan Transitional Charter that said southerners should select the members of the Council for the South, he selected Angelo Beda to replace Obur, when Obur became head of the government-supplied Anya-Nya II militia in Upper Nile.

5. *Sudan Times*, 11, 13, and 25 November 1986, 2 December 1986 on Islamic ex-

perts, 3 December 1986 on bar association, 3 February 1987 on NIF heckling al-Mahdi. The amendments would (1) let the government legislate while parliament was not in session, although decrees must be placed before the assembly within a fortnight of reconvening or else cease to be law; (2) enable parliament to amend the constitution by a simple majority, not two-thirds; (3) give parliament the right to unseat MPs who changed party affiliation; (4) reduce the quorum from 51 percent to 30 percent (90 MPs); (5) let the Council of State veto legislation, which parliament could override.

6. *Sudan Times*, 27 February, 3 and 11 March, 3 April 1987; *Le Monde*, 10 June 1987. Al-Mahdi tabled that version on 2 March 1987. Only SSPA voted against it, arguing that no changes should be made in the constitution before the final thirty-seven MPs were elected to represent the south.

7. SUNA, 15 December 1987 (FBIS-NES-87-241, 16 December 1987).

8. *Sudan Times*, 25 February 1988.

9. Speeches, *Sudan Times*, 13 and 16 March 1988.

10. Dr. Muhammad Yusif Abu Harira, *Sudan Times*, 6 February, 15, 17, 20 May and 5 June 1987. Hindi's comments in *Sudan Times*, 14 May 1987, and SUNA, 17 May 1987 (FBIS-NES 19 May 1987).

11. SUNA, 22 June 1987 (FBIS-NES 23 June 1987), 11 July 1987 (FBIS-NES 13 July 1987); Omdurman radio, 8 and 10 August 1987 (FBIS-NES 10 August 1987); Muhammad Uthman al-Mirghani in *Tadamun*, 19 August 1987 (FBIS-NES 3 September 1987); al-Mahdi in *October* (Cairo), 30 August 1987 (FBIS-NES 2 September 1987); *Sudan Times*, 14 May 1987 on Yassin's criticism of Ahmad al-Mirghani.

12. *Sudan Times*, 21 May 1987.

13. Omdurman Radio, 10 January 1988 (FBIS-NES-88-006 11 January 1988).

14. *Sudan Times*, 10 (text of 20 April charter), 14, 24, 25, 29 April 1988; SUNA, 28 April 1988 (FBIS-NES-88-082, 28 April 1988). Twenty-five MPs from African parties and SCP voted against al-Mahdi for prime minister.

15. A NIF member also became Khartoum commissioner: Major General Air Force al-Fatih Abdun, former chair of NIF's Khartoum branch. NIF's Muhammad Yusuf Muhammad replaced Umma's Dr. Muhammad Ibrahim Khalil as assembly speaker. Khalil had resigned in disgust at his own party. Al-Mahdi rejected two others whom NIF proposed as speaker: Lawyer Ahmad Sulaiman and former prime minister al-Jazouli Dafallah. SUNA, 28 April 1988 (FBIS-NES-88-083, 29 April 1988), 3 May 1988 (FBIS-NES-88-086, 4 May 1988), 5 May 1988 (FBIS-NES-88-087, 5 May 1988), 7 May 1988 (FBIS-NES-88-089, 9 May 1988). Al-Mahdi also wanted to reconfigure the council of state so that Umma would retain two seats but DUP, NIF, and the south would each have one (*Sudan Times*, 1 May 1988).

16. *Al-Sharq al-Awsat*, 3 June 1988 (FBIS-NES-88-116, 16 June 1988); interview in *al-Sha'ab* (Cairo), 30 August 1988 (FBIS-NES-88-174, 8 September 1988). Al-Mahdi statement in *Sudan Times*, 24 April 1988.

17. *Al-Sharq al-Awsat*: Turabi, 3 June 1988 (FBIS-NES-88-116, 16 June 1988) and long quote from 3 October 1988 (FBIS-NES-88-193, 5 October 1988); Taha in 18 July 1988 (FBIS-NES-88-141, 22 July 1988).

18. Hussain had been deputy prime minister and interior minister. SUNA, 30 April 1988 (FBIS-NES-88-084, 2 May 1988).

19. *Sudan Times*, 11 and 12 May 1988.

20. *Sudan Times*, 29 April and 1 May 1988.

21. NIF's Taha in SUNA, 6 September 1988 (FBIS-NES-88-175, 9 September 1988); African walkout in AFP, 20 September 1988 (FBIS-NES-99-182, 20 September 1988).

22. Quoted in Paul A. Hopkins, "Christianity, Islam and Politics in Sudan" (Philadelphia: memorandum for Presbyterian mission to Sudan, 1993), 7-8.

23. Angelo Beda, SUNA, 28 September 1988 (FBIS-NES-88-188, 28 September 1988).

24. SUNA, 16 November 1988 (FBIS-NES-88-222, 17 November 1988); text on SPLA Radio, 18 November 1988 (FBIS-NES-88-234, 21 November 1988).

25. Lt. Muhammad Chuol on Omdurman radio, 29 November 1988 (FBIS-NES-88-231, 1 December 1988).

26. DUP, SCP, and African parties voted against that delegation of power. SUNA, 14 December 1988 (FBIS-NES-88-240, 14 December 1988) and 19 December 1988 (FBIS-NES-88-240, 20 December 1988). NIF's Taha in *al-Sharq al-Awsat*, 3 December 1988 (FBIS-NES-88-234, 6 December 1988).

27. SUNA, 27 December 1988 (FBIS-NES-88-249, 28 December 1988).

28. Omdurman radio, 19 November 1988 (FBIS-NES-88-224, 21 November 1988); MENA, 20 November 1988 (FBIS-NES-88-224, 21 November 1988); SPLA radio, 21 November 1988 (FBIS-NES-88-225, 22 November 1988); Khalid, *Government They Deserve*, 400; Peter Nyot Kok, *Governance and Conflict in the Sudan* (Hamburg: Deutsches Orient-Institut, 1996), 68-69 and 83 fn 37.

29. Lt. Col. Hasan Nasr, an officer in the infantry academy, was arrested with some retired military officers and members of the former SSU. Although it was termed a pro-Numairi plot, the participants were released immediately after the June 1989 coup, which Nasr initially supported. *Al-Sharq al-Awsat*, 17 December 1988 (FBIS-NES-88-244, 20 December 1988); SUNA, 21 December 1988 (FBIS-NES-88-245, 21 December 1988).

30. Turabi in *Le Monde*, 24 December 1988 (FBIS-NES-89-009, 13 January 1989); SUNA, 10 January 1989 (FBIS-NES-89-007, 11 January 1989); Kok, 69. On February 1, Minister of State for Justice Hafiz al-Shaikh al-Zaki became attorney general and minister of justice. A NIF student leader at Khartoum University, he later worked in the attorney general's office under Turabi and was a judge in Numairi's "prompt justice" courts (1983-1985). After the 1989 coup, he became dean of the law faculty at Khartoum University.

31. Cases included Numairi's Minister of Energy Sharif Tuhami, Special Advisor Dr. Baha al-Din Muhammad Idris, and the manager of the State Petroleum Company. AFP and KUNA, 2 January 1989 (FBIS-NES-89-001, 3 January 1989); SUNA, 5 January 1989 (FBIS-NES-89-004, 6 January 1989), 11 January 1989 (FBIS-NES-89-008, 12 January 1989), 25 January 1989 (FBIS-NES-89-016, 26 January 1989).

32. Ambo Workshop, in Abel Alier, *Southern Sudan* (Exeter: Ithaca, 1990), 283-84.

33. Omdurman Radio, 1 February 1989 (FBIS-NES-89-021, 2 February 1989) and 21 February 1989 (FBIS-NES-89-034, 22 February 1989).

34. SUNA, 18 August 1988 (FBIS-NES-88-160, 18 August 1988); *al-Ahram*,

10 September 1988 (FBIS-NES-88-177, 13 September 1988). AFP, 22 May 1989 (FBIS-NES-89-098, 23 May 1989) reported that al-Mahdi withdrew the PDF plan after the change in government in March 1989; NIF revived it in December 1989.

35. Omdurman radio, 22 February 1989 (FBIS-NES-89-035, 23 February 1989).

36. Al-Mahdi angered DUP and the other groups by failing to mention the peace initiative in his press conference on 4 March and by refusing to resign along with the cabinet (MENA, 5 March 1989 in FBIS-NES-89-042, 6 March 1989). However, in his parliamentary speech on 13 March he did emphasize his commitment to the phased program, while omitting any reference to shari'a (MENA, 13 March 1989 in FBIS-NES-89-048, 14 March 1989).

37. MENA, 11 March 1989 (FBIS-NES-89-047, 13 March 1989).

38. Omdurman radio, 27 April 1989 (FBIS-NES-89-080, 27 April 1989).

39. Khartoum National Unity Radio, 26 March 1989 (FBIS-NES-89-057, 27 March 1989); AFP, 3 April 1989 (FBIS-NES-89-063, 4 April 1989).

40. The vote was 153 to 53; AFP, 10 April 1989 (FBIS-NES-89-068, 11 April 1989).

41. Turabi press conference; he chaired that executive bureau meeting and another on 13 March that reinforced the decision. MENA, 8 March 1989 (FBIS-NES-89-044, 8 March 1989); MENA and SUNA, 14 March 1989 (FBIS-NES-89-048, 14 March 1989).

42. Kok, 84 fn 42; first quote in Kok, 71, from *Al-Ray* (NIF newspaper), 24 March 1989; next quote by Turabi from *Ukaz* (Jeddah), 3 March 1989 (FBIS-NES-89-044, 8 March 1989).

43. SUNA, 2 March 1989 (FBIS-NES-89-041, 3 March 1989); MENA, 17 March 1989 (FBIS-NES-89-052, 20 March 1989) on another march after Friday prayers to the Council of Ministers and British Embassy. Further protests: MENA, 15 April 1989 (FBIS-NES-89-072, 17 April 1989) and 18 April 1989 (FBIS-NES-89-074, 19 April 1989); SUNA, 17 April 1989 (FBIS-NES-89-073, 18 April 1989) and 21 June 1989 (FBIS-NES-89-119, 22 June 1989).

44. Major General al-Fatih Abdun, *Al-Sharq al-Awsat*, 4 May 1989 (FBIS-NES-89-090, 11 May 1989).

45. *Al-Sharq al-Awsat*, 25 April 1989 (FBIS-NES-89-081, 28 April 1989).

46. *Al-Sharq al-Awsat*, 9 May 1989 (FBIS-NES-89-090, 11 May 1989).

47. By 20 June, seventy-six persons were arrested, including retired and serving military officers (including six brigadier generals and two colonels). They were released after the coup. *Al-Sharq al-Awsat*, 20 June 1989 (FBIS-NES-89-118, 21 June 1989); SUNA, 18 June 1989 and Omdurman radio, 18 June 1989 (FBIS-NES-89-116, 19 June 1989); MENA, 19 June 1989 (FBIS-NES-89-117, 20 June 1989), 20 June 1989 (FBIS-NES-89-118, 21 June 1989); BBC, 27 June 1989 (FBIS-NES-89-123, 28 June 1989).

48. Mubarak al-Fadhil al-Mahdi to *Ukaz* (Jeddah), 21 June 1989 (FBIS-NES-89-123, 28 June 1989).

6. Efforts to Resolve the Civil War

1. Quotations from Garang's address, 3 March 1984, speeches 22 March and 9 April 1985, and SPLM/SSPA joint communiqué of 8 February 1986, in Mansour

Khalid, ed., *John Garang Speaks* (London: Kegan Paul International, 1987), 21-23, 26, 43, 112.

2. Speech opening the Koka Dam Conference, 20 March 1986, Khalid, *John Garang Speaks*, 128-29.

3. Abel Alier, *Southern Sudan* (Exeter: Ithaca, 1990), 240-41; Robert O. Collins, *The Waters of the Nile* (Oxford: Clarendon, 1990), 393-95.

4. Garang detained Oduho, Martin Majer, and Kuot Mathews in 1985-1986. Oduho, a Latuko (Equatorian) member of the first SPLM executive and former Anya-Nya leader, wanted to head a civilian directorate. He went into exile in 1991 and died in the SPLA attack on an SPLA-United meeting in Kongor in March 1993. Former judge Majer from Bor, an ally of Oduho in the SPLM executive, was briefly released in 1991 but then rearrested and died in detention in March 1993. Mathews, Upper Nile governor (1983-1985) who supported Anya-Nya II, went into exile in 1987.

5. Gordon Kong and William Nyuon defected from the SPLA in September 1992. Nyuon freed from detention five SPLA commanders, including Kerubino and Arok Thon Arok, jailed for allegedly trying to kill Garang. Garang speech (26-27 May 1985) in Khalid, *John Garang Speaks*, 54. On Anya-Nya II: Alier, *Southern Sudan*, 251-55; *Africa Confidential*, 14 August 1985, 1 October 1985; SPLA radio, 7 August 1985 and 28 January 1988; Omdurman radio, 17 August 1985; BBC, 31 October 1985; and SUNA, 6 February 1988. Douglas H. Johnson, *Nuer Prophets* (Oxford: Clarendon, 1994), 342-44, provides a fascinating analysis of the intermingling of Nuer prophecies with the SPLA/Anya-Nya II conflict.

6. Ann Mosely Lesch, "External Involvement in the Sudanese Civil War," in *Making War and Waging Peace*, ed. David R. Smock (Washington: United States Institute of Peace, 1993), 85-87.

7. Garang's speech (20 March 1986) in Khalid, *John Garang Speaks*, 139; Omdurman radio, 31 January 1986.

8. *The Wall Street Journal*, 15 May 1984; Garang speech (26-27 May 1985) in Khalid, *John Garang Speaks*, 55. Collins argues, in correspondence with the author, that the attack at Bentiu was a rogue Anya-Nya II operation. Collins provides a detailed description of the SPLM actions vis-à-vis the canal project in *Waters*, 397-401. Johnson, *Nuer Prophets*, cites Nuer prophesy as to where the digging of the canal would suddenly halt, 341-42.

9. Libya lost three of four MiG-23's supplied to Sudan. The one surviving pilot was returned via the Red Cross. SPLA Radio, 18 December 1987 (FBIS-NES-87-244, 21 December 1987), 25 December 1987 (FBIS-NES-87-248, 28 December 1987), 21 January 1989 (FBIS-NES-89-013, 23 January 1989); Libyan appeals to return the pilots in SUNA, 15 January 1989 (FBIS-NES-89-012, 19 January 1989) and MENA, 20 January 1989 (FBIS-NES-89-013, 23 January 1989).

10. *Arab Times* (Kuwait), 21 January 1985; *Middle East Reporter*, 26 January 1985; *New York Times*, 1 February 1985; Reuters, 17 March 1985; SUNA, 7 February 1985 and 18, 19 March 1985.

11. Defense Minister Khalil on Omdurman Radio, 1 February 1989 (FBIS-NES-89-021, 2 February 1989); Alier, *Southern Sudan*, 247 on SPLA territory.

12. Fund for Peace, *Living on the Margin* (New York: 1995), 14-19; Human Rights Watch/Middle East, *Sudan: Destroying Ethnic Identity, the Secret War against*

the Nuba (New York: 1991), 5-6; John Prendergast and Nancy Hopkins, "*For Four Years I Have No Rest*": *Greed and Holy War in the Nuba Mountains of Sudan* (Washington: Center of Concern, 1994), 10-13.

13. *Living on the Margin*, 23; Alier, *Southern Sudan*, 256 on al-Da'ien; John Prendergast, "Roots of Famine," 117-18; "Sudan: The Forgotten War in Darfur Flares Again," *News from Africa Watch* (New York: 1990), 3-6; J. Millard Burr and Robert O. Collins, *Requiem for the Sudan* (Boulder: Westview, 1995), 81-82; Garang statement 12 July 1988 in Mansour Khalid, ed., *The Call for Democracy in Sudan* (London: Kegan Paul International, 1992), 161.

14. Interview with al-Mahdi, 21 September 1987.

15. Hassan Makki Mohamed Ahmed, *Sudan: The Christian Design* (London: Islamic Foundation, 1989), 137.

16. *Al-Sharq al-Awsat*, 16 July 1990 (FBIS-NES-90-138, 18 July 1990); MENA, 21 October 1989 (FBIS-NES-89-203, 23 October 1989); *al-Watan al-Arabi*, 9 February 1990 (JPRS-NEA-90-008-L, 27 April 1990). Umma's Dr. Bashir Umar Fadlallah, SUNA, 6 April 1987 (FBIS-NES 7 April 1987) and al-Mirghani in *al-Sharq al-Awsat*, 21 September 1988 (FBIS-NES-88-185, 23 September 1988).

17. Speech, 22 March 1985 in Khalid, *Call for Democracy*, 36.

18. Text, Lesch, "Transition in the Sudan," *UFSI Report* (1985), 2.

19. Mansour Khalid, *The Government They Deserve* (London: Kegan Paul International, 1987), 388. In his speech 9 April 1985, Garang detailed TMC members' responsibility for the war: Khalid, *Call for Democracy*, 44-45.

20. Suwar al-Dhahab press conference, SUNA, 10 April 1985.

21. Texts in Khalid, *Call for Democracy*, 84-86; Abdallah's earlier statement, SUNA, 16 April 1985. Dafallah's letter, dated 1 June 1985, was delivered to SPLM in Nairobi by Peter Gatkuoth, minister of transport and a senior member of SSPA. Abdallah's letter, dated 27 May 1985, was delivered by retired General Yusif Ahmad Yusif and Reverend Clement Janda. Yusif, who commanded absorbed troops in Upper Nile in the 1970s, opposed the violent suppression of the Bor mutiny in 1983. Yusif later participated in DUP negotiations with SPLM. Janda, secretary general of the Sudan Council of Churches, helped organize USAP-SPLM meetings in 1987. He told the author in September 1985 that Abdallah sent his letter in his personal capacity: it was not authorized by the TMC and did not reflect the views of TMC hardliners.

22. Khalid, *Government They Deserve*, 392, also 388-89.

23. It was unclear whether Abdallah backtracked or whether the hardliners in the TMC gained the upper hand. On hardliners Taj al-Din Abdullah Fadl (deputy chair of TMC) and Fadlallah Burma Nasir (a Baqqara Arab), *AC*, 14 August 1985, 4 September 1985, and 1 October 1985; Alier, *Southern Sudan*, 260.

24. SUNA, 25 August 1985.

25. Text in Khalid, *Call for Democracy*, 87-94 (specific quotation from 93). SPLA Major Dr. Yak Majer Deng delivered the letter to the Nasir garrison on 16 September 1985.

26. Prime Minister's letter in Khalid, *Call for Democracy*, 91-100; specific quotation on 99 (italics in original); comment on SPLA radio, 28 October 1985.

27. More likely the three units mutinied to protest being sent south to fight. SPLA radio, 8, 27 September 1985 and 2 October 1985; Omdurman radio, 28 Septem-

ber 1985; Agence France Presse (AFP), 26 September 1985; *International Herald Tribune*, 30 September 1985; BBC, 30 September 1985; and SUNA, 21 September 1985 and 3 October 1985; interview with Ghabboush, 6 January 1987.

28. Dr. Taisier Muhammad Ahmad Ali, political science professor at Khartoum University, was the National Alliance's special envoy. He met with Garang in early October and traveled frequently to Addis Ababa from 1985 to 1989; in spring 1989 he became a member of the official liaison group to finalize arrangements for the constitutional conference. Another interlocutor was Professor Mohamed Omer Bashir ("MOB") of Khartoum University, a central participant at the Round-Table and Addis Ababa conferences, who met with SPLM in fall 1985 for the government's reconciliation committee. Interviews with MOB in SUNA, 17 October 1985, and *al-Musawwar* (Cairo), 25 October 1985. Garang's letter to Deputy Prime Minister Samuel Aru Bol, 19 October 1985, in Khalid, *Call for Democracy*, 106-108.

29. SUNA, 6 and 7 November 1985, details the draft charter. Khalid, *Call for Democracy*, includes Garang and Yaji's letters, 101-106, 108 and Garang's comments on the Wad Medani conference, 126. TMC General Yusif Hasan al-Haj met SPLM officials in Addis Ababa on security arrangements, where he also transmitted TMC views on the constitution, according to *al-Khalij* (Sharja), 25 December 1985.

30. SCP-SPLM text on SPLA radio, 1 January 1986; interview with Ghabboush, 6 January 1987; SSPA-SPLM text in Khalid, *John Garang Speaks*, 110, and *Call for Democracy*, 108-11.

31. SUNA, 9 March 1986; Suwar al-Dhahab in SUNA, 10 March 1986; SUNA, 12 March 1986 on fall of Rumbek. Garang's speech mentions how bombing Rumbek delayed his travel to Koka Dam: Khalid, *Call for Democracy*, 121, 132.

32. Fourteen delegates from political parties, 12 from the National Alliance of professional and trade unions, and 24 from SPLM, headed by Kerubino Kuanyin Bol (deputy commander in chief of the SPLA and deputy chair of the SPLM provisional executive committee). Alliance Head Dr. Khalid Yaji's speech, on SPLA radio, 22 March 1986; Garang speech in Khalid, *John Garang Speaks*, 119-43, and *Call for Democracy*, 118-41. Text of declaration in *John Garang Speaks*, 145-46, and *Call for Democracy*, 142-44. Comments in Peter Nyot Kok, *Governance and Conflict in the Sudan* (Hamburg: Deutsches Orient-Institut, 1996), 57-58.

33. The liaison committee was chaired jointly by Major Arok Thon Arok (SPLM) and Dr. Taisier Muhammad Ahmad Ali (National Alliance). The proposed agenda covered nationalities, religion, human rights, the system of rule, culture, education, mass media, and foreign policy.

34. Khalid, *Call for Democracy*, 146, 148.

35. *Call for Democracy*, 115-17.

36. Interview with al-Mahdi, 21 September 1986; interview with Garang in *al-Musawwar*, 14 August 1987 (FBIS-NES 21 August 1987); Khalid, *Call for Democracy*, 150, 167; and Khalid, *Government They Deserve*, 395. Kok (59) notes that SPLM delegates (Garang, Lam Akol, Arok Thon, James Wani, and Yusuf Kuwa) participated fully in the discussion, whereas al-Mahdi alone spoke. Dr. Hamad Bagadi took minutes and three National Alliance members observed.

37. Comment 12 July 1988, Khalid, *Call for Democracy*, 167.

38. *Call for Democracy*, 150.

39. Press conference, 21 September 1986, which the author attended.

40. Interviews with Garang on SPLA radio, 9 November 1987 and in *al-Musaw-war*, 14 August 1987 (FBIS-NES 21 August 1987). Next quote from SPLA radio, 2 January 1987 (FBIS-NES 5 January 1987). Some SPLM members argued that downing the plane was a serious miscalculation that damaged the movement's credibility.

41. Interviews with Bona Malwal, Philip Peter Gadin (SSPA executive), Abd al-Basit Said (undersecretary of the Ministry of Peace), and Peter Nyot Kok, 6-10 January 1987.

42. *Al-Ittihad al-Usbu'i* (Abu Dhabi), 12 March 1987 (FBIS-NES 18 March 1987) and SPLA Radio, 6 April 1987.

43. Text on SPLA Radio, 20 April 1987; al-Mahdi comments in *al-Ittihad al-Usbu'i* (Abu Dhabi), 15 March 1987 (FBIS-NES 18 March 1987).

44. SPLA radio, 20 April 1987; Garang's initial comments on SPLA radio, 6 April 1987; formal response on SPLA radio, 8 August 1987. SPLM was annoyed that al-Mahdi sent the letter on plain paper with no official letterhead, signature, or date, addressed "to those who are still holding arms" rather than to the SPLM. Kok, 60, says that meant the letter was a "stunt."

45. Garang speech, SPLA Radio, 26 August 1987 (FBIS-NES 28 August 1987); text of joint statement on SPLA Radio and Addis Ababa radio, 25 August 1987 (FBIS-NES 26 August 1987); Garang press conference on Kampala radio, 10 September 1987 (FBIS-NES-87-179, 16 September 1987); text in *Kenya Times*, 23 September 1987 (FBIS-NES-87-185, 24 September 1987); Surur in SUNA, 29 September 1987 (FBIS-NES-87-191, 2 October 1987); interviews with PPP activists, 6 and 10 January 1987. The first meeting in Addis Ababa (20 to 25 August) was coordinated by Rev. Janda, secretary general of the Sudan Council of Churches; its communiqué was signed by Surur and William Nyuon Bany (SPLA chief of staff). The second meeting was in Kampala in early September. The communiqué from the third meeting, held in Nairobi (19 to 22 September), was signed by Surur and Lt. Col. Lual Deng Wol.

46. Alier, *Southern Sudan*, 274. Ex-TMC member Fadlallah Burma Nasir (a Baqqara Arab) participated. SPLA radio, 13 January 1988 (FBIS-NES-88-009, 14 January 1988); SUNA 7 February 1988 (FBIS-NES-88-025, 8 February 1988).

47. Text and al-Mahdi's speech in *Sudan Times* 12 January 1988; statement of government policy, 15 March 1988 in SUNA, 15 March 1988 (FBIS-NES-88-051, 16 March 1988). Dr. Pacifico Lado Lolik, the southern member of the Council of State, chaired the committee. Idris al-Banna headed the Council of Mercy's meetings with Garang in Addis Ababa (22-27 January 1988), arranged by the Islamic-Christian Peace Committee under the charter. Banna broke off talks on 6 February, on al-Mahdi's instructions. SPLA had captured Kapoeta on 12 January. Statement by Taisier Muhammad Ahmad Ali, SUNA, 28 February 1988 (FBIS-NES-88-039, 29 February 1988).

48. Statement, 12 July 1988, in Khalid, *Call for Democracy*, 152, 162-63, 170-72.

49. Andrew Wieu Riak (SANU) headed the USAP delegation to Addis Ababa (5-7 July). Joint communiqué, SPLA Radio, 9 July 1988 in Khalid, *Call for Democracy*, 172-74.

50. They met on 18-20 August with Lam Akol and 15-17 October with Akol and Yusif Kuwa, SPLA's senior Nuba officer; SUNA, 19 October 1988 (FBIS-NES-88-

203, 20 October 1988) and 25 October 1988 (FBIS-NES-88-207, 26 October 1988). DUP-SPLM joint statements broadcast by SPLA Radio, 22 August 1988 (FBIS-NES-88-163, 23 August 1988), 17 October 1988 (FBIS-NES-88-201, 18 October 1988), and 19 October 1988 (FBIS-NES-88-203, 20 October 1988). DUP politburo MP Abd al-Hakim Taifur met with SPLM in Addis Ababa and Nairobi in April 1987; SUNA, 27 April 1987 (FBIS-NES 28 April 1987).

51. This and most subsequent quotes from their joint press conference of 18 November 1988, on SPLA radio, 18 and 19 November 1988 (FBIS-NES-88-224, 21 November 1988); text of accord on SPLA radio and MENA, 17 November 1988 (FBIS-NES-88-223, 18 November 1988); and official statement, SPLA radio, 27 October 1988, which strongly criticized Turabi (FBIS-NES-88-209, 28 October 1988). Kok (68) says that, since "freeze" is not a legal term, they meant "recision."

52. SPLA radio, 18 November 1988 (FBIS-NES-88-224, 21 November 1988).

53. On 27 August 1988 al-Mahdi offered to meet Garang in two days, but SPLA said it required preliminary meetings at a lower level before the two leaders could meet.

54. SUNA, 14 December 1988 (FBIS-NES-88-240, 14 December 1988), 16 December 1988 (FBIS-NES-88-243, 19 December 1988), 19 December 1988 (FBIS-NES-88-244, 20 December 1988), and 22 December 1988 (FBIS-NES-88-246, 22 December 1988).

55. Garang said he would meet with the foreign and defense ministers only after the assembly vote; SPLA Radio, 21 December 1988 (FBIS-NES-88-246, 22 December 1988).

56. *Le Monde*, 24 December 1988 (FBIS-NES-89-009, 13 January 1989); SUNA, 10 January 1989 (FBIS-NES-89-007, 11 January 1989).

57. Alier, *Southern Sudan*, 283-84; SPLA Radio, 11 February 1989, and Addis Ababa Domestic Service, 9 February 1989 (FBIS-NES-89-028, 13 February 1989); MENA, 15 February 1989 (FBIS-NES-89-030, 15 February 1989).

58. SPLA Radio, 14 April 1989 (FBIS-NES-89-073, 18 April 1989) and 15 May 1989 (FBIS-NES-89-093, 16 May 1989).

59. SPLA Radio, 10 June 1989 (FBIS-NES-89-111, 12 June 1989) and 12 June 1989 (FBIS-NES-89-112, 13 June 1989); AFP, 12 June 1989 (FBIS-NES-89-112, 13 June 1989) and 13 June 1989 (FBIS-NES-89-113, 14 June 1989). The foreign ministry team included Dr. Taisier Muhammad Ahmad Ali, General Yusuf Ahmad Yusuf, and Dr. Umar Bagadi. Dr. Lam Akol was SPLM's chief negotiator.

60. SPLA Radio, 14 August 1989.

7. The Evolving Political System

1. *Sawt al-Sha'ab* (Amman), 23 February 1993 (FBIS-NES-93-034, 23 February 1993).

2. Hasan al-Turabi in *Islam, Democracy, the State and the West*, ed. Arthur L. Lowrie (Tampa: WISE, 1993), 22-24. The last phrase is *al-amr bil-ma'rouf wal-nahi an al-munkar* in Arabic.

3. *Middle East International* (*MEI*), 21 July 1995.

4. *Al-Dustur* (London), 21 August 1989 (JPRS-NEA-89-069, 23 October 1989).

5. *Al-Dustur*, 4 September 1989 (JPRS-NEA-89-069, 27 October 1989).

6. Bashir in *Uman* (Muscat), 7 December 1989 (FBIS-NES-89-240, 15 December 1989).

7. *Al-Sharq al-Awsat*, 11 October 1989 (FBIS-NES-89-199, 17 October 1989).

8. J. Millard Burr and Robert O. Collins, *Requiem for the Sudan* (Boulder: Westview, 1994), 206-207, 217. Bashir later said the leader of the conspirators was Air Colonel Mukhtar Muhammadain Ahmad, who died when his MiG fighter was shot down over Nasir on 21 January 1989; interview on Omdurman radio, 2 July 1989 (FBIS-NES-89-128, 6 July 1989).

9. *Africa Confidential (AC)* 36:14 (7 July 1995), 2; Burr and Collins (208, 253) state the council met daily in a Khartoum mosque after the evening curfew. Others reported later that it met every Thursday evening in Turabi's home. Members included RCC advisors Dr. Ghazi Salah al-Din al-Atabani, Dr. Mahdi Ibrahim, Dr. Ali al-Hajj, Ibrahim al-Sanusi, and Dr Naf'i Ali Naf'i; security chiefs Major Ibrahim Shams al-Din (RCC) and Colonel El-Hadi Abdullah (head of the committee that purged the army and police); Turabi's office manager, Abd al-Muhsin; former attorney general Hafiz al-Shaikh Zaki; Faisal Islamic Bank advisors including former security Brigadier Abbas Madani, Uthman Khalid Mudhawi, and economics professor Ibrahim Abdallah; Al-Fatih Hassanain, who coordinated policy toward Afghanistan, Pakistan, and Bosnia; and Abd al-Wahab "Gandhi" who handled finances in the Gulf from his base in Jeddah.

10. *Neue Zuercher Zeitung* (Zurich), 26 October 1994 (FBIS-NES-94-210, 31 October 1994); next quotation from *Keyhan* (Tehran), 1 March 1993 (FBIS-NES-93-044, 9 March 1993).

11. *Al-Hayat*, 30 October 1992 (FBIS-NES-92-218, 10 November 1992).

12. *Al-Majallah* (London), 10 March 1993 (FBIS-NES-93-048, 15 March 1993); Sulaiman to MENA, 31 July 1993 (FBIS-NES-93-138, 21 July 1993); Nuba negotiations in The Fund for Peace, *Living on the Margin* (New York: 1995), 22-23.

13. Omdurman radio, 6 August 1991 (FBIS-NES-91-153, 8 August 1991); *MEI*, 16 August 1991.

14. Kinga went abroad for an ILO meeting in Geneva and then remained in Egypt. MENA, 19 July 1992 (FBIS-NES-92-140, 21 July 1992); Omdurman radio, 30 July 1992 (FBIS-NES-92-148, 31 July 1992).

15. MENA, 23 June 1991 (FBIS-NES-91-121, 24 June 1991); renewed demands to abolish the RCC in *Sudan Update (SU)*, 10 July 1992 and *AC* 33:15 (31 July 1992).

16. Turabi to Reuters, 12 January 1993 (FBIS-NES-93-009, 14 January 1993), which Turabi denied despite Reuters' tape of the interview. *AC* 34:2 (22 January 1993), 8; *Middle East Times*, 19 January 1993, 6; *MEI*, 22 January 1993; *al-Hayat*, 5 February 1993 (FBIS-NES-93-026, 10 February 1993).

17. *Al-Hayat*, 13 January 1993 (FBIS-NES-93-010, 15 January 1993); Bashir on Turabi's role in *al-Sharq al-Awsat*, 21 January 1993 (FBIS-NES-93-014, 25 January 1993) and 8 September 1994 (FBIS-NES-94-175, 9 September 1994) and *Al-Arabi* (Cairo), 5 September 1994 (FBIS-NES-94-174, 8 September 1994).

18. Omdurman radio, 8 July 1993 (FBIS-NES-93-130, 9 July 1993); ministry goals in SUNA, 11 October 1993 (FBIS-NES-93-195, 12 October 1993).

19. *AC* 34:2 (22 January 1993); Omdurman radio, 19 January 1993 (FBIS-NES-93-011, n.d.).

20. Profile of al-Hajj by Peter Nyot Kok, *Sudan Democratic Gazette* (*SDG*) 35 (April 1993), 8.

21. *Al-Sharq al-Awsat*, 21 January 1993 (FBIS-NES-93-014, 25 January 1993).

22. Shiddu was defense attorney for Nimairi's vice president and minister of energy in 1986-1987. *Al-Hayat*, 20 February 1993 (FBIS-NES-93-035, 24 February 1993).

23. Abu Salih served in the transitional government and represented DUP in elected governments. *Al-Hayat*, 18 February 1993 (FBIS-NES-93-035, 23 February 1993) and 20 April 1993 (FBIS-NES-93-077, 23 April 1993).

24. Decrees on Omdurman radio, 16 October 1993 (FBIS-NES-93-199, 18 October 1993). Bashir speeches, Omdurman radio, 16 October 1993 (FBIS-NES-93-199, 18 October 1993) and 25 October 1993 (FBIS-NES-93-205, 26 October 1993).

25. Kongor was appointed on 15 February 1994 (Omdurman radio, 15 February 1994 in FBIS-NES-94-032, 16 February 1994).

26. Hamdi resurfaced as head of the new stock exchange. Omdurman radio, 30 October 1993 (FBIS-NES-93-209, 1 November 1993); *al-Hayat*, (1 November 1993) in *SU* 4:23 (10 November 1993).

27. *SDG* 41 (October 1993), 3, 5.

28. *AC* 35:15 (29 July 1994), 8; on civil defense, Omdurman radio, 16 August 1994 (FBIS-NES-94-160, 18 August 1994).

29. *AC* 35:18 (9 September 1994) and 35:20 (7 October 1994); on the UN conference, *SU*, 30 August 1994; dismissal in *MEI*, 17 February 1994.

30. Taha's first interview as foreign minister, *Al-Sharq al-Awsat*, 19 March 1995 (FBIS-NES-95-056, 23 March 1995).

31. *AC* 35:20 (7 October 1994), 8.

32. See Lesch, "The Sudan: Militancy and Isolation," in *The Middle East and the Peace Process*, ed. Robert O. Freedman (Miami: Universities of Florida Press, 1998), 325, 329; Omdurman radio, 12 August 1995 (FBIS-NES-95-156, 14 August 1995); MENA, 16 August 1995 (FBIS-NES-95-159, 17 August 1995); *al-Hayat*, 11 September 1995 (FBIS-NES-95-176, 12 September 1995); Col. Salih was already Bashir's security advisor: MENA, 14 December 1994 (FBIS-NES-94-240, 14 December 1994).

33. Cairo radio, 29 July 1995 (FBIS-NES-95-146, 31 July 1995); MENA, 31 July 1995, citing *al-Ra'y al-Akher* (FBIS-NES-95-147, 1 August 1995); MENA, 1 August 1995 (FBIS-NES-95-148, 2 August 1995).

34. *Al-Dustur*, 4 September 1989 (JPRS-NEA-89-069, 27 October 1989); comment by lawyer Ali Nasri, *al-Inqadh al-Watani* (Khartoum), 29 May 1990 (JPRS-NEA-90-037, 12 July 1990); Hasan al-Turabi, "Al-Shura wal-Dimukratiyyah" in his *Tajdid al-Fikr al-Islami* (Jiddah: Dar al-Sa'udiyya, 1987).

35. *Al-Sharq al-Awsat*, 11 October 1989 (FBIS-NES-89-199, 17 October 1989); Omdurman radio, 6 October 1991 (FBIS-NES-91-194, 7 October 1991).

36. *Al-Safir*, 24 February 1993 (FBIS-NES-93-041, 4 March 1993).

37. In a village in Kordofan, all the peoples' committee members were Arab or Arabized Nubians, excluding the Hausa and Burgo majority; Michael Kevane and Leslie Gray, "Local Politics in the Time of Turabi's Revolution," *Africa* 65:2 (1995), 280-81.

38. Omdurman radio, 4 January 1992 (FBIS-NES-92-004, 7 January 1992) and

13 February 1992 (FBIS-NES-92-031, 14 February 1992). Einas Ahmad, "The Dynamics of Local Politics and the Search for Local Legitimacy in Kassala State" (unpublished paper, 1997) notes (6, 8) that the four representatives to the TNA from Kassala State came from the most significant tribal and ethnic groups: Hadendowa (Beja), Beni Amer (Beja), and Rashaida (Arab), including the *nazir* (chief) of the Hadendowa.

39. *Al-Hayat*, 30 October 1992 (FBIS-NES-92-218, 10 November 1992). Malwal criticized the TNA in a letter sent to friends abroad.

40. Peter Nyot Kok, *Governance and Conflict in the Sudan* (Hamburg: Deutsches Orient-Institut, 1996), 144-45.

41. Kok, 149; *Sudan Newsletter*, fall 1993.

42. *Indian Ocean Newsletter*, 21 May 1994 (*SU* 5:11, 30 June 1994); *Sudan News and Views* (*SN&V*) 3 (29 May 1994). The tariff increase was the seventh in five years.

43. *SN&V* 6 (16 March 1995).

44. *Al-Hayat* and Omdurman radio, 12 January 1994 (FBIS-NES-94-009, 13 January 1994); *al-Sharq al-Awsat*, 12 January 1994 (FBIS-NES-94-010, 14 January 1994); Reuters, 13 January 1994 (*SU* 5:2, 17 January 1994); interview in *al-Ahram*, 17 January 1994 (FBIS-NES-94-015, 24 January 1994). He was replaced by Angelo Beda, who headed the Council of the South under al-Mahdi.

45. *Al-Safir*, 24 February 1993 (FBIS-NES-93-041, 4 March 1993); Turabi in *Islam, Democracy*, 26-27.

46. Omdurman radio, 4 March 1992 (FBIS-NES-92-044, 5 March 1992).

47. TNA member to Omdurman radio, 2 March 1993 (FBIS-NES-93-042, 5 March 1993); Abu Salih in *al-Sharq al-Awsat*, 17 April 1993 (FBIS-NES-93-075, 21 April 1993); Bashir in *al-Quds al-'Arabi*, 8 December 1993 (FBIS-NES-93-236, 10 December 1993). On the four regional-level sectoral congresses (youth, student, judiciary, economic) and eight national-level congresses (which added women, diplomats, administrators, security/defense): Bashir in *al-Hayat*, 3 August 1994 (FBIS-NES-94-150, 4 August 1994).

48. *SHR Voice*, 13 December 1994 (*SU* 5:21, 16 December 1994); *SDG* 56 (January 1995), 8. Detainees included businessmen, workers, civil servants, university students, and two physicians.

49. Speech to Lahamda tribe on Omdurman radio, 18 January 1995 (FBIS-NES-95-013, 20 January 1995).

50. *Al-Ahd* (Beirut), 21 April 1995 (FBIS-NES-95-090, 10 May 1995).

51. Chair in *SN&V*, 16 March 1995; *The Economist*, 24 June 1995; AFP, 2 July 1995 (FBIS-NES-95-129, 6 July 1995); *MEI*, 21 July 1995; Lawyers Committee, *Beset by Contradictions*, 73.

52. E. Ahmad, "The Dynamics of Local Politics," 7.

53. Kok, *Governance*, 220; appendix xix (352-82): text of Constitutional Decree #13.

54. Kok, 268.

55. Complaint against Turabi by Abd al-Rahman al-Sallawi; *SDG* 70 (March 1996), 11, and 71 (April 1996), 12.

56. Officially Bashir won 4,181,784 of 5,625,280 votes cast. His closest contestant was champion swimmer Abd al-Majid Kaijab, who received a reported 133,000 votes. *Le Monde*, 24-25 March 1996.

57. His acceptance speech. The cheers meant: "God Is Greatest" and "There Is No God but God." AFP, 1 April 1996 (FBIS-NES-96-063, 1 April 1996).

58. In a curious incident on 9 June 1996, however, Turabi refused to let MPs question the minister of finance and stressed that the assembly had only advisory powers. Turabi sent the assembly on a ten-week summer break starting 1 July to avoid further conflict. *SN&V* 20 (July 1996).

59. Press conference, 16 June 1996 in *SDG* 74 (July 1996), 7.

60. *SN&V* 20 (July 1996).

61. Benaiah Yongo-Bure, "Sudan's Deepening Crisis," *Middle East Report*, no. 172 (September-October 1991), 12; *al-Hayat*, 17 and 21 September 1993 (FBIS-NES-93-183, 23 September 1993 and FBIS-NES-93-186, 28 September 1993); *MEI*, 8 October 1993; Omdurman radio, 8 January 1995 (FBIS-NES-95-006, 10 January 1995).

62. Abel Alier, "The Political Charter: Observations and a Commentary," 1996, 5.

63. E. Ahmad, "The Dynamics of Local Politics," 9, 13.

64. Alier, "The Political Charter," 4.

65. Constitutional Decree #10, Sudan Embassy *Bulletin* (London), 1 February 1994 (*SU* 5:3, 7 February 1994); states listed in Sudan Embassy *Bulletin*, 8 February 1994; names of some southern governors in Reuters, 15 February 1994 (both in *SU* 5:4, 17 February 1994); Kok, 129-40. Analyses on Omdurman radio, 12 January 1994 (FBIS-NES-94-009, 13 January 1994) and 18 January 1994 (FBIS-NES-94-012, 19 January 1994).

66. Omdurman radio, 22 February 1994 (FBIS-NES-94-037, 24 February 1994). New governors on Omdurman radio, 28 May 1995 (FBIS-NES-95-014, 31 May 1995). Fund for poor states: SUNA, 8 August 1995 (FBIS-NES-95-153, 9 August 1995). Powers listed in SUNA, 16 August 1995 (FBIS-NES-95-159, 17 August 1995).

67. The government carved out a separate province for the Bitai family in Hamesh Koraib, which was detached from Aroma province which the rival Tirik family dominated. E. Ahmad, "The Dynamics of Local Politics," 9.

68. Kevane and Gray, "Local Politics," 290, 274-75; E. Ahmed, "The Dynamics of Local Politics," 6-7.

8. Indoctrination and Control

1. *Al-Shira* (Beirut), 17 May 1993 (FBIS-NES-93-098, 24 May 1993).

2. Peter Nyot Kok, *Governance and Conflict in the Sudan* (Hamburg: Deutsches Orient-Institut, 1996), 156-57.

3. Hasan al-Turabi, "The Islamic Awakening's New Wave," *New Perspectives Quarterly* 10:3 (summer 1993), 44.

4. Turabi in *Keyhan* (Tehran), 1 March 1993 (FBIS-NES-93-044, 9 March 1993); Bashir's speech to the TNA, Omdurman radio, 25 October 1993 (FBIS-NES-93-206, 27 October 1993); Bashir on the constitution, Omdurman radio, 1 November 1994 (FBIS-NES-94-213, 3 November 1994).

5. Fatwa issued on 24 April 1992 by the Conference of Religious Scientists, Mosque Imams, Shaikhs of Khalwas, and Sufis: *Sudan Update* 4:21 (8 October 1993); The Fund for Peace, *Living on the Margin* (New York: 1995), 7; Lawyers Committee for Human Rights, *Beset by Contradictions* (New York: 1996), 24.

6. For example, speech to Popular Defense Force graduates in Gadarif (Omdurman Radio, 30 January 1995, FBIS-NES-95-021, 30 January 1995). Reuters, 13 March 1996 (*SU* 7:5, 18 March 1996) reported that volunteers anointed themselves with perfume before battle to "smell sweet and pure when [they] met the virgins of paradise." Instead of funerals and reading the *Fatiha* (first chapter of the Quran) over the dead, families celebrated the martyr's wedding to the *houris*. Bashir's younger brother Uthman was one such martyr who received a posthumous wedding in 1996.

7. *Living on the Margin*, 25-28, 34.

8. Section 126. Abdullahi An-Na'im, "Whose Islamic Awakening? A Response," *New Perspectives Quarterly*, 10:3 (summer 1993), 47; Human Rights Watch/Africa, *Sudan: In the Name of God* (New York: 1994), 35-36. A Christian who converted to Islam would not be an apostate.

9. Turabi, "Islamic Awakening," 45, and Arthur L. Lowrie, ed. *Islam, Democracy, the State and the West* (Tampa: WISE, 1993), 41-44. Bashir granted a stay of execution for two men who had converted to Christianity many years earlier. The minister of justice facilitated the departure abroad of army officer Salvatore Ali Ahmad, convicted in 1994. *Beset by Contradictions*, 78.

10. Turabi, *Islam, Democracy*, 33-34; an-Na'im, "Whose Islamic Awakening?", 47; Riad Ibrahim, "Factors Contributing to the Political Ascendancy of the Muslim Brethren in Sudan," *Arab Studies Quarterly*, 12:3&4 (summer/fall 1990), 52-53.

11. Agence France Presse, 31 December 1990 (FBIS-NES-91-001, 2 January 1991); International League for Human Rights, *Sudan's Human Rights Record* (New York: 1991), 5-6, 16-17.

12. Turabi, *Islam, Democracy*, 16, 19; "Islamic Awakening," 43.

13. Constance L. Kirker, "'This Is Not Your Time Here': Islamic Fundamentalism and Art in Sudan: An African Artist Interviewed," *Issue: A Journal of Opinion* 20:2 (1992), 7-8. The Sudanese painter also discussed the flight of artists and the National Museum's closure of exhibits on pre-Islamic Nubia.

14. *Sudan Human Rights Voice* 3:11 (November 1994), AFP, 11 November 1994, and *Folk Roots* magazine, December 1994, in *Sudan Update* (*SU*) 5:20 (30 November 1994). *Sudan Democratic Gazette* (*SDG*) #55 (December 1994), 9: The famous singer Muhammad Wardi, president of the Musicians and Artists Union, was harassed until he left for England.

15. *The Guardian*, 8 December 1994 (*SU* 5:21, 16 December 1994). The attacker killed Khujali Uthman and wounded a violinist and a singer named Abd al-Gadir Salim, who played western Sudanese (Merdum) music. Security forces ordered Uthman buried that night to prevent disturbances by his fans.

16. Manager of Badr Company, *Africa Confidential* (*AC*), 3 March 1995; *Sudan News and Views* (*SN&V*), 16 March 1995; Horaya Hakim, *Proceedings: Human Rights Workshop* (Cairo: Arab Lawyers Union, 1992), 7-8; *SHR Voice* 5:5 (April 1996), 7.

17. Speech in January 1990, *In the Name of God*, 46, also 36-37; *Abuses against Women* (New York: Fund for Peace, 1992), 6; *Middle East International*, 20 November 1992; *SHR Voice* 2:4 (April 1993), 4; *The New York Times*, 27 October 1996; *SN&V* 21 (November 1996).

18. *Middle East International*, 6 December 1991; *al-Hayat*, 3 December 1991; Sondra Hale, "The Rise of Islam and Women of the National Islamic Front in Sudan,"

Review of African Political Economy 554 (1992), 40; *Abuses against Women*, 2-4; *In the Name of God*, 37; *Daily Telegraph* (London), 31 July 1995; *Beset by Contradictions*, 23.

19. Reuters, 11 February 1994 (*SU* 5:4, 17 February 1994); *Al-Sharq al-Awsat*, 4 January 1995 (*SU* 6:2, 6 February 1995). A Catholic girls' school in Khartoum won a partial exemption for non-Muslims, who had to wear long skirts without the veil.

20. Hale, 33, 39; *In the Name of God*, 22, 37-38, and The Fund for Peace, *Living on the Margin* (New York: 1995); First Christian Women's Conference on Women and the Law in Sudan Council of Churches, *Update*, June 1994 (*SU* 5:12, 14 July 1994).

21. Michael Kevane and Leslie Gray, "Local Politics in the Time of Turabi's Revolution," *Africa*, 65:2 (1995), 273, 277.

22. *Sudan's Human Rights Record*, 10; *Abuses against Women*, 2-4.

23. Four-phased plan described by Sennar minister of health, Muhammad Ahmad al-Arbab, *Al-Sharq al-Awsat*, 28 March 1995 (FBIS-NES-95-061, 30 March 1995).

24. *Keyhan* (Tehran), 1 March 1993 (FBIS-NES-93-044, 9 March 1993); Abdullahi an-Na'im and Peter Nyot Kok, *Fundamentalism and Militarism* (New York: Fund for Peace, 1991), 8-9.

25. *Middle East Times*, 9 February 1993; B. Yongo-Bure, "Sudan's Deepening Crisis," *Middle East Report* 172 (September-October 1991), 9; Ali Abdallah Abbas, "The National Islamic Front and the Politics of Education," *Middle East Report*, 172 (September-October 1991), 25, fn 1; Kok, *Governance*, 103, on al-Tayyib's role.

26. Taha Ibrahim, *Proceedings: Workshop on Human Rights*, 4; *Sudan's Human Rights Record*, 10-12; *Beset by Contradictions*, 41-44.

27. Turabi, *Islam, Democracy*, 94; Brig. Gen. Babiker Abd al-Mahmud, first PDF commander, *al-Inqadh al-Watani* (Khartoum), 9 March 1990 in *Sudan Human Rights Monitor* #12 (25 March 1990). Purges in *SU* 4:25 (15 December 1993) and 6:5 (3 April 1995).

28. Omdurman radio, 13 October 1993 (FBIS-NES-93-197, 14 October 1993) and 16 October 1993 (FBIS-NES-93-199, 18 October 1993); SUNA, 3 November 1993 (FBIS-NES-93-212, 4 November 1993).

29. *Living on the Margin*, 22; *In the Name of God*, 9.

30. *SHR Voice* 2:9 (22 September 1993); Reuters 22 August 1993 (*SU* 4:20, 22 September 1993); on Shabab al-Watan, Kevane and Gray, 272. Abd al-Khaliq Abdallah al-Turabi: *New African*, June 1994, in *SU* 5:11 (30 June 1994).

31. The Fund for Peace, *Abuses of Academic Freedom* (New York: 1992), 12-13; Human Rights Watch/Africa, *Sudan: The Copts* (New York: 1993), 8.

32. MENA, 9 April 1994 (FBIS-NES-94-069, 11 April 1994); Bashir on BBC, 17 November 1994 (FBIS-NES-94-223, 18 November 1994).

33. *SN&V*, May 1995; *In the Name of God*, 10 and 21-22.

34. Bashir on Omdurman radio, 17 November 1993 (FBIS-NES-93-221, 18 November 1993); PDF commander for Khartoum state in SUNA, 8 July 1995 (FBIS-NES-95-132, 11 July 1995).

35. Omdurman radio, 1 January 1995 (FBIS-NES-95-002, 4 January 1995) and 30 January 1995 (FBIS-NES-95-021, 1 February 1995); *SDG* 60 (May 1995), 9, on conscription and casualties.

36. *Al-Ahram*, 24 February 1993 (FBIS-NES-93-036, 25 February 1993); *Al-*

Hayat, 13 January 1995 (FBIS-NES-95-012, 19 January 1995). Some 130 soldiers based in al-Fashir (Dar Fur) joined local demonstrations, complaining they were not paid for six months and had not received rations. They were transferred under heavy guard to prison in Khartoum and fifteen "ringleaders" were executed. *SHRO*, 17 February 1995 (*SU* 6:5, 3 April 1995); *SDG* 58 (March 1995), 11.

37. Bashir attended a private dinner to honor Major General Muhammad Ahmad, due to leave the next day to become ambassador in Nairobi; instead, he landed in jail. *Al-Wafd*, 24 April 1994 (FBIS-NES-94-084, 2 May 1994).

38. BBC, 26 October 1989 (FBIS-NES-89-209, 31 October 1989); on multiple security organs, *AC* 36:14 (7 July 1995), 2.

39. Head of Revolutionary Security Guards Dr. Naf'i Ibrahim Naf'i, a former lecturer in the Faculty of Agriculture at Khartoum University, detained two colleagues—Dr. Abdin Muhammad Zain al-Abdin and Dr. Kamil Ibrahim—on the roof of the security headquarters in June 1990, where they collapsed from heat prostration. Numbers from *SDG* 35 (April 1993), 6; cases in Human Rights Watch/Africa, *Sudan: The Ghosts Remain* (New York: 1992), 4-8, and *Sudan: In the Name of God* (New York: 1994), 26-28. Brigadier (Retired) Muhammad Ahmad al-Raya al-Faki sent a handwritten letter to the minister of justice detailing torture in Shalla (Dar Fur) and Port Sudan: *SDG* 42 (November 1993), 4-5, and *AC* 34:21 (22 October 1993), 2.

40. Muhammad Ahmad al-Arbab, who defected in 1995, in *al-Wasat*, 17 July 1995 (FBIS-NES-95-140, 21 July 1995). Human Rights Watch/Africa, *Sudan: In the Name of God* (New York: 1994), 26.

41. *Africa Analysis*, 17 May 1991 in *SU* 3:1 (7 August 1991); *al-Sharq al-Awsat* 19 and 21 October 1991 in *SU* 3:6 (25 October 1991).

42. SUNA, 28 July 1991 (FBIS-NES-91-149, 2 August 1991); Omdurman Radio, 12 November 1992 (FBIS-NES-92-220, 13 November 1992); Omdurman radio, 14 December 1993 (FBIS-NES-93-239, 15 December 1993); *Guardian*, 8 December 1994 in *SU* 5:21 (16 December 1994); *SDG* 60 (May 1995), 8; *Beset by Contradictions*, 21-23, 29, 33, 80.

43. Constitutional Decree #2, article 6: *Sudan's Human Rights Record*, 5, 11.

44. Bashir on Omdurman radio, 3 December 1989 (FBIS-NES-89-232, 5 December 1989).

45. Amnesty International, *Sudan: A Permanent Human Rights Crisis* (New York: 1990), 12; Kok, *Governance*, 104.; *AC* 33:21 (23 October 1992); *In the Name of God*, 33; *Sudan's Human Rights Record*, 9-10.

46. BBC, 19 March 1991 (FBIS-NES-91-055, 21 March 1991); Human Rights Watch/Africa, *Sudan: Sudanese Human Rights Organizations* (New York: 1991), 2-5; *Beset by Contradictions*, 37-40. Chair Muhammad Ziyadh Hamur became head of the TNA in early 1992 but died suddenly on 29 March 1992. Ali Ahmad al-Nasri then headed the Bar Association and the official SHRO.

47. Omdurman radio, 23 November 1989 (FBIS-NES-89-227, 28 November 1989); *Sudan: The Copts*, 1, 3, 5-9; *In the Name of God*, 39.

48. *Daily Mail*, *Times* (London), and BBC, 7 September 1993 and *Independent*, 8 September 1993, in *SU* 4:20 (22 September 1993); *SDG* 41 (October 1993), 6, and 42 (November 1993), 5; *AC* 34:21 (22 October 1993), 1. The Right Reverend Peter al-Birish was charged with adultery in September 1993. A lower court threw out the

case for lack of evidence but the appeals court ruled against him and flogged him on his back and legs with a leather whip. The bishop said: "It is shameful as a leader to submit to this flogging [but] I will not run away and leave my people pastorless."

49. Giorgis Yustus Butrus, charged with possessing foreign currency. J. Millard Burr and Robert O. Collins, *Requiem for the Sudan* (Boulder: Westview, 1994), 257.

50. *SU* 3:19 (4 June 1992); *Sudan: The Copts*, 5; Human Rights Watch/Africa, *Sudan: Refugees in Their Own Country* (New York: 1992), 13; Amnesty International statement (London), 6 April 1992 in *SU* 3:18 (19 May 1992); *In the Name of God*, 9.

51. *The New York Times*, 1 June 1992; *Sudan: The Copts*, 5-6; and *In the Name of God*, 40.

52. Testimony to the UN Commission on Human Rights, Geneva, February 1993. *SHR Voice*, April 1993; *SDG* 34 (March 1993), 6.

53. *In the Name of God*, 40.

54. *Sudan: The Copts*, 7.

55. *SDG* 33 (February 1993), 3.

56. SUNA, 3 February 1993 (FBIS-NES-93-022, 4 February 1993); *The New York Times*, 12 February 1993; *AC* 34:3 (5 February 1993), 8, and 34:17 (27 August 1993), 8, and 34:21 (22 October 1993), 2, which noted that Turabi met for ten minutes with the Pope and an hour with the cardinal responsible for interreligious dialogue.

57. Sudan Embassy (London), *Bulletin*, 13 April 1993 (*SU* 4:14, 21 April 1993).

58. *SU* 5:19 (10 November 1994) and *SU* 5:20 (20 November 1994); Turabi in *De Volkskrant* (Amsterdam), 4 November 1993 (FBIS-NES-93-215, 9 November 1993); Comboni Press Network, 7 December 1994 (internet).

59. *Middle East Times*, 11 June 1995; *SDG* 55 (December 1994), 1, 4, on the new law.

60. Einas Ahmed, "The Dynamics of Local Politics and the Search for Local Legitimacy in Kassala State," unpublished paper (1997), 13.

61. *Sudan Monitor*, August 1990; *SDG* 29 (October 1992), 6; Omdurman radio, 26 May 1993 (FBIS-NES-93-101, 27 May 1993). NIF's rivalry with sufi orders: Ibrahim, "Factors Contributing," 40.

62. *Middle East Times*, 30 April 1993. Shaikh Muhammad al-Jimaiabi, a sufi preacher in a village north of Khartoum, was protected by his followers when security forces cordoned off the mosque. A full battalion returned the next day, attacked the mosque, killed two followers, and arrested the shaikh and several followers. They were released ten days later, without any charges or trial.

63. Shaikhs Muhammad al-Haddiya and Abu Zaid Muhammad Hamza. E. Ahmed, "The Dynamics of Local Politics," 2, 16; *al-Hayat*, 28 April 1994 (*SU* 5:9, 20 May 1994) and 7 November 1994 (FBIS-NES-94-217, 9 November 1994). *SDG* 46 (March 1994), 4, and 49 (June 1994), 12. There was a shoot-out between the surviving gunmen and guards for Turabi and Osama Bin Laden outside their villas in Khartoum: one version says the men sought sanctuary in the villas; another version says they wanted to kill those prominent leaders.

64. SUNA, 22 July 1995 (FBIS-NES-95-141, 24 July 1995).

65. E. Ahmad, "The Dynamics of Local Politics," 15-16.

66. Ali Abdallah Abbas and M. E. El-Tom, "Education and Fundamentalism in the Arab World: A Research Project Proposal" (1993), 3, 9, and 15.

67. Council head Ibrahim Ahmad Umar later became minister of higher education. Abbas, "The National Islamic Front," 23-24; *Abuses of Academic Freedom*; on the nursing college, *Living on the Margin*, 45.

68. Abbas, "The National Islamic Front," 24-25; *Abuses of Academic Freedom*: the nine were al-Sharq (East) University, Wadi el-Nil (Nile Valley) University in Atbara, el-Fatih min September University (First of September—named for the Libyan revolution of 1969) in Dar Fur, Kordofan University, African Islamic University (formerly the African Islamic Center), University of Ismail al-Azhari, the University of Imam al-Mahdi, Upper Nile University, and Bahr al-Ghazal University.

69. Statement by minister of education, IPS, 4 October 1994; music institute in *SU* 4:25 (15 December 1993) report on universities; Amnesty International, 30 July 1992 on southern reactions.

70. *The New York Times*, 1 June 1992.

71. Dr. Ma'mun Muhammad Ali Humaida in May 1994 (internet); Ali Abdallah Abbas, *Proceedings: Workshop on Human Rights*, 2; *Living on the Margin*, 48.

72. Dr. Abd al-Wahab Abd al-Rahim al-Mubarak became minister in April 1996; his predecessor was Dr. Ibrahim Ahmad Umar, NIF former chancellor of Khartoum University. The committee, chaired by Muddathir al-Tangari (former vice chancellor of Khartoum University), found that, in September 1996 alone, 26 staff left Sudan from Khartoum University, 53 from Sudan University (former Khartoum Polytechnic), 12 from Gezira University, and 8 from Nilain University (former Khartoum branch of Cairo University). *Al-Sharq al-Awsat*, 4 December 1996 in *SU* 7:23 (10 December 1996).

73. SUNA, 28 July 1991 (FBIS-NES-91-149, 2 August 1991); Abbas, "The National Islamic Front," 24; *Abuses of Academic Freedom*, 2-3.

74. *Middle East Times*, 10 January 1993; MENA, 5 January 1993 (FBIS-NES-93-003, 6 January 1993), 9 March 1993 (FBIS-NES-93-045, 10 March 1993), and 11 March 1993 (FBIS-NES-93-047, 12 March 1993).

75. SUNA, 28 February 1990 (FBIS-NES-90-042, 2 March 1990); *Africa Analysis*, 28 September 1990 (*SU* 2:8, 5 October 1990); Omdurman radio, 15 July 1993 (*SU* 4:18, 16 August 1993) and 23 July 1993 (FBIS-NES-93-134, 15 July 1993); *al-Hayat*, 14 June 1993 (FBIS-NES-93-114, 16 June 1993); Omdurman radio, 21 April 1993 (FBIS-NES-93-080, 28 April 1993). The three official newspapers were *al-Sudan al-Hadith*, *al-Inqadh al-Watani*, and *al-Quwat al-Musalaha*. A conference on information in February 1990 recommended greater independence for the media; instead, the government tightened restrictions.

76. Amnesty International statement, 3 March 1994 (*SU* 5:5, 15 March 1994); Omdurman radio, 4 April 1994 (FBIS-NES-94-065, 5 April 1994); Bashir in MENA, 7 April 1994 (FBIS-NES-94-067, 7 April 1994); article critiquing corruption in *al-Sudani al-Duwali*, reproduced in *al-Khalij* (8 April 1994) in *SU* 5:8 (30 April 1994); *AC* 35:8 (15 April 1994), 8; *SDG* 48 (May 1994), 10; *In the Name of God*, 34.

77. Brig. Faisal Madani Mukhtar. *SN&V*, 16 March 1995; BBC, 30 May 1995 (FBIS-NES-95-014, 31 May 1995); Omdurman radio, 1 June 1995 (FBIS-NES-95-106, 2 June 1995).

78. AFP and Reuters (20 September 1995) (FBIS-NES-95-183, 21 September 1995): the technical grounds for the suspension were the newspaper's failure to ap-

point a qualified editor-in-chief. The article on the south by al-Tayyib Zain al-Abdin, research director at Khartoum University, concluded that the south would opt to secede if a referendum were held; *SU* (6 February 1995) referred to Abdin as a "black sheep" among NIF intellectuals. *Al-Rai al-Akhar*, 17 May 1996 (*SN&V*, 19 June 1996).

79. SUNA, 4 September 1993 (*SU* 4:21, 8 October 1993); MENA, 13 July 1995 (FBIS-NES-95-135, 14 July 1995); Omdurman radio, 29 September 1995 (FBIS-NES-95-191, 3 October 1995).

9. The Fragmented Opposition

1. *Sudan News and Views* (*SN&V*) 13 (30 September 1995).

2. Brigadier General Ibrahim Nayil Idam, RCC, head of security, *Al-Watan al-Arabi*, 18 August 1989 (JPRS-NEA-89-060, 7 September 1989); International League for Human Rights, *Sudan's Human Rights Record* (New York: 1991), 9.

3. Garang in August 1989, *Call for Democracy*, ed. Mansour Khalid (London: Kegan Paul International, 1992), 267-68.

4. Amnesty International, *Sudan: A Permanent Human Rights Crisis* (New York: August 1990), 14; BBC, 25 November 1989 (FBIS-NES-89-227, 28 November 1989); SPLA radio, 28 November 1989 (FBIS-NES-89-228, 29 November 1989); Agence France Presse (AFP), 29 November 1989 (FBIS-NES-89-230, 1 December 1989) and 9 December 1989 (FBIS-NES-89-238, 13 December 1989); *al-Sharq al-Awsat*, 30 November 1989 and SUNA, 4 December 1989 (FBIS-NES-89-235, 8 December 1989); Omdurman radio and SUNA, 10 December 1989 (FBIS-NES-89-236, 11 December 1989).

5. Charged under Article 35 of the emergency laws (1989) and Articles 96K and 105 of the criminal code (1983), Dr. Ma'mun Muhammad Hussain, who had addressed the ten-minute planning meeting and announced the strike, was sentenced to death. Dr. Sayyid Muhammad Abdallah was sentenced to fifteen years in jail. Egyptian President Hosni Mubarak flew to Khartoum in December to oppose hanging Dr. Ma'mun. A human rights mission by the American Association for the Advancement of Science arrived in Khartoum the day after their release.

6. J. Millard Burr and Robert O. Collins, *Requiem for the Sudan* (Boulder: Westview, 1994), 249, 240.

7. Ibrahim al-Sanusi (NIF's Council of Forty), speech to PDF in Kosti, *al-Wafd* (Cairo), 13 February 1994 (FBIS-NES-94-033, 17 February 1994).

8. SPLA radio, 6 March 1990 (FBIS-NES-90-045, 7 March 1990).

9. The RCC commuted his sentence to life in prison. *Al-Sharq al-Awsat*, 31 August 1991 [*Sudan Update (SU)* 3:3 (7 September 1991)].

10. Led by Flight Lieutenant General Khalid al-Zain; Peter Nyot Kok, *Governance and Conflict in the Sudan* (Hamburg: Deutsches Orient-Institut, 1996), 105-106, 115 fn 88; Amnesty International August 1990, 16-17; *Sudan Monitor (SM)* 1:1 (July 1990) and 1:2 (August 1990).

11. Human Rights Watch/Africa, *Sudan: "In the Name of God"* (New York: 1994), 25; Amnesty International statement, 3 April 1992 and report on raiding private memorial services, Amnesty, 25 March 1994 in *SU* 5:8 (30 April 1994).

12. Conspirators included Major General Albino Akol. *SU* 2:7 (25 September 1990) and 2:8 (5 October 1990).

13. *SU* 2:8 (5 October 1990); *SM* 1:4 (October 1990); Bushra on Voice of Sudan (clandestine) radio, 2 January 1991 (FBIS-NES-91-003, 4 January 1991); Garang on SPLA radio, 4 January 1991 (FBIS-NES-91-006, 9 January 1991).

14. Twelve RCC members attended the summary court martial. The three RCC members who objected were purged. *SU* 2:21 (22 April 1991) and 2:22 (13 May 1991).

15. Led by Major General (ret.) Muhammad Ahmad Khalifa, with colonels who commanded the Armored Brigade Training School and a paratroop unit. KUNA and BBC, 22 August 1991 (FBIS-NES-91-164, 23 August 1991); *al-Hayat*, 23 August 1991, and MENA, 23 August 1991 (FBIS-NES-91-165, 26 August 1991); Omdurman radio, 23 August 1991 (FBIS-NES-91-167, 28 August 1991); *SU* 3:3 (7 September 1991).

16. *Al-Sharq al-Awsat*, 12 February 1992 (FBIS-NES-92-033, 19 February 1992).

17. *Al-Dustour* (Amman), 4 September 1989 (JPRS-NEA-89-069, 27 October 1989).

18. AFP, 29 December 1989 (FBIS-NES-90-002, 3 January 1990).

19. AFP, 16 December 1989 (FBIS-NES-89-244, 21 December 1989). Since students from SCP, Ba'ath, African parties, Umma, and independents posted separate lists, NIF could gain a plurality and control all the seats.

20. *Al-Sharq al-Awsat*, 7 September 1990 (*SU* 2:7, 25 September 1990) and 18 October 1990 (*SU* 2:10, 5 November 1990); *SM*, November 1990 and February 1991.

21. Ali Abdalla Abbas, "The National Islamic Front," *Middle East Report*, 172 (September-October 1991), 24-25; *SU*, 21 January 1991; *SM*, February 1991; SPLA radio, 6 March 1991 (FBIS-NES-91-045, 7 March 1991).

22. *Al-Sudan*, 25 April 1991; *al-Hayat*, 26 April 1991; *SM*, May 1991.

23. *Al-Sharq al-Awsat*, 18 July 1991 (FBIS-NES-91-141, 23 July 1991); *Abuses of Academic Freedom*, 3-6.

24. *Al-Sharq al-Awsat*, 23 September 1991 (FBIS-NES-91-187, 26 September 1991).

25. *Abuses of Academic Freedom*, 8-9; Monte Carlo radio, 8 February 1992 (FBIS-NES-92-027, 10 February 1992) and 15 February 1992 (FBIS-NES-92-032, 18 February 1992); *al-Sharq al-Awsat*, 5 January 1992 (FBIS-NES-92-006, 9 January 1992) and 12 February 1992 (FBIS-NES-92-033, 19 February 1992); *al-Hayat*, 9 April 1992 (*SU* 3:16, 17 April 1992) on dismissing professors.

26. Forty-nine students were dismissed. *Abuses of Academic Freedom* (New York: Fund for Peace, 1992), 9-10.

27. *SM*, August 1990; Amnesty, *Sudan: A Permanent Human Rights Crisis*, 13; death of union leader in *SU* 2:12 (5 December 1990) and railway protests in *SU* 2:11 (19 November 1990).

28. *Al-Sharq al-Awsat*, 30 September 1990 (*SU* 2:8, 5 October 1990).

29. *SM*, November 1990; *SU* 2:11 (19 November 1990).

30. Monte Carlo radio, 8 February 1992 (FBIS-NES-92-027, 10 February 1992).

31. *Al-Wafd*, 30 December 1992 (FBIS-NES-93-003, 6 January 1993); Amnesty International statement (London), 5 January 1993; on Wad Medani: *al-Sharq al-Awsat*, 7 January 1993 (FBIS-NES-93-005, 8 January 1993); *SU*, 16 January 1993.

32. *Africa Confidential (AC)* 34:20 (8 October 1993), 8; *Sudan Democratic Gazette (SDG)* 43 (December 1993), 6.

33. DUP's Uthman Umar al-Sharif was charged with instigating a shopkeeper strike in Wad Medani. *In the Name of God*, 32.

34. *SDG* 33 (February 1993), 5.

35. MENA, 23 April 1993 (FBIS-NES-93-077, 23 April 1993); *SU* 4:14 (21 April 1993) and 4:16 (6 June 1993).

36. Sentences 30 April 1994 included ten years (in absentia) to LC's Fathi, Bushra, and Sa'id. Training in Lebanon: *Al-Shira* (Beirut), 17 May 1993 (FBIS-NES-93-098, 24 May 1993). Umma-Ansar detentions included former minister of state for defense Fadlalla Burma Nasir and former governor of Kordofan Abd al-Rasul al-Nur: *SDG* 37 (June 1993), 2; *al-Sharq al-Awsat*, 30 September 1993 (FBIS-NES-93-191, 5 October 1993); *al-Hayat*, 2 October 1993 (FBIS-NES-93-192, 6 October 1993). Trials: Lawyers Committee for Human Rights, *Beset by Contradictions* (New York: 1996), 55-59; Omdurman radio, 13 December 1993 (FBIS-NES-93-238, 14 December 1993); BBC, 14 December 1993 (FBIS-NES-93-039, 15 December 1993); SUNA, 20 December 1993 (FBIS-NES-93-243, 21 December 1993) and 28 December 1993 (FBIS-NES-93-248, 29 December 1993); AFP, 30 April 1994 (FBIS-NES-94-084, 2 May 1994); *In the Name of God*, 28.

37. Bashir interview, in *al-Shaab* (Cairo) 9 July 1991 (FBIS-NES-91-136, 16 July 1991).

38. Press conference in London, 28 June 1991 (*SU*, 21 August 1991).

39. When other Nasir officers dissented, Machar executed seven and detained thirty-three, according to Khalid, *Call for Democracy*, 272, 280-81 (names and ranks). In October 1992 Kong joined Anya-Nya II forces and Nuer spiritual leader Wut Nyang to attack Malakal. Troops brought by steamer from Kosti recaptured the town after two days. Douglas H. Johnson, *Nuer Prophets* (Oxford: Clarendon, 1994), 350; *SDG* 31 (December 1992), 3. Kong's defection: SPLA-Nasir statements, 18 September 1992 (*SU* 4:1, 22 September 1992) and 29 September 1992 (*SU* 4:2, 30 September 1992); Omdurman radio, 2 November 1992 (FBIS-NES-92-216, 6 November 1992); *SDG* 30 (November 1992), 5.

40. Declaration in *SU* 3:4 (24 September 1991); BBC, 30 August 1991 (FBIS-NES-91-170, 3 September 1991); BBC, 2 September 1991, and AFP, 1 September 1991 (FBIS-NES-91-172, 5 September 1991); *AC* 32:18 (13 September 1991), 2-3; Khalid, *Call for Democracy*, 269-72.

41. *SM* 2:4 (October 1991), 6. Texts of the eighteen resolutions (September 12) in Khalid, *Call for Democracy*, 282-91 (appendix 2).

42. John Prendergast, *Diplomacy, Aid and Governance* (Washington: Center of Concern, 1995), 68-70; Omdurman Radio, 13 October 1991 (FBIS-NES-91-206, 24 October 1991); *SU* 3:8 (25 November 1991); AFP, 26 November 1991 (FBIS-NES-91-229, 27 November 1991); Machar on Bor killings on BBC, 17 December 1991 (FBIS-NES-91-244, 19 December 1991); Amnesty International, *Sudan: The Ravages of War* (29 September 1993), 21-23; Burr and Collins, 300-301.

43. *SDG* 36 (May 1993), 5-6; *AC* 34:7 (2 April 1993), 2; SPLA-Nasir statement, 29 March 1993. Machar, Akol, Nyuon, Arok, and Kerubino escaped, but fifteen officers and forty-five civilian politicians died, including veteran Equatorian politi-

cian Joseph Oduho, whom Garang detained from 1985 to 1991. John Prendergast details the overall devastation in "Multi-Layered Conflict in the Greater Horn of Africa" (Washington: Creative Associates International, 1996), 68-72.

44. Nyuon released Kerubino, former deputy chair of SPLM and deputy commander of SPLA, detained in 1987, possibly due to criticism of the SPLA's close relationship with Ethiopia; Cdr. Arok Thon Arok, former SPLA deputy chief of staff for administration and logistics, who criticized Garang's negotiating stance; and Alt. Cdr. Faustino Atem Gualdit. The defecting spokesmen were Alfred Lado-Gore (head of SPLM's political bureau, released after three years' detention in February 1992) and Richard Mulla (London spokesman and SPLM spokesman in Abuja I).

45. Amnesty, *Sudan: The Ravages of War*, 20-25; Burr passim; Africa Watch, *War in South Sudan: The Civilian Toll* (Washington: October 1993). Earlier attempts at cease-fires, December 1991 and February 1992: *Al-Sharq al-Awsat*, 19 December 1991 (FBIS-NES-91-246, 23 December 1991); Burr and Collins, 301. Fighting in "famine triangle" (Bor-Kongor-Ayod): *SHRV* 2:7 (July 1993), 6-7, and 2:8 (August 1993), 4; *SU* 4:18 (16 August 1993), 7.

46. Dr. Achol Mariel on BBC, 9 November 1992 (FBIS-NES-92-220, 13 November 1992); *SDG* 31 (December 1992), 6; Johnson, *Nuer Prophets*, 346-47.

47. Alfred Lado-Gore, Richard Mulla, and Barri Wanji press conference, Nairobi, 5 May 1993: AFP, 5 May 1993, and BBC, 6 May 1993 (FBIS-NES-93-086, 6 May 1993).

48. Al-Hajj and Ghazi Salah al-Din denied making any such assurance; *Al-Hayat*, 3 December 1991 (FBIS-NES-91-237, 10 December 1991); *Indian Ocean Newsletter*, 8 December 1991 (*SU* 3:9, 16 December 1991).

49. Akol's aides, Cdrs. Deng Ayuen and Telar Ring, who returned to SPLM-Mainstream, published their protest in Nairobi, 12 February 1992; SPLM radio, 14 February 1992; *Indian Ocean Newsletter*, 29 February 1992 (*SU* 3:13, 4 March 1992); Khalid, *Call for Democracy*, 279, 292.

50. *Southern Sudan Vision* (published by SPLA-United), 1 June 1993, in *SU* 4:16 (6 June 1993) lists delegates; Kok, 209 fn 81; Bashir on referendum: BBC, 2 November 1993 (FBIS-NES-93-212, 4 November 1993). NIF's Ali Uthman Muhammad Taha headed a government delegation that met SPLA-United in Nairobi on 23 April to discuss interim arrangements.

51. The meeting occurred in Fashoda in the context of the installation of the Shilluk *reth* (head). Akol then met regularly with government officials in Upper Nile. *AC*, 13 August 1993, 7. Pro-Machar *AC* expressed surprise at the Akol-government agreement, querying whether Akol went too far even for SPLA-United. New Sudan Council of Churches' open letter (11 August) criticized the splits and the Akol-government pact (*AC* 34:17, 17 August 1993, 8). SPLM-United's spokesman John Luk said criticism was unfair, since the Fashoda agreement was an extension of the Nairobi negotiations. In June 1994, Machar arrested Luk for siding with Akol.

52. The governor of Upper Nile and chair of the TNA peace committee died in a plane crash on 5 September traveling to Bentiu to meet Kerubino. *SDG* 41 (October 1993), 4, names those who died. Another delegation went to Bentiu on 22 September.

53. Turabi said 1,500 soldiers marched from Damazin into Ethiopia for 150 miles, crossing back at Pochala to surprise Garang's forces on 9 March 1992: on BBC, 27 April 1992 (FBIS-NES-92-082, 28 April 1992). This prompted an angry denial by Bashir. Ethiopian President Zenawi protested the violation of Ethiopian territory. The army recaptured Bor (4 April), Yirol (11 April), Pibor (23 April), Mongalla (25 April), Kapoeta (28 May), and Torit (13 July). Some 12,000 boys who had lived in camps in Ethiopia until May 1991 fled from UNHCR camps in Kapoeta to Kenya on 28 May: Human Rights Watch/Africa, *Sudan: Lost Boys* (New York: 1994), 16. The offensive is summarized in Burr and Collins, 306.

54. *AC* 33:15 (31 July 1992); *The New York Times*, 26 May 1992. On recruits: *SDG* 32 (January 1993), 3. PDF looted while escorting a train to Wau, February-March 1993: *Sudan Human Rights Voice* (*SHRV*) (London), May 1993, 5.

55. *Living on the Margin* (New York: Fund for Peace, 1995), 26.

56. Defectors accused SPLA-Mainstream of summarily executing twenty-eight Nuer, Acholi, Madi, and Dinka officers for treason and desertion after the attack failed. *AC* 33:15 (31 July 1992) and 32:18 (13 September 1992); Amnesty, *Sudan: The Ravages of War*, 16-20, 25; SPLM London, 7 July 1992; BBC and SUNA, 12 July 1992 (FBIS-NES-92-134, 13 July 1992); BBC, 14 July 1992 (FBIS-NES-92-136, 15 July 1992).

57. *MEI*, 5 March and 16 April 1993; *SU* 4:18 (16 August 1993), 1, citing *Guardian*, 9 August 1993, *AC* 34:16 (13 August 1993), *Independent*, 9 August 1993, and SPLA-Mainstream 17 and 27 July 1993. Battle reports include: SPLA-Mainstream communiqué on a six-hour battle (16 July) between Juba and Nimule, including aerial attacks by Antonov bombers and MiG jet fighters. The army moved on two axes from Juba toward Nimule and from Yei to Kaya (Ugandan border). By 11 August the army captured Morobo on the Juba-Yei-Kaya roads' junction; 100,000 fled to Uganda.

58. *SU*, 17 February 1995; *MEI*, 9 June 1995; *SDG* 61 (June 1995), 6.

59. *SDG* 67 (December 1995), 1, and 69 (February 1996), 2; Steven Wöndu, "Terrorism, Slavery, and Civil War," presentation to the Carnegie Endowment for International Peace (Washington: 20 November 1996), 4.

60. *Living on the Margin*, 19, cites a NIF-organized Arab tribal conference in Kordofan in 1986.

61. *Living on the Margin*, 20; Burr and Collins, 257; J. Millard Burr, *Quantifying Genocide* (Washington: U.S. Committee for Refugees, 1993), 41.

62. *Living on the Margin*, 24; Burr and Collins, 263-64; "Sudan: The Massacre at el Jebelein," *News from Africa Watch*, January 1990.

63. *Living on the Margin*, 18; John Prendergast and Nancy Hopkins, "*For Four Years I Have No Rest*": *Greed and Holy War in the Nuba Mountains of Sudan* (Washington: Center of Concern, 1994), 15-16; Human Rights Watch/Africa, *Sudan: Destroying Ethnic Identity: The Secret War against the Nuba* (New York: 1991).

64. "Sudan: The Forgotten War in Darfur Flares Again," *News from Africa Watch* (New York: April 1990), 5, 7; *Africa Confidential*, 15 June 1990; background in Gérard Prunier, "Ecologie, structures ethniques et conflits politiques au Dar Fur," in *Sudan*, ed. Hervé Bleuchot, Christian Delmet, and Derek Hopwood (Reading: Ithaca, 1991).

65. This culminated in killing 6,000 from Kawalib tribe (Heiban district), December 1992: *The Middle East* (June 1993), 12; *SU* 4:13 (31 March 1993). Burr, 55; Prendergast and Hopkins, 13-15; *Living on the Margin*, 25, 27-28, 32-33, 36; *SDG* 34 (March 1993), 5.

66. *SU* 4:13 (31 March 1993).

67. *Living on the Margin*, 34.

68. *Al-Hayat*, 24 October 1993 (FBIS-NES-93-207, 28 October 1993). Nyuon attacks: SPLA statement, 7 November 1993 in *SU* 4:24 (30 November 1993).

69. A government plane allegedly flew Akol from Nairobi to Tonga on 20 February 1994; he moved to the garrison near Fashoda. Sacking Kerubino and Nyuon: AFP, 25 January 1995 (FBIS-NES-95-017, 26 January 1995).

70. They were supported by Cdr. Arok Thon Arok (Dinka) and John Kulang (Nuer), a founder of SPLA jailed from 1989 to 1993. *SDG* 51 (August 1994); BBC, 15 August 1994 (FBIS-NES-94-158, 16 August 1994). Akol press statement, 25 March 1994 (*SU* 5:9, 20 May 1994); Kulang statement (AFP, 13 August 1994 in FBIS-NES-94-158, 16 August 1994). Arok (17 May 1994) said Machar dismissed Akol, forbade executive council members from using radios to prevent communication with each other, and refused to investigate corruption in handling relief aid (*SU* 5:12, 14 July 1994).

71. The army also used Nyuon's troops as porters. *SDG* 53 (October 1994), 5; *SDG* 54 (November 1994), 5; *SDG* 57 (February 1995), 2; *SDG* 61 (June 1995), 10.

72. BBC, 10 February 1995 (FBIS-NES-95-029, 13 February 1995); BBC, 24 February 1995 (FBIS-NES-95-038, 27 February 1995); Omdurman radio, 25 March 1995 (FBIS-NES-95-058, 27 March 1995).

73. *SDG* 60 (May 1995) on the complex events surrounding Nyuon's defection at Lavon, April 1-11. AFP, 21 August 1995 (FBIS-NES-95-161, 21 August 1995); KTN TV, 11 September 1995 (FBIS-NES-95-176, 12 September 1995); Voice of Sudan (clandestine), 29 September 1995 (FBIS-NES-95-191, 3 October 1995) and 4 October 1995 (FBIS-NES-95-193, 5 October 1995); AFP, 9 October 1995 (FBIS-NES-95-195, 10 October 1995).

74. Intra-Nuer fighting in eastern Upper Nile between Luo Nuer (Kong and Luk) and Jikany Nuer (Machar) was mediated in 1994 by the Protestant Church: *SU*, 30 June 1994; *Sudan: Lost Boys*, 23; New Sudan Council of Churches report, 15 September 1994; Julia Aker Duany, *Making Peace* (Bloomington, Ind.: Workshop on Political Theory and Policy Analysis, 1995); Wal Duany's research in *Creative Approaches to Managing Conflict in Africa*, ed. David R. Smock (Washington: United States Institute of Peace, 1997), 18-19.

75. Aru Bol letter in SSIM's *Southern Sudan Bulletin* 2:1 (March-June 1996), 18.

76. Charter and speeches in SSIM's *Southern Sudan Bulletin* (London: 2:1, March-June 1996), 3-9; Abel Alier, "The Political Charter: Observations and a Commentary" (Khartoum: mimeograph, 1996); Alier in *SDG* 78 (November 1996), 7-8.

77. Akol's *Southern Sudan Vision*, February 1996 (London) and SPLM/A United statements of 1 and 10 February 1996, in *SU* 7:3 (22 February 1996). Luk (a Lou Nuer), who replaced Nyuon, sustained heavy losses to Major Timothy Taban (Machar's Jikany Nuer commander), *SU* 7:23 (10 December 1996).

78. For example, James Othow Along—a former aide to Lam Akol, commis-

sioner of Tonga province and a PDF commander since January 1996—signed the charter on 16 May 1996. Omdurman radio, 16 May 1996 (FBIS-NES-96-097, 17 May 1996).

10. The Impasse in Negotiations

1. Reuters, 30 June 1989; Omdurman TV, 30 June 1989, and Omdurman Radio, 2 July 1989 (FBIS-NES-89-126, 3 July 1989).

2. Reuters, 7 July 1989 and 1 July 1989.

3. Text of *Final Report* from the conference; Alier, *Southern Sudan* (Exeter: Ithaca, 1990), 291-92; J. Millard Burr and Robert O. Collins, *Requiem for the Sudan* (Boulder: Westview, 1995), 229-31; Mansour Khalid, ed., *The Call for Democracy in Sudan* (London: Kegan Paul International, 1992), 233-34; Peter Nyot Kok, *Governance and Conflict in the Sudan* (Hamburg: Deutsches Orient-Institut, 1996), 174-76; MENA, 22 October 1989 (FBIS-NES-89-203, 23 October 1989); Agence France Presse (AFP), 2 November 1989 (FBIS-NES-89-211, 2 November 1989).

4. SPLA radio, 14 and 15 August 1989; Khalid, *Call for Democracy*, 237-68 (quotations from 240-45, 249, 261, 265-68).

5. MENA, 4 July 1989 (FBIS-NES-89-127, 5 July 1989); mission to Ethiopia: *al-Ahram* (Cairo), 8 July 1989, SUNA, 11 July 1989, and AFP, 12 July 1989 (FBIS-NES-89-130 to 133, 10 to 13 July 1989), *Akher Sa'a* (Cairo), 19 July 1989 (JPRS-NEA-89-057, 28 August 1989); Burr and Collins, 212, 217.

6. AFP and SPLA radio, 21 August 1989; SPLA radio, 22 August 1989; Omdurman radio, 22 August 1989, and *al-Sharq al-Awsat*, 22 August 1989 (FBIS-NES-89-162 to 164, 22 to 25 August 1989); Kok, 171-74; Burr and Collins, 217; Khalid, *Call for Democracy*, 232-33.

7. Burr and Collins, 233, 248-51; Kok, 177; Steven Wöndu and Ann Lesch, *The Battle for Peace in the Sudan* (draft ms), appendix F (Carter's statement); SPLA radio, 2, 4, and 6 December 1989; *al-Sharq al-Awsat*, 5 December 1989; SUNA, 7 December 1989, and Omdurman radio, 7 December 1989 (FBIS-NES-89-233-235, 6-8 December 1989).

8. Former Sudanese Ambassador Francis Deng and former Nigerian President Olusagun Obasanju were the emissaries, Wöndu and Lesch, n.p.; Kok, 178; Burr and Collins, 279-80.

9. SUNA, 30 November 1990 (FBIS-NES-90-236, 7 December 1990).

10. Press conference (London), 28 June 1991; *Sudan Update (SU)*, 21 August 1991; *SDG* 14 (July 1991), 4-5; *al-Hayat*, 22 June 1991 (FBIS-NES-91-125, 28 June 1991).

11. SUNA and BBC, 24 October 1991; Omdurman radio, 27 October 1991 (FBIS-NES-91-212, 1 November 1991); *Al-Hayat*, 3 December 1991 (FBIS-NES-91-237, 10 December 1991); Khalid, *Call for Democracy*, 278.

12. Details in Wöndu and Lesch, based on the Nigerian minutes; Kok, *Governance*, 180-85; 207 fn 57, 208 fn 61 and 70; KTN (Nairobi TV), 24 May 1992 (FBIS-NES-92-101, 27 May 1992). The head of the SPLM-Torit delegation was William Nyuon Bany, former Anya-Nya commander, since the designated heads—commanders Salva Kiir and James Iggi—were needed to stave off the army's offensive in Equatoria.

13. Omdurman radio, 23 February 1993 (FBIS-NES-93-035, 24 February 1993); Kok, 185.

14. Statement by Nuba Mountains Solidarity Abroad, 9 July 1992, criticizing the SPLM for not consulting Nuba, Fur, and Ingessana groups before revising the goals. *SU* 3:22 (29 July 1992).

15. *Al-Hayat*, 5 September 1992 and *al-Ra'i* (Amman), 9 September 1992 (FBIS-NES-92-177, 11 September 1992).

16. *SU*, 7 September 1992; Amnesty report on Juba on BBC, 23 September 1992 (*SU* 4:2, 30 September 1992); *AC* 34:7 (2 April 1993), 1-3.

17. Text in Wöndu and Lesch, 130-31.

18. *Al-Safir* (Beirut), 20 April 1993 (FBIS-NES-93-080, 28 April 1993).

19. "SPLM/SPLA Solution to the Sudanese Conflict: The Legal Framework for Abuja-2," *SPLM/SPLA Update* (Nairobi) 2:10 (14 March 1993).

20. Key differences in Wöndu and Lesch, 143-57, 167, 172-78; *Sudan Newsletter* (summer 1993), 8; *Middle East Times*, 25 May 1993; *The Independent*, 22 May 1993; *SDG* 37 (June 1993), 1, 3, 5, and 38 (July 1993), 6; numerous press reports in FBIS-NES-93-184-092 (6-14 May 1993); Kok, 192-97.

21. Wöndu and Lesch, 204-207.

22. IGADD, formed in 1986, comprised Sudan, Kenya, Uganda, Ethiopia, Djibouti, Somalia, and Eritrea. The Standing Committee consisted of Kenya (chair), Ethiopia, Eritrea, and Uganda. IGADD's name changed in 1996 to IGAD—Intergovernmental Authority on Development.

23. TNA statement on Omdurman radio, 29 November 1993 (FBIS-NES-93-228, 30 November 1993); Dr. Ghazi Salah al-Din in *Sawt al Shaab* (Amman), 11 December 1993 (FBIS-NES-93-237, 13 December 1993); AC 34:22 (5 November 1993), 5-6.

24. Text in *SDG* 45 (February 1994), 10.

25. Bashir press statement, January 24 in *SDG* 45 (February 1994), 9; Abu Salih statement in March in *SDG* 47 (April 1994), 6. IGADD presidents met on 9 March to prepare for peace talks. Moi invited Bashir to Kenya on 16 March. Bashir, Garang, and Machar all agreed to talks, but not a cease-fire.

26. Steven Wöndu, *IGADD: No Quick Fix for Sudan* (Nairobi: *New Sudan* Magazine, 1995), 2-4; *SDG* 47 (April 1994), 2, 6. Bashir spent two days in Nairobi, hoping to meet with the Eritrean president, who did not attend.

27. The subcommittee met in Nairobi April-May 1994; *Sudan News & Views* (*SN&V*), 23 June 1994; text in Wöndu, 11-14.

28. Quoted in Wöndu, 10.

29. Wöndu, 15-24.

30. *SPLM/A Update* 3:34 (Nairobi: 20 July 1994) and Wöndu, 28.

31. Bashir in *SDG* 49 (June 1994), 5; Khalifa memorandum, 26 May 1994 in Wöndu, 29-31.

32. Wöndu, 25 and 28; *SDG* 49 (June 1994), 2.

33. Khalifa headed the government delegation; Kiir and Kuwa led the SPLM delegation; and Richard Mulla led the SSIM delegation. Wöndu, 32-47. After Khalifa accused IGADD of adopting the SPLM position in its DOP, talks halted until he apologized: *SDG* 51 (August 1994), 3.

34. *SDG* 51 (August 1994), 2; *SDG* 52 (September 1994), 8.

35. Wöndu, 44-47.

36. Wöndu, 47. Khalifa was Berti and al-Hajj was Fur.

37. He agreed after meeting with U.S. Ambassador Melissa Wells; text in Wöndu, 42-43.

38. Al-Hajj in Wöndu, 48.

39. Wöndu, 51-54; analysis by Peter Nyot Kok, *SDG* 54 (November 1994), 12.

40. Wöndu, 56.

41. Bona Malwal argues in *SDG* 53 (October 1994), 9, that Turabi played the hardliner and Salah al-Din and Bashir played the softliners. Wöndu, 60, and *SDG* 53 (October 1994), 2; SPLM views in Wöndu, 62; Bashir on Omdurman radio, 20 September 1994 (FBIS-NES-94-183, 21 September 1994); Turabi in *al-Wasat*, 7 November 1994 [*SDG* 55 (December 1994), 8].

42. Moi's high-level delegation to Khartoum, Wöndu, 62; *SDG* 55 (December 1994), 8; Sudan's Supreme Council for Peace, formed 27 September 1994, *SU*, 31 October 1994, and *SDG* 54 (November 1994); Salah al-Din on Omdurman radio, 11 January 1995 (FBIS-NES-95-008, 12 January 1995). Turabi wanted a secret meeting with Garang inside Sudan in order to manipulate and discredit him, but agreed to meet in Nairobi on 10 April as proposed by the well-intentioned Sudanese businessman George Hajjar. Garang insisted they meet under IGADD auspices. Although Garang arrived on 8 April, Turabi failed to appear. *SDG* 60 (May 1995), 9, 11.

43. Khartoum rejected that. Wöndu, 64-65; *SDG* 57 (February 1995), 1.

44. *SDG* 60 (May 1995), 1-2; *SDG* 61 (June 1995), 6; *SDG* 64 (September 1995), 1-3.

45. Wöndu, 67, and other sources. "Friends of IGADD" comprised the Netherlands, France, Italy, United States, Canada, and Norway.

46. *MEI*, 9 June 1995.

11. The Emerging Consensus within the Opposition Movement

1. Signed by Mubarak al-Fadhil al-Mahdi for Umma (de facto party leader in exile) and Lual Deng Wol for SPLM on 22 February 1990. SPLA radio, 24 February 1990 (FBIS-NES-90-040, 28 February 1990).

2. *Sudan Monitor*, 1:1 (July 1990).

3. *Sudan Democratic Gazette (SDG)* 28 (September 1992), 5.

4. Statement by the U.S.-based branch of the NDA on 3 September 1991, signed by Muhammad Ibrahim Khalil, Umma member and former speaker of the national assembly.

5. Resolution #4, Mansour Khalid, ed., *Call for Democracy* (London: Kegan Paul International, 1992), 284.

6. Ibid., 276 and 277.

7. *Indian Ocean Newsletter*, 12 October 1991 in *Sudan Update (SU)* 3:6 (25 October 1991).

8. *Africa Confidential (AC)* 33:3 (7 February 1992); *al-Sharq al-Awsat*, 4 February 1992 (FBIS-NES-92-029, 12 February 1992).

9. 5 July 1992 [*SU* 3:21 (13 July 1992)].

10. *SDG* 31 (December 1992), 4.

11. Statement signed by representatives of SPLM/A, Umma (Mubarak al-

Mahdi), DUP, SCP, USAP, Legitimate Command, and Independent National Figures (Faruq Abu Isa) in *SU* 4:14 (21 April 1993) and *SDG* 36 (May 1993), 2. Garang interview in *al-Wasat*, 3 May 1993 (FBIS-NES-93-087, 7 May 1993). Peter Nyot Kok, *Governance and Conflict in the Sudan* (Hamburg: Deutsches Orient-Institut, 1996) 209 fn 87, states it was drafted by himself, Mansour Khalid (SPLM), and Taha Ibrahim in February 1991, at the first NDA meeting in Addis Ababa, but was rejected by DUP and Umma.

12. The meeting was hosted by the Africa Sub-Committee of the U.S. House of Representatives in Washington. *AC* 5, November 1993; *SDG* 44 (January 1994), 4; Kok's analysis in *SDG* 52 (September 1994), 9, and *Governance*, 217. Nuba concerns: *AC* 35:1 (7 January 1994).

13. *Sudan Democratic Voice*, 1:2 (September 1994). DUP-Kuwa accord in *SDG* 51 (August 1994), 5: Kuwa signed alone, not as part of an SPLM delegation; Mirghani invited Kuwa to Cairo, but did not sign the statement.

14. *De Volkskrant* (Amsterdam), 4 November 1993 (FBIS-NES-93-215, 9 November 1993); meeting with Turabi in *al-Sharq al-Awsat*, 21 January 1994 (FBIS-NES-94-015, 24 January 1994).

15. *Al-Sharq al-Awsat*, 17 December 1993 (FBIS-NES-93-242, 20 December 1993); Human Rights Watch/Africa, *Sudan: "In the Name of God"* (New York: 1994), 31; on Mahdi's march, *SDG* 47 (April 1994), 12. Umma detainees included Professor Sara Nugdallah, chair of the Umma women's committee; Abdallah Barakat, an Ansar leader who denounced the alleged rigging of student elections; and Abd al-Mahmud Abduh, who criticized the government in a sermon on the seventeenth day of Ramadan (27 February 1994), which marked the 110th anniversary of the Mahdi's revelation.

16. Other arrested politicians included Sara Nugdallah (7 April to 20 June) and former Kordofan government official, Abd al-Rasul al-Nur (9 April to 27 June), who was held in a ghost house. MENA, 1 June 1994 (FBIS-NES-94-106, 2 June 1994); *Sudan News and Views (SN&V)*, 10 May 1994.

17. The commemoration was held at the private Omdurman Ahlia University. Hussain had lost his right hand years earlier. While detained, his left hand was tied to his right leg during the day. At night he was forced to stand on three bricks while his left hand was tied to the window of his cell. *In the Name of God*, 28.

18. Security agents seized videos, so they could arrest speakers. *SDG* 49 (June 1994), 6.

19. *Al-Hayat*, 27 May 1994 (*SU* 5:11, 30 June 1994); Amnesty International, 16 June 1994 and 30 June 1994 on the detention of a leading defense lawyer; PEN "Freedom to Write" Bulletin, fall 1994; *In the Name of God*, 32-33. Sharif's detention July 1989 to May 1991: "Sudan: Bullets Aren't the Seeds of Life: The Detention of Mahjoub Sherif, Poet and Teacher," *News from Africa Watch* (New York: December 1990).

20. *In the Name of God*, 15.

21. Sudan Embassy (London) and *al-Sharq al-Awsat*, 20 April 1994 in *SU* 5:8 (30 April 1994).

22. *Al-Wasat* (London), 7 February 1994 (FBIS-NES-94-031, 15 February 1994).

23. "Umma Party: Self-Determination in the Sudan" (sent to the author by the

Umma representative in the United States on 3 February 1994); Kok, 211 fn 108, says the referendum would be three to six years after the change in government or earlier if the southern assembly decided on that; the statement does not specify the time period.

24. *Al-Sharq al-Awsat*, 19 February 1995 (FBIS-NES-95-037, 24 February 1995); Kok, 216; *SDG* 56 (January 1995), 1, 4 (text); the government confiscated Nur al-Da'im's house in retaliation [*SDG* 60 (May 1995), 6]. The accord was signed for SPLM by Cmdr. Salva Kiir and Cmdr. James Wani Igga. SPLM negotiators included journalist Bona Malwal and Aldo Ajo Deng, who defected in December 1993 (see chapter 7). SPLM and Umma formed a joint technical committee to resolve issues of power-sharing between the south and the center.

25. Sermon, 2 March 1995, at the Ansar mosque in Wad Nubawi, Omdurman, *SDG* 59 (April 1995), 3.

26. Khartoum University symposium, 11 February 1995 Kenya News Agency (Nairobi), 13 February 1995 (FBIS-NES-95-030, 14 February 1995); Id al-Adha address, 10 May 1995, in *SDG* 61 (June 1995), 2.

27. *AC* 36:3 (3 February 1995), 8. *SDG* 58 (March 1995) says DUP did not sign the document. DUP criticized the Chukudum statement but Mirghani urged DUP to support the Asmara document: *al-Sharq al-Awsat*, 30 January 1995 (FBIS-NES-95-022, 2 February 1995) and 7 February 1995 (FBIS-NES-95-026, 8 February 1995).

28. Hindi and Hussain were absent from the DUP conference, held in Cairo in March 1995. Hussain remained active in DUP, but Hindi broke away, met President Bashir during the latter's visit to Cairo in July 1996, and returned to Khartoum in 1997. *SDG* 58 (March 1995), 1, 2; 58 (April 1995), 11. *Al-Hayat*, 11 February 1995 (FBIS-NES-95-031, 15 February 1995) and *al-Sharq al-Awsat*, 17 February 1995 (FBIS-NES-95-047, 10 March 1995).

29. *AC* 35:24 (2 December 1994), 8.

30. Partial list of participants and decisions in *AC* 36:14 (7 July 1995), 3; text in *SDG* 63 (August 1995), 4-5; commentary in Kok, 217-18. The sixty participants came from Umma, DUP, SPLM, Legitimate Command, SCP, Surur's USAP parties, representatives of trade and professional unions, and prominent citizens. Absentees included Sharif al-Hindi (DUP dissident) and Ibrahim Khalil and al-Hadi al-Mahdi (Umma dissidents). Machar's SSIM and Akol's SPLA-United were not invited. Mirghani was elected chair, General Fathi vice-chair (Garang declined since he needed to lead the military effort at the front), Mubarak al-Fadhil al-Mahdi secretary general, and Faruq Abu Isa NDA spokesman.

31. *Al-Hayat*, 10 August 1995 (FBIS-NES-95-157, 15 August 1995).

32. *SDG* 62 (July 1995), 2, 4; *Nafir* (Nuba Mountains newsletter) 1:3 (October 1995) in *SU* 6:17 (6 November 1995), including an Umma politician's response that Umma and the Asmara Declaration endorsed self-determination "at any time by any people," that Umma was not responsible for Arab militias, and that Umma was never hostile to Nuba.

33. *SHR Voice*, August 1994 (*SU* 5:17, 13 October 1994); Beja Congress, 17 September 1995, on torturing to death a Beja arrested in the Eastern Region. Beja Congress' political leader was Muhammad Tahir Abubakr (a member of the NDA National Leadership Council) and its military commander was Musa Muhammad Ahmad; *The Guardian* (London), 11 May 1996.

34. *Al-Hayat*, 10 August 1995 (FBIS-NES-95-154, 10 August 1995); Omdurman TV, 10, 16, 20 August 1995 (FBIS-NES-95-155, 156, 160, 161, 11-21 August 1995).

35. *Al-Sharq al-Awsat*, 5 August 1995 (FBIS-NES-95-153, 9 August 1995); *SDG* 65 (October 1995), 8.

36. Reuters, 12 September 1995 (internet); *Middle East International*, 22 September 1995; Omdurman radio, quoted by *al-Sharq al-Awsat*, 14 September 1995; *SDG* 66 (November 1995), 9; AFP, 12 September 1995 (FBIS-NES-95-177, 13 September 1995). Twenty-two students were released on 21 September and another thirty-five on 26 September, after signing pledges to refrain from further protests: AFP, 22 September 1995; *SN&V*, 30 September 1995.

37. *SN&V*, 30 September 1995; council meeting on 13 September. The refugees were shown on television with swollen faces after beatings by security forces. Taha in *al-Sha'ab*, 22 September 1995 (FBIS-NES-95-190, 2 October 1995) and *al-Musawwar*, 29 September 1995 (FBIS-NES-95-192, 4 October 1995); Bashir's speech on Omdurman radio, 20 September 1995 (FBIS-NES-95-183, 21 September 1995), also *al-Quds al-Arabi*, 26 September 1995 (FBIS-NES-95-188, 28 September 1995) and *al-Sha'ab* (Cairo), 22 September 1995 (FBIS-NES-95-190, 2 October 1995); governors' Kassala Declaration: Omdurman radio, 20 September 1995 (FBIS-NES-95-183, 21 September 1995).

38. Abel Alier, Ezekiel M. Kodi, Joseph Ukel Abango, Isaiah Kulang Mabor, and Henry Tong Chol, former ministers in the southern regional government. *SDG* 67 (December 1995), 4, 6 (text); Reuters, 12 November 1995 (internet).

39. Text in *SDG* 69 (February 1996), 7-10.

40. SPLM response: MENA, 31 December 1995 (FBIS-NES-96-001, 2 January 1996).

41. Statement by al-Mahdi, *Al-Hayat*, 27 December 1995 (FBIS-NES-95-249, 28 December 1995); meeting with Turabi and sermon on 20 February 1996 in *SDG* 70 (March 1996), 11.

42. *SDG* 71 (April 1996), 3, 6. The DUP officials were Mirghani Abd al-Rahman and Hajj Mudawi Muhammad Ahmad.

43. Colonel Awad al-Karim Umar Ibrahim al-Nuqr of the Command and Staff Academy. On 14 September 1996 he retracted his confession, which he claimed was obtained by torture. The military court trial of the twenty-one officers and ten civilians began in fall 1996. Human Rights Watch/Africa wrote Bashir on 19 February 1997, calling for the transfer of the case to a civilian court.

44. *SDG* 72 (May 1996), 5.

45. Umma, DUP, SCP, USAP, Alier, and representatives of the organizations of women (Sara Nuqdallah of Umma), lawyers, trade unions, and journalists. *SDG* 76 (July 1996), 8, on al-Mahdi's endorsement (interview in *al-Sharq al-Awsat*, 15 June 1996).

46. Disturbances began on 2-3 April when Khartoum University postponed KUSU elections after pro-NDA students protested the efforts by NIF students to rig them; riots erupted on 21 April when Islamists won. Clashes on the Omdurman Ahlia University campus also involved student elections, which NDA won unopposed. They continued during June and July.

47. Press conference, 26 June 1996; *SDG* 75 (July 1996), 7.

48. Umma statement in *SU* 7:23 (10 December 1996). A DUP leader in Sennar was also arrested.

49. Statement issued in Asmara on 11 December 1996; see also *SDG* 80 (January 1997), 2, 3, 8; *SU* 7:23 (10 December 1996) report from Umma; *SU* 7:24 (30 December 1996); *SN&V* 22 (December 1996); *SU* 8:1 (15 January 1997); *MEI* 540 (20 December 1996), 15. His son Abd al-Rahman (a dismissed army officer) organized the flight in five cars with twenty-five armed guards who joined it along the route. Dr. Hasan Taj al-Din (Umma from Dar Fur, former member of the Council of State) delivered the letter to Bashir on 7 December. A short letter, delivered to Turabi's home, informed him of the letter to Bashir.

50. *SDG* 69 (February 1996), 6, 10; Kok, 219 covers the November meeting and provides the draft constitution's text. March 1997 meeting in *MEI* 543 (7 February 1997) and 4 April 1997, *MET*, 28 March 1997, *SDG* 83 (April 1997), and *SSA Newsletter* 17:2 (summer 1997) gives text of NDA press. DA press conference. June 1997 meeting in *SU* 8:15 (31 July 1997), *SN&V* 27 (June 1997), and *SDG* 87 (August 1997).

51. General Abd al-Rahman Said of the LC replaced General Fathi after he died of a heart attack on 28 April 1997.

52. *MEI*, 4 April 1997 and *ME*, June 1997.

53. *SDG* 48 (May 1994) and 49 (June 1994), 9.

54. Steven Wöndu, SPLM spokesman in Washington, D.C., 15 December 1996, quoting Garang. Speech by Garang in *Arbeiderbladet* (Oslo), 18 June 1996 (FBIS-NES-96-120, 20 June 1996) on the transition from emergency relief to building civil society. Key Equatorians included Governor Samuel Abujon, SPLM Secretary General James Igga Wani, and military Commander Thomas Cyrillo.

55. *SN&V* 21 (November 1996).

56. *MET*, 21 March, 11 April, and 16 May 1997; *Financial Times*, 26 March 1997; *MEI* 547 (4 April 1997); *SDG* 83 (April 1997), 2, and 84 (May 1997) and 88 (September 1997); *SU* 8:14 (19 July 1997), 8:17 (21 August 1997), and 8:18 (1 September 1997). Towns and garrisons seized by the SPLA included Kaya, Yei, Morobo, Kajo Kaji, and Lanya.

57. *SDG* 84 (May 1997), 85 (June 1997), 86 (July 1997), 87 (August 1997); *SU* 8:13 (9 July 1997) and 8:18 (1 September 1997). SPLA captured Rumbek (capital of Lakes state), Tonj, Warrap, and Yirol, and seized stolen cattle from Gogrial in a raid on 23 May 1997.

58. *SDG* 74 (July 1996), 4-5, and 75 (August 1996), 7; BBC, 14 June 1996 (FBIS-NES-96-117, 17 June 1996).

59. *SDG* 86 (July 1997) and *SU* 8:14 (19 July 1997).

60. *SDG* 87 (August 1997).

61. *SDG* 67 (December 1995), 7; 82 (February 1997), 4; 84 (May 1997).

62. Northern units came from SAF, Umma, and DUP. Statement by NDA office (UK), 11 January 1997 and BBC, 12-13 January 1997 in special *SU* edition (13 January 1997); *Financial Times*, 14 January 1997; *New York Times*, 21 January 1997; *SU* 8:1 (15 January 1997), 8:2 (27 January 1997), 8:13 (9 July 1997), and 8:18 (1 September 1997); *MEI* 542 (24 January 1997), 8; *SN&V* 23 (January 1997); *MET*, 7 March and 4 April 1997; *SDG* 83 (April 1997), 84 (May 1997), 86 (July 1997), 88 (September 1997).

63. *SDG* 69 (February 1996), 12, and 72 (May 1996); *SN&V* 5:5 (August 1996), 1. The reporter for *The Guardian* (London), 11 May 1996, visited an SAF training camp in Eritrea, where recruits used a picture of Turabi as the bull's-eye for target practice.

64. Brigadier General Abd al-Aziz al-Nur, mentioned by Brig. Khalid in *al-Watan al-Arabi* (Paris), 7 June 1996 (FBIS-NES-96-112, 10 June 1996).

65. *SN&V* 22 (11 January 1997) citing NDA Military Communiqué #1; also *SN&V* 22 (December 1996) and 27 (June 1997); *SU* 8:1 (15 January 1997); *SDG* 80 (January 1997), 81 (February 1997), 83 (April 1997), and 84 (May 1997); *NYT*, 24 December 1996; *MET*, 4 and 11 April, 13 and 27 June 1997.

66. Report of Christian Solidarity International, including Bitai statements in *SDG* 88 (September 1997), 10; also *SU* 8:18 (1 September 1997); on Bitai collaboration with the regime, Einas Ahmad, "The Dynamics of Local Politics and the Search for Local Legitimacy in Kassala State," 9.

67. *New York Times*, 21 January 1997 which includes citation from *al-Ahram*, 20 January 1997; *SU* 8:1 (15 January 1997) citing Reuters and Umma, 5 January 1997; Al-Sadiq's lengthy statement printed in full in *SU* 8:2 (27 January 1997).

68. The defendants were John Garang (SPLM), al-Sadiq al-Mahdi (Umma), General Abd al-Aziz Khalid (SAF), General Fathi Ahmad Ali (LC), Faruq Abu Isa (NDA), Mansour Khalid (SPLM), Mubarak al-Mahdi (Umma/NDA), and Umar Nur al-Da'im (Umma). *SN&V* 24 (February 1997).

69. Critiques from AFP, Inter Press Service, and *al-Sharia al-Siyasi* in *SU* 8:17 (21 August 1997); internet (Sudan Net) transcriptions of Deutsches Press Agency (DPA), 1 November 1997, AFP 26 November 1997 and 23 March 1998, and Reuters, 8 March 1998.

70. Although seventy-one southerners were appointed to the constitutional commission, only six regularly attended the sessions, since they protested its terms and its composition. Sudan Net internet transcriptions of AFP, 14 January 1998 and 23 March 1998.

71. Sudan Net internet transcriptions: AFP, 3 and 18 February 1998; ANEWS, 12 February 1998; Reuters, 9 March 1998.

72. Internet (Sudan Net) transcriptions: AFP, 6 January 1998; Salah al-Din quoted in AFP, 12 and 13 January 1998.

73. Internet (Sudan Net) transcription: AFP, 18 March 1998.

74. The vote was 261 (yes), 26 (no), and 11 (abstentions) (AFP, 28 March 1998). The constitutional commission's draft read: "the right to assemble and to establish political, cultural and scientific associations, and the state guarantees protection of this right." The final version read: citizens "have the right to form organizations for cultural, economic, social or professional purposes restricted only in accordance with the law." (Internet, Sudan Net, AFP, 11 March 1998).

75. Internet (Sudan Net) transcriptions: DPA and AFP, 31 March 1998.

76. The National Congress retained Bashir as chair and made Sharif Zain al-Abdin al-Hindi (former secretary general of the DUP) deputy chair. On 8 March Salah al-Din, the former secretary general, became minister of information and culture and Muhammad al-Amin Khalifa became minister for cabinet affairs. Hardline Al-Tayib Ibrahim Khair ("al-sikka") became minister of social planning, which placed him in charge of religious affairs, social welfare, and relief. [Internet (Sudan

Net) transcriptions: AFP, 18 February 1998; DPA and Reuters, 9 March 1998]. In December 1996 Bashir had backed his finance minister's demand that businesses run by NIF-controlled charities lose their tax-exempt status, a demand that Turabi sharply opposed [*SN&V* 22 (December 1996), *FT*, 18 June 1997]. Moreover, Turabi did not attend Bashir's address commemorating the eighth anniversary of the coup [*SDG* 87 (August 1997)].

77. *SU* 7:23 (10 December 1996), 8:17 (21 August 1997), and 8:19 (15 September 1997); *SDG* 80 (January 1997), 82 (March 1997), 83 (April 1997), 85 (June 1997), 88 (September 1997); *MET* 11, 25, 30 April 1997; *Diplomat* (London), June 1997; *MEI* 556 (8 August 1997).

78. Signed by Machar (SSIM), Kerubino (SPLM-Bahr al-Ghazal), Arok Thon Arok (another SPLM faction), Samuel Aru Bol (a faction of the Union of Sudan African Parties), Equatoria Defense Force, South Sudan Independent Group (Kuaj Mekwa), and a Nuba group (Muhammad Haroun Kafi). Lam Akol signed the agreement on 21 September 1997. Kerubino subsequently became a major-general, and Arok Thon Arok, Nikanora Atem Acek, and Faustino Atem Galdino became brigadiers, which reintegrated them into the armed forces. *MET*, 11, 25, and 30 April 1997; *SDG*, 84 (May 1997) and 85 (June 1997).

79. Kerubino's group replaced him as head with Lawrence Lual Lual Akwei (AFP, 6 February 1998). At Arok Thon Arok's funeral, Turabi announced that Arok had converted to Islam and, as a Muslim martyr, he would receive a Muslim burial. His family (supported by Machar) seized his body from the funeral procession and buried him in a Christian cemetery (DPA, 18 February 1998). Internet (Sudan Net) transcriptions: Radio Omdurman, 2 January 1998; BBC, 2 January 1998 and 20 February 1998; Reuters, 2, 12, 16, 29, and 31 January 1998 and 1 February 1998; AFP 6, 29, and 31 January 1998 and 2, 3, 4, 5, 6, and 18 February 1998; *MET*, 9 January 1998 and 20 February 1998; *NYT*, 13 February 1998.

80. Thirty-eight militiamen died when fighting broke out in Bentiu between factions backing rival candidates for governor: internet (Sudan Net) transcription of BBC, 19 January 1998; on the "elections" of the governors, DPA, 17 November 1997 and 1 December 1997; AFP, 23 November 1997; *MET*, 20 February 1998 on the plane crash at Nasir and DPA, 9 March 1998 on Akol joining the cabinet (the former governor of Bahr al-Jabal, Agnes Lukudu, became minister of labor and was the only female member of the cabinet).

81. *MEI*, 543 (7 February 1997); *MET*, 7 and 18 March 1997; *FT*, 26 March 1997; *SDG*, 83 (April 1997).

82. The Museveni-Bashir communiqué, issued at Eldoret on 10 May 1997, committed Sudan to return Ugandan schoolgirls whom the LRA had kidnapped, after which Sudanese POWs would be released. As of April 1998, the Sudan had not delivered on that exchange. The Ethiopian president insisted that Bashir resolve the issue of international terrorism and apologize for claiming that Ethiopian troops had invaded Sudan in January 1997, neither of which Bashir was prepared to do. Text of Eldoret communiqué; *SDG*, 85 (June 1997) and 86 (July 1997); *MET*, 15 May 1997: *SN&V*, 27 (June 1997).

83. SPLM press release, signed by Garang, 7 July 1997; *SU*, 8:15 (21 July 1997); *SDG*, 87 (August 1997); *MET*, 556 (8 August 1997).

84. *MET*, 15 and 29 August 1997; *SDG*, September 1997; *SU*, 8:17 (21 August

1997) and 8:18 (1 September 1997). Bashir met with Mandela on 12 August, using the Malaysian government as the intermediary; Garang met with Mandela on 28 August, just after a government delegation visited South Africa.

85. Carter claimed that three of the IGAD governments were "slanted against the Sudanese regime"—an implicit reference to Uganda, Eritrea, and Ethiopia. AFP, 29 August 1997 in *SU* 8:19 (15 September 1997).

86. The government delegation also included Khalifa, Ali al-Hajj, and Kerubino. Umar Nur al-Da'im headed the NDA delegation. Policy statements by SPLM and the government on 3-4 November 1997; final communiqué by IGAD on 11 November 1997; *SDG*, 95 (April 1998); internet (Sudan Net) transcriptions on IGAD: Inter Press Service, 28 October 1997; Reuters, 28 October and 4, 5, and 12 November 1997; AFP, 31 October and 1 November 1997; AP, 11 November 1997; Xinhua (China), 5 and 11 November 1997.

87. An SPLM spokesperson stated that publishing the draft constitution prior to the peace talks subverts the peace process; internet (Sudan Net) transcript of BBC, 31 March 1998.

88. Just as al-Mahdi feared a deal that would exclude the NDA, the SPLM, DUP, and northern secularists feared that al-Mahdi would cut a deal to establish a transitional government that would annul restrictive laws but would retain shari'a as the basis of public law. This option was encouraged by Hussain Abu Salih, the former foreign minister and former member of DUP, who formed the Popular Organization for National Dialogue (POND) in early 1998 to reach out to northern exiles and convince al-Mahdi to meet with Turabi. When al-Mahdi hinted that there were conditions under which he might meet Turabi, Mirghani accused him of violating the NDA charter and betraying his partners. Mubarak al-Mahdi stated on behalf of NDA that the movement rejected reconciliation talks since the government was not serious about restoring political pluralism and was merely trying to create divisions within the NDA. Internet (Sudan Net) transcriptions: AFP, 1 January 1998; BBC, 1 and 12 January 1998; ArabicNews.com, 13 January 1998.

89. Press conference in Cairo on 7 March 1998 in Reuters, 8 March 1998 (internet, Sudan Net) and *MET*, 13 March 1998; AFP, 18 March 1998 on planned NDA meeting; *SDG*, 95 (April 1998) on adding Egypt to IGAD.

12. Conclusion

1. Nelson Kasfir, "Peacemaking and Social Cleavages in Sudan," *Conflict and Peacemaking in Multiethnic Societies*, ed. Joseph V. Montville (Lexington: Lexington Books, 1990), 364-65.

2. T. Abdou Maliqalim Simone, *In Whose Image? Political Islam and Urban Practices in Sudan* (Chicago: University of Chicago Press, 1994), 79-80.

3. Jay O'Brien, "Toward a Reconstitution of Ethnicity: Capitalist Expansion and Cultural Dynamics in Sudan," *American Anthropologist* 88 (1986), 902, quoted in Michael Kevane and Leslie Gray, "Local Politics in the Time of Turabi's Revolution: Gender, Class and Ethnicity in Western Sudan," *Africa* 65:2 (1995), 281.

4. Kasfir, "Peacemaking," 366.

5. Ibid., 383.

6. John O. Voll, "Northern Muslim Perspectives," *Conflict and Peacemaking in*

Multiethnic Societies, ed. Joseph V. Montville (Lexington: Lexington Books, 1990), 389-90.

7. Kasfir, "Peacemaking," 367.

8. Martin Daly, "Islam, Secularism, and Ethnic Identity in the Sudan," *Religion and Political Power*, ed. Gustavo Benavides and M. W. Daly (SUNY Press, 1989), 83.

9. The banner was raised to celebrate the capture of a town in the south; *SDG* 45 (February 1994).

10. Simone, *In Whose Image?*, 76.

11. Abdelwahab El-Affendi, "'Discovering the South': Sudanese Dilemmas for Islam in Africa," *African Affairs* 89:356 (July 1990), 384, also 371.

12. Simone, *In Whose Image?*, 26.

13. El-Affendi, "Discovering the South," 385; his concluding remarks, 388-89.

14. *SDG* 44 (January 1994), 8.

15. Garang's comments at a symposium on the Sudan at the U.S. House of Representatives, Washington, D.C., 22 October 1993.

16. Comments by Manute Bol, Peter Nyot Kok, John Luk in the symposium on the south, U.S. House of Representatives, Washington, D.C., 22 October 1993.

17. Omar Nour Eldayem, "Statement," unpublished paper at the symposium on the Sudan, U.S. House of Representatives, Washington, D.C., 20 October 1993.

18. Text sent to the author by the Umma Party representative in Washington, D.C., 3 February 1994.

Selected Bibliography

Abbas, Ali Abdalla. "The National Islamic Front and the Politics of Education," *Middle East Report*, 172 (September-October 1991), 22-25.

—— and M. E. El-Tom. "Education and Fundamentalism in the Arab World: A Research Project." Cairo: unpublished proposal, 1993.

Abdel Rahim, Muddathir. *Imperialism and Nationalism in the Sudan: A Study in Constitutional and Political Development, 1899-1956*. Khartoum and London: Khartoum University Press and Ithaca, 1986.

Abdin, Hasan. *Early Sudanese Nationalism, 1919-1925*. Khartoum: Khartoum University Press, 1985.

Abu Hasabu, Afaf Abdel Majid. *Factional Conflict in the Sudanese Nationalist Movement, 1918-1948*. Khartoum and London: Graduate College Publication No. 12, University of Khartoum and Ithaca, 1985.

Abuses against Women. New York: Fund for Peace, 1992.

Abuses of Academic Freedom. New York: Fund for Peace, 1992.

Africa Confidential. London.

Ahmed, Einas. "The Dynamics of Local Politics and the Search for Local Legitimacy in Kassala State." Unpublished paper delivered at the International Sudan Studies Association Conference, Cairo (Egypt), June 1997.

Ahmed, Hassan Makki Mohamed. *Sudan: The Christian Design, a Study of the Missionary Factor in Sudan's Cultural and Political Integration: 1843-1986*. London: Islamic Foundation, 1989.

Alier, Abel. "The Political Charter: Observations and a Commentary." Khartoum: mimeographed document, 1996.

——. *Southern Sudan: Too Many Agreements Dishonored*. Exeter: Ithaca, 1990.

Amnesty International. *Sudan: Human Rights Violations in the Context of Civil War*. New York: 1989.

——. *Sudan: A Permanent Human Rights Crisis, The Military Government's First Year in Power*. New York: 1990.

——. *Sudan: Progress or Public Relations?* London: 1996.

——. *Sudan: The Ravages of War: Political Killings and Humanitarian Disaster*. New York: 1993.

An-Na'im, Abdullahi Ahmed. "Constitutionalism and Islamization in the Sudan," *Africa Today*, 36: 3&4 (1989), 11-28.

——. "Detention without Trial in the Sudan: The Use and Abuse of Legal Powers," *Columbia Human Rights Law Review*, 17 (spring-summer 1986), 159-87.

—— and Peter N. Kok. *Fundamentalism and Militarism: A Report on the Root Causes of Human Rights Violations in the Sudan.* New York: Fund for Peace, 1991.

——. "The Islamic Law of Apostasy and Its Modern Applicability: A Case from the Sudan," *Religion,* 16 (1986), 197-224.

——. *Toward an Islamic Reformation: Civil Liberties, Human Rights and International Law.* Syracuse: Syracuse University Press, 1990.

——. "Whose Islamic Awakening? A Response," *New Perspectives Quarterly,* 10:3 (summer 1993), 45-48.

The Arab Lawyers Union, The Fund for Peace, and The Sudan Human Rights Organization. *Proceedings: Workshop on Human Rights in the Sudan.* Cairo: November 1992.

Armstrong, John A. *Nations before Nationalism.* Chapel Hill: University of North Carolina Press, 1982.

Arou, Mom K. N., and B. Yongo-Bure, eds. *North-South Relations in the Sudan since the Addis Ababa Agreement.* Khartoum: Sudan Library Series No. 14, Institute of African and Asian Studies, University of Khartoum, 1988.

Assefa, Hizkias. *Mediation of Civil Wars: Approaches and Strategies—The Sudan Conflict.* Boulder: Westview, 1987.

Atabani, Ghazi Salahuddin. Untitled lecture, Conference on Human Rights in Islam, Sudan Bar Association, Khartoum, January 1993.

Badal, Raphael Koba. *Oil and Regional Sentiment in Southern Sudan.* Syracuse: Discussion Paper No. 80, Department of Geography, Syracuse University, 1983.

Bechtold, Peter K. *Politics in the Sudan: Parliamentary and Military Rule in an Emerging African Nation.* New York: Praeger, 1976.

Ben-Israel, Hedva. "Nationalism in Historical Perspective," *Journal of International Affairs,* 45 (winter 1992), 367-97.

Bernal, Victoria. "Gender, Culture, and Capitalism: Women and the Remaking of Islamic 'Tradition' in a Sudanese Village," *Comparative Studies in Society and History,* 36 (1994), 36-67.

Beshir, Mohamed Omer. "Ethnicity, Regionalism and National Cohesion in the Sudan," *Sudan Notes and Records,* 61 (1980), 1-14.

——. *Revolution and Nationalism in the Sudan.* London: Rex Collings, 1974.

——. *The Southern Sudan: Background to Conflict.* London: Hurst, 1968.

——, ed. *Southern Sudan: Regionalism and Religion.* Khartoum and London: Graduate College Publication No. 10, University of Khartoum and Ithaca, 1984.

——. *Terramedia.* London: Ithaca, 1982.

Beswick, Stephanie F. "Non-Acceptance of Islam in the Southern Sudan: The Case of the Dinka from the Pre-Colonial Period to Independence (1956)," *Northeast African Studies,* 1: 2&3 (1994), 19-47.

Biro, Gaspar. *Situation of Human Rights in the Sudan: Report of the Special Rapporteur.* Geneva: United Nations Commission on Human Rights, 1994.

Bleuchot, Hervé, Christian Delmet, and Derek Hopwood. *Sudan: History, Identity, Ideology.* Reading: Ithaca, 1991.

Buchanan, Allen. "Self-Determination and the Right to Secede," *The Journal of International Affairs,* 45 (winter 1992), 347-65.

Burr, J. Millard. *Quantifying Genocide in the Southern Sudan, 1983-1993.* Washington, D.C.: U.S. Committee for Refugees, 1993.

—— and Robert O. Collins. *Requiem for the Sudan: War, Drought, and Disaster Relief on the Nile.* Boulder: Westview, 1994.

Collins, Robert O. *Shadows in the Grass: Britain in the Southern Sudan, 1918-1956.* New Haven: Yale University Press, 1983.

——. *The Southern Sudan, 1883-1898: A Struggle for Control.* New York: Yale University Press, 1962.

——. *The Waters of the Nile: Hydropolitics and the Jonglei Canal, 1900-1988.* Oxford: Clarendon, 1990.

—— and Francis M. Deng, eds. *The British in the Sudan, 1898-1956.* Stanford: Hoover Institution Press, 1984.

Cunnison, Ian, and Wendy James, eds. *Essays in Sudan Ethnography.* London: Hurst, 1972.

Daly, M. W. *Empire on the Nile: The Anglo-Egyptian Sudan, 1898-1934.* New York: Cambridge University Press, 1986.

——, ed. *Al-Majdhubiyya and al-Mikashfiyya: Two Sufi Tariqas in the Sudan.* Khartoum and London: Graduate College Publication No. 13, University of Khartoum and Ithaca, 1985.

——. "Islam, Secularism, and Ethnic Identity in the Sudan." *Religion and Political Power,* ed. Gustavo Benavides and M. W. Daly, 83-97. SUNY Press, 1989.

——, ed. *Modernization in the Sudan.* New York: Lilian Barber, 1985.

Deng, Francis Mading. *The Dinka of the Sudan.* New York: Holt, Rinehart and Winston, 1972.

—— and Prosser Gifford, eds. *The Search for Peace and Unity in the Sudan.* Washington, D.C.: Wilson Center Press, 1987.

——. *War of Visions: Conflict of Identities in the Sudan.* Washington, D.C.: Brookings Institution, 1995.

Deutsch, Karl W. *Nationalism and Social Communication.* Cambridge: MIT Press, 1966.

Duany, Julia Aker. *Making Peace: A Report on Grassroots Peace Efforts by Women in South Sudan.* Bloomington, Ind.: Workshop on Political Theory and Policy Analysis, 1995.

Duany, Wal. "The Problem of Centralization in the Sudan," *Northeast African Studies,* 1: 2&3 (1994), 75-102.

—— and Julia A. Duany. *Genesis of the Crisis in the Sudan.* Bloomington, Ind.: Workshop on Political Theory and Policy Analysis, 1995.

Duffield, Mark. "Where Famine Is Functional," *Middle East Report,* 72 (September-October 1991), 26-30.

El-Affendi, Abdelwahab. "'Discovering the South': Sudanese Dilemmas for Islam in Africa," *African Affairs,* 89:356 (July 1990), 371-89.

——. *The Political and Ideological Development of the Muslim Brotherhood in Sudan, 1945-1986.* Reading: unpublished dissertation, University of Reading, 1989.

Eldayem, Omar Nour. "Statement." Washington, D.C.: unpublished paper, USIP conference, October 1993.

Eley, Geoff, and Ronald Grigor Suny, eds. *Becoming National.* New York: Oxford University Press, 1996.

Eltigani, Eltigani E, ed. *War and Drought in Sudan: Essays on Population Displacement.* Gainesville: University Press of Florida, 1995.

Emerson, Rupert. *From Empire to Nation.* Cambridge: Harvard University Press, 1967.

Etzioni, Amitai. "The Evils of Self-Determination," *Foreign Policy*, 89 (winter 1992-93), 21-35.

Fawzi, Saad ed Din. *The Labour Movement in the Sudan, 1946-1955*. London: Oxford University Press, 1957.

Fluehr-Lobban, Carolyn. *Islamic Law and Society in the Sudan*. London: Frank Cass, 1987.

Gordon, Carey N. "The Islamic Legal Revolution: The Case of Sudan," *International Lawyer*, 19 (summer 1985), 793-815.

Hale, Sondra. "The Rise of Islam and Women of the National Islamic Front in Sudan," *Review of African Political Economy*, 554 (1992), 27-41.

Hamid, Mohamed Beshir. "Confrontation and Reconciliation within an African Context: The Case of Sudan," *Third World Quarterly*, 5:3 (1983), 320-29.

———. *The Politics of National Reconciliation in the Sudan: The Numayri Regime and the National Front Opposition*. Washington, D.C.: Occasional Papers Series, Center for Contemporary Arab Studies, Georgetown University, 1984.

Hannum, Hurst. *Autonomy, Sovereignty, and Self-Determination: The Accommodation of Conflicting Rights*. Philadelphia: University of Pennsylvania Press, 1996.

Heraclides, Alexis. "Secession, Self-Determination and Non-intervention: In Quest of a Normative Symbiosis," *The Journal of International Affairs*, 45 (winter 1992), 399-420.

Hill, Richard. *Egypt in the Sudan, 1820-1881*. New York: Oxford University Press, 1959.

Holt, P. M., and M. W. Daly. *The History of the Sudan: From the Coming of Islam to the Present Day*. Boulder: Westview, 1979.

Hopkins, Paul A. "Christianity, Islam and Politics in Sudan." Philadelphia: Memorandum for Presbyterian mission to Sudan, 1993.

Human Rights Watch/Africa. *Academic Freedom and Human Rights Abuses in Africa*. New York: 1990.

———. *Children of Sudan: Slaves, Street Children and Child Soldiers*. New York: 1995.

———. *Civilian Devastation: Abuses by All Parties in the War in Southern Sudan*. New York: 1994.

———. *Denying "The Honor of Living": Sudan, a Human Rights Disaster*. New York: 1990.

———. "Political Detainees in Sudan," *News from Africa Watch*. New York: 1989.

———. "Political Detainees in Sudan: Academics," *News from Africa Watch*. New York: 1990.

———. "Political Detainees in Sudan: Journalists, Poets and Writers," *News from Africa Watch*. New York: 1990.

———. "Political Detainees in Sudan: Lawyers," *News from Africa Watch*. New York: 1990.

———. "Political Detainees in Sudan: Medical Doctors," *News from Africa Watch*. New York: 1990.

———. "Political Detainees in Sudan: Trade Unionists," *News from Africa Watch*. New York: 1990.

———. "Sudan: Bullets Aren't the Seeds of Life: The Detention of Mahjoub Sherif, Poet and Teacher," *News from Africa Watch*. New York: 1990.

———. *Sudan: The Copts: Passive Survivors under Threat*. New York: 1993.

———. *Sudan: Destroying Ethnic Identity, the Secret War against the Nuba*. New York: 1991.

———. "Sudan: Destruction of the Independent Secular Judiciary; Military Government Clamps Down on Press Freedom," *News from Africa Watch*. New York: 1989.

——. "Sudan: The Forgotten War in Darfur Flares Again," *News from Africa Watch*. New York: April 1990.

——. *Sudan: The Ghosts Remain*. New York: April 1992.

——. *Sudan: "In the Name of God," Repression Continues in Northern Sudan*. New York: 1994.

——. "Sudan: The June Coup d'État: Fifty Days On," *News from Africa Watch*. New York: 1989.

——. "Sudan: Khartoum: Government to Execute Peaceful Protesters, The Provinces: Militia Killings and Starvation Return," *News from Africa Watch*. New York: 1989.

——. *Sudan: The Lost Boys: Child Soldiers and Unaccompanied Boys in Southern Sudan*. New York: 1994.

——. "Sudan: The Massacre at el Jebelein," *News from Africa Watch*. New York: 1990.

——. *Sudan: New Islamic Penal Code Violates Basic Human Rights*. New York: 1991.

——. "Sudan: Officers Executed and Doctor Tortured to Death," *News from Africa Watch*. New York: 1990.

——. "Sudan: Recent Developments in Khartoum: An Update," *News from Africa Watch*. New York: 1989.

——. *Sudan: Refugees in Their Own Country: The Forced Relocation of Squatters and Displaced People from Khartoum*. New York: 1992.

——. "Sudan: Suppression of Information," *News from Africa Watch*. New York: 1990.

——. "Sudan: Threat to Women's Status from Fundamentalist Regime," *News from Africa Watch*. New York: 1990.

——. *Sudan: Violations of Academic Freedom*. New York: 1992.

——. *Sudanese Human Rights Organization*. New York: 1991.

——. *War in South Sudan: The Civilian Toll*. New York: 1993.

Ibrahim, Ahmed Uthman Muhammad. *The Dilemma of British Rule in the Nuba Mountains, 1898-1947*. Khartoum and London: Graduate College Publication No. 15, University of Khartoum and Ithaca Press, 1985.

Ibrahim, F. N. "The Southern Sudanese Migration to Khartoum and the Resultant Conflicts," *GeoJournal*, 25:1 (September 1991), 13-18.

Ibrahim, Riad. "Factors Contributing to the Political Ascendancy of the Muslim Brethren in Sudan," *Arab Studies Quarterly*, 12: 3&4 (summer/fall 1990), 33-53.

International League for Human Rights. *Sudan's Human Rights Record: Comments on the First Report of Sudan to the Human Rights Committee*. New York: July 1991.

Jamal, Abbashar. "Funding Fundamentalism: The Political Economy of an Islamist State," *Middle East Report*, 172 (September-October 1991), 14-17.

Johnson, Douglas H. *Nuer Prophets*. Oxford: Clarendon, 1994.

Johnston, Harry, and Ted Dagne. "The Crisis in Sudan: The North-South Conflict," *Mediterranean Quarterly*, 7:2 (spring 1996), 1-12.

Karklins, Rasma. *Ethnopolitics and Transition to Democracy: The Collapse of the USSR and Latvia*. Washington, D.C.: Woodrow Wilson Center Press, and Baltimore: Johns Hopkins University Press, 1994.

Kasfir, Nelson. "Peacemaking and Social Cleavages in Sudan." *Conflict and Peacemaking in Multiethnic Societies*, ed. Joseph V. Montville, 364-87. Lexington Books, 1990.

——. "Southern Sudanese Politics since the Addis Ababa Agreement," *African Affairs*, 76 (April 1977), 143-66.

Kevane, Michael, and Leslie Gray. "Local Politics in the Time of Turabi's Revolution: Gender, Class and Ethnicity in Western Sudan," *Africa*, 65:2 (1995), 271-96.

Khalid, Mansour, ed. *Call for Democracy in Sudan: John Garang*. London: Kegan Paul International, 1992.

——. *The Government They Deserve: The Role of the Elite in Sudan's Political Evolution*. London: Kegan Paul International, 1990.

——, ed. *John Garang Speaks*. London: Kegan Paul International, 1987.

——. *Nimeiri and the Revolution of Dis-May*. London: Routledge and Kegan Paul International, 1985.

Kirker, Constance L. "'This Is Not Your Time Here': Islamic Fundamentalism and Art in Sudan: An African Artist Interviewed," *Issue: A Journal of Opinion* (African Studies Association), 20:2 (1992), 5-11.

Kok, Peter Nyot. *Governance and Conflict in the Sudan, 1985-1995*. Hamburg: Deutsches Orient-Institut, 1996.

——. "The Ties That Will Not Bind: Conflict, and Racial Cleavage in the Sudan." *Arms and Daggers in the Heart of Africa: Studies on Internal Conflicts*, ed. P. Anyang' Nyong'o. Nairobi: African Academy of Sciences, 1993.

Lawyers Committee for Human Rights. *Beset by Contradictions: Islamization, Legal Reform and Human Rights in Sudan*. New York: 1996.

Lesch, Ann Mosely. "Confrontation in the Southern Sudan," *The Middle East Journal*, 40:3 (summer 1986), 410-28.

——. "Democratization in a Fragmented Society: The Sudan." *Political Liberalization and Democratization in the Arab World*, ed. Bahgat Korany, Paul Noble, and Rex Brynen. Boulder: Lynne Rienner, II (1998).

——. "The Destruction of Civil Society in the Sudan." *Civil Society in the Middle East*, ed. Augustus Richard Norton. Leiden: E. J. Brill, II (1996), 155-92.

——. "The Dialectical Relationship of Central and Local Politics in the Middle East," with Louis J. Cantori et al., *Journal of Arab Affairs*, 8:2 (fall 1989), 140-43.

——. "External Involvement in the Sudanese Civil War." *Foreign Intervention in Sub-Saharan Africa: Making War and Waging Peace*, ed. David R. Smock, 79-105. Washington, D.C.: U.S. Institute of Peace, 1993.

——. "The Fall of Numairi," *UFSI Report*. Indianapolis: 20, 1985.

——. "Khartoum Diary," *Middle East Report*, 162 (November-December 1989), 36-38.

——. "Military Disengagement from Politics: The Sudan." *Military Disengagement from Politics*, ed. Constantine P. Danopoulos, 19-46. New York: Routledge, 1988.

——. "Negotiations in the Sudan." *Foreign Intervention in Sub-Saharan Africa: Making War and Waging Peace*, ed. David R. Smock, 107-38. Washington, D.C.: U.S. Institute of Peace, 1993.

——. "The Parliamentary Election of 1986: Fatally Flawed?" *Northeast African Studies*, 1: 2&3 (1994), 129-58.

——. "Party Politics in the Sudan," *UFSI Report*. Indianapolis: 9, 1986.

——. "Prolonged Conflict in the Sudan." *Prolonged Wars: A Post-Nuclear Challenge*, ed. Karl P. Magyar and Constantine P. Danopoulos, 99-129. Air University Press, 1994.

——. "Rebellion in the Southern Sudan," *UFSI Report*. Indianapolis: 8, 1985.

——. "The Sudan: Militancy and Isolation." *The Middle East and the Peace Process*, ed. Robert O. Freedman. Miami: Universities of Florida Press, 1998.

——. "Transition in the Sudan," *UFSI Report*. Indianapolis: 20, 1985.

———. "A View from Khartoum," *Foreign Affairs*, 65:4 (spring 1987), 807-26.

Lind, Michael. "In Defense of Liberal Nationalism," *Foreign Affairs*, 73:3 (May-June 1994), 87-99.

Living on the Margin: The Struggle of Women and Minorities for Human Rights in Sudan. New York: Fund for Peace, 1995.

Lowrie, Arthur L., ed. *Islam, Democracy, the State and the West: A Round Table with Dr. Hasan Turabi.* Tampa, Fla.: Monograph #1, World and Islam Studies Enterprise, 1993.

Mahgoub, Mohamed Ahmed. *Democracy on Trial: Reflections on Arab and African Politics.* London: Andre Deutsch, 1974.

Mahmud, Ushari Ahmed, and Suleyman Ali Baldo. *Human Rights Abuses in the Sudan 1987: The Diein Massacre, Slavery in the Sudan.* Khartoum, 1987.

Makec, John Wuol. *The Customary Law of the Dinka (Jieng): A Comparative Analysis of an African Legal System.* Khartoum: St. George, 1986.

Malwal, Bona. *People and Power in Sudan: The Struggle for National Stability.* London: Ithaca, 1981.

———. *The Sudan: A Second Challenge to Nationhood.* New York: Thornton, 1985.

Mangan, J. A. "The Education of an Elite Imperial Administration: The Sudan Political Service and the British Public School System," *International Journal of African Historical Studies*, 15:4 (1982), 671-99.

Mawut, Lazarus Leek. *Dinka Resistance to Condominium Rule, 1902-1932.* Khartoum: Graduate College Publication No. 3, University of Khartoum, 1983.

———. *The Southern Sudan: Why Back to Arms?* Khartoum: St. George, 1986.

Mayo, David Nailo N. "The British Southern Policy in Sudan: An Inquiry into the Closed District Ordinances (1914-1946)," *Northeast African Studies*, 1: 2-3 (1994), 165-85.

Miller, David. *On Nationality.* Oxford: Clarendon, 1995.

Mitchell, Christopher R. *Conflict Resolution and Civil War: Reflections on the Sudanese Settlement of 1972.* Working Paper No. 3, Center for Conflict Analysis and Resolution, George Mason University, 1989.

Mohammed, Nadir A. L. "Militarization in Sudan: Trends and Determinants," *Armed Forces and Society* 19:3 (spring 1993), 411-32.

Mohed, Sayed, and Dunstan M. Wai. "The Fate of Human Rights in the Sudan," *Horn of Africa*, 3:2 (1980), 28-32.

Muhammad, Ahmad al-Awad. *Sudan Defence Force: Origin and Role, 1925-1955.* Occasional Paper No. 18, Institute of African and Asian Studies, University of Khartoum, n.d.

Nagi, Saad Z. "Ethnic Identification and Nationalist Movements," *Human Organization*, 51 (winter 1992), 307-16.

Niblock, Tim. *Class and Power in Sudan: The Dynamics of Sudanese Politics, 1898-1985.* Albany: State University of New York Press, 1987.

Norton, Augustus Richard. "The Future of Civil Society in the Middle East," *The Middle East Journal*, 47:2 (spring 1993), 205-16.

O'Brien, Jay. "Sudan's Killing Fields," *Middle East Report*, 161 (November-December 1989), 32-35.

O'Fahey, R. S. *State and Society in Dar Fur.* New York: St. Martin's, 1980.

Prendergast, John. *Dare to Hope: Children of War in Southern Sudan.* Washington, D.C.: Center of Concern, 1996.

——. *Diplomacy, Aid and Governance in Sudan.* Washington, D.C.: Center of Concern, 1995.

—— and Nancy Hopkins. *"For Four Years I Have No Rest": Greed and Holy War in the Nuba Mountains of Sudan.* Washington, D.C.: Horn of Africa Discussion Paper, Center of Concern, 1994.

——. "Humanitarian Intervention and Crisis Response in Africa," *Crosslines Global Report*, 16-17 (June-September 1995), 22-24.

——. "Is Aid Helping to Run the War?" *Africa Agenda*, 1:6 (summer 1995), 18-20.

——. "Multi-layered Conflict in the Greater Horn of Africa." Washington, D.C.: Creative Associates International, 1996.

——. "Roots of Famine." *Disaster and Development in the Horn of Africa*, ed. John Sorenson, 112-25. New York: St. Martin's, 1995.

——. *Sudanese Rebels at a Crossroads: Opportunities for Building Peace in a Shattered Land.* Washington, D.C.: Center of Concern, 1994.

Ranney, Austin. "Politics in the United States." *Comparative Politics*, ed. Gabriel A. Almond and G. Bingham Powell, Jr., 784-824. New York: HarperCollins College Publishers, sixth edition, 1996.

Rondinelli, Dennis A. "Administrative Decentralisation and Economic Development: The Sudan's Experiment with Devolution," *The Journal of Modern African Studies*, 19:4 (December 1981), 595-624.

Salih, Kamal Osman. "The Sudan, 1985-9: The Fading Democracy," *The Journal of Modern African Studies*, 28:2 (1990), 199-224.

El Sammani, Mohamed Osman. *Jonglei Canal: Dynamics of Planned Change in the Twic Area.* Khartoum and London: Graduate College Publication No. 8, University of Khartoum and Ithaca, 1984.

Sanderson, Lillian Passmore, and G. N. Sanderson. *Education, Religion and Politics in Southern Sudan, 1899-1964.* London: Ithaca, 1981.

Al-Sawi, Abdul-Aziz Hussein. *The Sudanese Dialogue on Identity and National Unity: A New Perspective.* Cairo: The Sudanese Studies Centre, 1996.

Sharkey, Heather J. "Luxury, Status and the Importance of Slavery in the 19th and early 20th Century Northern Sudan," *Northeast African Studies*, 1:2-3 (1994), 187-206.

Shebeika, Mekki. *The Independent Sudan.* New York: Robert Speller, 1959.

Sidahmed, Abdel Salam. "Sudan: Ideology and Pragmatism," *Islamic Fundamentalism*, ed. Abdel Salam Sidahmed and Anoushiravan Ehteshami, 179-98. Boulder: Westview, 1996.

Sikainga, Ahmad Alawad. *Slaves into Workers: Emancipation and Labor in Colonial Sudan.* Austin: University of Texas Press, 1995.

Simone, T. Abdou Maliqalim. *In Whose Image? Political Islam and Urban Practices in Sudan.* Chicago: The University of Chicago Press, 1994.

Smith, Anthony D. *The Ethnic Origins of Nations.* New York: Blackwell, 1986.

——. *National Identity.* London: Penguin, 1991.

Smooha, Sammy, and Theodore Hanf. "The Diverse Modes of Conflict-Regulation in Deeply Divided Societies," *International Journal of Comparative Sociology*, 33 (January-April 1992), 26-47.

Stevenson, R. C. *The Nuba People of Kordofan Province.* Khartoum and London: Graduate College Publication No. 7, University of Khartoum and Ithaca, 1984.

Sudan Cultural Digest Project. *A Concise Study of Some Ethnic Groups in Sudan.* Cairo: December 1996.

Sudanow. Perspective on the South: An Analysis of Trends and Events Leading to the Final Decree of Regionalisation for the Former Southern Region of the Sudan. Khartoum: Ministry of Guidance and National Information, August 1983.

Taha, Mahmoud Mohamed. *The Second Message of Islam.* Syracuse: Syracuse University Press, 1987.

Tier, Akolda Man. "Freedom of Religion under the Sudan Constitution and Laws," *Journal of African Law*, 26:2 (autumn 1982), 133-51.

——. "The Legal System of the Sudan," *Modern Legal Systems Cyclopedia*, 1983.

Al-Turabi, Hasan. "The Islamic Awakening's New Wave," *New Perspectives Quarterly*, 10:3 (summer 1993), 42-45.

——. *Tajdid al-Fikr al-Islami.* Jiddah: Dar al-Sa'udiyya, 1987.

University of Juba. *The Role of Southern Sudanese People in the Building of Modern Sudan: Selected Papers.* Khartoum: University of Juba, 1986.

Van Voorhis, Bruce. "Food as Weapon for Peace: Operation Lifeline Sudan," *Africa Today*, 36: 3&4 (1989), 29-42.

Viorst, Milton. "Sudan's Islamic Experiment," *Foreign Affairs*, 74:3 (May-June 1995), 45-58.

Voll, John Obert. *A History of the Khatmiyyah Tariqah in the Sudan.* Cambridge: unpublished dissertation, Harvard University, 1969.

——. "Northern Muslim Perspectives." *Conflict and Peacemaking in Multiethnic Societies*, ed. Joseph V. Montville, 389-409. Lexington, 1990.

——, ed. *Sudan: State and Society in Crisis.* Bloomington: Indiana University Press, 1991.

—— and Sarah Potts Voll. *The Sudan: Unity and Diversity in a Multicultural State.* Boulder: Westview, 1985.

Wai, Dunstan M. *The African-Arab Conflict in the Sudan.* New York: Africana, 1981.

——. "Revolution, Rhetoric and Reality in the Sudan," *The Journal of Modern African Studies*, 17:1 (March 1979), 71-93.

——, ed. *The Southern Sudan: The Problem of National Integration.* London: Frank Cass, 1973.

Warburg, Gabriel. *Historical Discord in the Nile Valley.* London: Hurst, 1992.

——. *Islam, Nationalism and Communism in a Traditional Society: The Case of Sudan.* London: Frank Cass, 1978.

——. "National Identity in the Sudan: Fact, Fiction and Prejudice in Ethnic and Religious Relations," *Asian and African Studies*, 24 (1990), 151-202.

Waterbury, John. *Hydropolitics of the Nile Valley.* Syracuse: Syracuse University Press, 1979.

Wöndu, Steven. *IGADD: No Quick Fix for Sudan.* Nairobi, Kenya: *New Sudan* Magazine, 1995.

——. "Terrorism, Slavery, and Civil War: Examining Sudan." Washington, D.C.: presentation to the Carnegie Endowment for International Peace, 1996.

—— and Ann Lesch. *The Battle for Peace: An Analysis of the Abuja Conferences, 1992-1993.* Unpublished manuscript, 1997.

Woodward, Peter. *Sudan, 1898-1989: The Unstable State.* Boulder: Lynne Rienner, 1990.

——. "Sudan after Numeiri," *Third World Quarterly*, 7:4 (October 1985), 958-72.

———. "Sudan's New Democracy," *Contemporary Review*, 251 (July-December 1987), 6-11.

———, ed. *Sudan after Nimeiri*. London: Routledge, 1991.

Yongo-Bure, Benaiah. "Islamism, Arabism and the Disintegration of Sudan," *Northeast African Studies*, 1: 2-3 (1994), 207-22.

———. "Sudan's Deepening Crisis," *Middle East Report*, 172 (September-October 1991), 8-13.

Index

Ann Mosely Lesch is Professor of Political Science at Villanova University and past President of the Middle East Studies Association of North America. She is coauthor (with Mark Tessler) of *Israel, Egypt, and the Palestinians* and principal author of *Transition to Palestinian Self-Government: Practical Steps toward Israeli-Palestinian Peace.*